Grains, Greens, and Grated Coconuts

Grains, Greens, and Grated Coconuts

Recipes and Remembrances
of a Vegetarian Legacy

Ammini Ramachandran
Foreword by Suvir Saran

iUniverse, Inc.
New York Lincoln Shanghai

Grains, Greens, and Grated Coconuts
Recipes and Remembrances of a Vegetarian Legacy

Copyright © 2007 by Ammini Ramachandran

All rights reserved. No part of this book may be used or reproduced by any means, graphic, electronic, or mechanical, including photocopying, recording, taping or by any information storage retrieval system without the written permission of the publisher except in the case of brief quotations embodied in critical articles and reviews.

iUniverse books may be ordered through booksellers or by contacting:

iUniverse
2021 Pine Lake Road, Suite 100
Lincoln, NE 68512
www.iuniverse.com
1-800-Authors (1-800-288-4677)

The views expressed in this work are solely those of the author and do not necessarily reflect the views of the publisher, and the publisher hereby disclaims any responsibility for them.

Photographs:
R. V. Ramachandran
Suresh Hinduja
Chirayil Infoteckh Pvt. Ltd.

ISBN-13: 978-0-595-40976-1 (pbk)
ISBN-13: 978-0-595-85332-8 (ebk)
ISBN-10: 0-595-40976-8 (pbk)
ISBN-10: 0-595-85332-3 (ebk)

Printed in the United States of America

For three people who influenced everything:
my husband, R. V. Ramachandran, and
in memory of my beloved parents, V. K. R. Menon and Ambica R. Menon

Contents

Foreword ix
Acknowledgments xiii

Part One

Introduction 1
Chapter One: Our History and Heritage 19
Chapter Two: Getting Started: Ingredients,
                Cooking Methods, and Utensils 42

Part Two

Chapter Three: Sacred Food: Rice and Rituals 80
Chapter Four: The World of Curries 98
    Popular Curries 100
    Seasonal Curries 118
    Curries from the *Madapilli* (Royal Kitchens) 142
Chapter Five: Hot off the Skillet: *Mezukkupurattis* and *Thorans* 155
Chapter Six: Chutneys and Pickles 168
Chapter Seven: Accompaniments and Sun-Dried Preserves 190
Chapter Eight: *Paayasams* (Puddings) 206
Chapter Nine: Breakfasts and Brunches 221
Chapter Ten: Savory Snacks 241
Chapter Eleven: Desserts: Sweet Treats 257
Chapter Twelve: Glittering Festivals and Revered Offerings 282

Part Three

Appendix I: Recipe Index 309
Appendix II: Menu Suggestions 316
Appendix III: Cooking Measurements and Syrup Consistencies 320
Appendix IV: Resources and Ordering Information 322

A Selective Bibliography 323
About the Author 329
Index 331

Foreword

In this richly flavored book on the household cooking of Kerala and its many vegetarian marvels, Ammini Ramachandran takes us into a journey that even tour guides driving you through Kerala's many vistas would be unable to share. How fortunate and blessed I feel to be able to introduce and perpetuate this brilliance. These are recipes gathered over a long, heartfelt, and celebrated lifetime. That Ammini calls Dallas, Texas, her home should be no surprise; hers is a passion and respect for the native land that only someone living outside of it can have. Lucky for us!

I first met Ammini through online chat forums that I moderated and that she contributed to. Always generous, never one to take credit, she posted meticulous and detailed missives on the magic of her region's culinary traditions. I was smitten at reading her first post. The rest is history. Her works soon became the stuff of midnight yearning. When hungry for good food, and being lazy to cook or eat, I found myself sating my hunger with the aromas that wafted through the computer screen as I read her writing. How exciting it is to finally see her passion in print, enabling us to cook like her, live her history, and celebrate her Kerala.

Having aristocratic blood from her father—yes, he was the son of the maharaja of Kochi (Cochin)—she found herself living in her mother's matrilineal family home at the age of eight. Her father had sadly passed away in a plane crash en route to New Delhi. Living in a joint family gave Ammini a new abundance that one can find peppered through the head notes that come with each recipe. A household of twenty-one family members made for great conversations, diverse tastes and palates, and, to the advantage of us readers, a cookbook that finds itself richer for it. Even a favorite recipe from her favorite chef at the family home finds itself into the curry section *(Varutharacha Sambar)*.

Having grown up vegetarian, Ammini was disappointed by the lack of vegetarian options shared in books of Kerala's cuisine. She was challenged by her husband, while waiting in a traffic jam over the Williamsburg Bridge in New York, to stop complaining and write her own book of favorite recipes. Fortunately for us, she has never been lazy, and here, after years of reflection, introspection, testing, and cooking, she has spilled her vast knowledge onto the pages of this book. And all of us, Malayali (people of Kerala) or not, Indian or not, shall be forever filled with great vegetarian options that not only give us healthful dishes to bring to our table, but flavorful foods, prepared in our modern kitchens, with respect for the past, true to authentic flavors, and never compromised.

Having grown up in New Delhi, I was delighted to see so many of our traditions find common practice across the different regions. The kitchen was the sanctum sanctorum in Ammini's home, just as it was in mine. And it was here that she found love, respect, intrigue, and a lifelong fascination with food. Daily fare, festival dishes, and puddings all enthralled her, as did the picking of sea salt from the *uppumarava* (wooden salt box), which kept the salt moisture free, even in the humid environs of Kerala. Homesick in the United States, having become a member of a cooking club, finding success in recipe development and creating, she submitted a recipe for her mother's coconut rice in a contest held by *Woman's Day* magazine. It should be no surprise that she won first place and found herself, a few weeks later, cooking coconut pancakes with the food editor of *The Providence Journal,* who then featured her recipes and story in an article in the food section the following week. Soon, recipes that came along with letters sent weekly by her mother in India found their way into a journal, and now these pages. Her two decades in the world of finance (and its exacting standards) have found their way into her recipes. The recipes from her mom, which had pinches and fistfuls and other not-so-precise adjectives, have been replaced with streamlined measurements and clear instructions. Even the clumsy amongst us can follow these recipes to roaring success.

If you crave coconut milk but want it to be healthy and flavorful at once, try the recipe for *Oolan.* Vegetables easily found in your supermarket will acquire a nod of sophistication, guided by Ammini. Okra will not be slimy again if you make the *Okra Kichadi* (fried okra in a coconut and mustard sauce); even you who love slime in okra will enjoy this for the aromatics that only add to the overall enjoyment. Could onion soup ever take on new heirs and flavors? Yes, and in the recipe for *Mulaku Varutha Puli,* Ammini empowers it with the fire of green chilies, the sourness of tamarind, and the comfort of savory shallots. That mustard seeds and curry leaves are in the recipe only adds to the overall decadence of this simple-to-prepare soup that shall replace any cravings you have for the most mundane, classic rendering of an onion soup. Any table, any time of the year will do well to have the recipe for *Mottakoozu Thoran* placed atop it. A great side dish, cabbage has never ever tasted the same in any other version. Indians are masters of treating cabbage well, and this recipe is a great specimen of their prowess. Fans of rice pudding will find a wonderful Kerala version of this comforting dessert in the recipe for *Neypaayasam*. With brown sugar in it, it is still wonderfully rich and different; if you use the jaggery Ammini suggests, you will have yourself holding a bowl of deeply flavored rice pudding that has texture and flavor, and that leaves a lasting, scintillating taste on your tongue that shall bring you back to flirt with these pages in your kitchen.

Foods that celebrate the gods, foods that celebrate mere mortals, and foods that celebrate mortal ancestors—all find a place in the pages Ammini has shared with us. Traditional dishes prepared for the days of the dead, dishes prepared to celebrate festivals in different seasons and regions, recipes from temples—all find places of pride in her repertoire and now in yours. You only need to cook from these pages, and you shall find yourself living traditions and cultures that you wish could have been yours in tender years. Evocative introductions, brilliant descriptions of flavors, and rich interplays of spices and aromatics never cease to excite the mind and coax you into trying these recipes, most of which, even to this Indian, are foreign and exotic. You will find yourself cooking these recipes in no time; and tasting these flavors, you will find yourself hooked on classics of Kerala, favorites of Ammini and tastes of an era that is dying and would be lost forever if it were not for this tome.

This book will portend the coming of age of Malayali cuisine. With the same ceremony that was attached to Ammini's *Thirandu Kalyaanam* (as you will read about in great detail in Chapter 12), Ammini has ensured that the passage of time has not deprived any of us of the magic that takes place around every moment of Kerala life. The dishes that marked the four-day celebration of her coming of age shall become yours and mine, just by our reading the intricacies shared here. She was bathed and jeweled in celebration, and for us, she has cleansed age-old recipes of bygone terminology but bedecked them with prose and instruction that at once relate them to the past and yet keep them fresh and meaningful to lives today. Ceremonies of the past have lost their social significance, as she tells us in this chapter and across the many other stories shared; but through these pages, you will find yourself reliving history, cooking delicious meals, and most of all, living Kerala without drama, right in your own kitchen and home.

May there always be Nagaswaram (drums and wind instruments) bands and men holding *valum parichayum* (swords and shields) for every young girl that comes of age in Kerala—and, even better, all over the world. I also wish every man could learn a lesson or two. The world then would be even better for it. We would be poorer if more Amminis are not able to share their magic with us. And to Ammini Ramachandran I give salutations for a book well written and long overdue, and for being a modest but powerful voice in the world of food and culture. I certainly cannot resist having this book perched on my kitchen counter, cooking and eating my way through the vegetarian jewels of Kerala.

Suvir Saran
Author of *Indian Home Cooking* (Clarkson Potter, Summer 2004) and *American Masala* (Clarkson Potter, Fall 2007)
www.indianhomecooking.com
www.americanmasala.com

Acknowledgments

Writing this book of recipes, history, traditions, memories, and tales was a labor of love. Over the past seven years, this book has gone through many incarnations before arriving at publication. I am eternally grateful to so many people for helping, teaching, advising, encouraging, supporting, and pushing me to complete it.

This book would not have been written if it were not for the love and encouragement of my devoted family. My husband, R. V. Ramachandran, has lived through my cook's trials, my writer's turmoil, and the highs and the lows. He is always relentlessly honest and generously supportive. And without his urging (and sometimes pushing), I would not have completed this book.

My late mother, Ambica R. Menon, my inspiration, was a great cook. She taught me the first and the most important lesson of good cooking: never skimp on the quality or quantity of ingredients. My sisters Girija Narayanan and Rathi Ramachandran and my cousin Usha Varma, my very patient research team, spent many hours collecting old recipes and the oral history of our cultural traditions. My brothers-in-law, C. Narayanan and P. Ramachandran, were always there, cheering me along.

My sons, Raghu Ramachandran and Rama Prasad Ramachandran; daughter-in-law, Jo-Ann Curley; nephews, Paddu Ramachandran, Vivek Varma, Ranjit Narayanan, Vivek Bhaman, and Vinay Golikeri; nieces, Radha Bhaman, Meena Golikeri, Kavita Varma White, and Prasanna Chandran; and grandnieces, Salonee Bhaman and Annika Bhaman, were always a source of encouragement. I give this collection to them, to whom this heritage belongs; may this collection be an enriching offering. I especially appreciate the many constructive suggestions from the four gourmets of our family—Raghu, Jo-Ann, Paddu, and Salonee. Jo-Ann's unbridled enthusiasm for *paal paayasam*, lemon rice, and *murukku* truly motivated me to finish this book.

I owe a big thank-you to my cousin Chechi (Kamala K. Menon); I was a picky eater in my childhood, and without her constant coaxing, I would not have tasted most of the dishes I am writing about today. My husband's late grandmother Kujippilla Thampuran, my late aunt Kamalam Menon, and my cousin's wife, Narayani B. Menon, gave me many fond food memories, some of which I have shared in this book. A compilation of royal family recipes would have been impossible without the generous help of K. T. Rama Varma, Usha Varma, Rajeswari Thampuran, Rugmini Varma, Uma Devi Thampuran, Ramabhadran Thampuran, Padma Menon, and my late mother-in-law, Padmam Varma. My warm gratitude goes to various family members and relatives who were kind enough to share their knowledge, treasured family recipes, memories, and tales. I cherish every contribution and the warmth that came with it.

My most heartfelt gratitude goes to Antonia Allegra, the best mentor and friend an aspiring writer could hope for. Toni was always there to extend a generous hand, guiding me, coaching me, and cheering me to the finish line. Thank you so very much, Toni, for believing in me even when I did not believe in myself, and for encouraging me to complete this book.

I am especially indebted to Suvir Saran, acclaimed Indian chef, cooking teacher, and cookbook author, for his interest in my writings and his enthusiasm for this book. Two wonderful friends—Monica Bhide, accomplished food writer and cookbook author, and Suneeta Vaswani, cookbook author and popular cooking school teacher—are always generous with their pearls of wisdom. Thank you, Monica, for introducing me to the world of online food forums, where I have met many fabulous cooks and food writers.

I tremendously value and appreciate the advice, support, and encouragement I have received from Tridib Biswas and Arnab Chakladar. My sincere thanks to David Leite, Jacqueline Newman, and Sally Bernstein; they were the first to accept my recipes and articles for publication in print and on the Internet. I don't have enough kind words to express my gratitude to Jill Hunting, whose erudite and meticulous approach helped me reshape my manuscript.

There are many from the wonderful world of food and food writing who have always inspired, advised, and encouraged me: Angela Miller, Linda Pelaccio, Ann Mendelson, Cathy Kaufman, Ken Ovitz, Grace Young, Judith Kern, Laura Shapiro, Nancy Harmon Jenkins, Rachel Laudan, Janie Hibler, Lynn Rosetto Kasper, Sharon Hudgins, Rathi Menon, Suresh Hinduja, Chef Farid Zadi, Judy Bart Kancigor, and Matt McMillan. My heartfelt thanks to all of you.

There are many dear friends, who share their passions for food and inspire me: Uma Iyer, Lalitha Visveswaran, Champa Bilwakesh, Vamadeva Gautam Bhattacharya, Shalini Nanda Nagappa, Rushina Munshaw Ghildiyal, Ji Young Park, Diana Buja, and Karen Ackerman. I sincerely appreciate the encouragement I have received from my many friends at anothersubcontinent.com, gourmetindia.com, bookofrai.com, and egullet.org food forums; unfortunately, there are far too many to name them all individually.

I am very grateful to my friends Melissa Wilson, Sany Abraham, Subhadra Nair, Lakshmi Devi Venugopal, Margaret Ravindranath, Neeru Biswas, Yolanda Ianniello, Marisol Caldas, Lillian Lepore, Nuccia Scapilato, Alina Kochumian, Anna Erbe, Maria Laura Baran, and Donna La Spina for patiently reading the several versions of my draft and giving me their valuable suggestions. I am especially thankful to my friends Babu and Jolly Chirayil of Chirayil Infoteckh and Suresh Hinduja for some of the photographs.

My warm gratitude to the creative teams at iUniverse for walking me through the publishing process. I wish to acknowledge my debt to a collection of cookbooks that I have used for reference. The one cookbook that truly motivated me to work on this is *Frida's Fiestas: Recipes and Reminiscences of Life with Frida Kahlo,* by Guadalupe Rivera and Marie-Pierre Colle. Cookbooks that present cuisines against a backdrop of culinary history and culture have always fascinated me; truly exceptional and inspiring to me were *Splendid Table,* by Lynne Rosetto Kasper; *Gefilte Variations,* by Jayne Cohen; *Italian Festival Foods,* by Anne Bianchi; and *The Food and Life of Oaxaca,* by Zarela Martinez.

I learned every recipe in this book from the generous and ingenious cooks of my home state. Mistakes, omissions, or any confusing statements are strictly mine; I give my sincere apologies for any such unforeseen errors.

Introduction

Morning begins before sunrise in India. I still remember, from my childhood in lush, tropical Kerala in southwestern India, the sounds of a large joint-family household coming alive before daybreak. I could hear the clatter of brass pots and copper pans being washed and the rhythmic creak of the granite grinding stone pureeing coconut and green chilies for fresh chutney. Temple bells rang in the distance, announcing predawn prayers. The fragrance from the wood-burning stoves and the aroma of fresh decoction coffee permeated the entire house. Soon, the sizzle of *dosa* batter falling on the hot griddle would entice everyone to get up and get ready for breakfast.

I grew up in Chittur, a small town nestled in a mountain pass in the Sahyaadri mountain range, in a large Nayar joint family. (Nayars are matrilineal, tracing their descent through the female line.) With its abundance of rice fields, Chittur was considered the rice granary of the old kingdom of Kochi (Cochin) in central Kerala. From the twelfth century to the middle of the twentieth century, Kerala was divided into three kingdoms: Kochi, Malabar, and Tiruvithamcore, ruled by three different royal families. Our household consisted of twenty-one family members, two cooks, and several servants. My father passed away in a plane crash when I was eight years old, after which, following the old matrilineal tradition, my mother and her children moved back to her joint family.

Needless to say, it was a noisy household. After our baths in the morning, we children would all make a quick run to the temple. Breakfasts were simple, mostly *idli* (soft, round steamed cakes made from a batter of rice and *urad* dal, a split legume) or *dosa* (thin, crisp pancakes made with rice and *urad* dal batter) with coffee or tea and perhaps a banana or a steamed ripe plantain. After we children went off to school, my mother and aunts began planning the lunch menu. Lunch was always the main meal of the day—invariably boiled rice; *ghee*; yogurt; two or three vegetable dishes; one or two spicy, hot pickles; and some crisp fried wafers called *pappadams*. One dish would be either *sambar* or *pulinkari* (spicy curries with dal and vegetables), while another would be a mild vegetable or fruit curry simmered with ground coconut, green chilies, and yogurt. There would also be some spicy pan-fried green beans, plantains, or black-eyed peas.

After lunch, the children returned to school, leaving the adults to plan the evening snack menu. We would interrupt their siesta as we came charging back at about four o'clock. Afternoon tea, probably a legacy of the long British rule, consisted of a couple of savory snacks, fruits, tea, coffee, and perhaps a sweet. Sometimes there might be crunchy pretzel-like *murukku* spiced with cumin and sesame seeds, or *thengavada,* rice crackers laced with crushed black pepper—or perhaps piping-hot plantain *pokavada,* or *vada,* fritters made of ground dal mixed with green chilies, curry leaves, and cilantro. During the summer months, there would also be platters of bananas, sliced mangoes, and jackfruit.

Our evenings were spent at the temple. At sunset, the grounds would be crowded with families, all barefoot, as is the custom. While adults chanted prayers and walked around the temple, we children ran and played in the courtyard. On festival days, we would be given a small serving of *nivedyam,* food prepared as an offering at the temple. Sometimes this treat might be rice pudding, or it might be *appam,* made with rice flour, ghee, and brown sugar. I particularly used to love the *kadala,* made with tiny brown chickpeas seasoned with mustard seeds and curry leaves. We would cup our right hands to receive small servings from the priest. All those little morsels of *prasadam* (food that had been blessed) had a very special taste—maybe because we received only a small serving, or maybe because it was God's favorite food.

After evening prayers, supper was served. Conversations were always quiet and subdued, as if speaking were a rude interruption of the serious business of eating.

For the first twenty-five years of my life, I knew only one kind of food, the simple vegetarian cuisine of my home. In fact, a non-vegetarian meal was a taboo in our home, even though traditionally the Nayars do not observe a strict vegetarian diet. But because the royal family and Brahmans always adhered to vegetarianism, and because certain Nayar families, such as mine, had close ties with them over several generations, often through marriage, our family has remained vegetarian.

Ironically, my true appreciation of this vegetarian cuisine was awakened only after I left home, and it has continued to grow during the three decades I have lived away from there. Moving to the United States with my graduate-student husband opened the door for me to a wonderful world of food. As the only married Indian student couple on the campus of Brown University in the early 1970s, our kitchen became the gathering place for a group of Indian graduate students longing for a home-cooked meal. Although we all came from the same country, I soon learned that the other students had not tasted most of the dishes I was preparing.

As my friends taught me how to make dishes from other parts of India, I came to realize for the first time how different the cuisine of Kerala is from the cooking of the rest of India. This really hit home when I first served banana *paayasam*—a form of banana pudding made with ripe plantains, brown sugar, and coconut milk—to my friends from other parts of India. They had no clue what it was! And even while they were complimenting me, I was baffled that such an old standby had suddenly become so new.

What makes this southwestern region of India—encompassing a diverse terrain of lush, dense rain forests; spectacular coastal towns and picturesque lagoons dotted with unspoiled beaches and soaring coconut palms; and, in between, peaceful, flat plains carpeted with rich, green rice fields—so different from the rest of the country? Just about everything: its culture, its language, and, most of all, its food. Regional differences are a salient feature of Indian cuisine because, until the British conquered India, each region was ruled by its own royal family and had its own provincial language, local customs, culture, and unique cuisine. And each region had its own history of foreign invasions and outside influences that affected its culture and cuisine. Our cuisine resonates with the influences of centuries of trade with outsiders.

In my part of the world, eating is an almost full-time occupation. Much of a family's energy is spent on planning meals or talking about food. There is as much pleasure in anticipating a meal and reminiscing about it afterward as there is in devouring it. It is a misconception that the vegetarian food of southern India is a slim repertoire of dishes: plain boiled rice, *sambar,* coconut chutney, and the ever-popular masala *dosa* (thin, crisp rice-and-dal pancakes stuffed with a spicy potato filling). On the contrary, our cuisine encompasses a full array of styles and flavors ranging from pungent to sweet, delicately balancing simplicity and subtlety.

The two most important aspects of this vegetarian cooking are seasonality and flexibility. This cuisine is all about creating the tastiest and most satisfying dishes from a few fresh, seasonally available ingredients. Our cooking does not require a professionally equipped kitchen or a pantry stocked with a vast array of spices and condiments. Rather, our recipes are based on the use of spices and herbs that are already to be found in many western kitchens—cumin, coriander, black pepper, hot green chilies, ginger, cilantro, and sesame seeds. This is pure comfort food: hearty, steaming stews (we call them *kootaan),* savory side dishes, and creamy, custard-like desserts. Several of our recipes use only two or three herbs or spices and some coconut. And once all the ingredients are assembled, many of these dishes can be prepared in less than thirty minutes.

Our cuisine has always been—and still is—one without rules. You need only to know your ingredients; the rest is up to your creativity and your ability to improvise. The pungency and character of most spices can be modified, depending on when during the cooking process you add them and how they are incorporated into a dish—whether they are used raw, toasted, or fried. In the warm climate of southern India, tamarind, coconut, and yogurt have a cooling effect on spicy food, while mustard seeds, black peppercorns, and hot red and green chilies provide pungent counterpoints. Fragrant curry leaves enliven any recipe to which they are added. The warm weather ferments batters to perfection without any leavening agent.

Although this vegetarian cuisine excludes all meat, fish, fowl, and eggs, it is healthy, delectable, and nutritionally well balanced. Unlike traditional Western menus, our meals do not have a main course. In the vegetarian South, rice is the heart of every meal. At lunch and dinner, a mound of plain boiled rice is always at the center of the plate or banana leaf (our substitute for paper plates), surrounded by various vegetarian preparations. If you were not raised eating rice, this might sound a bit monotonous, but good rice is like good bread—it always stimulates the appetite. It is simple to cook and goes well with an amazing number of different foods.

With the abundance of coconut palms, naturally the coconut is another indispensable ingredient. Coconut is used in various forms in spicy hot dishes as well as in desserts. While rice and coconut provide the starch and fat content of the meal, various kinds of beans and lentils are the major sources of protein. Plantains, both green and ripe, are also indispensable in our cooking. All kinds of tropical fruits (most importantly bananas, mangoes, and jackfruit) substitute for dessert. Sweets are generally served only on festive occasions, not with everyday meals.

It is my goal in this book to capture and recreate the simple vegetarian cuisine and age-old traditions of Kochi's royalty and the Nayars who served them.

Traditional Kitchens and the Pantry

The kitchen in my ancestral home was a spacious and special place, with wood-burning stoves and wooden racks filled with ceramic jars and pots made of copper, bronze, and soapstone. Like the kitchen of any orthodox Hindu home, it was always spotlessly clean, and no one was allowed to enter wearing shoes or without first taking a bath. To this day, cleanliness is of paramount importance, and people living outside the big cities still observe these rules.

As children, we were not allowed to go further than the doorway to the kitchen. My recollections are of sitting on a windowsill in the mornings and watching the cook churn a large pot of yogurt to make fresh butter and buttermilk; of lazy summer afternoons, when I tiptoed into the kitchen, when no one was there, to pick up a handful of sea salt from the *uppumarava* (wooden salt box) to eat with fresh, raw mangoes; of watching my mother continuously stir *paalpaayasam* (rice pudding) on festival days, while the cooks hurried around her, preparing traditional dishes with fresh vegetables from our farm; and of the many good times that made the kitchen the heart of our home. From the kitchen came amazingly diverse vegetarian dishes that were prepared with seemingly ordinary ingredients. To this day, the tastes and aromas that accompanied these simple creations remain vivid in my memory.

Across the back wall of the kitchen was the *aduppu* (wood-burning stove), a hollow brick construction with holes at the top that served as burners. Firewood was fed into the stove from another hole in front. On one side of the *aduppu* was a lower platform that was used to hold pots of cooked food and to drain cooked rice. (In my part of India, rice is cooked in a large quantity of water and then drained, just as you would prepare pasta.) Another corner of the kitchen was set up for cleaning vegetables and rice and for washing utensils. Across the wall stood long shelves, on which we kept copper and brass pots, and pans lined with tin. Because unlined copper and brass cookware can develop a highly poisonous substance, we tinned and periodically re-tinned all of our cookware, to be safe. At one end of the shelf sat the large steamer for *idli* and a stack of *idli* plates. An iron *Cheena chatti*, or wok, was used for deep frying, and shallow, heavy bronze pans called *uruli* were used for making curries and puddings. A flat iron griddle used exclusively for making *dosa* was kept at the bottom of the shelf.

Then there were pots called *kalchatti*, which were carved out of soapstone and used for cooking *sambar* and *rasam* (legume-based curries and soups). Even when removed from the stove, the *kalchatti* retained heat and kept their contents hot for a long time. Serving utensils included plates and glasses made of copper, bell metal, and silver. Today, the *aduppu* has been replaced by gas burners and the metal pots and pans have been replaced by stainless steel or aluminum alloy pots. Plates and tumblers are now made mainly of stainless steel and glass.

Just outside the kitchen was an open veranda, where we kept four different kinds of stone implements for grinding rice, dal, coconut, and various spice blends. The *ammi* sat on a raised platform and was used to grind spices and coconut in the right proportions. It was a large, rectangular, rough granite stone with a cylindrical stone piece on top that looked and worked exactly like the Mexican *matate*. Sometimes, in a rush, the cook would forget to rinse it off thoroughly, and instantaneously a couple of crows would fly in to feast on the leftover coconut. On a corner of the veranda majestically sat the *aattukal*, a large stone structure with a cavity in the middle and a cylindrical stone piece that tapered at the top and fit into the cavity. This was used every day for grinding the *idli* and *dosa* batters. Soaked rice and *urad* dal were fed into the cavity, and our cook sat there, rotating the cylinder until the batter was of perfect consistency. He would then lift the cylinder and scoop up the batter into a pot.

There were also the *ural* (a stone or wooden trough) and the *ulakka* (a long wooden or sometimes iron pole with a metal bottom), for pounding dry ingredients. Often, during summer afternoons, our maidservants Muttayi and Eennasu would pound chilies and other ingredients to be used for pickling. Muttayi would first fill the cavity of the *ural* with whole chilies. Each woman would then pick up an *ulakka*, and together they would start pulverizing the chilies. When Muttayi's pole went in, Eennasu's went up in the air, the two of them working in a synchronized motion that was fascinating to watch.

The *arakallu* was our food mill; it consisted of two massive stone disks, one on top of the other, connected with an iron rod. The bottom stone had an iron cylinder in the middle, and the top one had a wooden handle and a hole in the middle. Our cook would feed handfuls of grain into the hole and rotate the top stone over the bottom one, grinding the grains or dal between them. Coarsely ground flour trickled down the sides onto old newspapers spread underneath. Today, electric blenders and grinders have replaced these traditional appliances.

Close to the kitchen was the *kalavara*, or pantry. There, set on shelves running the length of one wall, were huge, lidded brass containers that stored a month's supply of various dried legumes. Smaller containers held dried spices and nuts. Lined up on another shelf were large ceramic jars containing a year's supply of homemade pickled mangoes, limes, and gooseberries, and fruit preserves made from ripe plantains, jackfruit, and mangoes. A huge earthenware pot with a lid contained tamarind. Large tins or ceramic jars stored coconut oil and sesame oil. The *ari mancha*, a huge wooden box with a lid, held a special place in our pantry. After the harvest, huge sacks of rice were emptied into it. A wooden partition kept the long-grain rice *(unakkalari)* away from the parboiled rice *(puzukkalari)*.

Sun-drying vegetables and spiced and cooked batters of rice was a major project every summer. Besides the vegetables from our farm, my mother bought large quantities of green chilies, okra, tender black-eyed peas in pods, various gourds, bitter melons, lotus stems, and bitter-tasting berries called *chundanga* and *manathankali*. After supper, the servants followed the ritual of washing and slicing the vegetables, which were stored overnight in large pots. Early in the morning, some of the vegetables would be blanched in salted boiling water, spiced, and spread out on mats to dry in the summer sun. Some others, like chili peppers, were soaked overnight in salted buttermilk and sun dried during the day. After they were completely dry, the vegetables were stored in airtight containers for use during the monsoon season.

When I was growing up, most households had their own cows, and yogurt and butter were prepared every day. The milk was boiled and allowed to cool; then yogurt culture was added, and the mixture was left to ferment overnight. In the morning, the set yogurt was poured into a tall vessel and stirred with a wooden churn to separate the butter. When the butter floated to the top, it was scooped up and placed in a bowl of cold water. The buttermilk that remained in the vessel was served with meals and used for cooking, while the butter was melted and clarified to make ghee. Now, milk and milk products are purchased from dairies, but many people still make their own yogurt and buttermilk.

Cooking and Dining Traditions

The skill of a traditional cook depends on his or her ability to judge taste with the eyes and nose. Tasting a dish while preparing it is a taboo. You are not allowed to serve another person the food you have already tasted. Some of these old traditions are so firmly engraved in my own mind that, even after thirty years in the United States, I still hesitate to taste anything I prepare before serving my guests or family. (All of the recipes for this book have been tested, however.)

There are various rules that govern the dining process. Although this may seem unrefined, the tradition of eating with the right hand is still very much alive, even in modern times. The left hand is considered unclean. Hygiene and cleanliness are paramount, and hands are always washed before sitting down to eat. At both lunch and dinner, rice and vegetable curries are shaped into small balls with the fingers of the right hand and scooped up to the mouth. Diners handle this motion with such finesse that one would think it was the only reasonable way to eat. All of the senses are experiencing a feast in unison: the eyes perceive the splendid meal, the nose inhales its hearty aromas, the hands sense the complex textures and temperatures of the food, and the tongue relishes the hot, sweet, sour, pungent, salty, and astringent flavors.

Drinking water is poured into the mouth from a metal tumbler, without the rim touching the lips. Traditionally, one should always allow food to be served, never attempting to serve oneself with the hand used for eating. Each dish on the banana leaf has a specific position, and the server is expected to know these rules.

Do not offer others any food that has already been served to you. To offer food from your plate to someone else is considered a social insult. Once the food is on your plate or banana leaf, it becomes "contaminated"—the closest English word I can think of, though it does not fully convey the hygienic nuances. The only exception to this rule applies to members of the royal family. In my parents' generation, each member of the royal family had a personal servant, who was entitled to the leftovers from his or her master's banana leaf. Also, after a coronation ceremony, the maharaja would offer an *urula* (small serving) from his banana leaf to a few chosen Nayar soldiers; by devouring this morsel, the Nayars sealed their unconditional loyalty to the throne. Those Nayars who were fortunate enough to receive the maharaja's food were called *chavor pada*, meaning that they would defend their king with their lives. When the Portuguese explorers arrived in India at the end of the fifteenth century, they were so impressed with this absolute loyalty that they employed many Nayars as guards for their warehouses at Kochi.

After the meal, both hands and mouth are washed clean, and often a betel leaf is chewed to cleanse the mouth and aid digestion. On religious and auspicious occasions, everyone sat on the floor on a *palaka* (wooden plank) or a *paya* (straw mat) facing east, and the food was served on banana leaves. On birthdays and holidays (such as Onam), the meal is first served on a banana leaf placed in front of a lighted oil lamp, as an offering to God.

Enormous importance is placed on hospitality. Guests are served lavish fare and are routinely coaxed to take second and third helpings, the host insisting that they have not eaten enough. My mother used to talk about her shock as a young bride when, during the course of one day, some thirty guests arrived at her in-laws' joint-family home unannounced and were graciously received and fed appropriately. The preparation of impromptu meals, made with a few simple ingredients to serve a large group of unexpected guests, was a challenge and a true test of the ingenuity of traditional vegetarian cooks. By custom, guests were always served first, followed by the men and children, and last, the women of the family. The women considered this a sign of graciousness rather than subservience. Today, the importance of hospitality remains strong, although, particularly with the breakup of large extended-family households and the availability of hotels for guests, all of these rules are no longer always observed.

It is difficult for my people to accept a compliment for good cooking. From childhood, we are taught to deny every compliment politely, as a sign of modesty. At the same time, a criticism about the quality of a dish is to be accepted with gratitude. The first opportunity I had to prepare a traditional vegetarian meal for a large group was when a famous *Kathakali* (dramatic dance) troupe came to Providence to perform at Brown University in 1972. The organizers of the event were worried about providing a vegetarian meal for such a large group, so my husband and I happily accepted the offer of front-row seats for the performance in exchange for providing a meal for the group. The performers, who were traveling in the United States for several weeks, were delighted to see the rice and vegetable curries we had prepared. In the most traditional way, they sat down and ate in silence, raising their heads only to ask for second servings. As this was our first attempt to cook for a large group, especially a respected group from back home, we were eager to hear their opinion of the meal. Finally, the leader of the group spoke. "We are very glad to get a home-cooked meal at last," he said. "We were living for weeks on a diet of cucumber salad and yogurt. But the *aviyal* (a mixed vegetable curry) was missing *chena* and *muringakkaya* (two tropical vegetables)." We thought that was the best compliment we could ever have hoped to receive!

Temple Festivals and Festive Fare

Some of my fondest childhood memories are of the numerous fun-filled, colorful, and glittering festivals that are celebrated throughout the year. Astrology, tradition, and creativity together have bestowed on the people of India a wealth of holy days, when one or another god of the Hindu pantheon has to be revered. Most festivals are held in honor of a patron god of a particular town, and they last for several days. These festivals give an opportunity to completely immerse oneself in tropical sounds, colors, costumes, and aromas.

All festivals, regardless of the deity they are honoring, have one thing in common—food! In addition to the popular snack foods sold by street vendors, each temple has its own *nivedyam*, food that is offered to the god being honored and later distributed to devotees. Each god has his favorite food: Ganapathi, the destroyer of all obstacles, loves fruits and coconuts, and his favorite dessert is *modakam*, made of rice flour and sweetened coconut flakes. Poornathrayesan, the one who bestows children upon childless couples, loves *paal paayasam* (rice pudding). Subrahmanya, who came to Earth to kill the demons and protect the world, prefers *panchamridam*, made of five sweet ingredients, and *paanakam*, a ginger-and-cardamom-flavored drink sweetened with jaggery, an Indian brown sugar. Durga, the goddess of strength, loves *neypaayasam*, a rice pudding made with ghee and jaggery.

Seasonal Festivals

Traditionally, there were four festivals to celebrate a rich rice harvest: Thiruvonam, Nira, Puthiri, and Kathir. Of these, only Thiruvonam is still observed today. On Thiruvonam, following the morning festivities, households enjoy a sumptuous noontime feast called Onasadya.

In summer, we celebrate Vishu, which is the first day of the month of Medam (mid-April to mid-May) on our regional calendar. Long ago, Vishu was our New Year's Day; it was changed to mid-September in 825 AD. (Whether it was changed to celebrate our king's victory over neighboring kingdoms or to mark the establishment of a new major seaport, Kollam, remains a topic of debate among historians.) It is believed that the first thing one sees on Vishu morning influences one's fortunes for the rest of the year. Before dawn, we wake up to see the Vishu Kani, a very pretty arrangement of several auspicious objects. Children light fireworks before dawn, and at noon, a fabulous feast is served.

During certain months of the year, Ekaadashi (the eleventh day of the moon calendar) is observed. On those days, no rice is cooked in the house. At lunch, other grains, such as wheat, *nivara,* and *chama* (two varieties of wild rice), are cooked and served. Supper consists of particular snacks made of wheat or cream of wheat. These days are called partial fast days; when no rice is served, it is considered fasting! Young women used to fast on Mondays to ensure that they would be blessed with good husbands.

In the month of Dhanu (mid-December to mid-January), the festival Thiruvathira celebrates the love between the goddess Parvathi and her husband, the god Siva. During this time, women observe partial fasting for the well-being of their husbands and children. They consume coconut, fruits, and dishes made with arrowroot.

An Uncommon Social Structure

Since very ancient times, matrilineal societies have existed around the world. Western Europe had a long matrilineal tradition in the Germanic regions of Austria, Germany, and Switzerland. European Celts were considered matrilineal, as were the Iroquois, a confederation of five groups of Native Americans. Matrilineal societies are known to have existed in other parts of Europe, Africa (the Toka of Zambia), South America, China, the Pacific Islands, and the Lakshadweep Islands in the Arabian Sea. Matrilineal clans called *kudi* were the dominant social organization among the Tamils and Muslims of eastern Sri Lanka. Kerala is one of the very few places (another being China, among the Mosuos) where remnants of a matrilineal system have survived to the present day.

For centuries, foreign visitors and anthropologists have been fascinated by the Nayars and royal families of Kerala for their matrilineal kinship and descent traced through the female line. Pliny, in his *Natural History*, referred to this community as *Nareae*. The first detailed accounts of Nayar society began to appear by the sixteenth century, as the Portuguese gained effective control of the Arabian Sea and the Kerala spice trade. Elie Reclus wrote in *Primitive Folk: Studies in Comparative Ethnology*, "No people have more fully appreciated the maternal family, nor developed it more logically than the Nayars, despite the accumulated obstacles thrown in its way."

Like the samurai of Japan, in ancient times, Nayars were the hereditary military aristocracy of Kerala. They were trained in Kalaripayattu (a traditional form of martial art) at village gymnasiums called *kalari*. Although tradition dictated that they defend their king with their own lives, not all of them were soldiers. Only the physically fit were recruited into the military. They formed the sword-bearing militia who fought for their king. In 1553, Luis de Cameons, a Portuguese soldier-poet, wrote about the Nayar soldiers:

> The proud *Nayres* the noble rank is claimed;
> The toils of culture and of art they scorn,
> The warrior's plumes their haughty brows adorn;
> The shining faulchion brandished in the right,
> Their left arm wields the target in the fight;
> Of danger scornful, ever armed they stand
> Around the king a stern barbarian band.

The sociological, cultural, and economic implications of matrilineal systems are the focus of much anthropological interest, even in modern times.

Rural settlements in medieval Kerala were mostly residential clusters focused around Nayar *tharavads* (joint families) living in their *naalukettu* homes. With a history dating back to hundreds of years, these beautiful homes are an interface between built world and the tropical greenery, with courtyards open to the sky in the center and open verandas both inside and out, lined with pillars. The ancestral homes belonged to the women, and they lived there with their children. Lineage was traced through women, who enjoyed equal rights, and children belonged to the mother's family. Nayar women were noted for their strength and confidence. By the latter half of the nineteenth century, many of them were educated. Several Nayar families had substantial land holdings (not all of them were rich), which were jointly owned by all members of the family and often were managed by the senior male, called the *Karanavar*. To belong to an aristocratic *tharavad* meant wealth, status, power, and privilege. The Nayars had a number of last names (caste-identifying names) including Nayar (Nair), Menon, Panikar, Pillai, Kaimal, and Unni. Today, a few continue this tradition, but many of them no longer use these last names.

In the old days, the matrilineal community had its own system of social governance. The customs and rituals of this matrilineal community were unique. In olden times, besides martial arts, Vattezhuthu, a descendant of the Tamil Brahmi script with thirty-letter alphabet from which Malayalam (Kerala's language) script evolved, was also taught to both boys and girls at various *kalaris*. (Tamil was the language of ancient south India. The Brahmi script was brought to the Tamil country in the third century BC by Jain and Buddhist monks. The term Tamil-Brahmi is used when the script is in Brahmi but the language is Tamil. The split of Malayalam from Tamil began sometime in the ninth century AD and evolved over a period of four to five centuries.)

The kingdoms of Kochi and Tiruvithamcore maintained Nayar brigades modeled after Western armies until India gained independence from the British in 1947. Many of the Nayars who returned home after the breakup of traditional armies in the last century were quick to take advantage of modern education and expanding employment opportunities.

The matrilineal system disintegrated over time. Land reform acts limited the size of the communal properties joint families could own. This substantially reduced the possessions of *tharavads,* and gradually they dwindled in size and wealth. Nayar reform movements challenged the unmitigated powers of the *Karanavar*. Economic changes and ideological and cultural perspectives of this period affected the *tharavads,* and the concept of the nuclear family gained acceptance. Today, life in a *tharavad* is merely an old memory. Several *naalukettu* homes were converted to favorite tourist destinations, where visitors enjoy their stay in ethnic surroundings. This style of architecture has today become a status symbol among the well-to-do in Kerala.

The selfishness and greed of the Nayar *Karanavars* and their ill treatment of poor relatives became the most captivating subject of popular Malayalam literature of the twentieth century. Unfortunately, some of the positive aspects of this ancient social system and their sociological, cultural, and economic implications were seldom found in Kerala's literature. Joint-family life was by no means flawless; like any other social structure, it had its share of issues. Personally, I have many fond memories of growing up in such a household. The breakup of a joint family into smaller units did not necessarily represent total rejection of the joint-family ideal. Many typically maintain strong bonds of kinship and attempt to provide each other with social and emotional support. Some of the royal families and Nayars of Kerala (including mine) continue to observe the ritual aspects of this ancient social system. The very close bond between a sister and brother—or, for that matter, between an uncle and his nieces and nephews—is often reaffirmed in time-honored ceremonies.

Celebration of the Life Cycle

Nowhere else in India is the birth of a baby girl received with greater joy than in Kerala's matrilineal community. A new baby girl is the next important link in the matrilineal chain. In my branch of the extended joint family, the first baby girl who was born outside India was my grandniece Annika. All of us had gathered at our ancestral home for the impending wedding of my nephew. Early on a monsoon-soaked June morning in 2001, my sister received a call from her daughter in Santa Monica—she had given birth to a little girl. Everyone was elated. "Ah! It is a girl." Someone else whispered, "Thank God for *santhathi* (a girl)."

The birth of another baby girl, an important matrilineal link that perpetuates the family, was indeed an occasion for celebration. My mother, the proud great-grandmother, sent a servant out to buy sweet candies. "Don't stand around talking at the store. Come back quickly with the sweets," someone warned her as she left. When she returned, all of us sat around making small packets of candies to give as gifts. It was amusing to think that even at the dawn of the twenty-first century, we were rejoicing like a true matrilineal clan.

Our maidservant, with a large shopping bag full of candy packets, left on a happy mission to deliver candies and good news of the birth of the little girl to our extended matrilineal clan. She didn't balk at going out in the pouring rain, because every time she delivered the candy packets and happy news, she would receive a small present of cash.

A baby's first lunar month and its first feeding of rice are all observed with much ceremony. At *Irupathettu*, a ceremony on the twenty-eighth day after a baby girl or boy is born, the child is given its name, its first meal of sweet porridge, its first piece of jewelry, and even its first chance to wear eye makeup. As on any special occasion, the mother and the baby take a bath in the morning, and the baby is clad in just a *konakam*, a small rectangular piece of red cotton fabric worn as a diaper. Relatives and friends are invited for the ceremony. The mother sits on the floor, facing east, with the baby on her lap. Her mother or an elder relative prepares the baby's first makeup of homemade eyeliner. A *mashioodam*, a round iron plate fitted with a chain, is dangled over a lighted oil lamp to collect soot; this soot is then smeared around the baby's eyes with the index finger. In the past, *Irupathettu* was also the time for ear piercing and adorning the baby with his or her first set of earrings. Traditional jewelry pieces at this ceremony include an *aranjanam* (a gold chain for the midriff) and *vala* and *thala* (gold bangles for arms and ankles). A black glass bangle is also included to ward off the evil eye. The baby is then fed a small spoonful of a freshly prepared herbal concoction called *vayambu*, which is believed to stimulate good digestion. Then the baby is fed a sweet porridge of dried raw-banana powder or *kora* (millet) cooked with milk and a touch of sugar. In some families, the baby's maternal uncle whispers the baby's name three times in his or her ears. Others wait to name the baby until the ceremony of feeding the first meal of rice. A sumptuous vegetarian feast follows the ceremonies.

Chooroonu, the occasion when rice is fed to the baby for the first time, is celebrated six months after birth. An astrologer is consulted to select an auspicious day for the ceremony. The baby is bathed, dressed in festive clothes, and taken to the temple. There, the baby is seated on the lap of his or her uncle or father. After offering special prayers for the baby, the priest ladles out a serving of *paal paayasam* (rice pudding that has been offered at the temple) onto a banana leaf. The baby is fed this *paayasam* by the uncle or father, followed by all family members. On this day, the baby also gets his or her first necklace. Needless to say, a sumptuous vegetarian feast follows this ceremony, to which extended family members are invited.

Every *pirannal,* or birthday, is observed with special prayers at the temple, followed by a sumptuous feast; but certain birthdays, such as the first, sixtieth, and eighty-fourth, are observed with more ceremony. Prayers are offered at the temple, and several guests are invited to the house for a festive meal on these occasions. A lighted oil lamp is kept in the dining room. A banana leaf laden with a festive meal is placed in front of the lamp as an offering to the Hindu god Ganapathi, destroyer of all obstacles. Mothers consider it a sacred duty to serve rice to children on their birthdays. They stand behind their son or daughter and serve rice on a banana leaf while praying for the long life, welfare, and happiness of the child.

Sixtieth and eighty-fourth birthdays are often celebrated like a wedding. During the days when the mortality rate was high, reaching the age of sixty was a big accomplishment, and it was celebrated accordingly. A person has witnessed one thousand full moons by living to eighty-four years, and that birthday is celebrated with much ceremony.

In ancient times, girls as young as six months and up to twelve years of age went through a symbolic wedding ceremony called *Kettukalyaanam.* This was purely ceremonial in nature, and it marked the girl's transition to adult life and legitimized the birth of her children. This ceremony, deeply connected to the matrilineal system, is no longer observed or celebrated.

In times past, as girls attained puberty, they were given a coming-of-age ceremony called *Thirandu Kalyaanam,* which lasted four days. The ceremony signaled the end of her childhood and her availability for marriage. Today, this ceremony has completely lost its old social significance. However, in the remote villages of Kerala and neighboring Tamil Nadu, it is still celebrated as a significant event in the life of a girl, with special feasts and traditional gifts.

I was very surprised to learn that a ceremony very similar to *Thirandu Kalyaanam* still exists among the Apache and Navajo Indian tribes in the United States. The Apaches call it *Naies* ("changing women ceremony"), while the Navajo Indians call it *Kinaalda.* In most Western cultures, puberty is greeted with little, if any, fanfare. Rather, it is a private, sometimes uncertain time for girls whose cultures have not sanctioned marriage and childbirth at this stage. In contrast, in many other societies, this new ability to be a reproductive female is publicly celebrated. The ceremony introduces the girl to her new life and ensures that her life will be long and productive. Although the details of ceremonies vary among tribes, the similarities between the American Indian ceremonies and Kerala's *Thirandu Kalyaanam* are quite remarkable.

All three celebrations are regarded as rites of passage into womanhood, and the festivities last for four days. Among the Navajo, the ritual begins with hair washing; in Kerala, the ceremonies begin with the girl taking a ritual bath. While American Indians bake cake made with their primary sustenance (corn) for the celebrations, in Kerala, rice (our primary food grain) is cooked in different ways for the ceremony. Special jewelry is placed on the girl celebrating *Kinaalda;* girls in Kerala were also adorned with several pieces of jewelry. In all three celebrations, the girl's family and members of her society are all considered participants and dances are performed. The American Indian dances express the girl's spiritual and physical transformation and acceptance of her as a woman. In Kerala, friends and relatives perform the hand-clapping folk dance around ceremonial food offerings on the third day of celebration. All three celebrations imply society's acknowledgement and acceptance of the girl as a woman.

In the old days, marriage as we know it today was uncommon in our society. In a very simple and silent wedding ceremony *(pudava kodukkal),* the groom presented the bride with a set of white cotton clothes in front of a lighted bronze oil lamp, marking the beginning of a visiting relationship. The woman stayed with her joint family, and the man of her choice visited her. Over the years, a type of traditional marriage arranged by the family became prevalent. Even today, the Kerala matrilineal wedding is probably the shortest wedding ceremony anywhere in India, or perhaps even in the world. It is held at the bride's home or temple, and her mother and maternal uncle's wife bring her to the wedding podium. The climax of the wedding is when the groom presents the bride with a *pudava mundu,* a traditional two-piece Kerala cotton sari with a golden border. Now weddings are celebrated on a grand scale, and guests often number five hundred to a thousand. The vegetarian feasts following the weddings are always exquisite and elaborate.

A woman's first pregnancy and the imminence of her giving birth to the next link in the family chain are celebrated in a ceremony called *Puliyoonu*. The expectant mother's brother (or matrilineal cousin) ceremoniously feeds her a type of tamarind soup. The tip of a sword or a long knife is placed on her tongue, and *puli*, a soup made from five kinds of sour fruits, is poured onto her tongue from a spoon made with a jackfruit leaf. Until the beginning of the nineteenth century, the Nayars were warriors, and the use of the sword is probably symbolic of their role and status. After the mother-to-be drinks the *puli*, her brother, father, and husband present her with new clothes. The event is celebrated with a feast.

The sad and somber occasion of death is observed with fifteen days of mourning. After this period, the life of the deceased person is honored in a ceremony called *Adiyanthiram*. It is a celebration of the long life of the person and an opportunity to show appreciation to neighbors and relatives for their help and support. Death anniversaries are observed with religious rites and feeding of the poor.

Food is such a vital part of our culture and tradition that every religious or family occasion—whether it is the birth of a baby, a marriage, the anniversary of a loved one's death, or any one of countless other small occasions—is observed by serving or giving a gift of food. Each of these ceremonies features specific dishes that are prepared only on these occasions. And in each family, the same festive dishes for each occasion continue to be prepared and served by one generation after another.

About the Recipes

Most of the recipes in this book were handed down from one generation to the next in my own extended family, and some of them are special gifts from relatives. I have purposely limited myself to a selection of family recipes here, and to the geographical, cultural, and historical context of this food, so as to present the subject in its proper perspective. With most recipes, I have given Western substitutes, following the traditional recipe.

In many cases, these everyday dishes have a very long history. As recipes tell only part of the story of this cuisine, I have included notes on the historical facts and anecdotes associated with several of them. Ancient Indian literature mentions certain recipes as far back as the fifth century AD. Several of the old recipes are associated with regional festivals, and some are traditionally prepared as offerings at famous temples.

Whenever one takes the regional dishes of a country to another part of the world, difficulties inevitably arise. Often, products are not readily available. The climate may not always cooperate. If I felt a recipe's authenticity and quality would suffer with changes and substitutions, I left it in its original form—but there are only a few recipes of this kind.

Back home, we are taught to cultivate a sense of smell and color, and we try to accomplish perfection in cooking through exploration. Almost every ingredient is measured only by hand—a handful, a little, a pinch, and so on. Cooking is an expression of the cook's personal tastes and preferences. The joy of it is in experimenting. The delight in cooking is not necessarily derived from the end product alone, but from the endless possibilities available for flavoring a dish. I urge you to use these recipes for ideas and suggestions. Improvise, but never let a cookbook order you around.

Chapter One
Our History and Heritage

Along the coastline of tropical southwestern India, where the Indian Ocean and the Arabian Sea converge, set among picturesque lagoons and backwaters and separated from the rest of the Indian subcontinent by the rugged Sahyadri mountain range (also called the Western Ghats), lies a land of spectacular beauty and proud heritage: Kerala, the land of coconut palms and spices.

The story of our spices is an ever-changing history of lands discovered or destroyed, favors sought or offered, treaties signed or broken, wars won or lost, and kingdoms built or brought down. Ever since ancient times, the monsoon-soaked rain forests of Kerala, home to several spices—including the world's most widely used spice, black pepper *(piper nigrum)*—were a prime destination for many explorers. The abundant black pepper attracted Arabs, Greeks, Romans, Portuguese, Dutch, and British from the west and Southeast Asians and Chinese from the east.

The spice trade not only brought prosperity to our region, but it also left an indelible imprint on Kerala's culture and cuisine. From the pre-Christian era onward, trade between the kingdoms of south India and ancient Israel and Arabia resulted in the formation of the earliest Jewish, Christian, and Muslim communities of Kerala. When foreign traders arrived at the port of Muziris, near the capital of the Chera kings (ancient rulers of Kerala), the reigning kings treated them with respect, extending facilities for their settlement and the establishment of their faiths in the land. The ancient travelers Sulaiman, al-Biruni, Marco Polo, and Ibn Battuta have all written about the religious tolerance of the kings and people of Kerala.

Foreign traders brought with them numerous new plants and trees, which thrived in our tropical weather. Several fruits, nuts, spices, and vegetables we associate today with Kerala cuisine were unknown in ancient times. All these were slowly but surely integrated into our cuisine.

This chapter presents a brief account of the development of the ancient spice trade that began before the birth of Christ, lasted many centuries, and greatly influenced our society. I will discuss the social and cultural diversity of Kerala; its gradual colonization by foreign traders, including the Portuguese, the Dutch, and the British; the unification of Kerala after India gained independence from the British; and the influences of foreign trade on our agriculture and cuisine.

Ancient Trade with the West

Legend has it that the ancient Phoenicians, the greatest travelers and traders of their time, traded with the southwest coast of India. The biblical King Solomon constructed a fleet of ships with the help of Hiram, the young king of Phoenicia, and the two allies jointly sent voyages to Ophir. Their navy returned every three years bringing gold, ivory, apes, peacocks, and almug wood (sandalwood). The exact location of Ophir, a place well known for its abundance of gold during early biblical days, remains a matter for speculation. One opinion is that Ophir probably was another name for southern Arabia, a region famous for its gold and precious gems, though sandalwood and peacocks are not native to the region. Perhaps Solomon's fleet, in search of sandalwood, traveled farther than Ophir, to the coasts of Africa or India. Gems, peacocks, and sandalwood were certainly some of the commodities traded at the port of Muziris in Kerala in ancient times.

> Substantial and lasting geographical changes took place along Kerala's coastline in 1341, when a great flood totally destroyed the ancient port at Muziris and opened up a large natural harbor at the nearby fishing village, Kochi. I distinctly remember, while living in this port city of Kochi during the 1950s and 1960s, the stevedores and workers transporting commodities in wooden carts, loudly reciting, "Elissa, eelam maali Elissa." It was an oral tradition passed on through generations, but no one knew what these words meant.
>
> One possible explanation is that they are emulating an ancient custom of Phoenician sailors, who are said to have carried, fixed on the prows of their ships, the image of Elissa, the legendary queen of Carthage and patroness of the mariners. I learned from an Italian friend that in Southern Italy, a region the Phoenicians frequented, port workers pushing heavy loads chanted Elissa's name to invoke her blessings. Is it possible that Phoenicians did come to the ancient port at Muziris in Kerala for sandalwood and peacocks? Perhaps the workers in Kochi were emulating the Phoenicians in evoking the goddess. Only further archeological research can shed some light on this interesting custom.

Arab Trade

Despite the fame of overland trade along the Silk Road, much of the significant trade between Europe and Asia was carried out in specific sailing seasons along the Indian Ocean. The Arabian Peninsula was home to Arabs, Hebrews, Ethiopians, and Syrians. These pre-Islamic tribes of central Asia, along with Indian and Southeast Asian merchants, were active traders and intermediaries in early Indian Ocean trade. They collected silk form China; cloves, nutmeg, pearls, and tortoise shells from Indonesia; and cinnamon, ivory, and tortoise shells from Sri Lanka. All of these commodities were transported to the port of Muziris and other ports along India's southwestern coast. Muziris became one of the main trans-shipment ports for goods from the east. Pepper was abundant in Kerala. Cinnamon and cassia were two other native spices. Cloves and nutmeg were introduced to Kerala early on. Spice traders took these native spices and other commodities that had arrived at the port across the great expanse of the Indian Ocean to Africa and Arabia, and from there, to points farther west.

The tradition of maritime trade expanded to unprecedented levels with the introduction of spices to the West. The Arab and Jewish merchants tolerated Indian traders in Africa, but they fiercely guarded the lucrative commerce within the Red Sea for themselves. Arabs also shrewdly withheld their sailing knowledge of the Indian Ocean from Greeks and Romans, in order to maintain their monopoly of Indian goods.

When the Romans occupied Egypt and made the Red Sea their main path of commerce, profits from caravan routes declined, and the kingdoms of southern Arabia lost much of their wealth. However, the old Arab channels of trade with India survived, thanks to age-old alliances and agreements between Arab and Hindu traders. Interestingly, cinnamon, the spice that made fortunes for the Arab traders in earlier times, remained an Arab monopoly. The Romans could find it only at Arab ports; the source of cinnamon in India was scrupulously guarded from them. Such was the loyalty between the ancient traders of the Indian Ocean. The Romans were offered only malabathrum, the leaves of the same tree that produce the fragrant cinnamon bark.

Discovery of the Maritime Trade Route

The seamen of Ptolemaic Egypt probably knew of the long coastal route to northern India, but they were reluctant to risk a long voyage close to the Arab-controlled shoreline. The Ptolemies of Egypt developed a series of ports on the Red Sea, initially to bring elephants from Africa for their armies. Then, during the second century BC, a Greek sailor is said to have taken advantage of the powerful monsoon winds to navigate his ship toward India's southwestern coast. This route to the coast of Kerala, primarily to the port of Muziris, was mostly from the Red Sea through the Arabian Sea, where trade winds helped push the ships toward the southern shores of India.

The primary Red Sea ports were Myos Hormos, Philoteras, Leukos Limen, and Berenike (Berenicé). In early times, Myos Hormos was the most frequented of these ports; this is perhaps because the desert roads were less secure during these times. Berenike eventually replaced Myos Hormos as the most prominent port. Once they mastered the use of the monsoons, the Greeks no longer needed the Arabs as expensive middlemen for African and Indian goods.

Roman Trade

When conducting trade through inland routes, Rome had to pay tolls to the Empire of Parthia and other Arab kingdoms. After they gained control of Egypt, the Romans began to exploit the Red Sea outposts. Ocean trade with India and Africa brought highly valued goods to Rome, and they began to rely heavily on sea trade for exotic spices and luxurious products from the east. When Emperor Augustus made Egypt a part of the Roman Empire, it ushered in a new era of trade. In Augustus's days, over a hundred dhow-type ships, manned primarily by Egyptian-Greek crews, set sail every year from Myos Hormos and Berenike toward India. They left in July, at the height of the southwestern monsoon season, to travel to the heart of the pepper country; carrying their precious cargo, they returned with the northwest monsoons in November. Many Indian goods arrived in great quantities at Red Sea ports before being transported to Alexandria.

By 40 AD, Alexandria became not only the greatest commercial center in the world but also the preeminent emporium for spices. Black pepper arrived in Rome in such great quantities that Emperor Domitian designated an area in the heart of the city as *horrea piperataria* (pepper sheds), for the exclusive use of spice merchants. The consumption of pepper grew astonishingly, and pepper became a status symbol of fine cookery. Pepper reigned as the paramount spice for several centuries.

Once the pepper shipments reached Roman Egypt, the governments collected customs duty on the imports—in some instances, from 25 to 50 percent of their value. Arab traders had to pay this duty in Alexandria. An ancient papyrus document dating back to the mid-second century AD is said to contain the text of a loan agreement drawn up in Muziris on one side; the other side recounts the period of shipment from Muziris until its arrival in Alexandria; it also gives details about the merchandise, its quantity, and its value as well as the 25-percent tax rate levied by the Romans. Some of the Roman merchants are believed to have remained at Muziris and served as middlemen between the local merchants and their own countrymen who arrived with cargoes to trade. *Tabula Peutingeriana,* a Roman map drawn up in the fifth century AD, shows a building identified as *Templum Augusti* (Temple of Augustus) near Muziris. Romans often paid dearly for the goods from India with gold and silver. Pliny the Elder worried that imports from India were costing Rome fifty million sesterces annually. Muziris's trade with Rome remained active and extensive for several centuries.

Rome's trade with southwest India, although dangerous because of storms and pirates, was highly profitable. Often, one ship carried the cargoes of several merchants, which included nard; malabathrum; pepper; gems such as turquoise, lapis lazuli, onyx, diamonds, sapphires, and pearls; ivory; sandalwood; tortoise shells; cotton; and silk. Ethiopian emeralds, Egyptian coral, gold, silver, and wine were some of the products Romans sold or bartered in Muziris.

Evidence of Roman Trade in Indian Literary Works

Ancient literary works, especially the poems of the Sangam literature of South India, provide graphic details of this ancient trade. Written in ancient Tamil during a period extending from about the third century BC to the second or the third century AD, Sangam literature is still the major source of information about the early Chera, Chola, and Pandya dynasties that ruled the greater Tamil country, encompassing most of southern India. (Kerala belonged to Chera rulers.) "Sangam" means the academy of poets and scholars patronized by the rulers. It is believed that there were three Sangams. Only *Tholkaappiyam,* a grammatical work from the second Sangam, and some of the literature of the third Sangam have survived.

The poems of the Sangam, composed by several poets and engraved on palm leaves, consist of hymns, ballads, erotic verses, and lyrics in praise of the country, of gods, and of kings. These literary works paint a picture of a cosmopolitan, trade-oriented, and tolerant society. They are collected in eight volumes of short poems in *Ettuthogai* ("Eight Anthologies") and ten volumes of longer poems, *Pattuppattu* ("Ten Idylls"). Many of these poems describe trade with the Romans. Translations of these poems by George L. Hart and J. V. Chelliah have brought some of this material to a wide English-reading audience.

Akananuru, part of *Ettuthogai,* describes the cargo ships of the Yavanas (Romans) at Muziris as:

> Masterpieces of the Yavanas
> That stirs white foam on the Periyaar,
> Arriving with gold and departing with pepper.

Maduraikanchi, part of *Pattuppattu,* describes the Indian merchants returning home:

> The ocean clear around it forms a deep moat
> And the place looks like a mountain overcast with clouds
> Large ships on which high flags on mast-tops wave
> Spread out their sails and cleave the rolling waves,
> Tossed by the wind of the great dark, treble season which rest clouds.
> They come to the sounds of drums to the port
> Their trade successful with the gold that much increases people's wealth.

Another stanza in *Maduraikanchi* describes foreign traders:

> Sea captains that sail over the ocean high in showy ships
> Those come from large and distant countries
> Take away the salt that is formed in black and clayey pans,
> Sweet tamarind and salted fish that look like sides of drums
> Prepared by fishermen on widespread sands
> They bring fine horses here and other precious things
> To barter them for jewels fine that are here made.

Several other poems in both *Ettuthogai and Pattuppattu,* including *Porunarattrupadi, Mullaipattu,* and *Nedunalvadi,* describe the Yavanas as sturdy and well-built men who enjoyed drinking toddy. Some were employed as construction workers, while others were artists.

The *Silappathikaram* ("The Ankle Bracelet") and its sequel, *Manimekalai* ("The Dancer with the Magic Bowl"), two post-Sangam works from early centuries, provide glimpses of the maritime wealth of the cosmopolitan cities of South India. Translations of these works by Alain Daniélou, Sridharam K. Guruswamy, and S. Srinivasan have brought these ancient Tamil works to a wide English-reading audience.

Silappathikaram was written by Prince Ilango Adigal, brother of the Chera (Kerala) king Shenguttavan, and *Manimekalai* was written by Shattan, a merchant poet and a protégé of King Shenguttavan. The stories takes place in the three southern kingdoms of Chera, Chola, and Pandya, and they contain various references to trade with Rome. They refer to the Yavanas as brave seafarers, some of whom were employed as bodyguards and palace guards of kings.

In Canto Two of *Silappathikaram*, the author describes a port city and its international trade:

> The riches of Puhar ship owners made
> The kings of faraway land envious
> The most costly merchandise, the rarest foreign produce,
> Reached the city by sea and caravans
> Such was the abundance that, had all the world's
> Inhabitants been assembled within the city walls,
> The stocks would have lasted for many years.

Canto Five of *Silappathikaram* describes foreign traders:

> In various quarters of the city the homes of
> Wealthy Greeks were seen, near the harbor
> Seamen from far-off lands appeared at home
> There were special streets for merchants of coral,
> Sandalwood, myrrh, jewelry, pearls, gold and precious gems.

In Canto Fourteen of Silappathikaram the author describes the hero of the story entering Madurai, the capital city of Pandyan kings, protected by Greek palace guards:

> The passage crossed the broad moat filled with
> Shining water, bordered by thick brushwork,
> Forming secure protection. Unnoticed by the
> Greek mercenaries, armed with swords,
> Who kept watch at the gate.

> **Location of Muziris:** Historians have long known about the ancient port of Muziris; however, its exact location still eludes them. It was a critical maritime trade link and a center of the pepper trade. *Periplus Maris Erythraei* ("The Periplus of the Erythraean Sea," a merchant's guidebook to the Red Sea, the Persian Gulf, and the Indian Ocean) describes it this way: "Muziris abounds in ships sent there with cargoes from Arabia, and by the Greeks; it is located on a river, distant from Tyndis by river and sea five hundred stadia, and up the river from the shore twenty stadia." It was described as *"primum emporium Indiae"* by Pliny the Elder in *Natural History*. Muziris appears in Ptolemy's *Geography*, suggesting that Roman merchants lived there. The port is celebrated in ancient Sangam literature. One of the most fascinating pieces of evidence about Muziris, however, is a papyrus discovered in Vienna in 1985 that sets out the details of a maritime loan agreement at Muziris between a ship owner and a merchant, using the ship as security.
>
> Despite the absence of much archaeological evidence, because of its association with the Chera kings and its location near the river Periyaar, Kodungallur in central Kerala was considered the location of Muziris. Recent archaeological excavations at Pattanam, a village south of Kodungallur in Kerala, have yielded strong evidence of sustained trade with the Roman Empire. The most salient finds from Pattanam are the rim and handle of a classic Italian wine amphora from Naples, a type common between the late first century BC and 79 AD, when pottery production in the region was disrupted by the eruption of Mt. Vesuvius. Islamic glazed ware from West Asia found at this site indicates that the site remained active beyond the early historic period and that Pattanam had trade not only with Rome, but also with other places in the Persian Gulf. Was Pattanam the ancient Muziris? Some research scholars are of the opinion that further research is required before it can be stated with finality that Pattanam was indeed the port of Muziris.

Archeological Excavations at Berenike

At the ancient Roman port town of Berenike along the Red Sea, nine seasons of survey and excavation unearthed extensive evidence of both international and regional trade in the Roman period (University of Delaware, Leiden University, and University of California, 1994 to 2002). Research show two periods of trade at Berenike: one at the beginning of the second century AD and the other in the mid- to late-fourth century AD. Evidence from the excavation site indicates that it was occupied from the third century BC until the sixth century AD. There was some contact with India during the first period, but trade between Berenike and India increased dramatically during the second. The site was gradually abandoned sometime during the sixth century AD.

The excavators found a very large Roman trash dump containing a variety of remains that suggest there was long-distance trade with India. Evidence of commercial contact found at the site includes fragments of sails of Indian origin; reused teak wood, which grows only in the east; gemstone beads; cotton textiles; sandalwood; and an abundance of black pepper. Although India traded two species of pepper (black pepper and long pepper), only black pepper was recovered at Berenike. They excavated a very large clay pot, originally buried in a courtyard, that was completely filled with peppercorns—probably one of the more abundant products coming through Berenike at regular intervals.

Pottery pieces found at the site, including cookware, also indicate evidence of an Indian presence at Berenike. An inscription in ancient Tamil Brahmi script was found on the base of a pot. (Tamil Brahmi is the root of both Tamil and Kerala's language, Malayalam.) Earlier archaeological excavations also found graffiti in Tamil Brahmi script at the port of Leukos Limen. Rice was also found at Berenike, but no remains of wheat, the grain cultivated in Egypt, were found. These findings suggest that there was contact with south India.

Ancient Muslim, Jewish, and Syrian Christian Settlements in Kerala

Kerala Muslims have always believed that their origins in Kerala go back to the seventh century AD, when Islam originated in Arabia. Their first mosque in Kerala, Cheraman Juma Masjid, at Kodungallur near Muziris, dates back to 629 AD. Trade with the Arab world brought prosperity, and Muslims enjoyed a privileged status. They began to settle down in Muziris and other port towns along the shores of Kerala.

There is no consensus of opinion among historians about the arrival of Jews in Kerala. According to local legends, contact with ancient Israel dates back to the time of King Solomon. The earliest Jewish settlers are said to have come to trade in teak, ivory, peacocks, and spices. Other legends put the date at 597 BC, following the destruction of their first temple. Another belief is that the Cochin Jews are the descendants of the Jews taken into captivity by Nebuchadnezzar and then released by Cyrus of Persia in the sixth century BC. Cochin Jews uphold that in 72 AD, after the destruction of the second temple of

Jerusalem, ten thousand more Jews migrated to Kerala. These early Jewish immigrants settled at Kodungallur in the Chera kingdom, known as Shingali in local Jewish tradition.

The earliest verifiable historical evidence about the arrival of Jews, perhaps several generations after their arrival, is the copper plate grant of Chera king Bhaskara Ravi Varman (962–1020 AD), predecessor of the royal families of Kerala. This document, engraved on copper plates, is the record of a royal gift of rights and privileges of high status, traditionally reserved for the feudal lords of the upper castes, granted to Joseph Rabban, chief of Anjuvannam, a prominent Jewish trade group. A remarkable collection of business papers that belonged to Jewish merchants from the period between 1000 AD and 1250 AD, discovered in a Cairo synagogue, provides ample proof of the activities of Jewish traders from Tunisia, Andalusia, and Sicily and their contacts with Kerala.

The introduction of Christianity and the history of the Christian church in Kerala are buried in obscurity, just as is the history of the Kerala Jews. According to tradition, the apostle St. Thomas introduced Christianity and established the original church in Kerala in the year 52 AD. He is said to have arrived at Muziris and founded seven churches and eight bishoprics. When St. Thomas visited Muziris, he is believed to have stayed in the Jewish quarter. The Chera ruler Sthanu Ravi granted several privileges to Christians. An ancient document of historical importance is the copper plate grant (1225 AD) issued by Chera king Veera Raghava Chakravarthi to the Christian merchant Iravi Korthan, granting him several privileges and rights.

The Revival of Arab Trade

Arab conquests and the political integration of Roman Egypt, Syria, Iran, and North Africa resulted in an expanded territory. After the fall of the Roman Empire, the resources of the Indian Ocean and its coastal lands came under the control of Arabs, and once again, they gained preeminence in the spice trade.

The meteoric rise of Islam closed off any further European exploration of the spice routes and opened new opportunities for traders from the Muslim world. Their newly found power allowed them to venture deep into the markets of the East. By the ninth century, the substantial volume of trade had greatly enriched the Islamic caliphate, while Europe sank into a dark age. Although Indian Ocean trade was mainly under the control of Arabs from the fall of the Roman Empire until the latter half of the fifteenth century, Jews, Syrian Christians, and Chinese also participated. Christian and Jewish trade guilds were very powerful in Kerala. Commerce between India and the Middle

East relied mostly on intermediaries; business was done on a consignment basis with friends and relatives in faraway ports, while the principal remained in India.

The Chinese were collecting cloves and nutmeg from the East Indies and delivering them to the port of Malacca. Merchants from India and Arabia transported these goods to India. In India, cinnamon from Ceylon and pepper from Kerala were added to the cargoes and sold to traders at the ports of Kochi, Kozikode, and Cannore. These Kerala ports, as well as the rest of the Indian Ocean, were controlled by Arabs. Regular shipments of spices went to Persia, Arabia, and East Africa. From Arabian and African ports, Arab traders took spices to Alexandria. Trade with regions farther west was under the control of the Venetians and the Genoese.

The Venetian Spice Monopoly

By the tenth century, Venice was beginning to prosper from the Indian Ocean spice trade. From Arabian and African ports, spices were shipped to Alexandria, and there they were bought and shipped by the Venetians and the Genoese.

Venetian merchants, strategically located midway between the Levant and Western Europe, became the great middlemen of the spice trade. By the dawn of the fifteenth century, Venice was a formidable trading power. The Venetians sold spices to northern and western European buyers at exorbitant prices. Europe had an insatiable appetite for spices. Marco Polo was sent on a voyage to explore the markets throughout Asia, and upon his return, he reported that there was an abundance of pepper, cinnamon, and ginger on the Kerala coast.

Other European nations knew the origin of the spices that reached Alexandria, but they were unable to break the strong hold of Venice. During the latter half of the fifteenth century, many European nations built ships and ventured abroad in search of a new route to the spice-producing countries. The conquest of Constantinople by the Turks in 1453 AD had already marked the decline of Venice. The Portuguese discovery of a new ocean route totally ended the pepper trade monopoly. In the following years, Lisbon became one of the wealthiest towns of Europe.

Ancient Trade with the East

Southeast Asian Trade

As early as 350 BC, sailors from the Malay Peninsula are believed to have undertaken expeditions across the Indian Ocean, reaching as far as China and the south of peninsular India and East Africa. They pioneered an all-sea route and developed an international market for fine spices. Indian and Arab merchants also traveled to Southeast Asia. During the height of Roman trade, contact with Southeast Asia increased. After the fall of the Roman Empire, this trade continued to flourish. Mariners of ancient South Indian kingdoms were able to borrow funds for their voyages from the treasuries of South Indian temples. Inscriptions dating back to the twelfth century AD reveal the presence of South Indian guilds in the ports of Sumatra.

By the time European merchants reached the shores of the Spice Islands in the sixteenth century, a number of large markets were already established in Southeast Asia. Dhows belonging to merchant guilds from India and Arabia, as well as huge junks from China, visited there regularly. This provided the early Portuguese, Spanish, and Dutch traders with the basic conditions for commercial expansion.

Chinese Trade

During the Song Dynasty (960–1227 AD), the first Chinese oceangoing trade ships were built. Their heavily planked and multi-decked ships, called junks, sailed to Southeast Asia and the markets on India's west coast. The Chinese brought silk, ceramic pots, camphor, and metals and returned home with black pepper, cardamom, ginger, coconut, and areca nut. By the early thirteenth century, China controlled the bulk of Indian Ocean trade. When rulers from the southern Song Dynasty prohibited the exchange of metals and coins, trade continued with the bartering of Chinese silk and ceramics.

In 1279, the Mongols, under Kublai Khan, controlled China, and emissaries were sent to South India and other countries bordering the Indian Ocean. External trade, while not forbidden, was made very difficult for the Chinese; however, this did not challenge the trade the South Asians and West Asians had pioneered. Foreign merchants were able to trade within China and were given privileges by the Yuan emperors. They were free of taxes and were allowed to travel throughout China without restrictions.

Emperors of the Ming Dynasty undertook the next ambitious series of voyages in the Indian Ocean. They sent seven naval expeditions led by the Chinese

Muslim admiral Zheng He (Cheng Ho). Chinese seagoing junks frequently arrived at and departed from the west coast of India. Ambassadors from the kingdom of Cochin (Kochi) are believed to have traveled to the Ming court in 1411. In 1416, Emperor Zhu Di sent an inscribed stone slab to the king of Cochin, to be erected on the mountaintop there. It is believed that Zhu Di personally composed the text for this tablet, in which he expressed his wish for the kingdom's prosperity and well-being.

Unfortunately, these expeditions were only an affirmation of the dynastic policy to monopolize all foreign trade and keep it away from individual Chinese traders. During the fourteenth century, Melaka (on the west coast of Malaysia) grew into a major trading center, enabling the Chinese to avoid long trips to the southwestern shores of India for trading. Their visits became less frequent by the latter half of the fifteenth century. In 1525, an imperial edict authorized the destruction of oceangoing ships, and China practically withdrew from Indian Ocean trade. Conical fishermen's hats (donned by local fishermen) and oil lamps dangling from the majestic Chinese fishing nets along Kochi's shoreline linger as a reminder of a flourishing ocean trade with China in centuries past.

Trade during the Colonial Era

Arrival of the Portuguese

In 1497, Portuguese explorer Vasco da Gama symbolized the emergence of the colonial era as he led an expedition of four ships through uncharted waters in search of spices. He rounded Africa's Cape of Good Hope and reached the port of Kozhikode (Calicut) in northern Kerala in 1498. As they landed on the shores of Kerala, his men shouted, "For Christ and spices!" They had arrived at the very heart of spice country. The opposition of Muslim traders in Kozhikode prevented him from establishing cordial relations during the three months he stayed. Vasco da Gama returned to Portugal with one practical piece of information: there was an abundance of pepper in Kerala as well as a lower market price.

In early 1500, a new fleet left Lisbon under the command of Pedro Álvarez Cabral. His goal was not only to bring back spices, but also to establish settlements on India's southwestern coast. Cabral brought expensive gifts to appease the Samoothiri (the ruler of Kozhikode), and he signed a treaty granting Portuguese the right to trade. But by the time the Portuguese collected enough spices to load two ships, a bitter fight between the Arab traders of Kozhikode and the newly arrived Portuguese turned the Arabian Sea into a battlefield.

The Portuguese found themselves surrounded by vengeful enemies in a hostile and aggressive atmosphere. They were eagerly looking for a helping hand from a friendly land along the coast, where they could find assistance and a regular supply of spices. On December 24, 1500 AD, Gaspar da Gama hastily navigated a fleet of Portuguese ships, under the command of Admiral Cabral, to the shores of Kochi.

The king of Kochi was waiting for an opportunity to overthrow the hegemony of the Samoothiri, and he welcomed the Portuguese to his shores wholeheartedly. Within nine days, a treaty of peace and friendship was signed by King Unni Goda Varma Koil Thirumulpad and the admiral, and all seven Portuguese ships were laden with pepper, nutmeg, cinnamon, and cloves. This was the beginning of a long-term alliance and friendship between Portugal and Kochi. It lasted over a century, until the Dutch overthrew the Portuguese in the late seventeenth century.

Vasco da Gama led a second expedition in 1502. He returned, leaving his uncle in charge of a squadron of five ships at Kochi. In 1503, Alfonso de Albuquerque was sent to Kochi to obtain permission to establish a Portuguese fort. In 1505, to establish a permanent presence and control of the spice trade, King Manuel I of Portugal appointed Francisco de Almeida to be the first viceroy of India. He set up his headquarters in Kochi. A few years later, Albuquerque was sent back again, to assume command from Francisco de Almeida. One of his goals was the capture of Goa. By the time the Portuguese seized Goa from Bijapur in 1510, Cabral had already founded the first European settlement on Indian soil at Kochi (1500); Vasco da Gama had established the first Portuguese trading station in India at Kochi (1502); and Alfonso de Albuquerque, with the permission of the king, had built Fort Immanuel, the first European fort in India (1503).

When the Portuguese arrived at Kochi, the new natural harbor (which was formed after the great floods of 1341) had gained strategic importance and was experiencing commercial prosperity. During the time of trade with the Portuguese, the town of Kochi grew into a flourishing city. In *The Coasts of Malabar and Coramandal*, published in 1732, Philip Baldaeus wrote, "This great shipping business had rendered the country of the Cochin (Kochi) king busy, rich, and opulent. The king and the inhabitants agree well with the Portuguese, the Jews, and the Moors and live in peace. The town of Cochin might compare with some of the best cities in Europe." It was a common saying among Portuguese traders that China was a good place to make money, and Cochin was a good place in which to spend it.

Dutch Trade

In 1602, the Dutch East India Company was founded. In 1663, the Dutch gained trade supremacy in Kochi by capturing the Portuguese fort. The spice trade was again the primary motive. Kochi was very prosperous during its trading days with the Dutch, which lasted through January 1791, when a new trade treaty was signed between the British and Kochi.

British Colonization

The British arrived in the latter part of the eighteenth century. They came initially for trade, but later, colonization of India became their goal. At that time, India was a large country ruled by more than 260 different royal families. The British knew they could not easily conquer such a large and fragmented nation. Their way was to enter into treaties with various royal families, under the pretext that the British would defend them. The kings continued to rule their kingdoms, with a British resident stationed in each kingdom to ensure that the maharaja did not deviate from the established British policies. Any changes in policies required the approval of the British. Slowly but surely, through these treaties, they took complete control of the country. The British ruled until August 15, 1947, when India gained independence through its successful nonviolent disobedience movement.

During British rule, our educational system received much attention. By 1818, British resident Colonel Monroe established several schools and tried to introduce free and compulsory education for all children above the age of five. Due to administrative and financial constraints, the effort to introduce compulsory education was not very successful; but it gave momentum to the educational system, and during the nineteenth century, many Christian missionaries and Muslim mosques set up schools. Toward the close of nineteenth century, education began to receive greater attention from the rulers. The maharajas of Kochi encouraged and provided financial help to European missionaries to set up schools and educate children from all religious backgrounds. Poor children were provided with free education, and children from all religious backgrounds attended these schools. My grandmother, born in 1881, was among those who benefited by learning English from British-born teachers. Beginning with the old tradition of schooling at Kalari, followed by Colonel Monroe's efforts, the royal patronage of education by the close of the nineteenth century, and the schools set up by various missionaries, all paved the foundation of Kerala's present 100-percent literacy rate.

The Royalty of Kochi

There is no tangible historical evidence on the split of Kerala, but according to some historians, a split may have occurred during the second Chera Dynasty, at the beginning of the twelfth century. The territories of Chera kings were divided into three major kingdoms (and several smaller ones); Kochi (Cochin), Malabar, and Thiruvithamcore were ruled by three different royal families who were believed to be the descendants of the Chera rulers. With the formation of a new harbor, the king of Kochi moved his capital from Thiruvanchikulam, near Kodungallur, to the new harbor town of Kochi. The Kochi royal family ruled the princely state of Kochi until India became an independent nation in 1947.

Hill Palace, a new official residence of the king of Kochi, was built in 1865 at Thrippunithura, a small town not far from the major port town of Kochi. This palace (shown at right) is an archaeological museum today. "Honor is our family treasure," the motto on the royal crest, speaks volumes about this kindhearted and caring family. Their homes, lifestyle, and eating habits are all very simple, even today.

Maharaja Rama Varma Sakthan Thampuran ruled Kochi for thirty-six years, from 1770 to 1806. The history of Kochi as a progressive princely state began with his reign. He laid the foundation for a centralized system of administration. He was mainly responsible for strengthening his kingdom and recapturing most of the territories that had been taken over by neighboring rulers, and for that, he earned the nickname of Sakthan ("Strong One"). Under his regime, Kochi became a unified territory and enjoyed peace and prosperity. Many of his successors were well educated in Sanskrit and ayurveda. They promoted Sanskrit education and the fine arts. By the close of the nineteenth century, the maharajas began to encourage the education of their subjects.

The Unification of Kerala

Under British rule, Kochi became a princely state within the British Empire, and the maharaja's powers were highly restricted. By the early twentieth century, the royalty of Kochi had adopted the progressive view that a group of people, democratically elected by the citizens, should have a voice in the region's administration. In 1912, Maharaja Rama Varma proposed the formation of an advisory council of the people and the eventual transfer of power to them. British authorities vehemently opposed this idea, and later, he abdicated his position as maharaja. In 1925, his successor was finally able to form a legislative council with limited powers. Maharaja Kerala Varma first proposed the unification of the kingdoms of Kochi, Malabar, and Thiruvithamcore to form a united Kerala. In May 1949, the maharajas of Kochi and Thiruvithamcore signed a form of accession to the Indian union, and Kochi ceased to exist as a separate princely state. Finally, on November 1, 1956, all regions speaking the Malayalam language were unified to form the state of Kerala.

The Royalty of Kochi and Foreign Relations

The cosmopolitan outlook and religious tolerance of ancient South Indian rulers was reflected in Kochi's good relationships with foreign traders. In spite of the rigidity of the caste system, Kochi was exceptionally hospitable to people of different beliefs and has a rare record of welcoming immigrants of all religious convictions.

Jews

Early Jewish settlers prospered in Kodungallur for hundreds of years. At the height of its glory, there were eighteen synagogues in and around Kodungallur. In 1524, blaming the Jews for interfering with their pepper trade, the Arabs attacked the Jews. They burned Jewish homes and synagogues and totally destroyed the Jewish settlement. Most of the remaining Jews deserted their ancient settlement and fled to the new port town of Kochi. King Kesava Rama Varma welcomed the Jewish immigrants, gave them land on which to build homes and synagogues (very close to his own palace), and granted them religious and cultural independence. The Jews repaid his kindness by helping the king in his military endeavors and advising him on economic and diplomatic affairs.

The Paradesi Synagogue, a complex of four buildings, was built in 1568 by the Jews on the land given to them by the king of Kochi. Reconstructed after the Portuguese bombardment in 1662 and restored in 1664, the Paradesi Synagogue is the oldest surviving synagogue in India. The most prized possessions of this Jewish synagogue are the two copper plates, inscribed in ancient script, containing the details of privileges granted to the Jews by King Bhaskara Ravi Varman.

During Dutch colonial rule, the close contact between the Jews of Amsterdam and Kochi brought another wave of Jewish immigration in the sixteenth century; Sephardic Jews came from Portugal, Spain, and Holland. In the seventeenth and eighteenth centuries, Kochi received several groups of Jewish settlers from the Middle East, North Africa, and Spain. In 1795, Kochi passed into the hands of the British. Under British rule, the Jews achieved their maximum wealth. The spice trade was dominated by the Jewish community. Jews were guaranteed a seat in the legislative assembly, as well as admission to colleges and professional education. Jews occupied virtually all the houses on Jew Town Road, where they sold spices, fruits, and vegetables.

With the establishment of Israel in 1948, most of the Jews immigrated to Israel, leaving only a few behind in Kochi. By 1970, the Jews from Kochi living in Israel numbered around 4,000. To mark the fiftieth anniversary of their immigration, these Jewish immigrants turned their settlement in Nevatim into a replica of the place of their origin in Kochi. There is a reproduction of the Paradesi Synagogue in southern Israel. A well, similar to the one near the synagogue in Kochi, was inaugurated in August 2004. In February 2005, the Jewish organization B'nai Brith honored the Kochi royal family with a humanitarian award.

Syrian Christians

From the ninth through the thirteenth centuries, many more Christians came from the Middle East to trade. Maharaja Sakthan Thampuran gave them land on which to build their churches. He also entrusted them with the management of farmland owned by him. He invited and encouraged Christian families to relocate to the major towns in Kochi from their business centers in adjoining areas, and he encouraged them to engage in commercial activities in the newly established markets.

Catholics also received several favors and generous contributions from the king. The *aanavilakku* (elephant lamp) used during festivities in the Catholic church at Kanjoor, near the king's birthplace, Vellarappilly Palace, was a gift from the king.

Portuguese Catholics

When Admiral Cabral arrived in Kochi in 1500, the king provided him with native guards and allowed the Portuguese to sleep within the walls of his palace; this was considered a great honor in those days. When Cabral returned to Portugal, the king sent along fourteen boats of spices and a letter engraved on a gold leaf as gifts to the king of Portugal. A Nayar youth accompanied Cabral as an envoy. Joao da Nova, who arrived at Kochi in 1501, noticed just before his departure that he was short of cash to purchase spices. When the maharaja was informed of this, he generously provided the security da Nova needed. In 1503, the first European church in India was built with wood within Fort Immanuel. In 1506, the king gave permission to Francisco de Almeida to refurbish the church with bricks and mortar, a privilege then confined to the palaces and temples of the king. This church, completed in 1516, was dedicated to St. Anthony. It is believed that the Anglicans later changed the patron saint to St. Francis and renamed it St. Francis Church.

In 1505, when Dom Francisco de Almeida arrived in Kochi as the first Portuguese viceroy of all of the Indies, he came with instructions from the king of Portugal to endow the maharaja of Kochi with a crown of gold set with jewels, in recognition of his chivalry in defending the Portuguese against the Samoothiri. He also arranged for an annual payment of five hundred crusadoes as a tariff on land given to the Portuguese for constructing Fort Immanuel.

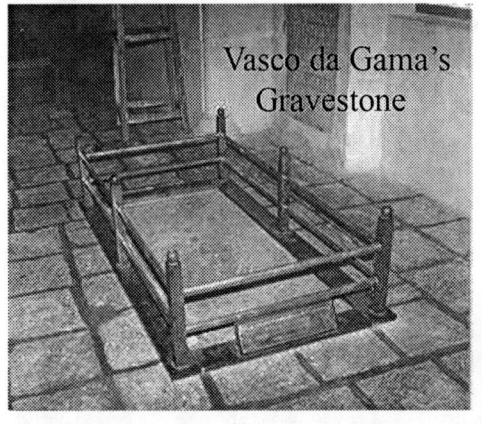

Vasco da Gama's Gravestone

On Christmas Eve, 1524, Vasco da Gama, the legendary navigator from Lisbon, died at Kochi and was laid to rest in this church. Fourteen years later, his remains were taken to Portugal. Vasco da Gama's original gravestone is tiled into the floor of St. Francis Church. The spacious and lofty Mattancheri palace, constructed in European fashion, was built by the Portuguese and presented to the maharaja in 1555.

Not far from St. Francis Church, there is another monumental house of worship, Santa Cruz Church (now Basilica), originally built by the Portuguese in 1505, under the initiative of Francisco de Almeida. Kochi became Kerala's first and India's second Catholic diocese in 1558, and the church was elevated to a cathedral by Pope Paul IV. When the British took over Kochi, they destroyed and demolished the Santa Cruz Cathedral. Over ninety years later, in 1887, Bishop Dom Gomez Ferreira commissioned a new building at the same site. A cathedral, with intricately carved wooden panels and pulpit and beautiful paintings on its ceiling, was rebuilt and consecrated on November 19, 1905. The cathedral was proclaimed a basilica in 1984 through a special decree by Pope John Paul II.

Muslims

By the eleventh century, Kozikode had become an important trading port, and it attracted many Muslim traders. The prosperity of the kingdom depended on Arab trade, and the Samoothiri rulers of Kozikode bestowed on them many privileges. According to tradition, Samoothiri took Muslim merchants into his service, and eventually they became the Marakkars (admirals) of his naval fleet. With the arrival of the Portuguese and their monopolization of trade at Kochi, Muslim trade was concentrated in Northern Kerala.

Dutch Protestants

After concluding a treaty with the maharaja of Kochi in March 1663, the Dutch also presented their ally Prince Veera Kerala Varma with a gold crown stamped with the symbol of the Dutch East India Company. Maharaja Sakthan Thampuran studied Dutch in order to communicate fluently with the Dutch. After the Dutch defeated the Portuguese in 1663, they made extensive renovations to the palace that had been built and given to the king by the Portuguese; from then onward it was known as the Dutch Palace. The hall where the kings of Kochi held their coronations is at the center of this building. It has a portrait gallery of the kings of Kochi and houses several ancient murals depicting scenes from the epic *Ramayana*.

The Dutch influence in Kerala's architecture is quite evident in several buildings constructed during this period. Vadakkekara Palace, today known as Shakthan Thampuran Palace, was reconstructed in Kerala Dutch style in 1795. The majestic Kalikotta Palace, where most royal-family events take place even today, was built during the Dutch period. The Bolgatty Palace at Kochi, the Dutch governor's mansion (later the British resident's mansion), and the Dutch Palace are some of the reminders of Dutch colonial rule. As a result of these friendships, the kingdom of Kochi enjoyed great prosperity during this period.

The Influence of Foreign Trade on Our Agriculture and Cuisine

Transplantation of trees and vegetation into India from other parts of the world is thought to have begun in prehistoric times. Tamarind is probably one of the earliest trees transplanted into India from tropical Africa; Arab texts from the Middle Ages refer to it as *tamr hindī*, or "dates of India." Okra is believed to have originated in tropical Africa and introduced to India early on. Fenugreek, coriander, and cumin, all native to either the Mediterranean or the Near East, are three other spice plants that were brought to India, probably by ancient Arab or Indian traders. Nutmeg, cloves, sugarcane, and numerous varieties of bananas and yams came from Southeast Asia.

Cashew was one of the earliest imports brought by Portuguese. In Malayalam, the cashew nut is called the *Parangi andi*—the nut brought by the *Parangi*, or Portuguese. In 1598, a Portuguese traveler described *caju* found in the gardens at Santa Cruz in the kingdom of Cochin. Kerala now grows and exports a significant portion of the cashew nuts consumed all over the world.

As the Portuguese sailed south on a circuitous route, they probably stumbled upon chilies at their trading posts in Brazil. Chilies traveled with them as they rounded the Cape of Good Hope and followed the monsoon winds to the southern shores of India. The chili had an enormous impact on the varied cuisines of India; it is hard to believe that it was not always grown in India. Because of their familiarity with pungent spices, Indians were quite taken with the fiery pod. The pungency of chilies was much greater than that of black pepper. The resemblance to long pepper may also have accelerated its acceptance. Above all, the chili was cheaper, it propagated easily, and it transplanted readily. And unlike black pepper or long pepper, it could be cultivated all over the country. In Malayalam, the red chili pepper is called *kappal mulagu*—"the pepper that came in the ship." Tolerance for hot chilies is substantial in tropical southern India. Chilies made such an impression that the famous sixteenth-century composer Purandara Dasa wrote a poem about it, which roughly translates as:

> I saw you green, then
> Turning redder as you ripened.
> Pleasant to look at and tasty in a dish,
> But too hot if excess is used.
> Savior of the poor, enhancer of good food,
> Fiery when bitten, this makes it difficult
> Even to think of the good lord himself!

Today, chilies appear in a variety of ways in Indian cuisine for their color, flavor, and heat. The diversity and intensity of peppers used in this cuisine rivals that of Mexico and the American Southwest.

Breadfruit, native to the Pacific Islands, was brought to Kerala by the Portuguese during the late seventeenth or early eighteenth century. Another plant brought by the Portuguese was pineapple, a native of Brazil. By the middle of the sixteenth century, pineapple cultivation began in South India. This tropical plant, which does not tolerate frost or prolonged cold weather, grew abundantly in Kerala's coastal as well as lower and moderately elevated lands.

Papaya, native to Central America, is another fruit that was introduced to the tropics of Asia by Portuguese and Spanish invaders. By the late sixteenth century, papaya reached India via the Philippines. Cassava (or tapioca, as it is known in India) is native to Central America and South America and was brought by the Portuguese. During the famine and rice shortage in Kerala more than a century ago, tapioca gained much prominence. Unlike rice, tapioca could be grown in every backyard and kept in the soil until required, making it a primary starch substitute during the days of famine. Although the increase in rice production resulted in the decline of tapioca consumption, cooked tapioca served with spicy fish is still considered a delicacy in southern Kerala.

Potato, another starchy root vegetable, was introduced in India during the early seventeenth century. Though it is not a staple food when compared to rice and legumes in south India, potato is used in a variety of dishes. The Dutch planted coffee on the higher elevations of the Sahyadri mountain range. The Spaniards took the tomato, native to the tropical Americas, to Western Europe by 1550. The tomato reached India much later, through England, around the late eighteenth century.

When the British lost their monopoly on the tea trade from China in the late 1830s, the East India Company began to cultivate tea in Assam, India. From the foothills of the Himalayas, tea cultivation expanded to the Sahyadri mountains in Kerala. And by the 1850s, tea was growing beautifully in all Kerala plantations. Slowly but surely, all of these new ingredients were incorporated into the regional cuisine.

The contribution of Chinese traders to this vegetarian cuisine was not a food product, but cooking utensils and storage containers. The Chinese wok, known as *Cheena chatti,* is indispensable in Kerala kitchens. Ceramic jars called *Cheena bharani* are still widely used for storing homemade pickles and yogurt.

Foreign trade substantially influenced even our regional language, as it assimilated several words and phrases from other languages. The Malayalam word for chair, *kasera,* closely resembles both the Greek and Portuguese words for chair, *kathedra* and *cedeira* respectively. The Malayalam word for table is *mesa,* which is the same in Portuguese. The fruits and vegetables they brought also still carry Portuguese-sounding names. Portuguese *papaiya* is papaya in Malayalam, while *pera* (pear) is the same in Portuguese and Malayalam. The Portuguese word for citrus fruits, *naranja* (pronounced nar-an-ha) is very similar to the Malayalam word *naranga.* And while the Portuguese call clove *cravoda,* in Malayalam it is *karayamboo;* and vinegar is *vinagre* in Portuguese and *vinnagiri* in Malayalam.

Many of the distinctive features of Kerala's vegetarian cuisine are derived from the use of ingredients brought by foreign traders. Today, no one back home thinks of chili peppers, cashew nuts, papayas, tomatoes, tea, coffee, pineapples, or breadfruit as foreign ingredients. They all have been completely integrated into the region's agriculture and cuisine, which combines the heartiness of spices, the interplay of sweet and acidic tastes, and the fiery heat of chilies.

In the following chapters, I invite you to explore, experiment with, and enjoy the vibrant vegetarian cuisine of the royal family and Nayars of Kochi.

Chapter Two
Getting Started: Ingredients, Cooking Methods, and Utensils

Before beginning to explore a new cuisine, one must delve into a few fundamentals: what, when, where, why, and how. The following alphabetical entries introduce the ingredients, simple techniques, and specific utensils used in this cuisine. Each entry contains useful information about appearance, availability, nutritional attributes, its significance in our cooking, the origin and history of the ingredient, medicinal qualities ascribed by ayurveda, the Indian holistic system of medicine, and interesting folklore.

My mother always insisted, "Never skimp on the quality or quantity of ingredients," and I believe it is the first lesson in good cooking. For each ingredient, I have listed the commonly used English name, followed by its name in Malayalam, in parentheses. Since ingredients are often labeled differently in Indian grocery stores, their botanical names are also included (in italics) to eliminate any confusion.

When I first came to live in Providence, Rhode Island, in the early 1970s, there were no Indian grocery stores in the whole state. In those days, the closest store that carried some Indian groceries was a Middle Eastern store, Kalusthyan's, in New York City. Being a lifelong vegetarian (I admit I am a stubborn vegetarian), I was determined to explore all possibilities. I went searching for anything even remotely Indian at American supermarkets. I was thrilled when I found the expensive little bottles of Spice Island brand coriander, crushed red pepper, and turmeric. Then I found a small packet of whole *tuvar* at an international store that carried Asian artifacts and fabrics.

As I hurriedly walked home, the thought of a plate of steaming rice with fragrant orange-red *sambar* was dancing in my head. Making *sambar* with that whole *tuvar* was indeed a major project (the hulled, split, and easy-to-cook *tuvar* dal is what we use). It took me an entire day to soak and remove the skin from the *tuvar* beans. Then it took another hour to cook. Months later, our friends discovered a Latin American grocery store that carried plantains and taro root. Even in those days when Indian ingredients were scarce, I was able to prepare South Indian vegetarian meals—maybe not truly authentic, but very close.

But today, just about every one of these ingredients is readily available in the United States. Perhaps you may not find them all in your neighborhood supermarket, but almost all of them are readily available at specialty stores, gourmet stores, or Indian, Southeast Asian, Mexican, and Chinese groceries. Every major city in the United States has at least one Indian grocery store. According to Linda Baldholm's *Indian Grocery Store Demystified,* there are over nine thousand Indian grocery stores in the United States. In addition, there are several Internet sources that ship ingredients directly to customers. A selection of Web sites that list Indian grocery stores across the United States (along with mail order and Internet sources) is included in Appendix IV. Unless you are buying them in a fancy gourmet store, none of these ingredients are very expensive.

The *Kalavara* (Pantry) Staples

The two indispensable ingredients of this vegetarian pantry are rice and coconuts. Jaggery (raw sugar) and salt are two other important components.

Rice *(ari)* is central to the diet throughout southern India. Rice's role in our cuisine is not limited to its appearance as the steaming serving of white rice around which meals are planned; it is also the main ingredient in a variety of dishes. The final product depends on what type of rice is used and how it is processed. Besides *puzukkalari* (ordinary parboiled rice) and *unakkalari* (medium- to long-grain raw rice), a mildly fragrant variety called *jeeraka chamban* is also grown in South India. The grains of this variety are small and thin, almost resembling cumin seeds. The wild rice navara (Latin: *Oryza nivara)* is cooked on religious partial-fasting days. However, the well-known, fragrant basmati rice is not generally used in southern Indian cooking. The distinct aroma of basmati or jasmine rice masks the flavors of the spices and the coconut used in South Indian preparations.

Generally, cooking rice means parboiled rice (converted rice) in our part of the world. Parboiling is an ancient technique that was developed in South India for improving the nutritional value of polished rice. The process involves immersing the harvested grains in boiling water and drying them before milling. This method forces the nutrients (vitamins and minerals) toward the center of the grain before it is milled, thus retaining the nutritional value. When the hull is removed by pounding the rice by hand instead of milling, part of the bran remains in the rice, giving it a reddish tinge. This manually hulled rice is called *kaikuthari*. Aging and parboiling hardens the rice and increases the yield. Since the rice grains have already been heated once, the starches in parboiled rice are harder in texture and take longer to cook. The cooked grains stay fluffy and do not stick together. Rice stored for three years after harvest is considered the most healthful in India. In the United States, Uncle Ben's, Carolina, and Golden Temple brands (though they all have larger-size grains) are ideal substitutes for Indian parboiled rice. For convenience, regular long-grain or medium-grain rice may be substituted.

Unakkalari is rice hulled without parboiling. It is used for preparing several breakfast dishes and desserts. Hand-pounded *unakkalari* has a delicate flavor and a consistency that has just the right cling, and it cooks to a perfect *paayasam* (pudding). It is either soaked and ground into a fine batter along with *urad* dal or powdered, pan-roasted, and mixed with freshly grated coconut to make breakfast dishes. *Unakkalari* flour combined with other flours and spices is used to make various snacks and sweets. In the absence of the real thing, medium-grain or long-grain white rice is the preferred substitute. I find Carolina and Adolphus brands long- and medium-grain rice excellent for making *idlis, dosas,* and *vellayappam.*

Rice is extremely adaptable and grows in a variety of environments, from flooded paddy fields at sea level to higher altitudes, and in both tropical heat and cooler climates. Rice contains a superior quality of protein, making it a healthy choice as the focus of a meal. Although it is high in starch content, a cup of cooked rice supplies about nine percent of the average daily protein requirement. The amount of the protein lysine in rice is one and a half times that of wheat and twice that of corn. When eaten with legumes, such as Indian dal, the nutritional benefit of rice is enhanced.

A Brief History of Rice

A primitive wild aquatic grass is believed to have existed in the great prehistoric continent of Gondwana, which, over one hundred million years or so ago, broke up into the areas of Africa, India, Australia, and South America. Many years later, early inhabitants of India and Africa gathered primitive wild rice for food and eventually realized it could be cultivated by sowing the seeds. During prehistoric times, rice was dispersed by the widespread movements of people throughout the world. From this ancient wild grass arose two major varieties of rice: *Oryza glaberrima* and *Oryza sativa*. From these, three species of rice developed: *indica, japonica,* and *javanica.* From its Asian and African origins, rice has become the staple food for a majority of the world's population, undergoing numerous incarnations in the diets of both East and West as it crossed cultural boundaries.

Flaked or pounded rice *(avil)* is an interesting mutation of rice. Unhulled rice is soaked in water and boiled for a longer time than for parboiling. The grains are drained and pounded hard until flattened. Pounding separates the husk from the grains and reveals paper-thin flattened grains with uneven edges. The quality of *avil* depends on the variety of rice and the method of pounding used. Since the grains are well cooked before pounding, they do not necessarily require further cooking. There are two kinds of *avil,* thick and thin, and they are available only in Indian grocery stores, where they are labeled *poha.* This versatile form of rice grain is used in cooking in several different ways. Soaked in milk and combined with sugar, ghee, honey, and raisins, it becomes *puthiri,* the rice dish made to celebrate the new harvest. It can be fried quickly in hot oil or ghee, or roasted in a dry pot and seasoned with salt and spices to make crunchy, savory snacks. Soaked in water and drained, it is used in preparing *puli avil,* another snack dish. Cooked in milk and sugar, it becomes *avil paayasam.* The recipes in this collection use the thick variety of avil.

Popped rice *(malar)* is made by dry roasting unhulled rice. It puffs up like tiny popcorn. It is available only in Indian grocery stores. Popped rice also has an auspicious significance: it is poured into sacred fire at Hindu religious ceremonies and presented as an offering at Hindu temples.

Coconut *(nalikeram),* the nut of the coconut palm *(Cocos nucifera),* is an essential ingredient in our cooking. Ninety-nine percent of the dishes served with rice are made with at least some coconut. Several snacks are served with coconut chutney, and coconut or coconut milk is used in making many sweets.

Coconuts from the tropics anywhere in the world are the sweetest and meatiest. There is at least one coconut palm, if not many more, in every backyard in Kerala. Coconut palms are grown here not just for coconuts. To a Malayali, the coconut palm's usefulness is manyfold. An old saying goes, "If you plant ten coconut palms when you can afford to, there will be at least ten coconuts when times are rough."

Every part of the tree is used in some way or other. The leaves of the tree are braided to make thatch for roofing, and the trunk is used in building huts. The inside hard shells of the coconut and the stem are used as firewood. Coconut shells are fitted with wooden handles to make ladles. The outer fibrous shell of the coconut is processed to make coir, which is used for ropes, mats, and rugs. The liquid inside the tender green coconut provides a refreshing drink, the milky white coconut inside the hard shell is indispensable in cooking, and dried coconut (or copra) is crushed to make coconut oil. The coconut residue left after pressing out the oil is used as feed for dairy cattle. The fermented sap from the flower-bearing shoots yields an alcoholic drink, toddy.

The origin of coconut is believed to be an island near Papua New Guinea. Coconuts float in the sea for months, and they sprout when they reach a beach, and thus they spread all over the warm southern shores of India. Ancient literature of India, dating back to 300 BC, refers to coconut. Its Sanskrit name, *nalikera*, is derived from two words of Southeast Asian origin: *niyoor* for oil and *kolai* for nut. The Portuguese sailors gave it the name coconut.

Breaking a coconut: Coconut is broken into two pieces in the middle to get the fresh white pieces. Personally, I prefer using a hammer. In the United States, the coconuts sold in supermarkets often have a groove marking the middle, and tapping along this line all around with a hammer and hitting the coconut hard a few times should open it into two equal halves.

Coconut can also be broken by piercing holes in its eyes (the three dark marks at one end), draining the liquid, and then placing the coconut in a preheated 400°F oven for ten to twelve minutes, until the shell cracks. Take out the coconut and crack it on a hard surface to open it. After opening the coconut, remove the white part from the shell with a sharp paring knife. The pieces will have a very thin brownish skin. They can be grated either manually or in a food processor fitted with the metal blade. If you insist on pure-white grated coconut, you may scrape off the skin with a potato peeler before grating, although the brown skin is quite edible and can be used in most curries. Back home, a *cherava*, a small, low wooden stool fitted with a metal scraper, is used to grate white coconut meat from the shell. Since this scrapes from the inside first, the grated coconut is milky white.

For making many of the curries that use freshly grated coconut, it is preferable to use fresh coconut. Frozen freshly grated coconut is available at Indian and Latin American grocery stores. In dishes where grated coconut is pan-roasted, dried coconut flakes may be substituted. Use the desiccated coconut available in Indian grocery stores, not the sweetened version from supermarkets.

Extracting coconut milk: Coconut milk is extracted in varying strengths from freshly grated coconut. There is the first extract, or the thick, creamy milk produced by tightly squeezing the scraped coconut in the palm of your hand. This is generally used at the final stage of cooking. The second extract, or thin milk, is squeezed after adding some water to the coconut scrapings from which the first milk has been extracted. A blender may be used in extracting second milk. This slightly watery milk is used for most cooking. Determined souls even attempt a third extract. For ease of use, you may substitute canned coconut milk, which is available in most supermarkets. As an easy alternative, I prefer using coconut milk powder, although it lacks authentic taste. By adjusting the quantity of water added, the powder allows you to make thick or thin coconut milk. Coconut milk powder is available in Southeast Asian and Indian grocery stores.

Jaggery *(sarkara)*, Indian unrefined brown sugar, is produced from the sap of sugarcane *(Saccharum officinarum)*, a giant grass resembling slender bamboo. An age-old process is still used in the villages to produce jaggery. The sugarcane crop is first burned to remove the leaves. The sugarcane stems are harvested and shredded in a primitive ox-driven press to extract the juice. The juice is boiled for hours to produce a concentrated liquid, and then lime is added to remove impurities. As impurities float up to the top, they are skimmed off. With continued boiling, the sugar begins to crystallize. At this point, the liquid is poured into wooden molds to set. This unrefined sugar comes in either small or large blocks. It is readily available in Indian grocery stores. Brown sugar, available in supermarkets, is an excellent substitute for jaggery.

Sugarcane is believed to have originated in Papua New Guinea. Thousands of years ago, the plant migrated to the Asian continent. In early Indian scripture, the *Atharvaveda* (circa 1500–800 BC) mentions sugarcane as a sacrificial offering. Ancient Buddhist literature also mentions jaggery. In 327 BC, Alexander the Great is believed to have sent back from India a reed tree that produced honey without bees. In the thirteenth century, Ibn Battuta wrote about the sugarcane of Kerala, which was unexcelled in the rest of the country.

Salt *(uppu)* is the basic seasoning, and without it, other flavors would not come together. When added to raw ingredients, salt draws out moisture. Always start with a smaller amount of salt, and increase it to your own taste. When I cook, I usually measure salt with my eyes.

Sea salt, the flaky crystallized variety, is a prized commodity. The production of sea salt in India in ancient times is described in the *Arthashasthra* (circa 300 BC) and *Charaka Samhita* (circa 200 BC). According to the *Arthashasthra*, the job of the *lavanadhyaksha* (salt superintendent) was an important one. He was the king's representative who oversaw the production and distribution of sea salt. He regulated the salt trade by using a licensing system and collecting sales tax revenues.

Gram and Dal (Beans, Peas, and Lentils)

Different kinds of grains and beans and peas form the mainstay of South Indian vegetarian cuisine. Beans and peas come in a variety of sizes and colors. There are three major branches of legumes: Old World, New World, and Asian and African. Old World legumes include fava beans, peas, and a variety of lentils. New World legumes include lima beans, runner beans, kidney beans, black beans, pinto beans, and white beans. Among Asian legumes are mung beans, several varieties of adzuki beans, urad beans, and soybeans; among African beans are cowpeas, yard-long beans, black-eyed peas, and pigeon peas. South Indian cooking uses every variety of bean that grows in our tropical climate.

The legumes we most commonly use are mung, *urad*, *chana*, and *tuvar*; they are different in shape, color, and taste, just like pinto, cannelloni, and black beans. In India, any type of legume—dried beans, peas, or lentils—is called gram or dal. Although gram means whole beans and dal means hulled and split, these words are often used interchangeably. Legumes are easy to grow and store, and are high in fiber content and essential vitamins and minerals. These complex carbohydrates are also a valuable source of protein in our meatless diet. It is easy to cook beans when they are hulled and split, and they are easily digested. Grains and dried beans and peas have a complementary relationship when they are served together. Whole beans, such as Indian chickpeas, small red beans (cowpeas), and whole mung beans are also used in several dishes.

Since the days of our ancient ancestors, legumes have been an important part of the human diet. They are among the oldest crops cultivated by the human race. According to ancient Sanskrit literature, mung and *urad* beans were cultivated in India as far back as 1500 BC and horse gram dates back to 1800 BC. *Chana* dal has been found in archeological excavations in India of sites dating as far back as 2500 BC, although finds in old Asia Minor in the Middle East go back to 5400 BC. *Tuvar* dal has been grown along the mountains of South India for centuries.

Cooking legumes: The first step in cooking dal is the same for all varieties: boiling it in water until it becomes very soft. On the other hand, whole beans are cooked until they are tender to the touch and can be mashed easily with fingers.

Soak the legumes thoroughly. The soaking process dissolves gas-causing elements into the soaking water. The longer you soak the beans (within reason), the more gas generators are removed. After soaking the legumes and discarding the soaking water, rinse the legumes thoroughly in several changes of water until the water runs clear. Whole beans cook faster if they are soaked overnight in plenty of water. After boiling the beans, if the recipe allows, discard that water and rinse the beans again. If you are using canned beans, drain the liquid from the beans and rinse.

Usually, legumes are boiled in four to five times their volume in water and seasoned only after they are well cooked. In India, pressure cooking is considered the ideal method for cooking legumes. Follow the manufacturer's directions when using a pressure cooker. Pressure-cooking time varies with each legume. Mung beans and mung dal take the least time to cook. Beans and dal are usually cooked along with turmeric in the pressure cooker, and salt is added afterward. When cooking in a pressure cooker, adding a few drops of cooking oil to the water will help prevent the clogging of the pressure cooker's vents. The most important thing about cooking dal is the combination of spices used in their flavoring.

Indian chickpeas and *chana* dal *(kadala* and *kadala parippu)*: Indian chickpeas *(Cicer arietinum)* are a close relative of European chickpeas. They are smaller and have dark-brown skins compared to the pale yellow-beige skin of European chickpeas. They are cooked whole and used in several dishes. Split and hulled, these peas are called *chana* dal and look very similar to yellow split peas. *Chana* dal is golden-yellow in color, very nutritious, and easily digested.

The chickpea, one of the oldest pulses used by man, was domesticated in the Middle East centuries ago. It is believed to have spread to the Mediterranean by 4000 BC and to India by 2000 BC. The Portuguese and the Spaniards took it to the New World in the sixteenth century. *Chana* dal has a much lower glycemic index and three times more fiber than the European variety of chickpea. It can be substituted for European chickpeas in just about any recipe.

Puffed *chana* dal *(porikadala)* is roasted, split, and skinned *chana* dal. It is made from brown-skinned Indian chickpeas. Making these is a small-scale cottage industry in India. They soak the chickpeas in water for several hours and then roast them in big cauldrons under controlled heat, continuously stirring them. Once the roasting process is completed, they remove the hulls and split each chickpea in half. This whole process intensifies the taste of the chickpeas and turns them into light yellow, mildly sweet puffed *chana* dal.

Mung and Mung dal *(cherupayaru and cheruparippu)*: Also known as green gram for its olive green skin, mung dal is the split bean of the plant *Vigna radiata*. This dal is widely used in three different forms in our cooking: whole, split with skin, and split and hulled. The split and hulled dal has a pale yellow color, is the easiest to digest, and has a delicate flavor when cooked. The whole and split-with-skin varieties have green skin covering the dal. A cup of cooked mung beans contain fourteen grams of protein. Mung beans are a good source of dietary fiber. They also contain thiamin, iron, magnesium, phosphorus, potassium, and copper.

Mung is believed to have originated in India. It is mentioned in Sanskrit literature dating back to around 1000 BC. Whole mung and dal are available in natural food stores, Chinese markets, and Indian stores.

Tuvar or *toor* **dal** *(tuvara parippu)*: Pigeon peas *(Cajanus cajan)*, when split and hulled, look like flat, split golden-yellow peas. They are called *tuvar* dal in India. *Tuvar* dal forms the base of our everyday dishes, such as *sambar* and *rasam*. The immature green peas are cooked like green beans or black-eyed peas. They have a mild, nutty flavor. Pigeon peas are a rich source of proteins, carbohydrates, and dietary minerals such as calcium, phosphorus, magnesium, iron, sulfur, and potassium. They are also a good source of soluble vitamins. In Indian stores, they are available either plain or coated with oil. The coated variety must be rinsed thoroughly in hot water to remove the oil before cooking.

Pigeon peas are an important crop in many parts of the world, including India, East Asia, Africa, Latin America, and the Caribbean; they are called *gandules* in Puerto Rico and *gungo* beans in Jamaica. They were called *adhaki* in ancient Buddhist literature.

Urad dal *(uzunnu parippu)*: Known as black gram in English, this bean, *Vigna mungo*, is believed to be indigenous to India. It shares a common ancestor with mung beans. These small oval beans have grayish-black skin and a white interior. They are widely used in Kerala cooking in three forms: split with skin, hulled whole, and split and hulled. *Urad* dal is substantially protein-rich, and when soaked, rinsed, and ground into batter, it has a glutinous texture. Ground-rice-and-*urad*-dal batters are used in preparing different breakfast dishes. *Urad* dal is also used in seasoning. When fried in oil, it takes on a nutty flavor.

Horse gram *(muthira or kollu)*: The tiny, flat, and slightly elongated brown-skinned bean from the plant *Macrotyloma uniflorum* is native to India. It has a strong, earthy aroma and is rich in protein. It is also used as a feed for horses, hence its English name, horse gram.

Cowpeas or small red beans *(vellapayaru)*: A native of tropical Africa, cowpeas are produced on the plant *Vigna unguiculata*. They are generally harvested early, and the immature peas are sold either dried or fresh. The variety of cowpeas grown in India has long pods and small, kidney-shaped, red beans. This annual legume was domesticated in West Africa around 3000 BC and reached India around 1500 BC. Just like the chickpea, it was carried to the New World by the Portuguese and the Spaniards in the seventeenth century. In the United States, cowpeas are grown in Texas, Georgia, and California.

Flours, Semolina, and *Semiya* Noodles

Flours made from rice, *chana* dal, and *urad* dal are the three most commonly used flours in Kerala cuisine. Others include all-purpose flour (called *maida*), fine wheat flour, and arrowroot flour. Coarsely ground whole wheat, processed wheat, and thin semolina noodles are other staples of the pantry.

Chana flour or *besan (kadalamavu)*: Hulled Indian brown chickpeas are powdered to make *chana* flour. Very fine in texture and pale yellow in color, it is widely used in making many snacks and sweets. It is low in gluten and high in protein. Indian stores sell two kinds of *chana* flour: extra-fine and slightly coarse. For the recipes in this collection, the extra-fine variety is recommended. Some gourmet food stores and natural food stores also carry this flour. It may be substituted for chickpea flour.

Rice flour *(arippodi)*: Long-grain rice is ground to a very fine texture to make rice flour. It is used in making several breakfast dishes and snacks. It is rich in starch but has no gluten.

Urad flour *(uzunnu podi)*: Hulled *urad* dal is ground to an extra-fine texture to make *urad* flour. It is grayish white in color.

Wheat flour *(gothambu mavu)*: Also called chapati flour or *atta,* this flour is made by powdering the kernels of hard whole wheat *(Triticum aestivum)*. Even though the bran and germ are powdered, it is sifted several times to remove any roughage. As a result, this flour is superfine in texture. The wheat flour available in supermarkets is not very fine in texture. Flour purchased from Indian groceries is recommended for the recipes in this book.

Arrowroot flour *(koova podi)*: This flour is produced from the rhizomes or rootstocks of the arrowroot plant *(Maranta arundinacea)*. The plant's creeping rootstock has fleshy tubers, which are harvested when they are gorged with starch, just before the plant's dormant season. The roots are peeled and grated directly into a pot of water. The resulting mixture is strained though cotton mesh. The process is repeated several times to purify the starch. The purified mass is dried and powdered. Arrowroot is pure starch; boiled in water or milk, it yields a transparent, pleasant-tasting jelly.

Semolina *(rava)*: Tiny grains of semolina made from processed wheat (called *rava*) and slightly coarser grains made from whole wheat (called *gothambu rava*) are used in making breakfast dishes and sweets. *Rava* has no aroma and is well suited to making either sweets or savory snacks. It has a nice, smooth texture similar to farina. Farina or cream of wheat, although slightly coarser in texture, may be used if *rava* is not available. Coarsely-ground whole wheat *(gothambu rava)* is used for making the breakfast dish *uppuma*. Both types are available at Indian grocery stores. Cracked wheat, available at American supermarkets, makes a good substitute for *gothambu rava*.

Semiya Noodles: Extremely thin Indian Durham wheat noodles, thinner than angelhair pasta, are used in making a savory snack and a dessert. Two kinds of noodles are available in Indian grocery stores; one is toasted, and the other is not toasted. The toasted noodles have a golden brown color. These thin noodles are very easy to break into tiny pieces.

Oils

In the traditional kitchen, coconut oil and sesame oil are preferred. Unless specifically mentioned in a recipe, these oils may be easily substituted with your choice of cooking oil.

Coconut oil *(velichenna)*: Coconut oil is extracted from sun-dried coconut pieces, called copra. This oil will turn to a creamy white solid in cold weather but will become clear when heated. With people becoming more health-conscious over the years, the use of coconut oil (which contains some saturated fat) has dwindled substantially. However, in certain dishes, such as *aviyal*, coconut oil is necessary to accomplish the authentic taste.

Sesame oil *(nallenna)*: This is a golden to brownish-gold-colored oil extracted from sesame seeds. It has a nutty fragrance and is used in pickling and making *dosa* and *ada*. When unavailable, sesame oil may be substituted with vegetable oil. Besides improving the flavor of food, oil extracted from roasted sesame seeds has a longer shelf life, resisting rancidity because of the antioxidants formed during seed roasting.

Sesame seeds and sesame oil are described in ancient Sanskrit literature from very early times. The *Rigveda* (circa 1700–1500 BC) and the *Atharvaveda* (circa 1500–800 BC) both frequently mention sesame.

Milk and Milk Products

It is believed that the Aryan invaders (the Iranian branch of the Indo-European nomads) who reached India around 1750 BC brought with them a food culture dominated by dairy products. Ever since, India's fascination for dairy products has remained unshaken. The reverence for cows developed against a background that was as much economic as it was religious. Cows provide us with milk and milk by-products. Before the days of mechanized cultivation, oxen also plowed our rice fields and carried the harvest home on their backs. Cow manure is still used as fertilizer in our gardens and farms. In ancient India, a milk cow was like the goose that laid the golden eggs: milk and milk products could feed more people than a cow's carcass. Cows and calves are treated almost as family members. At the festival of Vishu, the auspicious Vishu Kani is taken to the cowshed so that our cows also can start a good new year. Our neighboring state Tamil Nadu has a festival dedicated to cows: Maattu Pongal.

Vegetarianism remains popular among South Indian Hindus. However, authentic Indian vegetarian food does include certain animal products, such as milk, butter, and yogurt. Our vegetarianism is based on the principle of *ahimsa,* respect for life. We use milk and milk products because no killing of the animal is involved in the extraction of the milk. Calves are allowed to satisfy their hunger before the cow is milked. We offer milk, ghee, and yogurt at our temples and use ghee as the fuel in our temple lamps. We make *paayasams* with milk and ghee and offer them at our temples. We serve ghee and buttermilk with meals and use yogurt-based sauces in preparing several curries. Milk and milk products provide our diet with protein and calcium.

Until about the latter half of the twentieth century, most households had their own milk cows, a practice that continues in the present in some remote villages of Kerala. In the tropical heat of South India, milk is a highly perishable commodity. Fresh milk is always boiled before use. Before the days of refrigeration, the only way to use leftover milk was to ferment it daily to make yogurt. Yogurt is churned in the morning to separate butter from buttermilk. However, cheese-making was never a part of South Indian cuisine.

Yogurt or curd *(thayir)*: In the old days, most households prepared yogurt every day. Making fresh yogurt at home is very simple. It does not require fancy yogurt makers or special equipment. Milk is first boiled, and after it cools, yogurt culture is added and fermented for the next day. Homemade yogurt stays fresh in the refrigerator for up to two weeks. Store-bought plain yogurt makes a good substitute.

Buttermilk *(mooru)*: When set yogurt is churned to separate the butterfat, the remaining sour liquid is called buttermilk. Back home, yogurt is poured into a tall vessel and stirred with a wooden churn to separate the butter. When the butter floats to the top, it is scooped up and placed in a bowl of cold water. Buttermilk is served with meals and used for cooking. It also makes a refreshing cool drink, *sambharam*.

Ghee *(neyyu)*: Ghee is a form of clarified butter. Butter is melted and cooked over medium heat to remove all of the moisture and milk solids. Unlike butter, ghee can be stored at room temperature for several weeks and in the refrigerator or freezer for even longer periods. Ghee is excellent for frying, as it has a higher smoking point than butter. It also imparts a nutty aroma to dishes. Ghee is served with rice and used in making most desserts. The practice of frying in ghee is very old in India; it is mentioned in the ancient text *Rigveda*. The ancient Greek travel book *Periplus Maris Erythraei* describes the export of coconut oil and ghee to Rome. Ghee was sent in leather skins to Rome from Muziris for the use of the wealthy.

The Spice Rack

Spices have been important throughout history, both as a means to prestige and for preserving foods and enhancing their flavor. For Europe, spices were the envoys from the enchanted Orient. From ancient times, the monsoon-soaked rain forests of Kerala, home to several spices, became a prime destination for many explorers.

Nomadic Arabs were among the first who came to Kerala for trade. Spice trade and commerce between China and South India by sea began as early as the second century BC. The spice trade flourished during the Roman Empire, and after its fall, the Arabs regained control. During the latter half of the fifteenth century, the royal families of Spain and Portugal financed dozens of expeditions in search of a sea route to the spice coast of India. In 1498, Vasco da Gama heralded the emergence of the colonial era as he led an expedition to the spice-producing countries of the East.

Da Gama's rival, Columbus, went in the opposite direction (westward) in search of pepper. When he landed in the then-unknown Americas, his enthusiasm to convince his king—and himself—that he had succeeded in his mission led him to name the natives "Indians" and their red chili "pepper," two errors that have confused people to this day. The Dutch and the British followed the Portuguese. The spice trade was as profitable an undertaking as it was complex.

Today, spices hold the same magic. Understanding spices is the cornerstone of the art of Indian cooking; they provide endless possibilities for flavoring. Spices distinguish one dish from another, define the flavor, and heighten the taste. The essential ones used in Kerala vegetarian cuisine are asafetida, black pepper, cayenne pepper, cardamom, coriander, cumin, fenugreek, mustard seeds, sesame seeds, and turmeric. We prefer whole spices to powdered spices, as they impart fresher flavor. Even when they are used in powdered form, whole spices are generally either dry-roasted or pan-fried with a touch of oil and powdered just before using. Except for fenugreek and asafetida, all of the spices used in this cuisine are available in American supermarkets. Though it is traditionally used in a lot of recipes, asafetida can be omitted without really sacrificing the taste; in those recipes, I have noted that its use is optional.

Spices and aromatics are used not just as taste and flavor enhancers. According to ayurveda, the original purpose of the use of spices was not just for taste; it was also for their medicinal and therapeutic value. While some spices stimulate the appetite, others help digestion or reduce flatulence, and others have antiseptic value. The medicinal properties of certain spices are believed to compensate for harmful properties of some foods.

When working with a foreign cuisine, learning to balance flavors is very important. The flavors of spices can vary from brand to brand. Tropical produce grown in the West may have less flavor due to differences in climate and the nature of the soil; therefore, it is important to make adjustments in quantity to balance flavors. But believe me, none of these recipes are carved in stone! If you prefer a mild taste, reduce the amount of chili. If you like a sour taste, increase the quantity of tamarind, yogurt, or lemon juice. Start at the lower end, and increase slowly. Also, you do not have to buy a large variety of spices to try this cuisine.

In authentic Indian cooking, there is no spice or spice blend called "curry powder." Each dish is prepared with a different blend of spices. If you want the taste to be authentic, please do not substitute the spice blends with curry powder. If you do not want to go through the process of preparing spice blends, you can buy them at Indian grocery stores. As flavors tend to differ slightly among various brands, I have listed my personal preferences along with the recipes. Do not buy powdered spices in large quantities; they tend to lose their flavor over time. Whole spices have a longer shelf life. Keep them in jars with tight lids so that they will not lose their fragrance.

Though cinnamon, cloves, and nutmeg grow abundantly in this part of the world, our vegetarian cooking practically avoids them. Even black pepper, though native to our region, is used only sparingly. Although several foreign traders invaded Kerala for our black pepper, we prefer using the red pepper that the Portuguese introduced to us. The following are the spices used in this vegetarian cuisine.

Ajowan (*omam* or *ayamodakam*): This aromatic spice comes from the seeds of an umbelliferous plant, *Trachyspermum ammi,* that is native to India and the Near East. The tiny oval, ridged seeds look like miniature cumin seeds. The plant is closely related to dill, caraway, and cumin, and its flavor is a combination of anise and oregano with a hint of black pepper. It is known for its antioxidant and preservative qualities and is used in treating digestive disorders.

Asafetida (*kaayam*): Asafetida is a hard, aromatic, resinous gum collected from the roots of certain species of giant fennels, plants of the species *Ferula assafoetida.* It is sold in blocks or pieces as a gum and more frequently as a fine powder, sometimes crystalline or granulated. It is also known as "devil's dung" because of its strong, pungent smell due to the presence of sulfur compounds. The name asafetida is believed to have originated from the Persian word *azā* (mastic resin) and the Latin word *foetida,* meaning "stinking."

Asafetida is sold in powder and lump form at Indian grocery stores and certain gourmet food stores. The lump asafetida is the most common form of pure asafetida. In making commercially ground asafetida, the resins are combined with small quantities of rice, barley, or wheat flour to prevent lumping and to reduce the strong flavor. Processed asafetida often varies in color and texture because of the difference in additives. It is available as either mustard yellow powder or sandy-brown, coarse powder.

Asafetida has remained a part of the Indian spice box for centuries and continues to be used both in cooking and in medicine in India. South Indian vegetable curries are often garnished with a large pinch of asafetida that has been pan-fried in a spoonful of oil or ghee. When asafetida is added to hot oil, its strong and powerful smell changes to an enticing aroma that is similar to onion and garlic. Strict vegetarian diets of India forbid the use of onions and garlic, and asafetida is used in their place for its distinct aroma. It is used in the cooking of vegetables, certain savory snacks, pickles, and chutneys. As it helps to neutralize flatulence, it is widely used in dishes prepared with various beans and other legumes. In ayurveda, asafetida is used to stimulate appetite and digestion.

The ancient Sanskrit text *Kashyapa Samhita* (circa 200 BC) mentions the import of asafetida from Afghanistan. The great Indian epic *Mahabharata* (circa 400 BC to 300 AD) includes graphic descriptions of dishes prepared with spices, including asafetida.

The perennial asafetida plant is native to the region between the Mediterranean and Central Asia, especially Afghanistan and Iran. Three different species are used in the production of asafetida: *Ferula asafoetida, Ferula foetida,* and *Ferula narthex;* they are slightly different in color and properties. Even though most of the world's production of asafetida comes from Iran and Afghanistan, India is the major consumer of this spice. When the plants are about four or five years old, they develop very thick and fleshy carrot-shaped roots. The resin is collected from the roots just before the plants start flowering in spring or early summer. The milky liquid soon coagulates when exposed to air. The color darkens when it is sun dried into a solid form.

Asafetida's use as a tenderizer and preservative for meat was known centuries ago. Asafetida was a popular spice in Europe in Roman times and was in great demand during the Middle Ages. In Iranian cuisine, it is used for flavoring meatballs; in Afghanistan, it is used in the preparation of dried meat. Although this spice is practically unknown in modern Western cuisines, it is used in the United States and Europe in commercially prepared flavorings.

Asafetida's predecessor, silphium (also known as *silphion* or *laser),* the wonderful spice form the region of Cyrene (now in modern Libya), was in great demand in ancient times. The Greeks believed the plant was a gift from Apollo, because it appeared after a heavy rainstorm flooded the area at about the time the city of Cyrene was founded in the seventh century BC. However, true silphium became extinct by the end of the first century AD.

Asafetida became known as a result of the expeditions of Alexander the Great. While crossing the northeastern provinces of the Persian Empire, Alexander's soldiers discovered a plant that was almost identical to silphium.

They found that, although not quite so good, it could be substituted for silphium in cookery. Cooks who now recreate the ancient Roman recipes of Apicius (first-century author of *De re coquinaria*) use asafetida in place of silphium.

Black pepper *(kurumulaku)*: *Piper nigrum*, the black gold of Kerala, is native to tropical India. Black peppercorns are the sun-dried fruit of the pepper vine. Freshly crushed pepper has the best flavor and aroma. Black peppercorns are available in varying sizes, aroma, and pungency.

Black pepper is highly valued for its medicinal benefits and is an important component of many ayurvedic medicines. Applying a paste of crushed black pepper cooked in milk is considered to be a cure for migraine headaches. Black pepper soup relieves colds and sore throat.

Arab traders artfully withheld the source of pepper from Europeans for a long time. One of the fables they spread was that pepper was the seed or fruit of a tree that grew in the lush forests on the southern side of the Caucasus Mountains, in the hottest sunshine. The pepper forests were said to be full of poisonous snakes that guarded the trees, so when the peppercorns were ripe, people supposedly set fire to the forest, the snakes fled, and the thick flames blackened the pepper fruits and sharpened their taste.

Black pepper has a colorful history, as it followed the trade routes to the West. During much of the Middle Ages, pepper was such a prized spice that it was considered equivalent to money and was stored under lock and key. In Renaissance Italy, pasta dishes served at banquets were sprinkled with abundant quantities of black pepper and cinnamon, as a symbol of prosperity. When an English ship that sank in 1545 was raised from the ocean floor in the 1980s, nearly every sailor was found to have a bunch of peppercorns on his body.

Cardamom seeds *(elakkaya)*: These are the fragrant seeds of a tropical plant *(Elettaria cardamomum)* that grows abundantly in the tropical regions of South India and Sri Lanka. Cardamom is the world's third most expensive spice, right behind saffron and vanilla.

Cardamom is an herbaceous perennial plant belonging to the ginger family. Cardamom grows abundantly in higher altitudes with a warm humid atmosphere and evenly distributed rainfall. Cardamom plants flower for eight to nine months of the year. Each pod, or capsule, ripens slowly and is plucked when three-quarters ripe. Seeds are collected from well-ripened fruits from a healthy plant at least five years old. Today it is cultivated in partially cleared tropical rain forests of India, Nepal, Sri Lanka, Thailand, Mexico, Guatemala, and Tanzania.

India is the world's largest producer of cardamom. Indian cardamom is slightly smaller, but more aromatic. The brownish black seeds are enclosed in one-quarter to three-quarter inch long oval-shaped pods. The larger variety known as black cardamom is brown in color, and the smaller variety is called green cardamom. Green pods have an excellent fragrance compared to the yellow or white bleached ones. After harvest, the pods are washed and dried. The method of drying dictates the final color. White indicates that the pods have been dried for many days in the sun, leaving them bleached. Green pods have been dried for one day and one night in a heated room.

Cardamom is offered commercially in many forms. It is sold as whole pods, seeds, powder, and liquid extract. Cardamom has a pleasant flavor and aroma, and in India, it is either crushed coarsely or powdered finely and used in tea, cool drinks, and sweets, as well as in vegetarian and non-vegetarian dishes. In India, cardamom is another spice that is valued for its medicinal properties. It is considered to be a digestive aid; stirring a pinch of cardamom into milk is believed to reduce mucus produced by dairy products. It is also used for the treatment of dental diseases.

The ancient Egyptians chewed cardamom seeds as a tooth cleanser; the Greeks and Romans used it in perfumes. The Vikings came upon cardamom a thousand years ago, in Constantinople, and introduced it into Scandinavia, where it remains popular. Scandinavia consumes half of the world's cardamom production. Cardamom is a popular spice in North Africa and East Africa. Cardamom coffee is a symbol of Arab hospitality. In the West, cardamom essential oil is used as a food flavoring, in perfumery, and for flavoring liquor. The spice is often combined with cloves and cinnamon in all cuisines.

Cardamom seeds lose their flavor quickly when ground, and it is ideal to buy only whole pods and crush them just before using them.

Chili pepper *(kappal mulagu)*: *Capsicum annuum* and the tabasco-like *Capsicum frutescens* are the popular chilies in Indian cuisine. It is an herbaceous annual that has white flowers, and fruit that vary in length, color, and pungency. After harvesting part of the crop for use as fresh green chilies, the remaining crop is allowed to ripen on the plant until the pods are bright red. The harvested pods are sun dried and sold both whole and ground.

Capsicum has been known since the beginning of civilization in the western hemisphere. It is believed that capsicum has been a part of the human diet since about 7500 BC. Chili is one of the oldest cultivated crops of the Americas. The words "pepper," "chili," "chile," "chilli," "aji," "paprika," and "capsicum" are often used interchangeably. Based on scientific research, the word "chile" is a variation of "chil" from the Aztec dialect.

Until the beginning of the sixteenth century, hot chili pepper, one of the principal spices of Indian cuisine today, was totally unknown in India. The honor of introducing India to *Capsicum annuum* belongs to the Portuguese traders. When the Portuguese ventured abroad in search of a new sea route to the land of black pepper, chili pepper traveled on merchant ships, along with tobacco and cotton, to the next trading posts.

Indians were quite taken with the fiery red chili. Today chilies appear frequently in Indian cuisine, and tolerance for them is substantial, especially in tropical South India. The diversity and intensity of pepper used in this cuisine rivals that of Mexico and the southwestern United States. It is readily available in Indian and Mexican grocery stores and in grocery stores in the southwestern United States. If whole chili peppers are not readily available, substitute with crushed red pepper flakes.

The consumption of chili peppers may aggravate symptoms of ulcers, and excessive consumption can cause gastroenteritis and kidney damage. Chili pepper is the ultimate decongestant. Research studies have shown that chili peppers lower LDL cholesterol, the type associated with high blood pressure and heart disease. They are rich in vitamin C and beta carotene. As a medicinal plant, capsicum is used in ayurvedic remedies for colic, diarrhea, asthma, arthritis, muscle cramps, and toothache.

Coriander seeds *(kothamalli)*: Coriander seeds grow on the annual herb *Coriandrum sativum,* which belongs to the carrot family. The coriander plant yields both the fresh green herb and the spice seed. When ripe, the seeds have a distinctive sweet, musty aroma that has been valued over the centuries. They look like tiny beads with a yellowish brown color and have a distinctive fragrance and a mildly pungent taste.

Both the seeds and leaves of the plant are used in Middle Eastern, south Asian, and Latin American cuisines. It is also popular in Chinese cuisine. In Thailand, even the root of the plant is used. Although it is popular in the rest of Asia, it is practically unknown in Japan. In Indian cuisine, coriander is used extensively—whole, crushed, or ground—to flavor many different dishes. The use of coriander seeds is more widespread in Europe, the one exception being Portuguese cuisine. Coriander is a fairly recent arrival to the American kitchen. Coriander is used in gingerbread, cookies, yeast breads, sausages, stews, and chicken dishes.

Although cilantro and coriander seeds are most often associated with the cuisines of Mexico and Asia, this spice originated in the southern reaches of the Mediterranean. Coriander has been found in Egyptian tombs dating back 3,000 years. It was cultivated in ancient Egypt for both medicinal and culinary purposes. It is believed that the ancient Hebrews originally used cilantro root as the bitter herb in the symbolic Passover meal. Coriander seeds have been used in southern Europe since classical times. The Romans used coriander with cumin and vinegar as a preservative, which they rubbed into meat. The ancient Greeks and Romans took it to Europe, and the Arabs introduced it to India, China, and Southeast Asian countries.

In ayurveda, coriander is considered invaluable for digestion. It is a cooling spice with an astringent taste, and it enhances digestion and stimulates the appetite. Coriander is also considered helpful for promoting respiratory system health and enhancing natural defenses against allergens.

Cumin seeds *(jeerakam)* grow on a small annual herb of the parsley family called *Cuminum cyminum*. They are yellowish brown and are similar to caraway seeds, but a little longer. Cumin has a strong, slightly bitter, aromatic flavor and a warm taste due to the presence of volatile oils. Cumin is a popular spice used in Latin American, Mexican, North African, and most Asian cuisines. It is commercially sold as both seeds and powder. As any other spice, whole cumin seeds retain more aroma than powdered cumin. The main cumin-producing countries today are India, Iran, Indonesia, China, and countries in the south Mediterranean region. Cumin is one of the most commonly used spices of India; it is an important ingredient in several spice mixtures.

The seeds are used whole, and are fried or dry roasted before usage. The aroma of cumin seeds, like most spices, emerges best when dry roasted or added to hot oil. Similar spice mixtures are also much in use among the descendants of South Indian immigrants in Malaysia or Singapore. In Southeast Asia and East Asia, cumin is less valued but used occasionally.

Cumin is also very popular in West Asia to Central Asia; spice mixtures from this region featuring cumin include the Yemeni *zhoug,* the Saudi Arabian *baharat,* and the North African *tagines.* In Central and South American cooking, cumin is also an important spice. It is used in stews and breads in Spain. The popularity of Mexican dishes such as chili con carne, especially in the southwestern United States, has made cumin an important spice in the United States.

Cumin is believed to be a native of Egypt and the eastern Mediterranean region, where it has been cultivated since biblical times. Cumin is mentioned in the works of Hippocrates and Dioscorides. According to Pliny, the ancients took ground cumin seeds medicinally with bread, water, or wine. In the thirteenth and fourteenth centuries, it was much in use as a culinary spice in the West. In Italian cuisine, cumin has little use; however, it is referred to as Roman caraway in many European languages.

In ayurveda, cumin is considered a warming spice, invaluable for digestion. It is also a cleansing spice that helps burn toxins and enhances the appetite. A homemade antacid, *jeerakakashayam,* is prepared by boiling water with toasted and crushed cumin seeds and reducing it to one-fourth of the quantity. A couple of tablespoons of this liquid is believed to be a sure cure for indigestion.

Fenugreek *(uluva)***:** Fenugreek *(Trigonella foenum-graecum),* one of the earliest spices known to man, belongs to the bean family. The herb can grow to be about two feet tall. It blooms with white flowers in the summer and has very aromatic seeds. The small, oblong-shaped, yellowish brown seeds of the fenugreek plant have a warm and slightly bitter taste. Fenugreek is rich in vitamins and minerals and is high in protein.

Fenugreek is indigenous to western Asia and southeastern Europe. Now it is grown in India, Morocco, Egypt, and England. Iran has a very rich tradition of cooking with fenugreek leaves. The Ethiopian spice mixture *berebere* contains a small amount of fenugreek. It was introduced to India by Arab traders.

Fenugreek has a long history as both a culinary and medicinal herb in the ancient world. The Egyptians, Greeks, and Romans used fenugreek for medicinal and culinary purposes. In ancient Egypt, fenugreek was used in the mummification process. During the Middle Ages, it was used as a medicinal plant in Europe. Fenugreek is also known in North and East Africa. It is widely used in West, Central, and South Asia.

Although it is a legume, it is widely used as a spice in India and it is an integral part of many Indian spice blends. Both the fresh leaves and the seeds of fenugreek are used in Indian cuisine. Fenugreek leaves, which are high in iron, are used as a leaf vegetable in curries as well as in Indian flat breads. Uncooked fenugreek seeds have an unpleasant, bitter taste, so the seeds are usually roasted and ground before use to mellow the bitterness. Dry roasting enhances the flavor and reduces the bitterness of fenugreek seeds. The seeds need close attention while being toasted; they turn reddish brown and taste very bitter when over roasted. They are available at Indian grocery stores and natural food stores.

As a medicinal plant, fenugreek has traditionally been considered an expectorant and a laxative. It is used in the treatment oft bronchitis, diabetes, and ulcers. Fenugreek is used to promote lactation in nursing mothers. It is also used as an oral insulin substitute, and seed extracts have been reported to lower blood glucose levels in laboratory animals.

Mustard seeds *(kaduku)*: Mustard seeds belong to the genus *Brassica* and come in three varieties—black, brown, and yellow—which are used in various aspects of cooking. Mustard plants are valued for their spicy and pungent dried seeds. The aroma and flavor of mustard comes from the essential oil contained inside the seeds. Mustard seeds are available in whole form, as a powder, and, most popular, as a prepared paste. The sharp flavor complements vegetables, meats, eggs, and fish. Leaves of the mustard plant are edible and are high in magnesium and vitamins A and C. Left whole and undisturbed, the seeds are completely odorless; but crush them even slightly, and they transform into a spice whose pungency can be quite intense. But it is this very pungency that makes the mustard very nutritive.

Mustard grows easily in moderate climates and is cultivated all over the world today. Depending on the variety, the plants range from two to four feet tall. They have long, delicate, light green stems, narrow leaves, and yellow flowers. Mustards grown for seed have long, slender pods. As the summer progresses, these will turn from green to brown. The pods are harvested before they split open and placed on drying trays covered with tightly woven cloth. In about two weeks, they will have split open, and the seeds are ready to be used whole, ground into powder, or made into prepared mustard. There are several mustard varieties that are grown for their tasty leaves and not their seeds.

Mustard is one of the oldest spices and one of the most widely used. Mustard is native to the southern Mediterranean region. Leaf mustard has been cultivated in Asia and Europe for thousands of years. It is believed that it was first domesticated in central Asia and the Himalayas.

Mustard seeds are a well-traveled spice. Ancient Rome enjoyed them as a condiment and a medicine. Mustard was cultivated in France by the ninth century. Vasco da Gama carried mustard on his first voyage around the Cape of Good Hope in 1497. The Chinese were using mustard thousands of years ago, and the ancient Greeks considered it an everyday spice. In Europe, mustard was used by the poor who couldn't afford black pepper, a very expensive imported spice. However, with the advent of the high period of great feasts and banquets, especially during the Renaissance, mustard became more popular.

In India, black or brown mustard seeds are commonly toasted or fried in a little oil before being added as a garnish. When added to hot oil, these seeds pop and sputter, developing a nutty taste in the process. This flavor is particularly loved in South India. The brown seeds are also pounded with other spices in the preparation of spice blends. Mustard oil is popular in India, especially as a cooking oil in many parts of East India. Mustard leaves are also used in cooking.

Historically, mustard has always held an important place in medicine. The ancient Greeks believed it had been created by Asclepius, the god of healing, as a gift to mankind. As a medicinal plant, mustard is considered a digestive stimulant that aids digestion. It is used as a folk remedy against arthritis, rheumatism, inflammation, and toothache. Moderate use of mustard stimulates circulation, and so it is used as Ayurvedic medication for chest congestion, toothache, headache, and to relieve sprains and rheumatism.

> Other than their use in cooking, in Kerala, mustard seeds are seen as a powerful agent to ward off the evil eye. After special occasions such as a baby's twenty-eighth day ceremony or rice-giving ceremony, an adult holds a handful of mustard seeds and seven red peppers inside cupped palms, moves them around the baby's face seven times, and throws them into a wood-burning stove. When the mustard seeds splutter, instead of releasing their nutty aroma, they produce a foul smell—said to be the smell of warding off the evil eye.

Sesame seeds *(ellu)*: These tiny, flat, pear-shaped seeds grow on the plant *Sesamum indicum*. Gentle roasting brings out their nutty flavor. They are used with coconut and other spices in curry dishes, and with brown sugar in making a sweet called *ellunda*. Indian grocery stores sell two different forms: hulled brown and unhulled black. Both are equally good and are more fragrant than white sesame seeds, which undergo a special hulling process.

Sesame seeds contain three times more calcium than a comparable measure of milk. The term "sesame" traces back to the Arabic *simsim* and the early Egyptian *semsent*. One of the most ancient of oil seeds, sesame originated in Africa and was taken to India from there. It was a highly prized oil crop of Babylon and Assyria about 4,000 years ago. African slaves brought sesame seeds to America, where sesame became a popular ingredient in Southern recipes. Sesame is the basis for creamy, sweet, wholesome tahini.

Turmeric powder *(manja podi)*: Turmeric is an ancient spice native to Indonesia and India, where it has grown for more than 5,000 years. Its active ingredient is curcumin. Whole turmeric is a tuberous rhizome of the perennial plant *Curcuma longa*, which belongs to the ginger family. The name derives from the Latin *terra merita* ("meritorious earth"), referring to the color of ground turmeric, which resembles a mineral pigment. In many languages, turmeric is simply named "yellow root."

Today, turmeric is grown in the tropics and the subtropics. The plant requires a hot, moist environment and a fairly light soil. Turmeric powder is made from the root of the plant. It is yellowish brown in color, with an orange interior that turns bright yellow when dried and powdered. The harvested rhizomes are boiled and dried, then their rough skins are removed and powdered to make turmeric powder. It is usually sold ground, as a bright yellow, fine powder. The exception is in Southeast Asia, where the fresh spice is much preferred to the dried.

The powder maintains its coloring properties indefinitely, though its flavor tends to diminish over time. Turmeric powder should be kept in an airtight container and stored in a cool, dry place. Turmeric is a significant ingredient in most commercial curry powders. The leading commercial producers of turmeric include India, Indonesia, China, the Philippines, Taiwan, Haiti, and Jamaica. India is the leading producer and consumer of turmeric. India is also the largest exporter of turmeric to the Middle East, the United Kingdom, the United States, and Japan.

Turmeric was used in religious rites in ancient India and China. It is still used in Hindu rituals and as a dye for holy robes. It was used as a coloring agent in Assyrian herbal preparations dating back to 600 BC. Marco Polo, in 1280, mentioned turmeric in the notes of his travels in China: "There is also a vegetable that has all the properties of true saffron, as well as the smell and the color, and yet it is not really saffron." In medieval Europe, turmeric was known as "Indian saffron," because of its color. Arab traders introduced it to Europe.

This warm and aromatic spice with bitter undertones is also used extensively in Southeast Asian and Middle Eastern cuisines. Turmeric is an essential spice in Indian cuisine. It is added to nearly every dish, be it non-vegetarian or vegetarian. Its bright yellow color imparts an orange yellow hue to curries. Excessive use of turmeric in food will result in a slightly bitter taste. It is also used in spice blends in the Caribbean, North Africa, the Middle East, and Indonesia. Turmeric is also used to give a yellow color to some prepared mustards; it gives ballpark mustard its bright yellow color. It is also used in other prepared foods, often as a much cheaper replacement for saffron.

Turmeric has recently become popular in Western cultures. Much of its recent popularity is owed to the recent research highlighting its therapeutic properties. A new study has found that turmeric may be an effective enhancer of an enzyme that protects the brain against oxidative conditions. This research is an important first step in determining whether turmeric can be used as a preventive agent to help reduce the progression of chronic and age-associated neurodegenerative disorders, such as Alzheimer's disease. Studies have shown that two teaspoons of turmeric contains 1.88 milligrams of iron, 0.08 milligrams of vitamin B, 0.96 grams of dietary fiber, 114.48 milligrams of potassium, and 0.36 grams of manganese.

Both Indian ayurvedic and Chinese medicines use turmeric for the treatment of inflammatory and digestive disorders. Turmeric is warming, and it offers the pungent, bitter, and astringent tastes. Turmeric has both antioxidant and anti-inflammatory properties. It is a natural preservative. It enhances the digestion, strengthens the liver, and nourishes the body tissues. It also has antiseptic and antibacterial properties. Turmeric is considered a powerful purifier by ayurvedic physicians.

It is taken in Asian countries as a dietary supplement, which allegedly helps with stomach problems and other ailments. In southern India, buttermilk spiced with turmeric is considered a digestive aid that helps curtail stomach ailments. A puree of turmeric and Asian basil is applied as an antiseptic against insect bites. Turmeric water is an Asian cosmetic applied to impart a golden glow to the complexion.

The Herb and Vegetable Basket

Our cuisine uses many familiar fruits and vegetables, such as tomatoes, potatoes, onions, squash, cabbage, carrots, eggplant, green beans, black-eyed peas, okra, and lemon. In addition, many tropical fruits, vegetables, and herbs have been a part of this cuisine since ancient times. Fortunately, most of them are available in Indian, Southeast Asian, Chinese, or Latin American grocery stores. The following is a brief description of these tropical fruits, herbs, and vegetables.

Breadfruit *(kadachakka),* the starchy fruit of the tall tree *Artocarpus altilis,* is not a fruit in the popular sense of the term. It contains a considerable amount of starch and must be cooked before eating. Breadfruit grows in clusters of two or three, is rounded to cylindrical in shape, and has a green skin and a white, somewhat fibrous pulp. In Kerala, green breadfruit is cooked as a vegetable in curries, and firm breadfruit is sliced thin and deep fried to make *kadachakka* chips.

The introduction of breadfruit to the New World was connected with a famous historical incident: the mutiny on the *HMS Bounty* in 1789. Captain James Cook believed that breadfruit from the Pacific Islands would be a highly useful foodstuff for the slaves in the West Indies. Captain William Bligh was commissioned to carry breadfruit plants from Tahiti to be grown in the West Indies. After Bligh's infamous failed voyage, the tree was successfully established in Jamaica on the next attempt.

Cooking bananas *(kaya)*: In the tropics, bananas grow in countless varieties that differ greatly in appearance and flavor. With so many varieties, the botanical classification of bananas is complex, but two popular types are *Musa sapientium* and *Musa acuminata.* Although most varieties are consumed ripe, several are also cooked before they are fully ripe. These bananas are smaller in size and have a thinner skin compared to plantains.

Coriander leaves or cilantro *(pachakothamalli)*: Green coriander (also called cilantro and Chinese parsley), the leaf of the zesty coriander plant *Coriandrum sativam*, is probably one of the most commonly used flavorings in the world. The dark green leaves are fan-shaped and delicate and resemble flat-leaf parsley. The strong fragrance of coriander leaves is quite different from that of parsley, but in tropical cuisines of the world, the leaves are used in the same way as parsley. Although the coriander herb and spice come from the same plant, they are totally different from each other in taste and aroma. The leaves smell fresh with a hint of ginger, while coriander seeds have sweet aroma with a whiff of pine. Cilantro is also widely used in Mexican, Southeast Asian, and Chinese cuisines.

Curry leaves *(kariveppila)*: The leaf of the curry-leaf tree, *Murraya koenigii*, is a popular herb used in Indian cuisine for its characteristic flavor and distinctive aroma. These thin, shiny, dark green leaves are highly aromatic when used fresh, due to the presence of volatile oils. Dried leaves do not have the full flavor. Curry leaves are edible; however, they are generally removed from dishes before eating, just like bay leaves. Their antioxidant and anticarcinogenic potential has been reported in scientific studies.

Cucumbers, gourds, melons, pumpkins, and squash: These vegetables, which belong to the large food-plant family *Cucurbitaceae*, grow on climbing or trailing plants and generally have hard skins and soft, fleshy inner marrow and seeds. They contain a large amount of water, sometimes up to ninety percent, and small amounts of starch and sugar. They are largely used as vegetables. Several plants of this species have been cultivated in India since antiquity. The *Rigveda* mentions the use of cucumber.

Ash gourd *(elavan* or *kumbalanga)*: This large gourd with greenish-white skin and white flesh, *Benincasa hispida,* is thought to be of Malaysian origin. It is cultivated all over Asia and can be found in Chinese markets as *donggua* or winter melon. The fairly hard skin is peeled off and the seeds in the middle are scooped out. The remaining soft, white marrow is used in cooking various curries.

Bitter gourd or bitter melon *(paavakka* or *kaippaka)*: This bitter-tasting vegetable *(Momordica charantia)*, rich in minerals and vitamins, is believed to be of Indian origin. The *Rigveda* mentions the use of this vegetable in India. It grows on tropical climber plants and has a ribbed skin with tubercles. It is also popular in Chinese cuisine; the Chinese variety has softer ribs than the Indian variety. Besides its use in curries, this vegetable is also sun dried in summer, for use during the monsoon season. Bitter gourd contains vitamins A, B1, B2, and

C. It also contains minerals such as calcium, phosphorous, iron, copper, and potassium. From the ayurvedic perspective, bitter gourd is excellent for purifying blood tissue, enhancing digestion, and stimulating the liver. A tablespoon of juice from green bitter gourd, consumed every morning, is considered effective in controlling diabetes.

Yellow cucumber *(vellarikka)*: This pendulous and generally elongated vegetable, belonging to the *Cucumis sativus* family, varies in size and skin color depending upon the area where it is grown. It is thought to have originated in the foothills of the Himalayas, and it was cultivated in India more than three hundred years ago. While the European and American cucumber is smaller in size and has dark-green skin, the tropical varieties are much larger in size and the skin color may be yellow to rusty brown. The readily available green cucumbers may be substituted for the tropical variety. Tropical cucumbers are available at Indian grocery stores and some Mexican markets during the summer.

Pumpkin *(mathanga)*: This creamy orange-skinned squash, *Cucurbita pepo*, is round to oblong in shape with pale, golden yellow, or orange flesh. Its skin is fairly hard, but the marrow is soft and contains plenty of water. The center of the pumpkin is hollow, and the seeds are held together by a mass of fibers. Butternut squash is more comparable to the tropical pumpkins than other types commonly found in the United States. Roasted or sun-dried pumpkin seeds are a popular snack in India.

Snake gourd *(padavalanga)*: *Trichosanthes cucumerina*, a tropical climbing gourd, is native to India and grows all over Asia and Australia. This slender greenish-white vegetable grows up to four to five feet in length. Farmers attach small stones with threads to the bottom of the vegetable to prevent it twisting as it gets longer. Snake gourd is used in vegetable curries and is also sliced, parboiled, spiced, and sun dried for use during monsoon season.

It is a good source of carbohydrates, vitamin A, and vitamin C. It also contains magnesium, potassium, copper, and sulfur. Research studies using animals have shown that this gourd has the medicinal property of lowering cholesterol and blood sugar. From the ayurvedic point of view, it is excellent for the balancing of all five fundamental elements. It is easy to digest and assimilate into the body.

Drumstick or moringa *(muringakka)*: *Moringa oleifera* is a small, fast-growing tree characterized by its long, drumstick-shaped pods that contain its seeds. These long and slender pods with ribbed stems grow approximately twelve inches long and hang in clusters of three or four from the drumstick tree.

The outer green skin of the long pod is removed, and the pale green stem is cut into two-to three-inch pieces before cooking. The pods contain a whitish mass, inside of which several three-winged seeds are embedded. The outside of the pod is inedible and discarded, but the mucilaginous inside has a pleasant taste; it is usually eaten like artichoke, by sucking the contents and discarding the tough outer skin. The tender leaves of the drumstick tree are cooked as a leaf vegetable. Moringa pods are available frozen and canned in Indian grocery stores. Both fresh pods and leaves are available in season.

Because the tree produces leaves during times of drought, it is an excellent source of green vegetable. Rich in nutritive value, moringa leaves are believed to contain high amounts of vitamin A, vitamin C, protein, calcium, and potassium. Eating dishes prepared with the leaves is believed to increase a lactating mother's milk production. Both green and dried leaves are used in many ayurvedic medicines. The leaves are also said to help lower blood pressure, and the seeds inside the pods are used for water purification. Moringa seed is a natural coagulant. In ayurvedic medicine, the juice from the leaves is used to stabilize blood pressure, the flowers are used to cure inflammation, the pods are used for joint pain, and the roots are used to treat rheumatism.

Elephant's foot yam or telinga potato *(chena)*: This root vegetable, *Amorphophallus paeonifolius,* can reach a weight of twenty to twenty-five pounds. It is believed to have originated in India and then moved both eastward and westward as far as the New World. It is generally available both frozen and canned. During the summer months, it is available fresh in Indian grocery stores.

Ginger *(inji)*, the underground creeping rhizome of the tropical plant *Zingiber officinale,* is an important and valued spice worldwide. Ginger originated in Southeast Asia and grows abundantly in the tropics of India and in most of Asia. Today, it is a cash crop in Africa, Latin America, and Jamaica. African and Cochin ginger yield the most resin and volatile oil. Fresh ginger is now easily available in Western countries.

Fresh ginger root is pale beige in color with a creamy interior. The skin is thin and easy to peel off. Ginger's fragrance is sharp and aromatic, and its taste is spicy and biting. When shopping for fresh ginger, look for pieces with a plump, smooth, somewhat shiny skin. If it is wrinkled or cracked, then the ginger is drying and past its prime.

Ginger root must be kept in a cool, dry place or it will start sprouting little buds and will eventually get spoiled. It is best to store ginger at room temperature. Depending upon your recipe, fresh ginger may be sliced, diced, minced, grated, shredded, or juiced. Use either a vegetable peeler or a sharp knife to scrape off the skin.

When chopped ginger is fried, the hot and spicy taste gives way to a mild, rich flavor. If fresh ginger is cooked, it will increase in pungency but decrease in freshness. Fresh and dried ginger differs totally in taste. Don't substitute dried ground ginger for fresh. It simply doesn't taste the same. The taste of dry ginger is more aromatic than pungent.

Ginger helps digestion and has been proven to be effective in reducing nausea. Ginger tea, water boiled with grated ginger, and mixed with honey relieves a sore throat. Ginger has been used both as a spice and as a medicine in India and China since ancient times. Dried and powdered ginger is widely used in ayurvedic medicine. It was among the first Oriental spices to reach Europe. Ginger was one of the prized imports of the ancient Roman Empire; as far back as 2,000 years ago, it was imported to Rome in little clay jars. During the Renaissance, ginger had a high reputation in Europe. Ginger is used in the United States as a spice or a condiment, especially in carbonated beverages.

Gooseberry *(nellikka)*: Gooseberries, related to currants, have translucent flesh and pale veins that streak from top to bottom. They are mostly tart, but red-hued ones tend to be somewhat sweet. Two types of gooseberries grow in India: a tiny one with ridges and a slightly larger and smoother variety. The pale gooseberry, *Phyllanthus acidus* (Malay gooseberry), grows in dangling clusters on a small tree. It is light yellow or pale green, vertically ribbed, and acidic or sour. The fruit is less than an inch in diameter. These berries are used in making pickles. The other variety, *Phyllanthus emblica* (Indian gooseberry), grows tangy, pale green, translucent fruits with glossy skin and crunchy, crisp flesh. They are slightly larger in size, one-half inch to one inch in diameter, and are used in making both pickles and chutneys.

The fruit of the Indian gooseberry is acrid, cooling, diuretic, and laxative, and it is one of the richest natural sources of vitamin C. Clinical tests have shown that it is more quickly assimilated into the body than synthetic vitamin C. One hundred grams of gooseberry contains about 700 milligrams of vitamin C, which is thirty times the amount found in oranges. In addition to vitamin C, the berry contains calcium, iron, protein and tannic acids, sugar, phosphorus, and carbohydrates.

Indian gooseberries are used in preparing certain ayurvedic medicines. The fresh fruit is a light laxative and diuretic. The powder of the dried berries is considered an effective remedy for hyperacidity and ulcers. Along with the juice of the bitter gourd, the juice of these berries is used in the treatment of diabetes.

In England, the gooseberry *(Ribes uva-crispa)* is a familiar summer fruit and has thrived in gardens and cuisine since the sixteenth century. Growing conditions in America don't favor this berry, but pockets of it grow in some regions. Gooseberries are sometimes available at farmers' markets and specialty produce shops from mid- to late summer. Frozen and fresh berries (when available) are sold in Indian grocery stores.

Green chilies *(pacha mulagu)*: The green pods of various chilies belonging to the species *Capsicum annuum* and the tabasco-like *Capsicum frutescens* are used all over India for their color, flavor, and heat. Fresh chilies come in several shades of green, from pale lime to dark olive green. The level of heat depends on the amount of capsaicin in the seeds, veins, and skin. Almost all recipes in this collection are tested with moderately hot serrano peppers or hot Thai peppers. Jalapeno peppers may be substituted if serrano peppers are not available.

Jackfruit *(chakka)*: Jackfruit is the largest fruit on Earth. It grows on tropical trees *(Artocarpus heterophyllus)* belonging to the mulberry family. This tree is native to tropical India, and from there it spread to Southeast Asia, East Africa, and beyond. Today, it is widely grown throughout the tropics. The giant fruit is produced along the main trunk of the tree, as it is too heavy for the branches to support. The fruit grows up to two feet in length and weighs up to forty pounds. It has a dark green rind dotted with thorny hexagonal spines. Inside the rind is a layer of thick white pith, beneath which are layers of yellow, fig-like fruit pods that contain seeds. Unripe jackfruit is cooked as a vegetable, and when ripe, it is a very tasty fruit. The seeds are also used in cooking by either boiling them or roasting them. Roasted jackfruit seeds have a taste similar to roasted chestnuts. Both green and ripe jackfruit and seeds are readily available frozen and canned. In season, the fresh fruit is sometimes available in Indian grocery stores.

Lemons and lemon leaves *(cherunaranga* and *narakathinte ela)*: These are fruits and leaves of a variety of sweet lime (*Citrus limon*) indigenous to India. The fruits are less acidic than key limes but produce a mildly sour juice. They are rather small, about one and a half inches in diameter, with thin skin; they are greenish in color, changing to yellow as they ripen. Meyer lemon, the fruit of *Citrus meyeri,* is believed to be a hybrid of *Citrus limon* and *Citrus reticulata.* The lemons available in supermarkets are good substitutes for Indian lemons. Lemon leaves are available only in areas where the trees are grown (in the United States in California and Florida). They are used in preparing a very tasty chutney. Lemon is believed to be an effective cure for coughs and colds.

Mango *(maanga)*: The mango (about thirty-five species of the genus *Mangifera*) originated in the foothills of the Himalayas. Ancient literature dating back to 1700–1500 BC mentions the use of mangoes in India. Considered the king of tropical fruits, it was transplanted to East Asian countries centuries ago. The Portuguese and the Spaniards carried it to tropical Africa, South America, and the Pacific Ocean islands, especially Hawaii. Today, it is widely cultivated around the world and is the best known of tropical fruits. The mango tree often reaches fifty to sixty feet in height, is evergreen, and has plenty of branches full of long and lush green leaves. In India, the mango season lasts from April until the monsoon rains break in the middle of June. Several varieties of mangoes grow in India. Some are ideal for pickling, while the sweeter ones are consumed as fruit. Mangoes in their various stages—from tiny and green to fully ripe—are also used in cooking.

Plantains *(nenthra kaya)* are native to the Malayo-Polynesian islands. More than three thousand years ago, pioneers among the central Malayo-Polynesian-speaking populations are believed to have traveled across the Indian Ocean and brought plantains, water yams, and taro to India. Plantains are a variety of bananas from the plant *Musa*

paradisiaca, which have thicker skins than regular bananas. Even when ripe, they are not very sweet, and they are not eaten raw. Both green and ripe plantains are central ingredients in our cuisine.

Plantain stems *(unnithandu)*: Both cooking bananas and plantains produce only one crop. After the fruits are harvested, the plants are usually cut and removed in order to plant the next crop. Removing the green outer skin of the trunk reveals the edible white, slender stem. It is about four to five inches in diameter and rather stringy. The strings are removed by twirling them around with a knife. The plantain stems are then cut into small pieces and used in cooking.

Tamarind *(puli)* is the pod-like fruit of a shade tree *(Tamarindus indica)* that originated in tropical Africa. It grows throughout tropical Africa and Asia. Ancient Arabic traders found this tree in India and gave it the name *tamr hindi*, "dry dates of India."

Tamarind grows on trees and is shaped like large bean pods. As it matures, the outer skin changes from green to sandy brown and becomes hard. Inside the pod is the sticky, dark brown pulp covering black seeds. There are a few thick strands that run along the length and hold the pulp in place. Fresh tamarind pulp is brownish black in color and has a sour taste with a hint of sweetness. The dried pulp is available in two different forms, either as small blocks of pulp or as a jelly-like concentrate. Both are equally good, though the concentrate is easier to use. In the West, tamarind is used in the preparation of commercially prepared sauces.

The medicinal uses of the tamarind are many. Alone or in combination with lime juice, honey, milk, dates, spices, or camphor, the pulp is considered effective as a digestive and as a remedy for bile disorders. Tamarind leaves and flowers, dried or boiled, are used as poultices for swollen joints, sprains, and boils. In the old days in Kerala, new mothers bathed in water that had been boiled with tamarind leaves for hours and then cooled.

Taro root *(chembu)*: *Colocasia esculenta* is a very starchy spherical underground root vegetable that resembles small, dark, hairy potatoes. It is believed to have originated in India and Southeast Asia. A root vegetable well suited to primitive agriculture, it has been cultivated in these regions since ancient times. It is cut into cubes and used in preparing various curries. In Hawaii, this starchy vegetable is cooked and mashed to make poi. It is available in Indian, Latin American, Mexican, and Southeast Asian markets.

Yams *(cherukizangu, kaachil,* and *koorka)*: Yam is the common name for the several species of edible tubers of the genus *Dioscorea*. They vary widely in shape, size, color, taste, and appearance. Yams are botanically distinct from the sweet potato that is often called "yam" in the United States. There are several different kinds of yams in India, including a small variety called *cherukizangu* and the large variety called *kaachil*. The skin of the yam is usually hairy, and the color of the flesh ranges from white to pink. Another variety of tuber, *koorka*, commonly known as coleus tuber or Malabar catmint, thrives in tropical and subtropical regions. It is rather small in size: a little more than inch long and less than an inch wide. The leaves of this plant resemble mint leaves and have an aroma loved by cats.

All edible yams are cooked before consumption to destroy the bitter toxin they contain in their raw state. When cooked, they are starchy and bland and sometimes slightly sweet. Because of their long shelf life, they are a staple during the monsoon season. Pieces of large yams can be cut off for cooking when needed; the tuber's juices naturally seal any exposed surface and keep it fresh. These root vegetables are available in Latin American, Mexican, African, and Indian grocery stores.

Cooking Methods

Simple cooking methods—steaming, boiling, simmering, seasoning, panfrying at low heat, dry roasting, and deep-frying—are used in our cuisine. The two methods that are slightly different from Western ways of cooking are seasoning and the special way of salting while deep-frying. They are not complicated and are described in detail.

Steaming: Cooking by moist heat allows food to retain its natural flavor and nutrients, and this method requires very little oil, if any. Steamed foods retain moisture and are digested easily. A regular pot with a steamer insert and a tight lid is all that is required for steaming. Fill the pot or saucepan with water just to the level of the steamer insert, but not touching it. Bring the water to a boil. Spread the items to be steamed on the insert, and cover them with a tight-fitting lid. This method is used in preparing breakfast dishes such as *idlis* and *kozhukkatta* and sweets such as *ela ada* and *kumbilappam*. *Idlis* are traditionally steamed in vessels called *idli pathram*. (Please see the picture and description of the vessel in the section on utensils.) *Puttu* is traditionally made in a utensil called a *puttu kudam*. Both *puttu* and *kozhukkatta* may be steamed in a regular pot with a steamer insert. As *ela ada* and *kumbilappam* are first wrapped in banana leaves, the steaming process is exactly the same as for tamales.

Boiling and simmering: Boiling is the standard method for preparing most curries. Vegetables cut into cubes or strips are cooked in just enough water to cover them. Water is the preferred cooking medium in our cuisine; stock is never used. Both vegetables and spices add flavor to the dish. After the cooked vegetables become fork-tender, spice blends and seasonings are stirred in and simmered. For curries that call for cooking in coconut milk, simmering is the preferred method; coconut milk separates when cooked over high heat.

Seasoning or tempering *(kaduku varakkal)*: Seasoning food with spices pan-fried in oil is a technique fundamental to many dishes. Most curries are seasoned with spices and herbs fried in a few spoons of oil. Heat the oil in a small skillet over medium heat, and add mustard seeds. When the mustard seeds start sputtering, add halved dry chili peppers and curry leaves and remove the skillet from the stove. Pour the contents into the cooked curry. For certain curries, asafetida and *urad* and *chana* dal or coconut flakes are also fried with the mustard seeds and chili peppers. In some curries, instead of the seasoned oil, fresh curry leaves and a couple of tablespoons of coconut oil are stirred in.

Panfrying at low heat: *Mezukkupurattis* and *thorans*—mildly spiced vegetable dishes with no sauce—are an important part of everyday meals. They are prepared by cooking vegetables with very little water, or in their own natural juices. The subtle seasoning for these dishes is prepared in a frying pan, and the cooked vegetables are added to the pan. Unlike in stir-frying (in which fresh vegetables are quickly fried to a crispy, crunchy texture), in panfrying at low heat, cooked vegetables are combined with spices and a very small amount of oil and cooked over low heat for a longer time. This method allows the vegetables to absorb the flavors of the spices.

Dry Roasting: When making curry pastes or powders, blends of spices are often dry roasted over medium heat in a heavy skillet. Vegetables such as okra, which turns slimy when boiled in water, are pan roasted with a touch of oil over medium heat for a few minutes before boiling them for further cooking.

Deep-frying gives food a delicious crunchiness. It is important to use oils that can be heated to high temperatures. The oil must be well heated before adding the foods for frying; otherwise, the oil will seep into the food and make it soggy. Hot oil sears the surface to a firm crispiness. Heat the oil in a wok or another heavy saucepan with some depth. When the oil is hot (approximately

360° to 365°F), slide in the vegetables or dough and deep-fry them until they are golden and crisp.

Salting while deep-frying: While frying plantain, jackfruit, and breadfruit chips, we use a unique method of salting. Chips are salted at the last stage of frying by adding concentrated salt water to the oil. Add one tablespoon of salt to one-half cup of water and stir well; if there is no salt sediment at the bottom, add more salt and stir until some salt residue is left at the bottom and the water is saturated with salt. Fry the thinly sliced pieces until they are just about golden and crisp. Add a teaspoon of the concentrated salt water to the oil carefully, and immediately cover with a splatter screen. The water in the hot oil will really splatter and make a lot of noise. In a minute or so, when the water has stopped sputtering, remove the cover. By now all the water should have evaporated and the crispy chips should be golden brown and evenly salted. Remove the fried pieces from the hot oil with a slotted spoon, and drain them. A good way to drain deep-fried food is to use a cake cooling rack placed over a cookie tray; excess oil will drip through the cooling rack and fall on the cookie tray. (Paper towels will absorb too much oil, and if the food stays on the paper, it tends to get soggy.) Store the chips in airtight containers. When the chips are salted this way, there will be no salt residue on top of the chips (compared to sprinkling salt over fried chips).

Utensils

As all dishes in our cuisine are cooked on the stove top, a couple of heavy skillets; a chef's pan or other deep-frying pan, such as a wok; a Dutch oven; a variety of regular pots, such as two-, three-, and four-quart vessels; a steamer insert that fits inside a vessel; perhaps a pressure cooker (in which to cook beans and dal quickly); and a heavy griddle are sufficient for most cooking. As for appliances, a coffee grinder for powdering dry spices; a blender to grind wet spice blends, rice, and dal; and a food processor to prepare thick batters and dough would be more than enough.

Following is a description of six utensils required to make certain recipes in a traditional South Indian kitchen. For all of them except for the snack press, there are alternatives. A snack press is used in making several sweets and snacks.

Appakkara: This is a bronze pan, about eight inches in diameter, with three or more large cavities in it. To make *appams,* the pan is heated over the stove and a spoonful of ghee is poured into each cavity. The *appam* batter, made with rice flour and jaggery, is poured on top of the ghee and cooked over medium heat. When the bottom part is cooked, the *appams* are turned over and the other sides are cooked. An ideal substitute for an *appakkara* is the cast-iron, nonstick utensil used for making the Danish pancake balls known as *aebleskiver.* It is often referred to as a "munk pan" or a Danish cake pan.

Dosa kallu: This is a heavy, flat cast-iron griddle that has been seasoned with use. It is strictly used for making *dosas* and *adas.* The type of cast-iron griddle available in the United States is an ideal substitute. When it is brand new, smear it with a couple of tablespoons of cooking oil and three tablespoons of salt. Set it aside for several hours, and then wipe it clean with a paper towel. If the first *dosa* starts to stick, scrape it off, smear a little oil on the griddle, and try again. A nonstick spray also may be used. After you finish making *dosas,* wipe the griddle clean. If you want to wash it, be sure to dry it thoroughly and smear it with a few drops of oil before storing it. A well-seasoned griddle lasts a lifetime. Any flat griddle, either cast iron or nonstick, may be used to make *dosas.* Use a cast-iron griddle if you prefer crispy *dosas.*

Idli pathram: This is the traditional steamer for making *idlis.* It is a large vessel with a tight lid and a stack of *idli* trays. The trays have three to six round cavities, each approximately two to three inches in diameter. The traditional *idli* plates have small holes. A piece of wet cotton cloth is spread over the cavity and the batter is poured into it. The modern stainless-steel plates have cavities without holes. They fit perfectly inside a four- or six-quart pot. These *idli* plate stacks are available at most Indian grocery stores. An egg poacher is an alternative.

Murukku naazi or snack press: This gadget can be filled with any dough and used to make several different shapes. Just like a cookie press, it has several flat disks with differently shaped holes. For example, disks with three round holes or disks with three star-shaped holes are used for making *murukkus*. A disk with several thin holes is for *noolpittu* and *sev* noodles. There is one with two tiny rectangular holes for making ribbon *pokavada*. It is an inexpensive gadget, and one can be purchased at an Indian grocery store for under ten dollars.

Puttu kudam: This is a pot with a covered tubular attachment on top. A flat disk with holes fits onto the bottom of the tube. It also has a cover with three holes that allow steam to escape. To make *puttu,* the disk is inserted in the tube and the tube is filled with a rice flour and grated coconut mixture. Fill the pot with water almost halfway, and fit the tube on top. Place the pot on the stove, and cook over medium heat.

When the *puttu* is cooked, steam will start coming through the holes in the top of the tube. This vessel is made with bell metal, aluminum, or stainless steel. If you are not particular about the cylindrical shape, a regular pot with a steamer insert may be used. In the old days, a bamboo log (one to one and a half feet long) was used as the steaming tube. *Puttu* cooked this way absorbed a pleasant earthy aroma from the bamboo.

Vellayappam chatti: In order to get the proper shape—a thick, spongy center and lacy, crisp edges—*vellayappam* has to be made in *vellayappam chatti* or small, wok-like pans called *Cheena chatti* with deep, more pointed centers. These pans are inexpensive and available in Indian stores. Lacking these pans, however, an eight-inch nonstick skillet is the perfect substitute. The shape may not be perfect, but the taste certainly will be.

Chapter Three
Sacred Food: Rice and Rituals

Enraptured by our last meal of rice and curries, and eagerly anticipating the next, even as we hungrily devour the rice before us, people in Kerala never get tired of eating rice. The relationship we have with rice is deep-rooted and imbued with meaning and importance; it is magical and mystical. Rice is not just the integral part of our food; it is also part of our religious rituals and celebrations as well as our social ceremonies. Centuries-old traditions dictate the manner of rice cultivation, harvesting, and consumption. As the rice cycle moves from plowing to seedlings to planting and fertilizing, to scarecrows in lush green fields as the grains ripen, and then to golden stacks of harvested rice drying in the sun, so does village life.

The cultivation of rice itself is a slow, meditative process, passed down through generations. When the soaking monsoon rains flood the baked, cracked rice terraces, they are ploughed by oxen and buffalo. When the land is ready, farmers sow the grain and wait for a few days to replant the tender new shoots. Rice is traditionally farmed by hand; under cloudy or clear skies, men and women stoop in the deep mud and plant the rice, stalk by stalk. Soon the countryside becomes dotted with bright green bristles. The green gold clings to mountainsides, cascades down valleys, meanders across flat plains, and grows even below sea level on temporarily reclaimed lands. (The seasoned farmers along the upper reaches of Kerala backwaters have developed ingenious methods to reclaim land from the lagoons and deltas in order to grow rice below sea level.) Weeks later, the land is draped in vivid emerald, speckled with pools of reflective water. Slowly, the tall sheaves ripen, hanging in golden bunches.

When the leaves of the rice stalks start to turn yellow, the rice paddies are drained and dried in preparation for the harvest. Stalks are cut with iron sickles and tied in bundles to dry in farmyards and on roadsides. Whole villages become large drying areas. There is the constant sound of pounding and threshing as the grains are separated from the dried stacks. The languid air becomes heavy with dust. After threshing, the rice is ready for milling. The dried rice grains are then packed into burlap bags and taken to storage. The rice grains are husked, either mechanically or manually. They are then sifted to separate the grains from the bran.

The antiquity and continuity of rice as a staple food in India are remarkable. It is believed that South India began cultivating rice during the first half of the second millennium BC. Countless varieties of rice are described in ancient literature, reflecting the sustained development of rice varieties in India. The *Susrutha Samhita,* a medical treatise written during the golden age of Indian medicine (circa 800 BC to 1000 AD), describes several varieties of rice and their effects on human body. Another ancient Sanskrit text, the *Kashyapa Samhita* (written around 200 BC), gives detailed accounts of every aspect of ancient rice cultivation. The significance of rice continues to survive, and its influence can be traced throughout our culture.

"If you do not cultivate rice in your land, you may have to beg for your meal," begins an old collection of poems, *Krishigeetha* ("farming songs"), in Malayalam. The poems document the process of the selection of farmland and of planting, fertilizing, and harvesting rice. It continues with a description of our rich, fertile farmlands, the ideal variety of rice seeds for each kind of soil, what types of animals should be used to plough the fields, and how often the fields should be watered and fertilized. Another section narrates the qualities of a good farmer ("honest, hardworking, and caring") and tells how he should store the rice harvest in a separate rice granary and generously reward his farmhands for their help.

Rice doubled as currency in olden days; farm workers were paid their wages in measures of rice. Tenants leasing land for cultivation made their lease payments, called *paattam,* to landlords in measures of rice. Land ownership was not measured in acres of land owned but in measures of rice the landowner received as lease payments.

Every part of the rice plant is used in some form or other. Once the rice is harvested, what remains of the plant is straw. It is dried in the sun and stored in the middle of the field in the form of a pyramid. Straw is used as fodder for cattle. It is also used as roofing material for huts. It is widely used as packaging material—nature's answer to plastic bubble wrap! During the summer, when mangoes are harvested, they are spread on a thick layer of rice straw for ripening. The straw bed cradles and insulates the mangoes while letting warm air circulate around the fruit.

After husking, the rice is sifted to remove bran. The dried bran *(thavidu)* is powdered fine and used as fodder for cattle. It is also burned till it turns black, and villagers use this coarse powder *(umikkari),* mixed with salt, to cleanse their teeth. A wet index finger dipped in the powder becomes a makeshift toothbrush.

We celebrate and honor this grain of life from planting to harvesting to consuming. The ceremonial and religious aspects of rice planting and harvesting are not that important to modern-day city dwellers, but rice as food continues to maintain its impressive significance in our lives.

Rice Festivals

Wherever rice grows in Kerala, planting and harvesting cycles are celebrated with spectacle and ritual, events as old as the land itself. With monsoon season comes a renewal of the life cycle of farming, and cultivation begins with the onset of rain. Once the seedlings are planted, more water is needed to ensure a good harvest. The arrival of the monsoon is welcomed with many rituals and ceremonies.

Ancient agrarian practices of Kerala depended solely on the movement of the sun. Farmland is considered sacred, and prayers are offered before starting cultivation. Based on astrology, Vishu festival represents the passing of the sun into Aries at the vernal equinox, a solar event that marks the beginning of a new astrological year. According to Indian astrology, this solar event is believed to be the ideal time for commencing rice cultivation.

On Vishu morning, farmers observe a ritual called *chaal* (furrow), the auspicious commencement of rice farming. They decorate the eastern corner of the rice field with yellow *kanikonna* flowers and rice-flour designs. They pin up leaves in the shape of bowls, fill them with *navadhaanyam* (nine different kinds of grains), and place them near the lamps. Early that morning, farmers bathe their oxen and wash and clean their plows. They decorate both the animals and the ploughs with rice-flour batter and fresh flowers and take them to the rice field. They light oil lamps and offer bananas, popped rice, and a sweet dish made with rice and coconut, to propitiate the goddess of earth. They pray for her blessings for a good crop, the proper working of their plows, and the good health of their farm animals. They plough a few yards and sow a few grains. The first ten days of the New Year are considered ideal for sowing. In olden days, landlords consulted the astrologer to pick an auspicious day for sowing.

Harvest season is the time for the biggest celebrations. In times past, Nira and Puthiri were a big part of harvest celebrations in agricultural families. Nira celebrated the bringing of the first stalks from the new harvest to the house. Puthiri celebrated the cooking and serving of new rice. These festivals were celebrated mostly by farming families and landlords. With the enactment of the land reform act of Kerala in the 1960s, land holdings reverted to cultivating tenants, and now Nira and Puthiri are mostly observed at Hindu temples. A few days later, in late August or early September (depending on when the holiday is, according to lunar calendar), we celebrate the four-day-long Thiruvonam (or Onam for short) festival. Onam continues to be celebrated all over Kerala. In November, we used to celebrate Kathir, the second rice crop, with processions of decorated mock palanquins, tribal bands, and folk dancers.

Nira, the agricultural festival that celebrated bringing home the harvest of the first rice stalks, is one of my fond childhood memories. In our extended family, it was celebrated at our ancestral home, a large *naalukettu*, a sprawling structure with over thirty rooms. The whole extended family gathered around the courtyard for the festivities.

The house was cleaned and the floor of the *nadumittam* (inner courtyard) was decorated with lighted bronze oil lamps and *kolam*, an intricate design drawn with rice flour. Much more than just an aesthetic art, it symbolized happiness and prosperity. As the farmhands brought in the stacks of rice, we would chant:

> *Nira nirayoodu nira nira nira,*
> *Poli poliyodu poli poli poli,*
> *Ellum nira vallam nira vallotti nira.*

This loosely translates as: "Fill the home with rice, and fill the *vallam* and *vallotti* (rattan seed-storage containers) with rice." The rice stacks were placed on a large banana leaf spread in the middle of the courtyard. Following the festive rituals, stacks of paddy were distributed to everyone. After hanging a few stacks on the doors of the ancestral home, we took the remaining stacks to our individual homes and hung them on doors and placed them in our *ari mancha,* the huge wooden box where rice is stored.

Puthiri (short for *puthiya ari,* "new rice") celebrated the cooking and eating of new rice. In the early morning, a couple of farm workers brought new rattan baskets filled with the first batch of parboiled rice and freshly prepared *avil* (pounded rice). These baskets were placed in front of a *nilavilakku,* a traditional oil lamp.

In our home, my mother prepared *puthiri* in a large silver bowl. We would each cup the palm of our right hand, place a piece of fresh banana leaf on it, and receive a small serving of *puthiri* from our uncle. In the kitchen, my mother continuously stirred the *paalpaayasam* (rice pudding), and the cooks hurried around her, preparing traditional vegetable dishes with fresh vegetables from our farm. When all the cooking was done, pots of food were moved to the center of the kitchen floor and arranged in a circle. With an oil lamp in hand, Mother walked three times around the assembled food. My uncle walked behind her, sprinkling a few grains of *avil* on all of the dishes.

The Puthiri feast was served in a unique way. Festival food is always served on banana leaves, spread horizontally in front of each person. But on this occasion, the leaves were arranged vertically, and the first dish served was *paayasam* (rice pudding). A meal starting with dessert! Children loved this change in order. After we relished the small serving of *paayasam* along with ghee and honey, the leaves were turned horizontally—very carefully, of course—and the rest of the meal was served. *Enn* curry, a simple curry made of eight different vegetables, is a typical special dish that was prepared only for this festival.

Thiruvonam continues to be celebrated all over Kerala (and wherever Malayalis live) with colorful flowers, sumptuous feasts, graceful folk dances, and gifts of new clothes. Bedecked elephants sway to the tune of the *panchavaadyam* band at the famous temple at Trikkakkara. Spectacular boat races take place along our fabulously long coastline and along crisscrossing rivers and inland waterways.

Children dressed in festive clothes start collecting flowers to decorate the courtyard with *pookkalam,* an intricate flower design. In the middle of the flower design, mothers place pyramidal images of Trikkakarayappan (Vamana), also fondly called Onathappan, made of clay or wood, and decorated with fresh flowers. They light bronze oil lamps and fragrant incense sticks, and they offer ripe plantains and *ela ada,* steamed sweet coconut in flat rice cakes, to the lord.

The big event at Onam is the *sadya* (feast), which is served around noon. When all the dishes are ready, a huge banana leaf is spread in front of Onathappan, and the feast is served. After this offering of food, everyone enjoys a sumptuous feast served on fresh, green banana leaves. After the meal, girls and women dance *kaikottikali*, a hand-clapping folk dance, around Onathappan.

At Onam, the traditional gift is *onapudava*, a thin cotton fabric laced with colorful, sometimes golden, borders. In my childhood, farmer tenants leasing our land for cultivation used to bring bunches of green and ripe plantains and other vegetables to the house as *onakazhcha* (Onam gifts). After receiving these gifts, my uncle presented them with *onapudava*. Banana bunches and large pumpkins were hung from coir hangings around the *nadumittam* (inner courtyard).

The religious anecdote about Onam goes back to the fifth incarnation of Vishnu as Vamana, a dwarf Brahman. According to Hindu mythology, Lord Vishnu took this incarnation to expel the demon King Mahabali from his throne. The story goes that during the reign of King Mahabali, Kerala was a land of peace and prosperity. King Mahabali was very proud of performing the *Aswamedha Yaga* (sacrifice of a horse) to gain strength and power. Lord Vishnu entered the *yagasala* (place of sacrifice) disguised as a dwarf Brahman. Not knowing that the visitor was a god, in an arrogant tone, the king asked him, "What is your preferred gift, young man?"

Vamana replied politely, "All I want is three steps of land that I can measure with my foot."

Mahabali laughed and told Vamana, "Measure the land anywhere you want, with your little feet."

Assuming the cosmic form, with two steps, the lord measured the earth and the sky. Then he asked the king, "Where should I put my foot for the third step?" Mahabali, realizing the presence of the almighty, removed his crown and asked Vamana to place his third step on his head. In recognition of Mahabali's humility, Vishnu granted him his wish to return to Earth, once a year, to visit his people. At Onam, the people of Kerala try to recapture the glory of King Mahabali's days.

Onam of a bygone era: During the early centuries, Onam was popular festival celebrating the birthday of Lord Vamana. It was celebrated all over southern India before becoming confined to Kerala around the tenth century AD. At the portals of the famous Ranganatha temple at Srirangam, in Tamil Nadu, Vamana is worshipped as Sri Vamanaperumaal. In times past, Vamana Jayanthi celebrations were held on a large scale at this temple. Another famous temple celebrating Vamana Jayanthi is the famous Vishnu temple of Sri Venkateswara at Tirupathi, in Andhra Pradesh. The ancient Tamil text *Pattuppattu*, from the Sangam age, includes a poem called *Maduraikanchi* by Mangudy Marudanar, one of the noted poets of the period. This poem describes the Onam celebrations at the Pandyan capital of Madurai, in Tamil Nadu. For reasons unknown, by the tenth century AD, Onam became confined to Kerala, and the celebrations became focused on Mahabali's visit and the bounty of the rice harvest.

During the reign of the maharajas of Kochi, the ten-day celebration at Thrippunithura (the town where Kochi's royal palaces were situated) began with Athachamayam. According to the story, this procession was symbolic of the maharaja's trip to a nearby Trikkakkara Vamana temple to celebrate the Onam festival. The maharaja commanded the procession while sitting in a decorated *pallakku* or palanquin, a covered seat for one person carried by poles on men's shoulders. He was accompanied by the Nayar brigade (militia brigade), police, the cavalry, and three decorated elephants. After the parade, the maharaja held a meeting at Kalikotta Palace, a palace built during the Dutch period. At this time, the officers paid their respects to the maharaja and received presents of *puthans* (coins wrapped in fresh banana leaves). Afterward, they were treated to a sumptuous Onam *sadya*. The general public also was offered food at the *sarvani* (public feast), along with some oil and one *puthan* as a gift. After India became independent and opted for a democratic rule, the princely states ceased to exist, and Athachamayam also faded away. Today a state government-sponsored Athachamayam procession takes place at Thrippunithura.

An interesting anecdote is that instead of wearing his crown on his head, the maharaja would place it on his lap during the Athachamayam procession. This custom originated because of a feud with the Samoothiri, the king of neighboring Malabar. During the late 1600s, the king of Malabar went to war against Kochi and succeeded in annexing certain territories, including the village of Perumpadappu, which housed the Chitrakutam palace, where the maharajas of Kochi were crowned. During the early 1700s, Prince Rama Varma, with the help of the Dutch, defeated Samoothiri and recovered most of the possessions of his ancestors. However, Samoothiri held onto the village of Perumpadappu tenaciously, knowing full well that it was the place of coronation for the maharajas of Kochi. Prince Rama Varma took a solemn oath on his accession to the throne that he would not be crowned anywhere but at Chitrakutam, and that he will never wear the crown on his head until he went through the coronation ceremony. Unfortunately, Kochi never regained possession of Perumpadappu, and the king's successors, respecting his oath, never went through a coronation ceremony at Chitrakutam, nor did they ever wear the crown at Athachamayam.

Onam is a festival that has evolved and changed over time. From its start as a purely Hindu religious festival, today it is a celebration of good will and good food by Kerala's Hindus, Christians, and Muslims. Gone are the days when the entire household assembled in the kitchen to prepare Onam *sadya*. Life in Kerala is in the fast lane today. Hotels and resorts across the state work overtime to give tourists a taste of our most important festival. Other than tourists, the hotels also cater to modern-day Malayalis who might be too busy to cook a traditional feast at home. The one good thing is that today, Thiruvonam is celebrated as a social event by all the people of Kerala.

Kathir ("new buds") was an agricultural festival celebrated in the northern rice-growing regions of Kochi. It was a big event in my hometown, Chittur, and in its neighboring villages. While Thiruvonam celebrates the first rice harvest of the year, Kathir celebrated the emerald rice stalks of the second rice harvest. (Since the passage of the land reform act of Kerala, this festival is no longer celebrated.) The farmhands assembled several *koodu* (grains covered in straw and encased in palm leaves in the shape of a ball) and mock palanquins made with the stems of banana plants and decorated them with colorful flowers and *kuruthola* (palm leaves). During the evening hours, accompanied by tribal bands and folk dancers, several small processions came to the homes of landlords. It was a competition between the various groups to assemble the best-looking palanquin, tribal band, and folk dancers. When they reached the landlord's house, the palanquin was brought to the front of the house, and the folk dancers and the tribal bands put together a terrific and boisterous show at the front courtyard. People crowded along the streets to see the continuing saga of processions going to various homes. The palanquins were left at the landlord's house, and the *koodu* were taken to the local temple. The landlords rewarded the farmhands amply for their efforts, and they returned home drumming and dancing through the streets.

Rice in Religious and Social Rituals

Rice in temple rituals: Besides being the traditional staple grain in our culture, rice has a broader significance. It has an important place in our religious and social ceremonies. Uncooked rice, colored yellow with turmeric, is offered during prayers at our temples. Ancient Sanskrit scriptures say: *"Annam Brahm?"* ("Rice is God"). The offering of both raw rice and rice-based dishes at our temples is an indispensable part of Hindu religious rituals.

The enshrined deities of the Hindu temples are faithfully fed twice a day with formal offerings of food, even today. Famous temples of Kerala have some of the very best traditional cooks, who prepare food offerings. They do not follow any written recipes, nor are they trained at any culinary schools. They perfect their art through practice, under the watchful eyes of senior priests. But the proof of their culinary repertoire is in the most delicious *prasadam* (food that has been offered to God) that devotees receive from the temples.

The food offerings at temples are always the most excellent food. The priests and their helpers prepare offerings every day in the temple kitchen. Hand-pounded rice *(unakkalari)*, the aristocrat of rice varieties, is used for preparing temple offerings. It has a delicate flavor and a consistency that has just the right cling, and it cooks to a perfect creamy texture. A rice offering may be cooked rice, or rice cooked in milk and sugar, or rice cooked with brown sugar and ghee, or griddle cakes made of rice flour and brown sugar. These offerings may express sincere devotion; sometimes they plead for favors or convey thanks for prayers answered and wishes fulfilled. They are presented with great ceremony. The grander the festival, the more numerous the offerings. Once the ceremony is over, the offerings are removed from the inner shrine, and the priests and devotees share the food as blessings.

In ancient times, many temples had huge land holdings, which were given to them by kings and devotees; the proceeds from the land were used for the upkeep of the temples. Even today, several days before the major temple festivals, the image of the temple deity is carried around on top of a decorated elephant to the homes in the village. Devotees present the deity with *paras* (old wooden measuring barrels that contain approximately twenty pounds of rice) of unhulled rice and popped rice as offerings.

Both the sacrifice and denial of this precious grain is perceived as an act of worship. Traditionally, during certain days of religious observances in Hindu homes, no rice is cooked. While some of these observances require total fasting, others are partial fasting days, when other varieties of grains such as wheat, *nivara* (wild rice), and *ragi* (finger millet) are served. When no rice is served, it is considered fasting.

Rice in social rituals: The coronation of the maharaja of Kochi was known as *ariyittuvaazcha*, because priests sprinkled rice grains on his head. A traditional matrilineal wedding takes place in front of a *para* filled with unhulled rice and decorated with a fresh flower stack from a coconut palm. The bride's mother ceremoniously fills the wooden barrel with the rice before the wedding ceremony. At weddings, elders bless young couples by sprinkling rice on their heads. In Malayalam, people call their meals *uoonu,* a word that also means eating cooked rice. Six months after their birth, babies are fed rice for the first time in a ceremony called *Chooroonu*. On birthdays, one's mother serves extra rice on a banana leaf, signifying prosperity. Later the leftover rice is fed to fish in the pond.

Rice also plays an important part in the annual memorial observances of departed family members. As rice was their staple food, ancestors are offered the same on their death anniversaries. Early-morning religious rites include the offering of cooked rice sprinkled with black sesame seeds for the peace of the departed souls. Later, this rice is fed to crows. Crows are considered messengers of the dead; if plenty of crows come by to eat, it is believed that departed souls are pleased with the memorial ceremony.

Feeding rice or rice soup to the poor is considered the ultimate good deed. During my childhood, Mondays were *dharmam* (charity) days. Beggars lined up in front of the house in the morning, and we gave each one a few handfuls of rice. In the old days, our family had a *sathram* (a place where poor people are fed), where a man was employed to cook and serve *kanji* (rice soup) to the poor every day of the year. Revenues from some of the joint family's land holdings were assigned for the upkeep of the *sathram*.

Rice, the principal staple: In Kerala, this carbohydrate-rich staple is so important to our life that it even has its own place in our language. It is not just a steaming serving of white rice around which meals are planned, but it is *nellu* when it is unhusked, *ari* after it is husked, *choru* when it is cooked plain, *uoonu* when it is consumed, *palahaaram* when it is made into savory breakfast dishes, and *paayasam* when it is cooked in milk or coconut milk along with sugar or jaggery. Rice is also the main ingredient in a variety of dishes from appetizer to main course, to snacks and desserts; the final product depends on how the rice is processed and what type of rice is used. Naturally, people tend to consider the rice they are used to eating as the most delicious variety; for us, it is the non-aromatic parboiled rice. Plain boiled rice is served with various vegetable dishes at both lunch and supper. Fragrant varieties like basmati or jasmine do not bring out the flavors of the spices and coconut used in our cuisine. Different varieties of rice are used for preparing various breakfast dishes, snacks, and desserts.

The attitude toward rice varies from one country to another. In South India, as in other rice-eating parts of the world, rice is revered as divine, and it is still cooked in the plainest possible way, and it is typically eaten at least two or three times a day. The variety of dishes that accompany rice may be elaborate and exquisite, but rice by itself is too precious to be treated as an ingredient. Since the preferred method of cooking rice is simple boiling, we do not have a rich variety of rice dishes. However, no grain of precious rice is allowed to go to waste. Before the days of refrigeration, leftover rice was kept overnight in an earthenware pot filled with cold water. Cold rice and fresh yogurt made the next day's breakfast.

> There is an old anecdote about rice and the royal family. The story goes that Maharaja Sakthan Thampuran, the most powerful king of this dynasty and a widower, remarried when he was in his fifties. His young bride, a Nayar lady named Chimmukkutty Amma (my father's great-grandaunt), was almost three decades younger than him. She was overwhelmed by her sudden ascendance to being the *Valiya Neythiyaramma* (consort of the king). He was anxious to fulfill every whim of his young bride, but he also enjoyed playing practical jokes on her. When she asked for a new house in her hometown, the king granted her wish immediately. When the construction of the house was completed, she wanted a sumptuous *sadya* for her housewarming ceremony. The king asked her to make a list of all of the dishes she wished to be prepared for the *sadya*. She gave an elaborate list, but rice was taken for granted and not mentioned. When it was time for the *sadya,* she was shocked to realize that there was no cooked rice. When she complained to her husband, he replied, "But rice was not in your list." Although the anecdote ends here, I am sure no one would have allowed all those dishes to go to waste, and someone would have come up with some cooked rice.

Choru: Plain Boiled Rice

Parboiled rice is the preferred variety, because its grains do not stick together when cooked. Nevertheless, when blended with various curries, the grains will easily hold together. Traditionally, rice is cooked with excess water and then drained. This method allows the cooked grains to remain fluffy and separate. The Uncle Ben's and Golden Temple brands of converted rice, though larger in grain size, are ideal substitutes for Indian parboiled rice. Converted rice takes longer to cook. For convenience, regular long-grain or medium-grain rice may be cooked.

2 cups parboiled rice
12 cups water

In a heavy, large saucepan, bring twelve cups of water to a boil. Wash and clean the rice in several changes of water. Add the rice to the boiling water, and cook it uncovered over medium heat for approximately forty-five minutes, until the rice is tender to the touch. To test if the rice is cooked, take out some grains with a spoon and mash them with your fingers. If they are soft to the touch and mash easily, the rice is ready. Place a colander in the sink and drain the rice. Let it sit there for a few minutes to drain completely. Serve it hot with various curries and other accompaniments.

Makes approximately 6 cups of cooked rice.

Kanji: Rice Soup

Kanji is simple, basic rice soup. It is often served for breakfast in our villages. Because *kanji* requires less rice to feed the same number of people, it is considered a poor man's meal. In olden days, it was the preferred breakfast dish among farming and seafaring families. It is served warm with salt and cooked red beans. The soup spoons for eating this rice soup were made of folded jackfruit tree leaves pinned with the stems of coconut palm leaves.

Kanji is not just a dish served as part of a meal; it is also a base for therapeutic treatment. *Kashyapa Samhita*, the ancient Sanskrit text (circa the second century BC) describes rice soup made with parched rice, long pepper, ginger, and pomegranates. *Kanjika,* sour rice gruel, was popular among the ancient seafaring Dravidians of ancient South India. *Kanji,* a dish with ancient origins, is popular all over Asia and remains the comfort food of millions, with flavor differences from one country to another.

Kanji is my favorite comfort food. We enjoy it for supper on cold and snowy winter evenings. As the dollop of ghee melts and spreads over the hot *kanji* and the steam from it clouds my eyeglasses, I am transported, for an instant, to my tropical homeland.

The best *kanji* is made with *podiari,* or broken rice. When rice is hulled manually, a bit of the hull remains on the grain, giving it a reddish tinge. Manual hulling also results in several broken rice grains. These are separated from the whole grains by sifting the grains with a flat rattan tray called a *muram.* Since *podiari* is not always readily available, parboiled rice may be substituted.

1 cup parboiled rice
6 cups water

Wash and rinse the rice. In a saucepan, bring the water to a boil and add the cleaned rice. Lower the heat to medium, and cook the rice until it is very soft (approximately one hour). Cover the pot and set it aside for half an hour before serving. During this time, the rice will continue to soften and absorb more water. If the pot is not covered, a thin film will form on the top. Just before serving, stir the *kanji* gently. If it is too thick for your taste, add a little boiling water and stir.

Makes 6 cups.

> My grandfather loved *kanji*. In fact, he loved it so much that he insisted on having it every day. There was nothing wrong with this, except that it posed a slight problem when he became the maharaja of Kochi—a king insisting on having a poor man's meal!
>
> Grandfather passed away two months before I was born, so I never knew him, but I have heard several stories about his brilliant mind, his knowledge of Sanskrit and ayurveda, and his eccentricities. In fact, his nickname was *Midukkan,* "Smart One." My father-in-law (also from the royal family) had an interesting anecdote about Grandfather's obsession with *kanji*. In his day, tradition dictated the menu for a king. When he became king, the man in charge of the royal pantry and the cooks were confused about his food preferences. Finally someone came up with an amicable solution. When Grandfather sat down to eat with other family members, a large banana leaf was spread in front of him, and various vegetable dishes were served. This was followed by servings of rice and other curries. Finally, the cook came out with a silver bowl filled with Grandfather's favorite *kanji* and placed it at the center of his banana leaf. Grandfather would totally ignore the small pile of rice and devour his *kanji,* as if he was eating the same food as the others.

Kanji is served in a shallow bowl with salt sprinkled over it. Accompanying dishes enhance the taste of *kanji*. Ghee or yogurt is served, according to preference. Other accompaniments include fried *pappadams,* any of the deep-fried dehydrated vegetables, fresh or toasted coconut chutney, any type of *puzukku* (vegetable curry with coconut), any of the dry vegetable dishes called *mezukkupurattis* or *thorans,* and any of the hot pickles. (Recipes for these dishes are included in the following chapters.)

Flavored Rice Dishes

The following four rice dishes are prepared by combining cooked long grain rice with various ingredients. All of them make good brunch dishes. Since they are already spiced, flavored varieties are generally served with a dry vegetable dish, deep-fried *pappadams,* and pickles. A store-bought bottle of pickles and a bag of potato chips make a quick substitute for *pappadams* and homemade pickles.

Thayir Choru: Yogurt Rice

Milky white yogurt spooned on top of the last course of white rice, served on green plantain leaves, to be enjoyed with some seasonal pickle—for the South Indian born, it is the taste of heaven. We are perfectly satisfied with an entire meal of yogurt rice and pickles. The preparation of yogurt rice is simple, but it is also a complex affair, with as many variations of the process as there are consumers. For starters, the balance of rice and yogurt differs with each hand that blends it. Some like a cake-like firmness, while others want it to dribble sensuously from the serving spoon. Some add milk to make it less sour, while others insist that the yogurt should be set to reach the right sour-sweet balance.

Thayir choru is also an easy way to use leftover plain rice. Freshly grated ginger and green chilies complement the tanginess of the yogurt. This dish is always served cold or at room temperature.

4 cups cooked rice, at room temperature
Salt to taste
1½ cups thick plain yogurt
2 tablespoons vegetable oil
1 teaspoon mustard seeds
1½ teaspoons each cleaned *urad* dal and *chana* dal
2 tablespoons coarsely chopped cashew nuts
3 fresh green chilies (serrano or Thai), thinly sliced (less for a milder taste)
1 tablespoon freshly grated ginger
15 to 20 fresh curry leaves

In a large bowl, combine rice, salt, and yogurt and stir well. Heat the oil in a small skillet over medium heat and add the mustard seeds. When the mustard seeds start sputtering, add *urad* dal, *chana* dal, and cashew nuts. When the dal and cashews start turning golden brown (in about thirty seconds), add green chilies, grated ginger, and curry leaves and keep stirring for a minute or two.

Remove the skillet and pour this spice blend over the rice and yogurt. Stir and mix well. Serve with *pappadams* and pickles.

This old recipe has evolved over the years to include various ingredients for added crunch. Finely diced raw mango, carrot, cucumber, grape, pineapple, and pomegranate have all become favorite additions to embellish this simple dish.

Makes 4½ to 5 cups.

Thenga Choru: Coconut Rice

My mother's coconut rice is an unforgettable dish. The distinct tastes of toasted coconut and tender rice meld into each other, and every grain of rice is flavored by the rich, fragrant ghee, the nutty fried dal and cashew nuts, and the curry leaves.

Coconut rice is made in many different ways. Some cooks add fresh coconut, while others fry it before mixing it with the rice. Another version calls for rice cooked in coconut milk. The following is my mother's version, rich with fresh coconut toasted in ghee.

4 cups cooked long-grain rice
Salt to taste
½ cup ghee
3 cups freshly grated coconut
1½ teaspoons mustard seeds
1½ tablespoons each cleaned *urad* dal and *chana* dal
2 dried red cayenne, serrano, or Thai chilies, halved
½ cup halved cashew nuts
¼ teaspoon asafetida powder
15 to 20 fresh curry leaves

Spread the cooked rice in a large, flat dish, sprinkle it with salt, and stir to combine. Heat half of the ghee in a large heavy skillet over medium heat, and add the grated coconut. Reduce the heat, and panfry the coconut over medium-low heat until the flakes turn golden brown, approximately six to eight minutes. Remove it from the stove and spread the coconut over the rice.

Heat the remaining ghee in the skillet and add the mustard seeds. When the mustard seeds start sputtering, add the dal and fry them until they turn golden brown. Lower the heat, and add red chili peppers, cashew nuts, asafetida powder, and curry leaves. Fry until the cashew pieces are slightly browned. Remove it from the stove and pour it over the rice. Stir gently to coat the rice with fried coconut and spices. This rice dish tastes good served warm or cold.

Makes 6 cups.

Naaranga Choru: Lemon Rice

Variations of this rice dish are made throughout southern India. Lemon rice, flavored with fresh lemon juice and colored yellow with turmeric, is gently spiced with curry leaves and cilantro leaves. It makes a good brunch dish when served with *rasam, thoran,* and *vadas* (recipes given in following chapters).

2 cups long-grain rice
½ teaspoon turmeric
Salt to taste
2 tablespoons fresh lemon juice
½ cup sesame oil*
1½ teaspoons mustard seeds
1½ tablespoons each cleaned *urad* dal and *chana* dal
2 dried red cayenne, serrano, or Thai chilies, halved
¼ cup halved cashew nuts
¼ cup roasted unsalted peanuts
¼ teaspoon asafetida powder
12 to 15 fresh curry leaves
2 tablespoons chopped cilantro leaves

Cook the rice according to package directions along with salt and turmeric. Transfer the cooked rice to a large, flat serving bowl or dish. Sprinkle with lemon juice and toss well.

Heat the sesame oil in a heavy skillet and add mustard seeds. When the mustard seeds start sputtering, add the dal, and fry until they turn golden brown. Lower the heat, and add the red chili peppers, nuts, asafetida powder, and curry leaves. Fry until the nuts are slightly browned. Remove from the stove and pour this spice mixture over the rice. Stir gently to coat the rice with the spice mix. Garnish with the cilantro leaves.

*Sesame oil is used in the traditional recipe. It may be substituted with either ghee or vegetable oil.

Makes approximately 4 cups.

Pothichoru: Spiced Rice in Banana-Leaf Packets

In the month of Dhanu (mid-December to mid-January) in the lunar calendar, we observe Thiruvathira, a festival celebrating the love of the goddess Parvathi and the god Siva. It is believed that Parvathi spent years praying that Siva would marry her. Finally, with a little help from Kamadeva, the god of love, her wish was fulfilled. During Thiruvathira, women and young girls offer special prayers in the hope that they too will have good husbands and lead happily married lives.

Four days before Thiruvathira, an hour or two before daybreak, my sisters, cousins, friends, and I gathered at the temple pond. As we walked through the early morning fog, we sang Thiruvathira songs—songs in praise of goddess Parvathi's love for her husband, Siva. Once we were in the water, we splashed to the rhythm of the songs. After the bath, we went to the temple for predawn prayers. Our breakfast included tender coconut and bananas offered at the temple.

On the day before Thiruvathira, all mothers undertake a partial fast for the well-being of their children. On this day, a special dish, *ettangadi*, is prepared as a prayer offering and later served to all of the women and girls of the extended family. On Thiruvathira, all of the women and young girls in our extended family observed partial fasting for the well-being of their husbands and future husbands. Fasting means the avoidance of our staple food: rice. We ate other cooked grains for lunch, and in the evening, we ate a light meal of wheat flour *dosas* or cracked-wheat *uppuma*. Certain special dishes—Thiruvathira *puzukku,* Thiruvathira *koottu, koova paayasam,* and both sweet and sour *koova varattiyathu* were also served on this occasion. (Recipes for these dishes can be found in following chapters.) We spent the rest of the night sitting on swings, singing Thiruvathira songs, and dancing the hand-clapping fold dance Thiruvathira Kali.

Giving a gift of rice was also a part of the Thiruvathira ceremonies. Two days before Thiruvathira, it was customary to send rice packets to relatives living in the same town or village. A rice packet consists of cooked long-grain rice mixed with yogurt, milk, and butter and seasoned with fresh ginger and curry leaves. The rice is packed in fresh banana leaves and placed in stainless steel or brass containers, to be delivered along with deep-fried, sun-dried vegetables (recipes for these are included in a later chapter).

1 cup long-grain rice
1 cup plain yogurt
¼ cup boiled whole milk
3 tablespoons butter
1 tablespoon freshly grated ginger
Salt to taste
12 to 15 fresh curry leaves

Cook the rice, and spread it in a large tray or a flat glass dish to cool to room temperature. Combine yogurt, milk, and butter in a large bowl. Sprinkle the milk mixture with the grated ginger and salt, and whisk to combine. Pour this over the cooled rice and mix thoroughly. Sprinkle curry leaves on top. This rice dish will have the consistency of risotto. Makes 2½ to 3 cups, enough to make two rice packets.

To make two rice packets, you will need four large banana leaves, approximately 8 to 10 inches long, and another small piece to make into strings to tie the packets. In warmer climates, banana leaves are available fresh at Mexican markets. They are also imported to the United States frozen and sold in Chinese, Mexican, and Thai markets. Wash the banana leaves under running water. To make them pliable, pick up a large piece with tongs and toast it over a medium flame, holding it high, for ten seconds. The leaf will become darker in color, limp, and flexible. Because they have horizontal ribs that tear easily, crisscross the ribs of two pieces when stacking them to wrap food or for cooking.

Lay the toasted leaf on a large cutting board. Toast another large piece of banana leaf and spread it on top of the first one. Place half the rice in the center of the leaf. Bring both sides of the leaf to the center, and fold it like a package. Bring the other two sides of the leaf to the top, and secure the packet with a toothpick. Tear a small toasted banana leaf into thin strips, and tie the pieces together to make long strings. Tie the rice packet with this string, and remove the toothpick. Repeat the process with the remaining banana leaves and rice. Let the packets rest for two hours to allow the rice to absorb the fragrance of the banana leaves. *Pothichoru* is served at room temperature along with various deep-fried dehydrated vegetables and *pappadams*.

Makes 2 rice packets.

Chapter Four
The World of Curries

There is nothing more satisfying than sopping up the last drops of curry from the plate with a few grains of rice. The word "curry," a corruption of the Tamil word *kari*, is a generic name used in the West for every Indian dish cooked in a spicy liquid. The western notion that curry derives its color from the sprinkling of a distinctly yellow curry powder is unfortunately a misconception. And as for curry powder, it does not come from one spice plant called "curry."

South Indian vegetable curries are dishes that contain a few or many ingredients, thoughtfully seasoned and cooked in a thick or thin sauce and served with plain boiled rice. There is a lot of room to be creative in the world of curries. The spectrum of vegetable curries varies greatly in terms of taste, texture, color and complexity. Our traditional food has a very simple cooking style. The spices used are comparatively limited, but they have the ability to bring out and highlight the taste of the ingredients used, particularly the original taste of the vegetables. Variety comes from innovative methods of preparing vegetables with different herbs and spices. Everyday home curries are robust and full flavored, yet mild enough to be enjoyed by children and adults alike.

South India is blessed with an overwhelming variety of vegetables and fruits. Legumes are plenty; there are over a dozen varieties of green, black, yellow, red, and white beans and peas in all sorts of shapes—small, large, round, and flat. Each legume is used in a particular way for individual curries that require the special characteristics of that one kind of legume above any other.

The spicy curry base, masala, is made with a blend of spices. Added to this masala is an array of herbs along with liquids like water, yogurt, coconut milk, or pureed lentils. The spice blend should be vivid enough to give sparkle to the vegetables, but not so strong that the character of the vegetable is obscured. As they cook in the sauce, the vegetables impart their flavors to one another, resulting in an outstanding dish. There are set rules dictating the use of specific spices for each curry. Our vegetable curries traditionally do not use any stocks or thickeners such as flour or cornstarch.

This chapter on curries is divided into three segments: popular curries, seasonal curries, and curries from the *madapilli* (royal kitchen).

Popular curries: These are the standard fare at any feast. In a way, the concept of these dishes is similar to the turkey and fixings served at Thanksgiving and Christmas; they are always the same and yet infinitely varied, depending on individual family recipes and traditions. They are served traditionally on a large banana leaf spread on a clean floor or a simple table, with rice in the center.

Seasonal curries: There are only two seasons in our region: summer and monsoon. The abundance of fresh summer vegetables is perfect for our lighter, more fragrant vegetable curries flavored with tamarind, mango, coconut, and green chilies. In stark contrast to summer's abundance, hardly any vegetables grow in our monsoon-flooded soil. Preparing meals during this season is a challenge and a true test of the ingenuity of the vegetarian cook. Several root vegetables (which have longer shelf lives than fresh vegetables), edible leaves, and various kinds of dried beans are the mainstays of the vegetarian kitchen during this season. While I was growing up in Kerala, the use of frozen or canned vegetables was not popular in our part of the world. All of the drying and preserving done during the summer months also come in handy.

Curries from the *madapilli*: Family recipes are treasured possessions of every society. Some of the simplest and tastiest vegetable curries of our region come from the kitchens of the royal family of Kochi. Over the years, I have collected recipes for several simple delicacies that are traditionally prepared at the *madapilli*. Most of them require only a few ingredients and are very easy to prepare.

Serving suggestions: Most recipes for curries and dry vegetables in this book yield approximately four to six servings. When the number of dishes is increased, these recipes are sufficient to serve even more people.

Despite their tropical roots, many the ingredients for these curries are commonly found in most American supermarkets. Explore and enjoy the wonderful world of curries.

Popular Curries

Whether it is a wedding or a religious holiday or a birthday, the recipes in this section are the standard fare at any *sadya* (feast). At a traditional *sadya*, there are no fancy table settings or beautiful vases of fresh-cut flowers, and there is no particular main course. The perfection of the dishes is more important than the presentation itself. They come just as they are, served on a large banana leaf spread on a clean floor or a simple table, with rice in the center accompanied by several vegetable dishes, both wet and dry, and several different accompaniments. And as you begin to relish the meal, so many different flavors are blended on the palate that each bite tastes different and better than the one before. Food's greatest glory is in its infinite variety of textures and flavors.

The traditional vegetarian feast, *naalukari sadya,* refers to four curries—*kaalan, oolan, aviyal,* and *erisseri*—all prepared with plenty of fresh coconut. At more festive events, the number of curries is doubled to eight curries *(ettukootan)*. Over the years, the traditional *sadya* menu has evolved to include *sambar* and *rasam,* two curries that originated in our neighboring state of Tamil Nadu, brought to us by Brahman cooks. All dishes for a *sadya* are customarily served with plain boiled rice, preferably parboiled rice. In a way, the concept of this menu is similar to the traditional fare at Western holidays such as Thanksgiving and Christmas; they are always the same and yet considerably diverse, depending on individual family recipes and customs.

However, these curries are not strictly reserved for *sadyas.* A typical everyday vegetarian lunch or dinner will consist of two curries and a dry vegetable dish, along with ghee, yogurt, *pappadams,* and a pickle. For lunch, a spicy *sambar* normally appears at least three or four times during the week, if not more. *Kaalan, pachadi, rasam,* and *kichadi* often appear as a second curry at everyday meals. *Oolan* and *aviyal* are generally considered *sadya* dishes.

Almost all of the following recipes have a very long history. Ancient Sanskrit texts dating back to 1485 AD describe a recipe for *pachadi.* Historical records show that *erisseri, kaalan,* and *oolan* were some of the dishes served at the *oottupuras* (dining halls serving free meals) during the reign of Maharaja Sakthan Thampuran (1770–1806). A recipe for *sambar* was found in an ancient cookbook from 1648. Traditionally, our vegetarian cuisine avoids the use of certain vegetables and spices that are associated with non-vegetarian cooking—onions, garlic, shallots, cloves, and cinnamon. Even today, on religious and festive occasions, they are avoided. Believe me, dry spices, fresh ginger, cilantro, green chilies, curry leaves, and coconut impart plenty of flavor.

The reason I call these popular curries is because various versions of these recipes are found in many Indian cookbooks. Open any South Indian cookbook, and without a doubt, there will be recipes for *sambar* and *rasam*. One of our traditional vegetarian dishes that creeps into most Indian cookbooks is the mixed vegetable curry, *aviyal*. There are many versions of these popular recipes. Here I describe how these curries are prepared at the homes of the royal family and the Nayar of Kochi.

Serving a Sadya

In the old days, people sat cross-legged on a *paaya* (straw mat) or a *palaka* (wooden plank), and food was served on a banana leaf placed on the floor in front of them. Although banana leaves are still used, they are mostly spread on dining tables. There are specific places for each of the dishes on the banana leaf, and the servers are expected to know these rules.

When one is seated in front of a banana leaf, the wider end of the leaf should be to your right and the tapering end of the leaf to your left. Often, the side dishes are already served on the leaf before everyone is seated. There will be small piles of *varuthupperi, sarkara upperi,* and *chena varuthathu* at the tapering end of the leaf. A couple of fried *pappadams, pazzam nurukku,* finger bananas, *puliingi,* and *naranga* curry are served next to these. On the half section of the leaf that is away from you, beginning from left to right, there are servings of *thoran* or *mezukkupuratti,* followed by *oolan, aviyal, pachadi, kaalan,* and *erisseri* at the farthest, wider end. On the half of the leaf that is next to you, toward the wider end to your right, there is a very small serving of *parippu*. After you are seated, rice is served in the middle of the leaf (on the half that is near to you). A small serving of ghee over the rice is followed by *sambar*.

A small portion of the rice is mixed with the ghee and *parippu* (with the right hand, of course) and eaten as the start of the meal. Next, some rice is mixed with *sambar* and devoured with the other curries served on the leaf along with *thoran* or *mezukkupuratti,* chips, and *pappadam*. This is followed by more rice with *rasam*. After the *rasam* course, you practically clean the half of the leaf with your fingers and get ready for the *paayasam;* that's right—the dessert is served in the middle of the meal, not at the end. To scoop up the thick liquid *paayasam* with the palm of your right hand and take it to your mouth without spilling it all over is a feat in itself. If you cannot do this, *paayasam* is served in a small metal glass. Bits of *pappadam* and finger bananas and morsels of spicy *naranga* curry or *puliingi* are nibbled along with the *paayasam* to enhance its taste. Often, more than one type of *paayasam* is served, one followed by the other. And finally, to soothe the palate, there is another small serving of rice with yogurt or buttermilk. Needless to say, the servers will coax everyone to have second servings of each item. Recipes for *thorans, mezukkupurattis,* pickles, accompaniments, and *paayasams* mentioned above are included in following chapters.

After the meal is finished, the hands and mouth are washed. At wedding feasts and other festive occasions, elaborate trays containing betel leaves and various accompaniments are served after the meal. Ancient Sanskrit literature associate the practice of chewing betel leaves with southern India, then called Malaya. The botanical names "areca" for the nut and "betel" for the leaves comes via the Portuguese, who derived them from the Malayalam (and Tamil) words *adakka* and *vettila.*

The presentation of betel leaves has turned into an art form. On auspicious occasions, guests are served betel leaves on large brass or silver trays called *vettila thambaalam.* These trays have beautiful carvings, and the leaves are arranged in several layers in a circle around the edge of the tray. Brass or silver slaked-lime containers shaped like mangoes, leaves, or swans and carved small bowls holding *adakkapodi* (chopped *Areca catechu),* cloves, cardamom, and sugar crystals are kept in the center of the tray. The areca nut is chopped into thin pieces and several fragrant spices are added to make *adakkapodi.* In Kerala, the nut is also processed to make *kaliadakka;* the nuts are cut into thin rounds and cooked in their own juices until all the liquid is absorbed, then they are mixed with thick brown-sugar syrup sprinkled with dried ginger powder. Both betel leaves and areca nuts (whole nuts and *adakkapodi)* are available at Indian grocery stores.

> There are several myths about betel chewing. The betel leaf and areca nut are regarded as auspicious items and symbols of prosperity. They are offered at the temples along with flowers and fruit. An ancient myth about the betel leaf is that it was brought to Earth from Nagaloka, the land of the serpents. The story goes that when Nagaraja (king of the serpents) was bringing the leaf to Earth, a snake's mouth touched the ends of the leaf; this is why, even today, all betel leaf chewers break off the ends of the leaf before chewing, supposedly to remove any poison left on the tip. When betel leaves are offered to elders or priests, they are usually given with the end of the leaf turned toward the person making the offering.

People who chew betel leaves on a daily basis have their own metal containers called *chellam.* These boxes are often artistically carved and have separate compartments for the areca nuts and nutcrackers used to split and shred the nuts, slaked lime, and other ingredients.

Before chewing, the ends of the betel leaf are snipped off, the leaf is turned upside down, and a very small serving of lime paste is spread all over it. About half a teaspoon of *adakkapodi,* a few cardamom seeds, and perhaps a clove and a pinch of sugar are placed in the middle of the leaf. It is folded tightly, put into the mouth, and chewed leisurely. Betel leaves leave a reddish color on the lips and tongue.

Neyyum Parippum: Mashed Mung Dal with Ghee

A simple combination—a small serving of boiled mung dal *(parippu)* with a dollop of golden ghee—marks the beginning of a vegetarian feast.

1 cup mung dal
½ teaspoon turmeric powder
Salt to taste
¼ cup ghee

Wash and clean the mung dal in several changes of water, until the water runs clear. Bring 2 to 2½ cups of water to a boil and add the mung dal. Sprinkle turmeric on top, reduce the heat to medium low, and simmer until the dal is well cooked and can be mashed with the back of a spoon. Stir to make sure that it does not stick to the pan. If necessary, add more water while cooking. Sprinkle salt on top and stir. Remove from the stove and keep covered. Serve with ghee.

Makes 4 to 6 servings if served with another curry, as is traditional.

Erisseri: Butternut Squash and Mung Dal in Coconut Cumin Sauce

Succulent and chunky, the taste of this curry is dominated by vegetables and creamy coconut. It arrives at the dinner table as golden yellow chunks floating in a pool of creamy mung dal thickened with toasted coconut and spiced with cumin seeds. *Erisseri* may be prepared with a variety of vegetables such as potatoes, plantains, jackfruit, Indian pumpkin, and drumsticks *(Moringa oleifera,* not chicken). The following recipe uses the readily available butternut squash.

¾ cup mung dal
½ teaspoon turmeric

2 teaspoons dried red cayenne, serrano, or Thai chili pepper powder (less for a milder taste)
Half of a butternut squash, peeled, seeded, and cut into half-inch cubes
Salt to taste
1½ cups freshly grated coconut
1 teaspoon cumin seeds

For seasoning and garnish:
2 tablespoons vegetable oil
1 teaspoon mustard seeds
1 dried red cayenne, serrano, or Thai chili, halved
12 to 15 fresh curry leaves
½ cup freshly grated coconut

In a heavy skillet, dry roast the dal until it is golden. Wash and clean the mung dal in several changes of water, until the water runs clear. Transfer to a saucepan along with 2 cups of water, add turmeric and chili powder, and cook over medium heat, until it is well cooked and can be mashed easily with a potato masher or the back of a large spoon (approximately fifteen to twenty minutes). Stir the dal to make sure that it does not stick to the bottom of the pan. When the dal is well cooked, mash thoroughly, add cubed squash, salt, and half a cup of water and cook until the squash cubes are fork tender, approximately six to eight minutes. The squash and dal may also be cooked separately and then combined.

In a blender, grind 1½ cups of the coconut with the cumin seeds and just enough water to make a smooth puree. Combine this with the cooked dal and squash. Stir gently to combine all the ingredients. Cook over medium heat for four to five minutes, and remove from the stove.

Heat a tablespoon of oil in a skillet and add the mustard seeds. When the mustard seeds start sputtering, add the halved chili pepper and the curry leaves, and remove from the stove. Pour over the *erisseri*. Toast the remaining coconut flakes in one tablespoon of oil until golden brown, add them to the curry, and stir gently. Cover and set aside for ten minutes, to allow flavors to blend. Serve hot with plain boiled rice.

Makes 4 to 6 servings if served with another curry, as is traditional.

Varutha Erisseri: Green Plantains in Toasted Coconut and Cumin Sauce

When making *varutha erisseri,* a different version of the previous recipe, chunks of green plantain are cooked in a sauce of golden-brown toasted coconut. It has a complexity and aroma peculiarly and delightfully its own.

2 green plantains, peeled and cut into half-inch cubes
Salt to taste
1 teaspoon dried red cayenne, serrano, or Thai chili powder (less for a milder taste)
½ teaspoon turmeric powder
2 cups freshly grated coconut
1 tablespoon vegetable oil
1 teaspoon cumin seeds

For seasoning and garnish:
1 tablespoon vegetable oil
1 teaspoon mustard seeds
1 dried red cayenne, serrano, or Thai chili, halved
12 to 15 fresh curry leaves

Wash the peeled and cubed plantains, and place them in a saucepan with just enough water to cover. Add salt, chili powder, and turmeric, and cook over medium heat until the plantains are tender. In the meantime, toast the grated coconut in one tablespoon of oil until it is golden brown. Grind half of this toasted coconut with cumin seeds and just enough water to make a thick, smooth puree. Add the puree to the plantains. Stir gently, so that the plantains are not mashed. Simmer for another three to five minutes, and remove from the stove.

Heat the oil in a skillet and add the mustard seeds. When the mustard seeds start sputtering, add the halved chili pepper and the curry leaves, and remove from the stove. Pour over the *varutha erisseri.* Sprinkle in the remaining toasted coconut flakes, and stir gently. Cover and set aside for ten minutes, to allow flavors to blend. Serve hot with plain boiled rice.

Makes 4 to 6 servings if served with another curry, as is traditional.

Kaalan: Ripe Plantains with Coconut, Green Chilies, and Yogurt

The word "curry" often evokes a sense of tropical spiciness. Although in Kerala we prepare a variety of spicy curries, we also have some mildly sweet, tropical fruit curries that are cooked in a mellow coconut and yogurt sauce. The spiciness of the curry is balanced with the addition of brown sugar. One thing to remember when cooking with yogurt: Don't let the curry boil at high heat. Always simmer over medium-low heat, and the curry will have a creamy texture with a hint of sourness.

Kaalan may be prepared with a variety of vegetables or fruits. At the Onam festival, ripe plantains generally are plentiful, and they are used in preparing this curry. Other vegetables used for *kaalan* include ripe mangoes, ash gourd, spinach, and taro root.

2 firm, ripe plantains
1 teaspoon crushed black pepper
Salt to taste
½ teaspoon turmeric powder
2½ cups freshly grated coconut
3 to 4 fresh green chilies (serrano or Thai) (less for a milder taste)
2 cups thick yogurt

For seasoning and garnish:
2 tablespoons vegetable oil
1 teaspoon mustard seeds
1 dried red cayenne, serrano, or Thai chili, halved
12 to 15 fresh curry leaves
1 teaspoon fenugreek seeds, panfried and crushed
2 tablespoons jaggery or brown sugar

Peel and cut the plantains into half-inch chunks. Place the plantain chunks in a saucepan and pour in enough water to cover them. Stir in black pepper, salt, and turmeric, and cook over medium heat until the plantains are fork tender. Stir periodically while cooking, and add more water if necessary. While the plantains are cooking, grind the coconut, green chilies, and one cup of yogurt into a thick, smooth puree. Add this to the cooked banana pieces along with the remaining yogurt, and stir well. Cook over medium-low heat until it comes to a boil. Remove from the stove.

Heat the oil in a skillet, and add the mustard seeds. When the mustard seeds start sputtering, add the halved chili pepper and the curry leaves, and remove from the stove. Add crushed fenugreek to the skillet, and pour the spices over the *kaalan*. Stir in the jaggery or brown sugar. Cover and set aside for ten minutes, to allow flavors to blend. Serve hot with plain boiled rice.

Makes 4 to 6 servings if served with another curry, as is traditional.

Oolan: Vegetables in Coconut-Milk Sauce

This simple dish of delicate vegetables cooked in coconut milk and spiced with fresh green chilies and curry leaves is a must at all feasts. Coconut milk has a tendency to separate when cooked at high temperatures, so be careful not to let it get too hot.

1 cup ash gourd or zucchini, cut into half-inch cubes
1 cup shelled black-eyed peas (thawed if frozen), or 1 cup tender black-eyed peas in pods, cut into 1-inch pieces
3 to 4 fresh green chilies (serrano or Thai), slit lengthwise (less for a milder taste)
Salt to taste
3 cups coconut milk*

For seasoning and garnish:
2 tablespoons coconut oil
12 to 15 fresh curry leaves

Place the cut vegetables and green chilies in a saucepan and pour in enough water to cover. Stir in the salt, and cook over medium heat, until the vegetable cubes are fork tender. Pour in coconut milk and bring to a slow boil. Reduce the heat, and simmer for five minutes. Remove from the stove, and garnish with coconut oil and fresh curry leaves. Stir gently and keep covered for ten minutes, to allow flavors to blend. Serve hot with plain boiled rice.

Makes 4 to 6 servings if served with another curry, as is traditional.

* Coconut milk is prepared by grating fresh coconut and squeezing the thick coconut milk from it. Then a few handfuls of water are sprinkled over the coconut flakes, and the thin coconut milk is squeezed out.

For greater ease, you may substitute with canned coconut milk, which is available in most supermarkets. As an easy alternative, I prefer using coconut milk powder. By adjusting the quantity of water added, you can make thick or thin coconut milk with the powder. Coconut milk powder is available in Southeast Asian and Indian grocery stores.

As a last resort, use half-and-half or whole milk as a substitute for thin coconut milk. However, this last version will definitely lack the flavor of coconut.

Aviyal: Mixed Vegetable Medley in Coconut Cumin Sauce

Aviyal is one recipe that captures the spirit of Kerala. A tangy, full-flavored dish, it is a medley of vegetables cooked with coarsely pureed fresh coconut, cumin, green chili peppers, and yogurt and seasoned with curry leaves and a liberal drizzling of coconut oil. Like most scrumptious Kerala recipes, the flavors are robust but not heavy-handed, and the ingredients mix perfectly, melding without any one flavor standing out.

Traditionally, ash gourd, snake gourd, yellow cucumbers, green plantains, string beans, telinga potatoes *(suran)*, and drumsticks *(Moringa oleifera)* are used in the preparation of *aviyal*. In the United States, green plantains are available in Latin American grocery stores and sometimes even at American supermarkets. Long string beans, ash gourd, snake gourd, yellow cucumbers, drumsticks (fresh, frozen, and canned), and telinga potatoes *(suran* or *zimikand)* are available in Indian food stores, and ash gourd (with light green skin and white flesh) is readily available at Chinese markets. Although not traditional, zucchini, carrots, butternut squash, green beans, and potatoes also may be used in this curry. The idea is to use as many vegetables as possible. This is one dish that definitely needs curry leaves. Curry leaves, fresh coconut, and coconut oil give *aviyal* its authentic flavor.

1 green plantain
2 medium-sized carrots
1 zucchini
1 medium-sized potato
1 cup ash gourd pieces
8 pieces of drumstick*
1 cup telinga potato pieces*
¼ pound green beans or string beans
Salt to taste
½ teaspoon turmeric powder

1½ cups plain yogurt
3 cups grated fresh coconut
4 to 5 fresh green chilies (serrano or Thai) (less for a milder taste)
1 teaspoon cumin seeds

For seasoning and garnish:
3 tablespoons coconut oil
12 to 15 fresh curry leaves

Peel and cut the plantains, carrots, zucchini, potato, ash gourd, drumstick, and telinga potato into pieces 2½ to 3 inches long (approximately the size of thick french fries). Cut the green beans or string beans into pieces of about the same size. Place the vegetables in a colander, wash them under running water, and drain. Place the cut potatoes, carrots, drumsticks, telinga potato, and beans in a heavy saucepan, and add just enough water to cover. Sprinkle with salt and turmeric and cook over medium heat. When they are partly cooked, add the remaining vegetable pieces and combine. Cook for five to six minutes, until all the vegetables are cooked; add a couple of tablespoons of water if necessary. Stir the yogurt with a tablespoon and pour it over the cooked vegetables. Simmer for three to five minutes. Grind the coconut, green chilies, and cumin seeds with just enough water to make a coarse, thick puree. Remove the puree from the blender, and stir it into the cooked vegetables. Simmer gently for five minutes over low heat (to prevent the yogurt from curdling). Remove from the stove and garnish with coconut oil and fresh curry leaves. Cover and set aside for ten minutes, to allow flavors to blend. Serve with plain boiled rice.

*Both frozen and canned drumsticks and telinga potatoes (labeled *suran*) are available at Indian grocery stores. If using the canned vegetables, first drain them, wash them under running water, and drain them again. After cooking the fresh vegetables, add them along with the ground coconut puree and mix.

Makes 4 to 6 servings if served with another curry, as is traditional.

Sambar: Vegetables and *Tuvar* Dal in a Spicy Tamarind Sauce

A spicy *sambar* served with simple boiled rice is the quintessential first course in a South Indian vegetarian meal. *Sambar,* one of my favorite curries, has an ancient lineage, dating back to at least 1648. Its taste is robust yet elegant, and it blends well with rice and the myriad dishes served with it. There are several interpretations of this curry within Kerala, and there are many more in other parts of southern India.

Sambar may be prepared with many different kinds of vegetables. When two or three vegetables are used, there is a subtle blending of flavors. For a distinctive flavor, cook the *sambar* with only one type of vegetable. Shallots and pearl onions are two of those vegetables that are often used alone in making *sambar*. Okra, potatoes, drumsticks, eggplant, red and green bell peppers, tomatoes, ash gourd, pumpkin, and taro root are other vegetables often used in making *sambar*.

1 cup *tuvar* dal
1 teaspoon turmeric powder
½ tablespoon vegetable oil
2 cups fresh okra, cut into pieces two inches long
2 fresh hot green chilies (serrano or Thai), slit lengthwise (less for a milder taste)
2 tomatoes cut into half-inch cubes
Salt to taste
¾ teaspoon tamarind concentrate
3 tablespoons *sambar* powder (recipe below)

For seasoning and garnish:
1 tablespoon ghee or vegetable oil
1 teaspoon mustard seeds
1 dried cayenne, serrano, or Thai chili pepper, halved
¼ teaspoon fenugreek seeds
¼ teaspoon asafetida powder
12 to 15 fresh curry leaves
3 tablespoons finely chopped fresh cilantro leaves

Wash and clean the *tuvar* dal in several changes of water until the water runs clear. If using oily *tuvar* dal, the oil must be washed off before starting to cook. Place the *tuvar* dal in a saucepan, add 2½ cups water and ½ teaspoon turmeric powder, and bring to a boil over medium heat. Turn down the heat, and cook for twenty-five to thirty minutes. (Alternatively, you may use a pressure cooker to cook the dal, following manufacturer's directions. It will take about six to eight minutes to cook in a pressure cooker.) As the dal cooks, it should be fairly thick but still liquid; stir in another half-cup of water if it is too thick. Thoroughly mash the cooked *tuvar* dal with a spoon. Set aside.

Heat ½ tablespoon of oil in a skillet over medium heat, and add the okra pieces. Panfry for two to three minutes over medium heat. Keep stirring so that the okra skin does not turn dark brown. Remove from the stove. In another saucepan, cook the okra, green chilies, and tomato with 2 cups of water, salt, and the remaining turmeric powder for six to eight minutes.

Stir in the tamarind concentrate, and cook for another five minutes. Add the cooked dal, and mix well. Stir in the *sambar* powder and cook for five minutes more, over medium heat. Remove from the stove.

Heat the ghee or oil in a skillet, and add the mustard seeds. When the mustard seeds start sputtering, add the halved chili pepper, fenugreek seeds, asafetida, and curry leaves. Remove from the stove, and pour over the *sambar*. Garnish with thinly chopped cilantro leaves. Cover and set aside for ten minutes, to allow the flavors to blend. Serve hot with plain boiled rice.

Makes 4 to 6 servings if served with another curry, as is traditional.

Sambar powder: Homemade *sambar* powder tastes better any day; but for convenience, you may use the ready-made powders available at Indian grocery stores. The MTR brand Madras *sambar* powder is my personal favorite. Look for the word "Madras." MTR also manufactures a *sambar* powder that contains cinnamon. 777 and Ambi's are other good brand names.

1 cup coriander seeds
3 tablespoons fenugreek seeds
½ tablespoon oil
½ cup *urad* dal
1 cup dried red cayenne, serrano, or Thai chilies (less for a milder taste)

Dry roast the coriander seeds in a heavy skillet for about three minutes over medium heat, taking care not to burn them. It will produce a strong aroma. Remove them to a plate, and let them cool. Toast the fenugreek seeds over medium heat for a minute or two; if over-toasted, they will taste bitter. Combine them with the coriander seeds. Add the oil to the pan, and roast the *urad* dal to a golden-brown color. Add the red chili peppers, and toast for another minute. Let all of the ingredients cool. Using a coffee grinder or a blender, grind them into a smooth powder. Store it in airtight containers.

Varutharacha Sambar: Vegetables and *Tuvar* Dal in a Toasted-Coconut and Tamarind Sauce

Sambar is prepared in two different ways in our family: one using *sambar* powder, and the other using freshly ground *sambar* puree. In some Nayar homes, especially those closer to the mountain ranges, the *sambar* puree method is more prevalent. This is the way *sambar* was made at home by our cook Sreedharan Nayar. For *sadya,* he used to prepare this excellent sambar with drumsticks and taro root. The spicy sauce is thickened with the addition of toasted coconut flakes.

¾ cup *tuvar* dal
1 teaspoon turmeric powder
3 or 4 drumsticks, peeled, washed, and cut into two-inch pieces
Taro root, peeled, washed, and cut into small cubes (about 1 cup)
Salt to taste
1 level teaspoon tamarind concentrate

For sambar *paste:*
1 tablespoon vegetable oil
½ tablespoon cleaned and washed *urad* dal
½ tablespoon cleaned and washed *chana* dal
1½ tablespoons coriander seeds
1 cup freshly grated coconut
8 dried red cayenne, serrano, or Thai chilies (less for a milder taste)
½ teaspoon fenugreek seeds

For seasoning and garnish:
1 tablespoon vegetable oil
1 teaspoon mustard seeds
1 dried cayenne, serrano, or Thai chili pepper, halved
¼ teaspoon fenugreek seeds
¼ teaspoon asafetida powder
12 to 15 fresh curry leaves
3 tablespoons finely chopped fresh cilantro leaves

Wash and clean the *tuvar* dal in several changes of water, until the water runs clear. If you are using oily *tuvar* dal, the oil must be washed off before starting to cook. In a saucepan, bring the *tuvar* dal, 2½ cups of water, and ½ teaspoon of turmeric powder to a boil over medium heat. Turn down the heat, and cook for twenty-five to thirty minutes. (Alternately, you may use a pressure cooker to cook the dal, following manufacturer's directions. It will take about six to eight minutes to cook in a pressure cooker.) As the dal cooks, it should be fairly thick but still liquid; stir in another half-cup of water if it gets too thick. Mash the cooked *tuvar* dal thoroughly with a spoon, and set it aside.

Place drumsticks and taro root cubes in a saucepan and pour in enough water to cover the vegetables. Add salt and the remaining turmeric to the pot, and cook until the vegetables are fork tender. Stir in the tamarind concentrate and one half cup of water, and cook for another five minutes.

Heat a tablespoon of oil in a skillet over medium heat. Add the *urad* dal and *chana* dal and fry till the dal is well toasted, stirring continuously so that they are evenly toasted. Stir in the coriander, grated coconut, and red chilies, and fry until the coconut turns golden brown. Stir in the fenugreek seeds, and toast for a minute. Remove from the stove, and let it cool. In a blender, grind the spice blend and just enough water to make a thick puree. Combine the puree and the cooked dal, add it to the vegetables, and mix well. Bring to a boil, reduce the heat, and simmer for another five minutes. Remove from the stove.

Heat oil in a skillet, and add the mustard seeds. When the mustard seeds start sputtering, add the halved red chili pepper, fenugreek seeds, asafetida, and curry leaves. Remove from the stove, and pour over the *sambar*. Garnish with thinly chopped cilantro leaves. Cover and set aside for ten minutes, to allow flavors to blend. Serve hot with plain boiled rice.

Makes 4 to 6 servings if served with another curry, as is traditional.

Thakkali Rasam: Tomato and *Tuvar* Dal Soup

Rasam is a thin and deliciously spicy soup. Served with rice, it is the traditional second course in a South Indian vegetarian meal. Lemon and tomato come together in this refreshing dish. There are as many variations of *rasam* as there are cooks. In our home, *rasam* is always made with tomatoes cooked with *tuvar* dal. Some prefer to drink it as soup rather than mixing it with rice. Crispy fried *vadas* served in *rasam* make an excellent snack. *Rasam* may also be prepared without the dal, but the consistency is thinner.

½ cup tuvar dal
½ teaspoon turmeric powder
4 medium-sized tomatoes, cut into small cubes
Salt to taste
1½ tablespoons *rasam* powder (recipe follows)
Juice of 1 small lemon or ½ teaspoon tamarind concentrate*

For seasoning and garnish:
1 tablespoon ghee or vegetable oil
1 teaspoon mustard seeds
1 dried cayenne, serrano, or Thai chili pepper, halved (less for a milder taste)
¼ teaspoon asafetida powder (optional)
12 to 15 fresh curry leaves
2 tablespoons finely chopped fresh cilantro leaves

> The predecessor of the famed mulligatawny soup, *rasam* is a favorite South Indian soup traditionally served with rice. The British were enamored of this spicy, thin broth. Its Tamil pronunciation, *molagu thanni* ("pepper water"), was corrupted to "mulligatawny" when it arrived at British dining tables many incarnations later, totally different from the original recipe.

Wash and clean the *tuvar* dal in several changes of water, until the water runs clear. If you are using oily *tuvar* dal, the oil must be washed off before starting to cook. In a saucepan, bring the *tuvar* dal, 2½ cups of water, and ½ teaspoon turmeric powder to a boil over medium heat. Turn down the heat, and cook for twenty-five to thirty minutes. (Alternately, you may use a pressure cooker to cook the dal, following manufacturer's directions. It will take about six to eight minutes to cook in a pressure cooker.) If the cooked dal is thick add another cup of boiling water to it. Mash the cooked *tuvar* dal thoroughly with a spoon. Set aside. Dal for *rasam* should be more watery than dal used for *sambar*.

Cook cubed tomatoes in 2 cups of water along with salt and turmeric for three to four minutes. Add the *rasam* powder and the cooked dal. Cook for another five minutes. Remove from the stove. Stir in lemon juice. If using tamarind, add it along with *rasam* powder.

Heat oil in a skillet, and add the mustard seeds. When the mustard seeds start sputtering, add the halved red chili pepper, asafetida, and curry leaves. Remove from the stove, and pour over *rasam*. Garnish with thinly chopped cilantro leaves. Cover and set aside for ten minutes, to allow flavors to blend. Serve hot with plain boiled rice.

*When tamarind is used, *rasam* appears darker. For a paler, golden yellow color, use lemon juice instead.

Makes 4 to 6 servings if served with another curry, as is traditional.

Rasam Powder:
1 cup coriander seeds
2 cups dried red cayenne, serrano, or Thai chilies (less for a milder taste)
2 tablespoons black peppercorns
2 tablespoons cumin seeds
1½ tablespoons fenugreek seeds
1 teaspoon turmeric powder

In a heavy skillet, dry roast the spices over medium heat, stirring constantly, starting with the coriander. After a minute or two, add the red chilies and black pepper. After another minute, add cumin seeds and then fenugreek. (Cumin and fenugreek have a tendency to burn quickly.) Fry for another minute, then remove the spice mixture from the heat and stir in the turmeric powder. Let it cool. Using a coffee grinder or a blender, grind the spices to a smooth powder. Store *rasam* powder in airtight containers.

Tomato *Pachadi:* Tomatoes in a Fresh Coconut and Yogurt Sauce

According to Indian food historian K. T. Achaya, the earliest recipe for *pachadi* was found in our neighboring state Karnataka, in a text dating back to 1485. Since ancient times, cooks have come to Kerala from our bordering states Karnataka and Tamil Nadu. They brought with them many recipes, which later became part of our own cuisine.

In Kerala, this dish is traditionally prepared with tomatoes, cucumbers, or ash gourd; only one type of vegetable at a time is used in this dish. For an unusual twist, use cubed pineapple pieces instead of traditional vegetables. My mother-in-law used to make this curry with tomatoes just before we all sat down to eat, and it would always be the best among the many dishes served.

3 medium-sized tomatoes, washed and cut into cubes
Salt to taste
½ teaspoon turmeric powder
2 cups freshly grated coconut
3 or 4 fresh green chilies (serrano or Thai) (less for a milder taste)
1 cup plain yogurt

For seasoning and garnish:
1 tablespoon vegetable oil
1 teaspoon mustard seeds
1 dried red cayenne, serrano, or Thai chili, halved
12 to 15 fresh curry leaves
½ tablespoons jaggery or brown sugar

Bring ½ cup of water to a boil in a saucepan, and add the cubed tomatoes. Stir in the salt and turmeric and cook for three to four minutes over medium heat. Using a blender, grind the coconut and green chilies with a very small amount of water into a fine thick puree. Remove from the blender, and stir in the yogurt. Add this to the cooked tomatoes, mix well, and simmer over low heat until the mixture starts to bubble. Remove from the stove.

Heat the oil in a skillet, and add the mustard seeds. When the mustard seeds start sputtering, add the halved red chili pepper and curry leaves. Remove from the stove, and pour over the *pachadi*. Sprinkle with jaggery or brown sugar, and stir gently. Cover and set aside for ten minutes, to allow flavors to blend. Serve hot with plain boiled rice.

Makes 4 to 6 servings if served with another curry, as is traditional.

Okra *Kichadi:* Fried Okra in a Coconut and Mustard Sauce

Okra, the quintessential ingredient in gumbo, has a tendency to become slimy when cooked. In this mildly spiced curry, diced okra is panfried before being added to the sauce, which prevents it from turning slimy. It is spiced mainly with mustard seeds. This curry delicately balances the heat of the *sambar* and spicy pickles that are typically served along with it.

2 cups freshly grated coconut
1 tablespoon mustard seeds
3 or 4 fresh green chilies (serrano or Thai) (less for a milder taste)
Salt to taste
½ tablespoon vegetable oil
2 cups okra cut into eighth-inch rounds
1 cup plain yogurt

For seasoning and garnish:
1 tablespoon vegetable oil
1 teaspoon mustard seeds
1 dried red cayenne, serrano, or Thai chili, halved
12 to 15 fresh curry leaves

In a blender, grind the grated coconut, 1 tablespoon mustard seeds, the green chilies, and the salt to a fine thick puree. Heat 1 tablespoon of the oil in a skillet, and panfry the okra pieces until they are tender and slightly browned at the edges, approximately ten to twelve minutes. Remove from the stove and set aside.

    Heat the remaining oil in a skillet, and add the mustard seeds. When the mustard seeds start sputtering, add the halved red chili pepper and curry leaves. Mix the yogurt with the ground coconut, and pour it over the fried spices. Cook over low heat until the sauce simmers. Stir in the fried okra pieces. Cover and set aside for ten minutes, to allow flavors to blend. Serve hot with plain boiled rice.

Makes 4 to 6 servings if served with another curry, as is traditional.

Seasonal Curries

There are only two seasons in Kerala: summer and monsoon. This section on seasonal curries includes recipes for both summer and monsoon season curries.

In the outermost reaches of southwestern India, the soundtrack of summer has a deeper bass and a heavier beat than the rest of the year. As the bright rays of sunshine come fluttering through the swaying coconut palm leaves, the pace of life slows and afternoon siestas become the norm of the day. Some of us wait for summer all year long. We dream not only of lazy afternoons and sun-drenched beaches, but of cool lemonade and plump, sweet summer fruits. Golden-yellow mangoes hide seductively under lush, green leaves, and giant, thorny green jackfruits dangle languidly from tree trunks. Chirping, tiny black birds jump among broad, green banana leaves, looking for the nectar in banana flowers.

As one wanders around the open-air marketplace, the food is so fresh and the smell of the earth itself is the strongest and most assertive odor. Ripe, golden-striped, large cucumbers glow next to mounds of brilliantly green chilies and curry leaves. Pausing beside a pile of coconuts, I pick up one and shake it gently, listening to the sound of coconut water splashing inside, indicating its freshness. Who would argue that open jackfruit—its humble, thorny, dark green exterior yielding to a juicy, bright yellow fig-like flesh—does not offer a promise of unqualified delight? Sibling members of the gourd family, various squashes and large cucumbers, green and golden skinned and white fleshed, mostly water, they are the perfect antidotes to the sultry heat of summer. The abundance of fresh seasonal vegetables is perfect for the lighter and more fragrant summer vegetable curries. Despite their tropical roots, many of the ingredients in these curries are commonly found in most American supermarkets.

Vishu Festival: A Celebration of Summer's Bounty

In mid-April, we celebrate the bounty of tropical summer with a festival called Vishu. It is a festival of promise, of expectation, and of the hope for another good harvest season. Houses are cleaned, and children anticipate with excitement the Vishu firecrackers that they will burst on this auspicious dawn. Sometimes even the sky resonates with the children's mood, unleashing the sparklers of nature, the thunder and the flashes of lightning, and drenching the dry fields and drying water wells.

Mothers prepare beautiful displays of Vishu Kani, which every Hindu Malayali wishes to see before the first rays of the Vishu dawn. It is believed that what one sees first on Vishu morning influences one's fortunes for the rest of the year. Vishu Kani, the auspicious first sight of the day, is a very pretty arrangement of rice, coconut, various vegetables and fruits, gold jewelry and coins, flowers, and *vaalkannadi* (bell-metal mirror), all displayed in a large bell-metal pan *(uruli)*. The *uruli* is half filled with raw rice, and a large yellow cucumber is placed in the middle. Gold necklaces and gold coins are spread over the cucumber. Lemons, mangoes, and bananas are arranged around the cucumber. A large jackfruit sits outside the *uruli*. A coconut is broken into two pieces and filled with *kanikonna* (tiny, bright yellow flowers) and fresh *puliavaraka* (a type of seasonal bean similar to the lima bean). A lighted bronze *nilavilakku* (oil lamp) and a small bowl filled with coins are placed in front of the *uruli*.

At home, we were awakened before dawn and led, with eyes tightly shut, to where the Vishu Kani was displayed. To open my eyes to such light and color never failed to evoke wonder. Children received *vishukainettam* (presents of money), and they rejoiced in lighting firecrackers. Anyone who came by the house got a "lucky coin" and wishes for more to come in the new year. On Vishu morning, farmers marked the auspicious beginning of rice farming with chaal, a ritual furrow. Cultivation began with the onset of rainy season.

No celebration is complete without a sumptuous vegetarian feast around noon. The dishes for this *sadya* are similar to those for Thiruvonam, but more dishes are cooked with mangoes and jackfruit, instead of plantains and black-eyed peas. *Pazza pradhaman* is substituted with *chakka pradhaman,* and the *kaalan* is made with ripe mangos instead of ripe plantains. The *erisseri* is made with raw jackfruit, and there are jackfruit chips instead of banana chips. In my hometown, Chittur, a special dish called Vishu *kanji* (rice soup with coconut milk) is also prepared for Vishu.

Moloshyam: Vegetables in Coconut and Cumin Sauce

This satisfying stew of summer vegetables with mung dal and coconut, gently spiced with cumin, has a delicate flavor. Any one of a variety of vegetables—potatoes, green beans, peas, ash gourd, snake gourd, and spinach—is used in this curry. Cucumbers and zucchini also work well with this recipe. The following is a recipe using potatoes, which are readily available. While root vegetables and gourds are peeled and cut into small cubes, leaf vegetables are panfried in a little oil before cooking. Muringa leaves, the tiny leaves of the drumstick tree, are used to prepare this dish during the monsoon season.

1 cup mung dal
2 medium-sized potatoes, peeled and cut into cubes
½ teaspoon turmeric powder

½ teaspoon dried red cayenne, serrano, or Thai chili powder
Salt to taste
2 cups freshly grated coconut
2 teaspoons cumin seeds

For seasoning and garnish:
1 tablespoon vegetable oil (plus ½ tablespoon when cooking leaf vegetables)
½ teaspoon mustard seeds
1 dried red cayenne, serrano, or Thai chili, halved
12 to 15 fresh curry leaves

Wash and clean the mung dal in several changes of water, until the water runs clear. In a saucepan, bring the mung dal and two cups of water to a boil over medium heat. Lower the heat, and simmer, stirring occasionally, for fifteen to twenty minutes, or until the dal is tender.

In another saucepan, bring three cups of water, the potato cubes, turmeric powder, red pepper powder, and salt to a boil over medium heat. Reduce the heat, and simmer for ten minutes, or until the potato cubes are soft and fork tender.

Grind the grated coconut and cumin seeds along with half a cup of water to a smooth, thick puree. Mix the ground coconut with potatoes, and cook for another three to four minutes. Add the cooked mung dal to the saucepan, and stir gently. Simmer for another two minutes, and remove from the stove.

Heat the oil in a skillet, and add the mustard seeds. When the mustard seeds start sputtering, add the halved red chili pepper and the curry leaves. Remove from the stove, and pour over the *moloshyam.* Cover and set aside for ten minutes, to allow flavors to blend. Serve hot with plain boiled rice.

Makes 4 to 6 servings if served with another curry, as is traditional.

Variations: When preparing this curry with leaf vegetables such as spinach, panfry the leaves in oil before cooking. Before boiling the mung dal, panfry it over medium heat until it turns golden brown. Follow the remaining steps as detailed in the recipe above.

Moloshyam is also prepared without coconut. In this version, mung dal is substituted with *tuvar* dal. Cucumber, zucchini, ash gourd, snake gourd, or spinach is cooked with salt, turmeric, and red chili powder. Stir in the cooked dal, and garnish with a tablespoon of coconut oil and 15 to 18 curry leaves.

Pulinkari: Vegetables with Spicy *Tuvar* Dal

Pulinkari is probably an earlier version of the *sambar* prevalent in Kerala. This curry is prepared with *tuvar* dal and any one of a variety of vegetables, such as summer squash, ash gourd, papaya, plantain stem, eggplant, red and green bell peppers, okra, and taro root. The following recipe uses unripe papaya.

1 cup *tuvar* dal
2 cups papaya, peeled and cut into cubes
3 or 4 fresh green chilies (serrano or Thai), slit lengthwise (less for a milder taste)
1 teaspoon turmeric powder
1 teaspoon dried red cayenne, serrano, or Thai chili powder (less for a milder taste)
Salt to taste
1 teaspoon tamarind concentrate mixed with ½ cup water

For seasoning and garnish:
1½ tablespoons vegetable oil
1 teaspoon mustard seeds
1 dried cayenne, serrano, or Thai chili pepper, halved
¼ teaspoon fenugreek seeds
¼ teaspoon asafetida powder
12 to 15 fresh curry leaves
3 tablespoons finely chopped fresh cilantro leaves

Wash and clean the *tuvar* dal in several changes of water, until the water runs clear. If you are using oily *tuvar* dal, the oil must be washed off before starting to cook. In a saucepan, bring the *tuvar* dal, 2½ cups of water, and ½ teaspoon turmeric powder to a boil over medium heat. Turn down the heat and cook for twenty-five to thirty minutes. (Alternately, you may use a pressure cooker to cook the dal, following the manufacturer's directions. It will take about six to eight minutes to cook in a pressure cooker.) As the dal cooks, it should be fairly thick but still liquid; stir in another half-cup of water if it becomes too thick. Mash the cooked *tuvar* dal thoroughly with a spoon, and set it aside.

In another saucepan, bring three cups of water, the cubed papaya, green chili pepper, turmeric powder, red pepper powder, and salt to a boil over medium heat. Reduce the heat, and simmer for eight to ten minutes, or until papaya is soft and fork tender. Stir in the tamarind liquid, and cook for another five minutes over medium heat. Add the cooked dal, mix well, and simmer for another three minutes, then remove the pan from the stove.

Heat the oil in a skillet, and add the mustard seeds. When the mustard seeds start sputtering, add the halved red chili pepper, fenugreek seeds, asafetida, and curry leaves. Remove it from the stove, and pour it over the *pulinkari*. Garnish with thinly chopped cilantro leaves. Cover and set aside for ten minutes, to allow flavors to blend. Serve hot with plain boiled rice.

Makes 4 to 6 servings if served with another curry, as is traditional.

Vazuthaninga Varutharacha Kootan: Eggplant in Spicy Toasted-Coconut Sauce

When the summer heat fades the appetite, the lively flavors of coriander, mustard, tamarind, curry leaves, and cayenne can certainly whet it. Eggplant is a vegetable that maintains its individuality while mixing well with a blend of spices. Cubed eggplant is first panfried in oil and then simmered in a spicy toasted-coconut sauce. This may not be one of the most visually appealing dishes, but hidden within the thick, brown toasted-coconut puree are the hardy flavors of eggplant infused with a hint of toasted coriander and hot red chili pepper.

Long, thin Japanese eggplants or the small, bulb-shaped Indian eggplants are the preferred varieties for this curry. Regular large eggplant has a slightly bitter taste. When this variety is used, place the cubed eggplant in a colander set on a plate or in the kitchen sink, sprinkle on a teaspoon of salt, place a heavy pot over the eggplant, and let it sit for about thirty minutes to allow the bitter juices to drip out. Then proceed with the recipe below.

1½ tablespoons vegetable oil
1 cup freshly grated coconut
    or ¾ cup dry, unsweetened coconut flakes
1 tablespoon coriander seeds
4 to 6 dried red cayenne, serrano, or Thai chilies (less for a milder taste)
2 cups eggplant, cut into one-inch cubes

Salt to taste
½ teaspoon turmeric powder
1 teaspoon tamarind concentrate

For seasoning and garnish:
1 tablespoon vegetable oil
1 teaspoon mustard seeds
1 dried red cayenne, serrano, or Thai chili, halved
12 to 15 fresh curry leaves

Heat half a tablespoon of the oil in a heavy skillet over medium heat, and fry the coconut flakes until they begin to turn golden brown. Add the coriander seeds and the red chili pepper to the fried coconut, and stir well. Fry for another two to three minutes, until the coriander seeds are well toasted. Remove from the stove, and let it cool to room temperature. Transfer to a blender, and grind with just enough water to make a very smooth, thick puree.

Heat a tablespoon of the oil in a saucepan over low to medium heat, and panfry the eggplant pieces until they are slightly browned at the edges. Panfrying will keep them from becoming mushy when they are cooked. Sprinkle on the salt and the turmeric, and stir well.

Add the spicy coconut puree to the fried eggplant. Add another cup of water and bring to a boil, then reduce the heat, and simmer for approximately five to six minutes. Stir in the tamarind concentrate, and cook for another five minutes before removing the pan from the stove. This curry will be fairly thick.

Heat the remaining oil in a skillet, and add the mustard seeds. When the mustard seeds start sputtering, add the halved red chili pepper and curry leaves. Remove from the stove, and pour over the curry. Cover and set aside for ten minutes, to allow the flavors to blend. Serve hot with plain boiled rice. This curry also goes well with any kind of warm flatbread, such as pita bread or Indian tandoori bread, which is available in Indian grocery stores as well as in some supermarkets.

Makes 4 to 6 servings if served with another curry, as is traditional.

Variation: Panfry a cup of thinly sliced onion until the edges begin to brown. Combine with toasted coconut and spices, and grind to make the puree. Follow the recipe above.

Paavakka Varutharacha Kootan: Bitter Gourd in Spicy Toasted-Coconut Sauce

Bitter gourd or bitter melon is a popular vegetable in Indian and Chinese cuisine. It is believed to contain chemicals that help control diabetes. This plant-based cure has no side effects, and diabetic patients in India consume this vegetable whenever it is available.

In this bitter-melon curry, the bitterness of the vegetable is tamed with a combination of the tartness tamarind and the sweetness of shallots (or onions). As the name suggests, bitter melons have a strong, bitter taste. To mellow the flavor, the pieces of bitter melon are cooked with salt and turmeric for five minutes and drained.

5 or 6 medium-sized bitter gourds (or Chinese bitter melons)
Salt to taste
½ teaspoon turmeric powder
2 tablespoons vegetable oil
1 cup freshly grated coconut
    or ¾ cup dried, unsweetened coconut flakes
1 tablespoon coriander seeds
4 dried red cayenne, serrano, or Thai chilies (less for a milder taste)
1 cup thinly sliced shallots or onions
1 teaspoon tamarind concentrate mixed with a cup of water

For seasoning and garnish:
1 tablespoon vegetable oil
1 teaspoon mustard seeds
1 dried red cayenne, serrano, or Thai chili, halved
12 to 15 fresh curry leaves

Wash and cut the bitter melons into thin rounds. In a saucepan, bring two cups of water to a boil. Add the sliced bitter melon, salt, and turmeric, and cook for five minutes, then drain.

Heat one tablespoon of oil in a heavy skillet over medium heat, and fry the grated coconut flakes until they begin to turn golden brown. Add the coriander seeds and red chili pepper to the skillet, and stir well. Fry for another two to three minutes, until the coriander seeds are well toasted. Remove from the stove, and let it cool. Heat half a tablespoon of oil in a small skillet, and panfry the shallots or onions until they are slightly browned. Combine with toasted coconut and spices, and grind with just enough water to make a very smooth, thick puree.

Heat half a tablespoon of oil in a heavy saucepan, and panfry the cooked bitter melon pieces for three to four minutes. Add the spicy coconut puree, salt, and a cup of water, and stir gently. Bring it to a boil, then reduce the heat and simmer for six to eight minutes. Stir in the tamarind, and cook for another five minutes.

To make the garnish, heat the oil in a skillet, and add the mustard seeds. When the mustard seeds start sputtering, add the halved red chili pepper and curry leaves. Remove it from the stove, and pour it over the curry. This curry will be fairly thick. Cover and set aside for ten minutes, to allow the flavors to blend. Serve hot with plain boiled rice.

Makes 4 to 6 servings if served with another curry, as is traditional.

Koottu Curry: Butternut Squash and *Chana* Dal in a Coconut-Cumin Sauce

The humble summer squash, bathed in a nutty, mildly spiced coconut sauce, often appears as a second curry during summer lunches. This is another curry prepared with several different summer vegetables. Yam, green plantain, Indian pumpkin, snake gourd, and ash gourd are some of the vegetables traditionally used in preparing *koottu* curry. The following recipe uses the readily available butternut squash.

½ cup *chana* dal
1 teaspoon turmeric powder
½ tablespoon vegetable oil
2 tablespoons *urad* dal
6 dried red cayenne, serrano, or Thai chilies (less for a milder taste)
¾ cup freshly grated coconut
3 teaspoons cumin seeds
Half of a butternut squash, peeled, seeded, and cut into half-inch cubes
Salt to taste

For seasoning and garnish:
1 tablespoon vegetable oil
1 teaspoon mustard seeds
1 dried red cayenne, serrano, or Thai chili, halved
12 to 15 fresh curry leaves

Wash and clean the *chana* dal in several changes of water until the water runs clear. In a saucepan, bring the dal, half a teaspoon of turmeric powder, and two cups of water to a boil over medium heat. Lower the heat and simmer, stirring occasionally, for twenty to twenty-five minutes, or until the dal is tender. The dal should be well cooked but not mashed. Remove it from the stove, and set it aside.

Heat half a tablespoon of oil in a heavy skillet, add the *urad* dal and red chili peppers, and panfry until the dal is slightly browned. Turn off the heat, and stir in the coconut and the cumin seeds, then remove it from the stove. When it has cooled, grind it into a smooth thick puree.

Bring two cups of water to a boil in a saucepan. Add the squash cubes, half a teaspoon of turmeric powder, and salt. Reduce the heat, and cook until the squash is fork tender. Transfer the cooked dal to the pot, and stir gently. Simmer for two to three minutes. Stir in the coconut-spice puree, and mix well. Cook for another five minutes over medium heat.

For the garnish, heat the oil in a skillet, and add the mustard seeds. When the mustard seeds start sputtering, add the halved red chili pepper and curry leaves. Remove it from the stove, and pour it over the curry. This curry is fairly thick. Cover and set aside for ten minutes, to allow the flavors to blend. Serve hot with plain boiled rice.

Makes 4 to 6 servings if served with another curry, as is traditional.

Cheera Udachathu: Spicy Mashed Spinach

During summer holidays when I was a child, I always woke up at the crack of dawn to the loud calls of street vendors selling vegetables. Their call was almost like a song. "*Vendakka, pacha mulagu, thakkali, padavalanga, cheeraiii!*" ("Okra, green chilies, tomatoes, snake gourd, spinach"—they always lengthened the name of the last vegetable.) It was fun watching our cook bargain with the vendor for another handful of green chilies. Some extra curry leaves were always thrown in as a bonus. Our cook used to turn simple spinach into this delicious side dish for lunch. The fragrance of fenugreek seeds roasting in an iron wok over wooden logs filled the house.

Cheera udachathu is literally "mashed spinach." Toasted fenugreek seeds impart a pleasant aroma to this dish.

2 large bunches of fresh spinach leaves
    or 2 ten-ounce packages of frozen chopped spinach
½ teaspoon turmeric powder
Salt to taste

For seasoning and garnish:
1 teaspoon fenugreek seeds
2 tablespoons vegetable oil
1 teaspoon mustard seeds
1 teaspoon *urad* dal
2 dried red cayenne, serrano, or Thai chilies, halved
12 to 15 fresh curry leaves

Wash the spinach leaves, and cut them into fine strips. Bring one-quarter cup of water to a boil in a saucepan. Reduce the heat, and add the spinach to the pan. Sprinkle it with salt and turmeric, and cook over medium heat. Spinach leaves contain plenty of water. When cooked, it should be a thick mass. Drain the excess water, and let the spinach cool, then run it through a food processor to make a thick, smooth puree.

In a skillet, toast the fenugreek seeds over medium heat. (Dry roasting enhances the flavor and reduces the bitterness of fenugreek seeds. Fenugreek needs close attention while toasting; it turns reddish brown and tastes very bitter when over-roasted.) Using a mortar and pestle, crush it into a coarse powder.

Heat the oil in a skillet, and add the mustard seeds. When the mustard seeds start sputtering, add the *urad* dal, the halved chili peppers and the curry leaves, and fry until the dal turns golden. Transfer the mashed spinach to the skillet. Sprinkle the toasted fenugreek powder on top, mix well, and cook for another minute or two. Cover and set aside for ten minutes, to allow flavors to blend. Serve hot with plain boiled rice.

Makes 4 to 6 servings if served with another curry, as is traditional.

Maampaza Pachadi: Ripe Mangoes in a Coconut and Mustard Sauce

During summer in Kerala, mangoes turn up in some form in just about every meal. This simple curry is easy to prepare and very tasty.

2 ripe mangoes
Salt to taste
½ teaspoon turmeric powder
3 cups freshly grated coconut
4 fresh green chilies (serrano or Thai) (less for a milder taste)
½ teaspoon mustard seeds
1½ cups yogurt

For seasoning and garnish:
2 tablespoons coconut oil (or vegetable oil)
12 to 15 fresh curry leaves

Wash and peel the mangoes. Cut them into medium-sized cubes. In a saucepan, combine the mango pieces with a cup of water. Add salt and turmeric, and cook over medium heat for five to six minutes.

Meanwhile, grind the coconut, green chilies, and mustard seeds with half a cup of yogurt to make a thick, smooth puree. Stir the puree into the cooking mango pieces, and simmer for five minutes. Beat the remaining yogurt with a large spoon to make a smooth, thick liquid. Pour this over the mango pieces. When the liquid in the pot starts bubbling, remove it from the stove. Pour the oil into the *pachadi* and garnish with curry leaves. Stir gently, cover, and set aside for ten minutes, to allow flavors to blend. Serve hot with plain boiled rice.

Makes 4 to 6 servings if served with another curry, as is traditional.

Kadachakka Masalakkari: Breadfruit in Spicy Coconut Sauce

Breadfruit, a Portuguese contribution to our cuisine, is not a fruit in the popular sense of the term. It is cylindrical in shape, with a green skin and a white, somewhat fibrous pulp. It contains a considerable amount of starch, and it is seldom eaten raw. It is available fresh in Latin American grocery stores and sometimes in Indian stores. Peeled and cubed frozen pieces of breadfruit are available at Indian grocery stores. In this curry, a combination of assertive seasonings gives the breadfruit an enticing aroma.

1 medium-sized breadfruit, peeled and cut into one-inch cubes
½ teaspoon turmeric powder
Salt to taste
½ tablespoon vegetable oil
½ cup thinly sliced shallots **or** ½ cup thinly chopped onions
2 cup freshly grated coconut
1 tablespoon coriander seeds
8 dried red cayenne, serrano, or Thai chilies (less for a milder taste)
1 teaspoon cloves
1 small stick of cinnamon

For seasoning and garnish:
12 to 15 fresh curry leaves
2 tablespoons vegetable oil

Place the breadfruit pieces in a saucepan, and pour in just enough water to cover them. Sprinkle with turmeric powder and salt, and cook over medium heat until the vegetable is fork tender.

Heat half a tablespoon of oil in a skillet, and panfry the chopped shallots or onions. When they start to turn slightly brown, remove them from the skillet to a plate, and set it aside. Add the coconut to the same skillet, and fry it until the coconut flakes are golden brown in color. Add coriander seeds and red chili peppers to the coconut flakes, and fry until the spices are well toasted. Remove from the stove.

Dry roast the cloves and cinnamon in a skillet for two to three minutes, and add them to the toasted coconut and spices. Using a blender, grind the shallots (or onions), spices, and coconut to a very smooth thick puree.

Add the puree to the cooked breadfruit pieces, and mix well. If it appears to be very thick, add a little water and stir well. Cook for six to eight minutes over medium heat, then remove it from the stove. Pour in two tablespoons of oil, and add the curry leaves. Cover and set aside for ten minutes, to allow the flavors to blend. Serve hot with plain boiled rice.

Makes 4 to 6 servings if served with another curry, as is traditional.

Vellarikka Tharichathu: Cucumbers in a Mustard and Coconut Sauce

There is practically no effort in putting together this crunchy, cool salad—a refreshing side dish at a summer lunch or brunch. But there are two requirements: the cucumber should be crisp and tender, and the yogurt must be fresh. This salad is subtly seasoned with mustard seeds and fresh green chilies.

1 small, tender cucumber, peeled and seeded
1 teaspoon mustard seeds
1½ cups freshly grated coconut
3 or 4 fresh green chilies (serrano or Thai) (less for a milder taste)
Salt to taste
1 cup yogurt

For seasoning and garnish:
1 tablespoon vegetable oil
½ teaspoons mustard seeds
1 dried red cayenne, serrano, or Thai chili, halved
12 to 15 fresh curry leaves

Cut the cucumber into very small pieces. Sprinkle them with salt, and put them in a large sieve to drain. Grind the coconut, with one teaspoon of mustard seeds and the green chilies, to a fine, thick puree. Combine it with the yogurt, and stir well.

Heat the oil in a saucepan, and add the mustard seeds. When the mustard seeds start sputtering, add the halved chili pepper and the curry leaves. A minute later, stir in the coconut yogurt sauce, and simmer over medium heat. When it just starts bubbling, remove it from the stove. Add the cucumber pieces to the sauce, and stir gently. Cover and set aside for ten minutes, to allow the flavors to blend.

Makes 4 to 6 servings if served with another curry, as is traditional.

Monsoon Treats

For me, monsoon is a word that stirs up many fond memories of growing up in Kerala. Monsoon mornings bring an invigorating smell of damp earth, budding leaves, washed streets, knee-deep water, crisp air, and dark, ominous clouds rolling across the sky. Every morning, we woke up at dawn to the sound of rainwater gushing through the drains into the inner courtyard.

The arrival of monsoon clouds over the Arabian Sea is an eagerly awaited event. After the dry spell of summer, the muggy air becomes unbearable. The sun baked dry earth give off heat. The parched earth seems to call out for the first drop of rain. And then, one day, the unbearable wait comes to an end.

Accompanied by howling winds and rumbling thunder, torrential rains break a lengthy spell of scorching temperatures. Monsoon rain is no ordinary heavy downpour. Gusts of wind blow away everything in their path. The tranquil sea becomes a restless pool of water. Loud thunder, bright streaks of lightning, blowing winds, and swaying coconut palms all add to the spectacle. The most spectacular clouds and rain occur against the Sahyaadri mountain range, where the early monsoonal airstream piles up against the steep slopes, then recedes and piles up again to a greater height. Each time, it pushes thicker clouds upward, until the wind and clouds roll over the barrier and, after a few brief spells of absorption by the dry inland air, cascade toward the interior. The monsoon season stretches from June through mid-August.

When the monsoon was late, farmers in my hometown performed a ritual, pleading to God to bring rain to the rice fields. Rainfall is crucial to the cultivation of rice, and a drought meant famine. The farmers believed that rain did not fall because the village was home to a sinner. A gigantic human form—*Kodumpaavi* (ultimate sinner)—was made of rice straw, and a thick rope was attached to it. Several people pulled this symbol of the evil person around the streets, while others accompanied them singing a song, pleading for rainfall: "*Kodumpaavi chakaathe koda mazza peyyathe.*" This roughly translates to: "The sinner is not dead, and the rain is not falling. Please take him away and give us rain." And sure enough, when it rained in a couple of days (as it always does in this tropical climate), the farmers firmly believed that their ritual had brought the rain.

Rice cultivation begins with the onset of the rainy season, and seedlings need more water to ensure a good harvest. The climatic shift in the elements is considered to be nothing less than a holy event, and many rituals are observed to propitiate the gods. We welcome Sridevi, goddess of plenty and prosperity, to our midst. On the last day of the month of Midhunam in the lunar calendar (mid-July), houses get a thorough cleaning: floors are scrubbed and mopped, cobwebs are cleared, and furniture is dusted. In days past, towards dusk, one of our maidservants, with a pail of trash in hand, would walk out of the front door of our home. We children accompanied her, shouting, "*Chetta purathu poo, Sridevi akathuvaa!*" ("Let all the dirt and evil go out the door, and let cleanliness and goodness come inside!" My mother or aunt walked behind her, sprinkling handfuls of water on the floor, performing a symbolic purification ritual.

From the next day onward, a special place was set up in our prayer room to honor the goddess. Every day before dawn, the goddess was invoked and worshipped. My mother decorated a wooden plank symbolizing the goddess with sandalwood paste, bright red *kumkumam* powder, and garlands of seasonal yellow *mukkutti* flowers and dark-green *karuka* grass. Among the lighted bronze oil lamps and platters of fruits and flowers rested a silver bowl filled with *nivedyam* (popped rice mixed with fresh coconut and brown sugar), to propitiate the goddess. The delicate fragrance of burning sandalwood incense sticks and the distinct scent of lighted camphor cubes, enveloping the whole house. Throughout the month of Karkitakam (mid-July to mid-August), at sundown, Hindu homes reverberate with readings from the epic *Ramayana*.

The dark days of monsoon are also a time for ancestral remembrance. On Karkitaka *vaavu* (new moon), special prayers are offered in memory of deceased ancestors. In the belief systems of the East, fasting (or at least depriving the body of certain luxury foods) is considered a means of achieving a higher state of consciousness. In my childhood, a symbolic observation of this belief was practiced on every new moon, especially on new moons during the monsoon season, by serving only *kanji* (rice soup) instead of cooked rice.

In stark contrast to summer's abundance, hardly any vegetable grows in our monsoon-flooded soil. Preparing meals during this season is a challenge and a true test of the ingenuity of the vegetarian cook. Several root vegetables (which have longer shelf lives than fresh vegetables), edible leaves, and various kinds of dried beans are the mainstays of the vegetarian kitchen during this season. The use of frozen or canned vegetables is not popular in our part of the world. All of the drying and preserving done during the summer months also come in handy. On the first Tuesday and Friday of the month of Karkitakam, two special dishes, *thalu kootan* and *chuttathu,* are prepared for the royal family. Spicy, hot shallot soup and Indian garbanzo beans cooked in coconut and coriander sauce are some of the monsoon season favorites in our village.

Urulakkizangu Stew: Potato Stew

The base of this curry is fresh coconut milk, an ingredient most prevalent in Thai and Malaysian dishes. Don't be misled by the word "stew"—this is definitely not a stew in the western sense of the word. This is one curry that can be made practically mild; it was probably served to the British during their long stay in India. I wonder whether the British christened it "stew."

3 or 4 medium-sized potatoes, peeled and cut into cubes
3 or 4 fresh green chilies (serrano or Thai), cut lengthwise into thin strips (less for a milder taste)
2 tablespoons freshly grated ginger
Salt to taste
6 cups fresh thin coconut milk*
1 cup fresh thick coconut milk**

For seasoning and garnish:
2 tablespoons coconut oil or ghee
20 to 25 fresh curry leaves

Place the potatoes, green chilies, and ginger in a saucepan, and pour in the thin coconut milk. Sprinkle with salt, and cook over medium-low heat until potatoes are fork tender, approximately eight to ten minutes. Coconut milk should be always simmered, not boiled. When boiled, it has a tendency to separate. Stir in the thick coconut milk, reduce the heat to low, and bring it to a simmer. Remove it from the stove, add the curry leaves, and stir in the coconut oil. Keep it covered for ten minutes before serving. This allows the stew to absorb the flavors of the coconut oil and curry leaves.

Makes 4 to 6 servings if served with another curry, as is traditional.

Variation: This is the way potato stew is prepared at our house. For a change, add about two cups of thinly sliced onions to the potatoes when cooking.

*Coconut milk is prepared by grating fresh coconut and squeezing the thick coconut milk from it. Then sprinkle a few handfuls of water over the coconut flakes and squeeze out the thin coconut milk.

**For ease of use, you may substitute with canned coconut milk, available in most supermarkets. As an easy alternative, I prefer using coconut milk powder. By adjusting the quantity of water added, you can make thick or thin coconut milk using the powder. Coconut milk powder is available in Southeast Asian and Indian grocery stores.

As a last resort, use heavy cream as a substitute for thick coconut milk and whole milk as a substitute for thin coconut milk. However, this last version will definitely lack the flavor of coconut.

Brown Stew: Potatoes in Spicy Coconut Milk

This spicy potato curry in coconut milk is a specialty of my cousin's wife, Narayani B. Menon. The sauce is a delicious combination of a smooth béchamel-textured coconut milk with the intense flavors of the tropical south—ginger, shallots, cloves, cinnamon, and curry leaves. This curry is usually served with the breakfast dishes *vellayappam* and *dosa*. Its myriad flavors also mingle well with warm, fluffy rice.

4 medium potatoes, peeled and cut into large cubes
2 tablespoons freshly grated ginger
4 fresh green chilies (serrano or Thai), cut lengthwise into thin strips (less for a mild taste)
6 cups fresh thin coconut milk*
Salt to taste
1 teaspoon vegetable oil

2 medium onions, chopped **or** 1 cup thinly chopped shallots
1 one- inch piece of cinnamon
1 teaspoon cloves
1 tablespoon coriander seeds
6 dried red cayenne, serrano, or Thai chilies (reduce for a mild taste)
1 cup thick coconut milk**

For seasoning and garnish:
20 to 25 fresh curry leaves
2 tablespoons coconut oil or ghee

Place the potatoes ginger, and green chilies in a saucepan, and pour in the thin coconut milk. Sprinkle with salt, and cook over medium heat until the potatoes are fork tender, approximately eight to ten minutes. Coconut milk should be always simmered, not boiled.

While the potatoes are cooking, heat the teaspoon of oil in a heavy skillet, and fry the onions until they turn golden brown. Add cinnamon, cloves, coriander seeds, and red chili peppers, and fry for two more minutes. Remove the mixture from the stove, and let it cool. Using a blender, grind the fried spices and onions with just enough water to make a thick, smooth puree. Add the puree to the potatoes cooking in coconut milk, and stir. Simmer over low heat for five minutes. Stir in the thick coconut milk, bring it to a simmer, and remove from the stove. Garnish with the fresh curry leaves and coconut oil or ghee. Keep it covered for ten minutes to allow the flavors of the coconut oil and curry leaves to blend.

Makes 4 to 6 servings if served with another curry, as is traditional.

*Coconut milk is prepared by grating fresh coconut and squeezing the thick coconut milk from it. Then sprinkle a few handfuls of water over the coconut flakes and squeeze out the thin coconut milk.

**For ease of use, you may substitute with canned coconut milk, which is available in most supermarkets. As an easy alternative, I prefer using coconut milk powder. By adjusting the quantity of water added, you can make thick or thin coconut milk using the powder. Coconut milk powder is available in Southeast Asian and Indian grocery stores.

As a last resort, use heavy cream as a substitute for thick coconut milk and whole milk as a substitute for thin coconut milk. However, this last version will definitely lack the flavor of coconut.

Kadalakari: Spicy Chickpea Curry

This spicy Indian brown chickpea curry is generally served with the breakfast dish *puttu*. It also goes well with any type of flatbread. Garbanzo beans may be substituted for Indian brown chickpeas.

2 cups Indian brown chickpeas
½ teaspoon turmeric
½ tablespoon vegetable oil
1 cup freshly grated coconut
1 tablespoon coriander seeds
5 or 6 dried red cayenne, serrano, or Thai chilies (or less for a milder taste)
Salt to taste

For seasoning and garnish:
1 tablespoon vegetable oil
1 teaspoon mustard seeds
1 dried red cayenne, serrano, or Thai chili, halved
¼ teaspoon asafetida powder (optional)
12 to 15 fresh curry leaves
1 tablespoon finely chopped cilantro leaves

Soak chickpeas overnight in plenty of water. Rinse in several changes of water until the water runs clear, and drain. Place the chickpeas in a saucepan with four cups water and the turmeric powder, and bring it to a boil over medium-high heat. Cook until the chickpeas are very tender, approximately fifty minutes to one hour. Alternatively, you may cook the chickpeas in a pressure cooker (following the manufacturer's instructions) for six to eight minutes to speed up the process.

Heat half a tablespoon of the oil in a skillet over medium heat, and fry the grated coconut, stirring constantly, until it turns golden brown. Add the coriander seeds and red pepper, and fry for another minute or two. Remove from the stove, and let it cool. In a blender, grind the coconut and spices with just enough water to make a thick, smooth puree. If there is excess water in the chickpeas, drain some of it. When the spice puree is stirred in, the curry should be fairly thick. Combine the spice puree and the chickpeas, add salt to taste, and simmer for six to eight minutes.

Heat oil in a skillet, and add the mustard seeds. When the mustard seeds start sputtering, add the halved red chili pepper, asafetida, and curry leaves. Remove it from the stove, and pour it over the *kadalakari*. Garnish with thinly chopped cilantro leaves. Cover and set aside for ten minutes, to allow flavors to blend. Serve hot with *puttu* or plain boiled rice.

Makes 4 to 6 servings if served with another curry, as is traditional.

Variation: Instead of using asafetida, substitute with half a cup of finely chopped onions that have been browned in a teaspoon of oil.

Easy versions: Instead of making the fresh spice puree, add two tablespoons of *sambar* powder, which is available in Indian grocery stores, to the cooked chickpeas, and continue with the remaining steps of the recipe. An even easier version is to use canned chickpeas. Rinse the canned chickpeas under cold running water and drain them before proceeding with the remaining steps of the recipe.

Kurumulaku Rasam: Black Pepper Soup

Although black pepper grows abundantly in our part of the world, it is used only sparingly in our cuisine. Black pepper enticed many foreign traders to our shores, but we prefer using the fiery red chili pepper the Portuguese introduced to us. This is one of the rare recipes that uses black pepper.

1 teaspoon tamarind concentrate
Salt to taste
½ teaspoon turmeric powder
2 tablespoons black peppercorns
1 tablespoon cumin seeds
1 cup curry leaves
1 tablespoon vegetable oil
2 medium-sized tomatoes, seeded and cubed
3 fresh green chilies (serrano or Thai), cut into thin strips (less for a milder taste)

For seasoning and garnish:
1 tablespoon thinly chopped fresh cilantro leaves

In a saucepan, mix the tamarind concentrate with three cups of water, add salt and turmeric powder, and bring it to a boil. Reduce the heat, and simmer for five minutes.

Using a mortar and pestle or a food processor, crush the peppercorns, cumin seeds, and curry leaves. Heat the oil in a heavy skillet over medium heat, and fry the crushed ingredients for three to four minutes. Add the cubed tomato and green chili strips, and fry for another minute or two. Transfer the contents of the skillet to the simmering tamarind water, and stir well. Simmer for five minutes. Remove it from the stove, and garnish it with chopped cilantro leaves. Cover and set aside for ten minutes, to allow flavors to blend. Serve hot as a soup or with boiled plain rice and *pappadams*.

Makes 4 to 6 servings if served with another curry, as is traditional.

Variation: Cut a medium-sized onion into thin pieces, fry it in a teaspoon of oil, and stir it into the soup.

Mulaku Varutha Puli: Onions and Green Chilies in Spicy Tamarind Sauce

This aromatic, brownish broth crowded with bits of panfried shallots and green chilies is a monsoon season curry traditionally served with rice. Accompanied by deep-fried *pappadams* or any type of flatbread, it makes a delicious, warming winter soup—a South Indian version of onion soup.

2 tablespoons vegetable oil
2 cups finely chopped shallots or onions
6 fresh green chilies (serrano or Thai), thinly sliced (less for a milder taste)
½ teaspoon turmeric
Salt to taste
1 tablespoon tamarind concentrate

For seasoning and garnish:
1 tablespoon oil
1 teaspoon mustard seeds
1 dried red cayenne, serrano, or Thai chili, halved
12 to 15 fresh curry leaves

Heat two tablespoons of oil in a skillet. Add the shallots and green chilies, and fry over medium heat for six to eight minutes, until the shallots are slightly browned. Add turmeric and salt, and stir well. While the shallots are browning, dissolve the tamarind concentrate in three cups of water. Add the tamarind liquid to the fried ingredients, and cook for ten minutes over medium heat. Remove it from the stove, and set it aside.

Heat one tablespoon of oil in a skillet, and add the mustard seeds. When the mustard seeds start sputtering, add the halved chili pepper and the curry leaves. Remove it from the stove, and pour it over the curry. Cover and set aside for ten minutes, to allow the flavors to blend. Serve hot, as soup or with rice.

Makes 4 to 6 servings if served with another curry, as is traditional.

Uppuparippu: Mung Dal with Fresh Green Chilies and Curry Leaves

There is something inviting about the earthy aroma and wholesome taste of gently simmered mung beans. This hardy mung dal curry, flavored with green chilies and curry leaves, is a staple during the monsoon season. It is protein rich and very easy to prepare.

2 cups split mung dal with skin
½ teaspoon turmeric powder
4 or 5 fresh green chilies (serrano or Thai) (less for a milder taste)
Salt to taste

For seasoning and garnish:
12 to 15 fresh curry leaves
2 tablespoons vegetable oil

In a heavy skillet, dry roast the dal until it is golden. Then wash and clean it in several changes of water, until the water runs clear, and drain well. Heat four cups of water in a saucepan. Stir in the toasted mung dal and the turmeric, and cook over medium heat. Cut the green chilies lengthwise into thin strips, and add them to the cooking dal. Stir periodically to make sure that the dal does not stick to the bottom of the pan. By the time it is fully cooked, there should be very little water left in the pot. If it becomes too dry, add some more water. When it is well cooked, add salt, stir well, then remove it from the stove. Garnish with curry leaves and oil. Cover and set aside for ten minutes, to allow the flavors to blend. Serve hot with rice and ghee.

Makes 4 to 6 servings if served with another curry, as is traditional.

Mathan Puzukku: Pumpkin and Red Beans with Coconut and Curry Leaves

Puzukku is a thick curry made with lots of fresh coconut, beans, and vegetables. It is usually served with our rice soup, *kanji*. It is prepared with a variety of vegetables and beans: green plantains, ash gourd, pumpkins, fresh black-eyed peas in pods, red beans, and mung beans. The following recipe uses pumpkin and red beans. Butternut squash makes an ideal substitute for Indian pumpkin.

1 cup small red beans
1 teaspoon turmeric powder
1 medium-sized butternut squash
Salt to taste
2 or 3 fresh green chilies (serrano or Thai) (less for a milder taste)

For seasoning and garnish:
2 cups freshly grated coconut
12 to 15 fresh curry leaves
2 tablespoons coconut oil

Soak red beans for eight hours (or overnight), then wash them in several changes of water until the water runs clear. Bring three cups of water to a boil in a saucepan. Add the red beans and a half-teaspoon of turmeric, and cook over medium heat. Reduce the heat to medium, and cook until the beans are very soft to the touch and can be easily mashed between two fingers (approximately forty to fifty minutes). If necessary, add more water and continue cooking until they are soft. Alternatively, the beans may be cooked in a pressure cooker (following the manufacturer's directions) for six to eight minutes.

Peel the squash, and cut into two-inch long pieces (like for french fries). When the beans are almost cooked, add the squash pieces, the remaining turmeric, and salt, and cook over medium heat. Stir to make sure that the curry does not stick to the bottom of the pot. Slice the green chilies lengthwise into thin strips, and add them to the pot. When the squash is cooked (about five minutes), remove it from the stove, and sprinkle on grated coconut and curry leaves. Pour coconut oil on top. Cover and set aside for ten minutes, to allow the flavors to blend. Serve with *kanji* or plain boiled rice.

Makes 4 to 6 servings if served with another curry, as is traditional.

Variations:

Puzukku **with green plantains, telinga potatoes *(suran)*, and fresh black-eyed peas in pods**

½ cup whole mung beans
½ teaspoon turmeric powder
2 green plantains
1 cup telinga potatoes, cut into one-inch pieces
1 cup black-eyed peas in pods, cut into one-inch pieces
2 fresh green chilies (serrano or Thai), cut into thin strips (less for a milder taste)
Salt to taste

For seasoning and garnish:
2 cups freshly grated coconut
12 to 15 fresh curry leaves
2 tablespoons coconut oil

Soak the mung beans for eight hours (or overnight), then wash them in several changes of water until the water runs clear. Bring three cups of water to a boil in a saucepan. Add the mung beans and a half-teaspoon of turmeric, and cook over medium heat until the mung beans are soft. Add more water if necessary.

Peel the green plantains, and cut them into one-inch pieces. In a saucepan, heat three cups of water, and add the plantain cubes, telinga potatoes, black-eyed peas, and green chilies, along with salt and turmeric. Cook over medium heat until the vegetables are fork tender. Add the cooked mung beans to the saucepan and stir gently, then remove it from the heat. Add the grated coconut and the curry leaves, and pour coconut oil on top. Cover and set aside for ten minutes, to allow the flavors to blend. Serve with *kanji* or plain boiled rice.

When using canned telinga potatoes *(suran)*, first open the can and drain them. Rinse the vegetable cubes under cold running water, and drain again. As they are already cooked, add to the pot after the plantains are cooked.

Puzzukku with Jackfruit

2 cups green jackfruit segments, cut into pieces*
Salt to taste
½ teaspoon turmeric powder
½ teaspoon dry cayenne, serrano, or Thai chili powder (less for a milder taste)
1 cup freshly grated coconut
3 or 4 fresh green chilies (serrano or Thai) (less for a milder taste)
1 teaspoon cumin seeds

For seasoning and garnish:
12 to 15 fresh curry leaves
2 tablespoons coconut oil

In a saucepan, bring one cup of water to a boil, and add the jackfruit segments, salt, turmeric, and red pepper powder. The water should just cover the vegetables. Roughly grind the coconut, green chilies, and cumin seeds in a blender to a thick, coarse puree. When the jackfruit is cooked, stir in the ground coconut, and bring it to a boil. Reduce the heat, and simmer for three to four minutes before removing the pan from the stove. Add the coconut oil and curry leaves. Cover and set aside for ten minutes, to allow the flavors to blend. Serve with *kanji* or plain boiled rice.

*Canned green jackfruit pieces are readily available in Indian, Chinese, and Thai food stores. When using canned jackfruit, first open the can and drain the liquid. Wash the jackfruit under running water, then drain again. As these pieces are already partially cooked, the cooking time should be reduced.

Curries from the *Madapilli* (Royal Kitchen)

Culinary traditions and cherished family recipes are prized possessions in every society. The best Indian dishes are never found in restaurants. Maybe this is because we are not by tradition (or preference) avid restaurant goers. It is in private homes that you find the most varied dishes, treasured family recipes, and traditional formalities about serving food. Some of the simplest and tastiest curries come from the royal kitchens of Kochi—but please don't let the title misled you.

Words such as "royal kitchen" invoke visions of elaborate, multi-course feasts. The following recipes are not by any means fancy, nor do they call for exotic ingredients. The food habits of the Cochin royal family are quite unassuming. They prefer tasteful, simple vegetarian meals prepared with local ingredients, served on banana leaves, and eaten by hand. In the old days, cooking in a *madapilli* was done by either Namboodiris (Kerala Brahmans) or Brahmans from the neighboring states of Tamil Nadu or Karnataka; the influence of their cuisines is clearly reflected in these recipes. Most of them require only a few ingredients and are very easy to prepare.

My paternal grandfather was a maharaja of Kochi, but he passed away before I was born. After my father's demise, I grew up in my mother's matrilineal Nayar family. My personal experience with the royal family really began after my marriage; my father-in-law was also from the royal family. My earliest memory of a meal from a *madapilli* is still fresh in my memory.

Within a few months after marriage, I was to attend a birthday feast at the *kovilakam* (palace) of my husband's grandmother. It was my father-in-law's birthday. It was also the birthday of his older sister and his mother.

My mother gave me a briefing on the proper etiquette when one visits a *kovilakam*. "When you go there for lunch," Mom said seriously, "remember to hold the water glass high and pour the water into your mouth. Don't let the glass touch your lips. Don't talk while you are eating, and do not forget to fold the banana leaf in half when you finish eating." The list went on.

Honestly, by the time I put down the telephone, I was a nervous wreck. As we walked in the front gate, my husband's *achaama* (father's mother) came out, smiling, to welcome us—a slim, tiny figure dressed in freshly laundered white cotton clothes. We sat around the several huge pillars, each about two feet in diameter, that stood tall and firm on the portico of the *kovilakam*. From there, we could see bright red hibiscus and purple bougainvillea flowers swaying in the breeze.

When it was time for lunch, we were ushered into a room adjacent to the *madapilli*, a bare dining room with terra cotta-tiled floors and whitewashed walls. The plain dining table and chairs were pushed into a corner. We sat down cross-legged on the mats, which were spread on the floor. A huge banana leaf, laden with various vegetable dishes, was spread in front of each person. At the tapered end of each banana leaf were deep-fried puffed wafers called *pappadams* and small piles of salted *varuthupperi* and sweet *sarkara upperi*, both plantain chips. A couple of servings of spicy hot pickles hid under the *pappadams*. On one half of the leaf were servings of vegetables—*thoran, oolan, aviyal, pachadi,* and *kaalan*—and a thick brown curry with the distinct fragrance of black sesame seeds and curry leaves. That was *ellukari*, a specialty of the palace kitchen: mildly hot, sour, and sweet. Once everyone was seated, there came servings of rice, followed by *sambar* and then *rasam*. After the *rasam* course, we had to practically clean that half of the leaf with our fingers to get ready for the *pantheeraazi paayasam*, a special rice pudding offered at the temple. Bits of *pappadam* and morsels of spicy *puliingi* (ginger pickle) were nibbled along with the *paayasam* to enhance its taste. And finally, to soothe the palate, came another small serving of rice with homemade buttermilk.

I did remember to pour the water into my mouth without the brass tumbler touching my lips. And when I finished eating, I did fold the banana leaf in half. Even after I returned home, the taste of that *ellukari* lingered on my palate; it was so good and so different. During my many later visits to the palace, I devoured even more sumptuous delicacies: *varuthupperi kootaan*, deep-fried chunks of plantain in a thick fresh coconut and yogurt sauce, spiced with fresh green chilies and curry leaves; irresistible *maampaza kaalan*, ripe mango slices floating in a mouthwatering silky-smooth coconut sauce, colored yellow with turmeric and garnished with fresh green curry leaves; *kadumaanga*, a fiery-hot and flavorful mango pickle made with tiny green *chandrakkaran* mangoes; and *adamaanga* and *maangaathera*, two sweet and hot dried mango preserves. The list goes on and on. Every time I return from India, I bring back packages of these special preserves. Although some mango dishes are made all over Kerala, I believe that mangoes get the real royal treatment at the *kovilakams* of Kochi.

Over the years, I have collected several recipes from various royal family members for vegetable curries, pickles, and desserts, all passed down by word of mouth. These so-called recipes were strictly lists of ingredients and methods of preparation, not including any kinds of measurements. After several trials, I have developed the following collection of recipes from the *madapilli*. These simple delicacies are easy to prepare and don't call for any fancy ingredients. I hope you enjoy them as much as I do. I am deeply indebted to K. T. Rama Varma, Usha Varma, Rajeswari Thampuran, Rugmini Varma, Uma Devi Thampuran, Ramabhadran Thampuran, Padma Menon, and my late mother-in-law, Padmam Varma, for several of these recipes.

Ellukari: **Vegetables in Spicy Coconut and Sesame Sauce**

Sweet, sour, and mildly spiced, *ellukari* symbolizes *madapilli* cuisine at its best. The toasted coconut and sesame seeds impart a nutty flavor, while tamarind and jaggery contribute sweet and sour contrasts. *Ellukari* is traditionally prepared with either plantains, as called for here, or telinga potatoes, but even russet potatoes can be substituted in a pinch.

1 firm green (unripe) plantain, peeled and cubed*
Salt to taste
½ teaspoon turmeric powder
1½ teaspoons vegetable oil
1½ tablespoons *urad* dal
½ cup grated fresh coconut or dried coconut flakes
1½ tablespoons black or brown sesame seeds

5 dried red cayenne, serrano, or Thai chilies (less for a milder taste)
1 teaspoon tamarind concentrate

For seasoning and garnish:
1 tablespoon vegetable oil
½ teaspoon mustard seeds
1 dried red cayenne, serrano, or Thai chili pepper, halved
¼ teaspoon asafetida powder
12 to 15 fresh curry leaves (if available)
2 tablespoons crushed jaggery or lightly packed brown sugar

Place the plantain, salt, and turmeric in a heavy pot over medium heat, and add just enough water to cover it. Cook for six to eight minutes, or until plantain is fork tender.

Heat one and a half teaspoons of oil over medium heat in a heavy skillet. Add the *urad* dal, and keep stirring until it begins to turn light brown. Add the coconut, and stir until it starts to turn golden brown. Add the sesame seeds and red chilies, and stir for another two to three minutes more. (The sesame seeds will start popping.) Remove the pan from the heat, and let the mixture cool to room temperature. In a blender, grind the spice mix with just enough water to make a fairly smooth, thick puree. Stir the puree into the cooked plantain. Dissolve the tamarind concentrate in a cup of water, add it to the pot, and cook over medium-low heat for six to eight minutes, until the mixture is fairly thick.

Heat the oil in a heavy skillet over medium heat, and add the mustard seeds. When the mustard seeds start sputtering, add the halved red chili pepper, asafetida, and curry leaves to the oil. Remove the skillet, and pour the seasoning into the curry. Add the jaggery, and mix well. Cover and set aside for ten minutes, to allow the flavors to blend. Serve hot with rice and a second curry.

Makes 4 to 6 servings if served with another curry, as is traditional.

*Fresh or canned telinga potato (a large tropical yam labeled *suran* in Indian grocery stores) or even russet potato can be substituted for plantain in this recipe. If you are using canned telinga potatoes, drain them and rinse them under hot running water, then drain again. Simmer with the turmeric and salt for three to four minutes before proceeding with the following steps of the recipe.

Pacha Sambar: **Sambar with Fresh Green Spices**

Sambar is a staple curry of South India. It is always served with rice and often served for breakfast. *Pacha* ("green" in Malayalam) *sambar* is a version prepared only with fresh spices. In this curry, not only must the vegetables be fresh, most of the spices are also green (not dried). For tartness, many curries rely on tamarind; here, it comes from lemon juice.

1 cup *tuvar* dal
1 medium russet potato or 3 taro, peeled and cubed
2 medium tomatoes cubed
Salt to taste
½ teaspoon turmeric powder
¾ cup finely chopped cilantro leaves
¼ cup finely chopped fresh fenugreek leaves (preferred, if available)
    or ½ teaspoon ground fenugreek
6 fresh green chilies (serrano or Thai), thinly sliced (less for a milder taste)
4 tablespoons lemon juice

For seasoning and garnish:
2 tablespoons vegetable oil
1 teaspoon mustard seeds
1 dried red cayenne, serrano, or Thai chili, halved
¼ teaspoon asafetida powder
20 to 25 fresh curry leaves

Wash and clean the *tuvar* dal in several changes of water, until the water runs clear. If you are using oily *tuvar* dal, the oil must be washed off before starting to cook. Place the *tuvar* dal in a saucepan with two and a half cups of water and a half-teaspoon of turmeric powder. Bring it to a boil over medium heat, then turn down the heat, and cook for twenty-five to thirty minutes. (As an alternative, you may use a pressure cooker to cook the dal, following the manufacturer's directions. It will take about six to eight minutes to cook in a pressure cooker.) As the dal cooks, it should be fairly thick but still liquid; stir in another half-cup of water if it is too thick. Mash the cooked *tuvar* dal thoroughly with a spoon, and set it aside.

Combine the potato (or taro), tomatoes, salt, turmeric, and two cups of water in a saucepan over medium heat, and bring it to a boil. Stir in the cilantro, fenugreek, and green chilies. Reduce the heat, and cook until the potatoes are fork tender. Stir in the cooked *tuvar* dal, and simmer for four to five minutes. Stir in the lemon juice. Remove it from the heat, and set it aside.

Heat two tablespoons of oil in a small skillet, and add the mustard seeds. When the mustard seeds start sputtering, add the halved red chili, asafetida, and curry leaves. Remove it from the stove, and pour the seasoning over the cooked curry. Cover and set aside for ten minutes, to allow the flavors to blend. Serve hot with rice and a second curry.

Makes 4 to 6 servings if served with another curry, as is traditional.

Varuthupperi Kootaan: Fried Plantains in Coconut Yogurt Sauce

It was in the kitchen of my mother-in-law, Padmam Varma, that I learned the essentials of *madapilli* cuisine. Some of the dishes in her kitchen came from the same tradition I had grown up with; others used familiar ingredients but expressed them with an accent new to me. This dish of fried plantain chunks in fresh coconut and yogurt sauce reminds me most vividly of her simple style of cooking.

1 green plantain
3 cups vegetable oil (for frying the plantain pieces)
2 cups freshly grated coconut
3 fresh green chilies (serrano or Thai) (less for a milder taste)
Salt to taste
1 cup plain yogurt

For seasoning and garnish:
1 tablespoon vegetable oil
1 teaspoon mustard seeds
1 dried red cayenne, serrano, or Thai chili, halved
12 to 15 fresh curry leaves

Peel the plantain, and slit it lengthwise through the middle. Cut each half into quarter-inch thick slices. Heat the oil in a heavy pot, and deep-fry the plantain pieces. (It will take about five to six minutes, as the slices are thick.) When the slices are golden in color and crisp, remove them with a slotted spoon, and drain.

While the plantain chunks are frying, grind the grated coconut, green chilies, salt, and yogurt in a blender to make a thick puree. If the mixture is too thick, add a few tablespoons of water to speed up the process. In a saucepan, heat one tablespoon of oil, and add the mustard seeds. When the mustard seeds start sputtering, add the halved red chili pepper and the curry leaves. Add the coconut puree to the saucepan, and stir well. Simmer the mixture for three minutes over low heat, and remove it from the stove. Add the fried plantain pieces, and mix well. Cover and set aside for ten minutes, to allow the flavors to blend. This is generally served as a second curry.

Makes 4 to 6 servings if served with another (hot) curry, as is traditional.

Chakka Madhura Curry: Sweet Jackfruit Curry

Long before the days of printed cookbooks, there were poems detailing the ingredients and cooking methods for various curries. I have translated (and developed) this recipe from a Malayalam poem collection called *Curry Slokangal* ("Culinary Ballads"), a part of the ancient Sangha Kali songs. Sangha Kali is an ancient art form that had an integral connection with the rituals of society. Reciting poems describing the quality of the curries was part of the ceremonial dinner at Sangha Kali performances.

Traditionally prepared with ripe jackfruit, this mild curry uses only two spices, cumin and dried ginger. Ripe jackfruit is available both bottled and canned in Indian grocery stores. Pineapple or pears make good substitutes for jackfruit.

1 cup ripe jackfruit, cut into one-inch pieces
Salt to taste
½ teaspoon turmeric powder
1 teaspoon ginger powder
1 teaspoon toasted cumin seeds
1½ cups freshly grated coconut

For seasoning and garnish:
1 tablespoon coconut oil
1 tablespoon jaggery or brown sugar
12 to 15 fresh curry leaves

Place the jackfruit pieces in a saucepan with just enough water to cover. Sprinkle salt and turmeric over the fruit pieces, and cook for five minutes. While it is simmering, using a blender, grind the cumin, dried ginger, and coconut into a smooth, thick puree. Add the spicy coconut puree to the cooked jackfruit, and stir well. Simmer for five minutes. Remove it from the stove, add the coconut oil, jaggery, and curry leaves, and stir gently. Cover and set aside for ten minutes, to allow the flavors to blend. Serve with rice.

Makes 4 to 6 servings if served with another curry, as is traditional.

Pappadavalli: Fried *Pappadams* in Spicy Sauce

Pappadavalli is one of those innovative, simple curries that appear on the dinner table during the monsoon season. When fresh vegetables are scarce, sundried summer vegetables and even *pappadams* are substituted in their place. Following is a recipe using store-bought *pappadams*.

2 cups plus 2½ tablespoons vegetable oil
2 tablespoons *urad* dal
1½ cups freshly grated coconut
4 or 5 dried red cayenne, serrano, or Thai chilies (less for a milder taste)
½ cup fresh curry leaves
1 teaspoon tamarind concentrate
Salt to taste
½ teaspoon turmeric powder
6 store-bought *pappadams,* cut into one-inch pieces

Heat a half-tablespoon of the oil in a heavy skillet over medium heat, and panfry the *urad* dal. When the dal turns pink, add the coconut and red chili peppers, and panfry until the coconut turns golden brown. Reserving eight curry leaves for the garnish, add the remaining leaves to the skillet. Stir well, remove from the stove, and cool for five minutes. Using a blender, grind the panfried ingredients with just enough water to make a thick, smooth puree. Dissolve the tamarind concentrate in two cups of warm water. Combine the tamarind water with salt and turmeric, and cook over medium heat. When it starts boiling, add the spicy coconut blend, and stir well. Bring it back to a boil, reduce the heat, and simmer for ten minutes. Heat two cups of oil in a skillet and deep-fry the *pappadam* pieces. Remove the cooked curry from the stove, add the remaining two tablespoons of oil and the reserved fresh curry leaves, and sprinkle the fried *pappadam* pieces on top. Stir gently. Serve hot, with rice.

Makes 4 to 6 servings if served with another curry, as is traditional.

Varikkasseri: Green Bananas and Taro Root in Coconut Buttermilk Sauce

In this mild curry of raw plantains and taro root, a combination of coconut milk and buttermilk is used to produce a creamy, tart sauce. Taro root is readily available in South American, Indian, and Chinese grocery stores.

1 cup green plantain, cubed and 1 cup taro root, cubed
4 fresh green chilies (serrano or Thai), cut lengthwise into thin strips (less for a milder taste)
Salt to taste
1½ cups buttermilk
1½ cups coconut milk

For seasoning and garnish:
1 tablespoon coconut oil
12 to 15 curry leaves

Place the vegetable cubes and green chilies in a heavy saucepan, and pour in just enough water to cover them. Add salt, and simmer until the vegetables are fork tender. Add the buttermilk and coconut milk, and simmer over low heat for about three to four minutes, until it just bubbles and rises to the top. Remove it from the stove. Add the coconut oil and curry leaves, and stir gently. Serve hot with rice.

Makes 4 to 6 servings if served with another curry, as is traditional.

Karutha Moloshyam: Telinga Potatoes *(Suran)* in Black Pepper and Coconut Sauce

Karutha moloshyam is a very old, simple dish from the days before the arrival of hot chili peppers in Kerala. It is prepared with two of the most popular crops from our region: coconut and black pepper. A garnish of coconut oil and fresh curry leaves really enhances the flavor.

1 cup telinga potato or regular white potato, cubed
1½ teaspoons crushed black pepper
Salt to taste
1 cup freshly grated coconut

For seasoning and garnish:
12 to 15 fresh curry leaves
1 tablespoon coconut oil

Place the potato cubes in a heavy saucepan, and add just enough water to cover them. Season them with the salt and pepper, and simmer until the potato is fork tender, about five to seven minutes. Meanwhile, in a blender, grind the grated coconut with just enough water to make a smooth, thick puree. Add the puree to the cooked potato, stir, and simmer for four to five minutes. Remove it from the stove, and garnish it with the curry leaves and coconut oil. Serve hot, with rice and ghee.

Makes 4 to 6 servings if served with another curry, as is traditional.

Kaattu Kootan: Green Bananas, Cucumber, and Yam in a Sweet and Sour Sauce

When monsoon rains relentlessly fall, home cooks in Kerala produce curries with whatever vegetable they can find. Giant telinga potatoes *(suran)* are always a staple. A large yellow cucumber from a late summer crop may be still there in the pantry, and plantains may be still available in the vegetable market. All of them cooked together in a sweet and sour sauce, and served with rice, was just right for a monsoon season lunch.

½ cup plantains, cubed
½ cup cucumber, cubed
½ cup telinga potato **or** potato **or** yam, cubed
Salt to taste
½ teaspoon turmeric powder
1 teaspoon tamarind concentrate
2 tablespoons brown sugar
1 tablespoon *urad* dal
5 to 6 dried red cayenne, serrano, or Thai chilies
1 cup freshly grated coconut

For seasoning and garnish:
1½ tablespoons coconut oil
½ teaspoon mustard seeds
1 dried red cayenne, serrano, or Thai chili, halved
12 to 15 curry leaves

Place the vegetable cubes in a heavy saucepan, and pour in just enough water to cover them. Sprinkle on salt and turmeric, and simmer over medium heat. After five minutes, add the tamarind dissolved in a cup of water and brown sugar, and simmer for another five minutes. While is the vegetables are simmering, toast the *urad* dal in a dry frying pan until it is golden brown in color. Add red chili peppers, and fry for another two minutes. Remove it from the stove and let it cool. Using a blender, grind the toasted dal, red pepper, and fresh coconut, using just enough water in the blender to make a thick, smooth puree. Combine the ground coconut mixture and the cooked vegetables, and simmer for another four to five minutes. Remove it from the stove. Heat the oil in a small skillet, and add the mustard seeds. When the mustard seeds start sputtering, add the halved red chili pepper and the curry leaves. Pour this over the cooked vegetables. Serve hot with rice.

Makes 4 to 6 servings if served with another curry, as is traditional.

Maampaza Kaalan: Ripe Mangoes in Coconut Yogurt Sauce

This irresistible delicacy is a staple for lunch during the mango season. Golden, ripe mango slices and large mango seeds float in a mouthwatering thick coconut and yogurt sauce, colored yellow with turmeric and garnished with fresh green curry leaves and mustard seeds—a feast for the eyes and the mouth.

2 ripe mangoes
Salt to taste
½ teaspoon turmeric powder
3 cups freshly grated coconut
4 fresh green chilies (serrano or Thai) (less for a milder taste)
1 teaspoon black pepper
1½ cups yogurt
2 tablespoons jaggery or brown sugar

For seasoning and garnish:
1 tablespoon vegetable oil
1 teaspoon mustard seeds
1 dried red cayenne, serrano, or Thai chili, halved
½ teaspoon fenugreek seeds
12 to 15 fresh curry leaves

Wash and peel the mangoes. Cut them into medium-sized cubes. Do not discard the seeds. In a heavy saucepan, combine the mango pieces and seeds with two cups of water. Sprinkle salt and turmeric on top, and cook over medium heat for five to six minutes. Meanwhile, grind the coconut, green chilies, and black pepper with just enough water to make a thick, smooth puree. Add the coconut puree to the cooking mango pieces, stir, and simmer for five minutes. With a large spoon, beat the yogurt into a smooth, thick liquid, and pour it over the mango pieces. Reduce the heat, and simmer. When the liquid in the pot starts bubbling, remove it from the stove, sprinkle jaggery or brown sugar on top, and stir gently. Heat the oil in a skillet, and add the mustard seeds. When the mustard seeds start sputtering, add the halved red chili pepper, fenugreek seeds, and curry leaves, and remove it from the stove. Pour this over the cooked curry. Serve hot with rice.

Makes 4 to 6 servings if served with another curry, as is traditional.

Kurukku Kaalan: Vegetables in Slow-Cooked Sour Buttermilk Sauce

In the tropical heat of South India, milk and milk products are highly perishable. Before the days of refrigeration, the only way to use leftover milk was to ferment it daily to make yogurt. Yogurt was churned in the morning to separate the butter from the buttermilk. Even buttermilk turns sour quickly in tropical heat. To preserve sour buttermilk from further fermentation, it was cooked down over slow heat. In the old days, *kurukku kaalan* was prepared with reduced sour buttermilk and stored in ceramic jars for several days. Ground coconut and seasoning spices were added only just before serving.

1 green plantain, peeled and cut into cubes
1½ cup telinga potatoes *(suran)*, peeled and cubed
2 teaspoons crushed black pepper
Salt to taste
½ teaspoon turmeric powder
3 tablespoons ghee
10 cups sour buttermilk*
10 curry leaves
2 cups freshly grated coconut
6 to 8 fresh green chilies (serrano or Thai) (less for a milder taste)
1 teaspoon cumin seeds

For seasoning and garnish:
1 teaspoon fenugreek seeds, toasted in a quarter-teaspoon of ghee and powdered
2 tablespoons coconut oil
1 teaspoon mustard seeds
10 to 12 fresh curry leaves

Place the plantain and telinga potato cubes in a pot and pour in just enough water to cover them. Sprinkle on black pepper, salt, and turmeric, and cook over medium heat until the vegetables are fork tender. Most of the water will have evaporated by the time the vegetables are cooked. Add the ghee, and keep stirring until all of the water has evaporated. Pour the sour buttermilk on top, sprinkle half of the curry leaves, and cook over low heat for several minutes, until the buttermilk has been reduced to half its original quantity.

While it is cooking, grind the coconut, green chilies, and cumin seeds into a very thick, smooth puree. Add the puree to the vegetables, and cook over medium to low heat until it just begins to boil. Remove it from the stove, and set it aside. Stir in the powdered fenugreek seeds.

Heat the oil in a small skillet, and add the mustard seeds. When the mustard seeds start sputtering, add the curry leaves, and remove it from the stove. Pour it over the cooked curry. Keep the dish covered until it is time to serve.

Makes 4 to 6 servings if served with another curry, as is traditional.

Chapter Five
Hot off the Skillet:
Mezukkupurattis and *Thorans*

The concept of serving raw vegetables tossed with a salad dressing was unknown to Kerala until the arrival of colonial conquerors. The only kind of salad that was prepared in our home is a combination of sliced raw tomatoes, green chilies, and onions in a yogurt dressing. Even today, salads take a back seat to cooked vegetables in our cuisine.

We have two kinds of panfried vegetables: *mezukkupurattis* and *thorans.* Both are dry vegetable dishes with no sauce. Unlike Chinese stir-fries, in which vegetables are sautéed at very high heat, *mezukkupurattis* are prepared by panfrying cooked vegetables or cooked dried beans over very low heat, which allows the vegetables to absorb the oil and the fragrance of the spices. They become crisp on the outside and fluffy-soft on the inside. For *thorans,* vegetables are thinly sliced and steam-cooked, or cooked in very little water or their own natural juices. This method helps preserve the freshness of the vegetables. Then they are tossed with panfried seasoning made with *urad* dal, mustard seeds, cayenne pepper, curry leaves, fresh coconut flakes, and green chilies. They are not very spicy, but at the same time, they are extremely flavorful. These are homey dishes that yield tremendous flavor. Once the ingredients are assembled, they can be prepared in thirty to forty minutes.

Kaya Mezukkupuratti: Panfried Green Plantains with Curry Leaves

Here is a dish that is as unfussy and simple as you can imagine, but believe me, it is also unimaginably good comfort food. This simple vegetable dish balances the bold flavors of curries in a vegetarian meal. It is more or less the equivalent of mashed potatoes in a Western meal. *Kaya mezukkupuratti* may be made with a variety of green raw bananas. In the tropical regions where bananas grow, there are countless varieties that differ widely in appearance and eating qualities. Although most varieties are consumed when they are ripe, several of them are used in cooking when they are unripe. In the following recipe, cooked green plantains are panfried over low heat until they are fluffy and absorb the flavor of the curry leaves and oil.

3 green plantains
Salt to taste
½ teaspoon turmeric
2 tablespoons vegetable oil
12 to 15 fresh curry leaves

Peel off the thick green skin from the plantains, and cut them in half lengthwise. Slice each half lengthwise again, and then cut them into small pieces. Wash the plantain slices to remove any dark stains from the outside, then transfer them to a saucepan. Add salt, turmeric, and water, just enough to cover the plantain cubes. Cook over medium heat until the plantain pieces are very soft (ten to twelve minutes). Stir, and if necessary add a little more water. If the plantains are done and there is still excess water in the pot, drain them in a colander.

Heat oil in a large, heavy skillet, and panfry the curry leaves for two minutes. Transfer the cooked plantain cubes to the skillet, and stir. Cook over low heat for half an hour, stirring occasionally. Serve warm, along with rice and curries.

Makes 4 to 6 servings.

Kaya and *Achinga Mezukkupuratti:* Panfried Green Plantains and Fresh Black-Eyed Peas with Mustard Seeds and Curry Leaves

Here is another old standby: green plantain cubes combined with fresh black-eyed peas. This simple and healthy dish is rich in fiber, carbohydrates, and protein.

2 green plantains
2 cups tender black-eyed peas in pods, cut into one-inch lengths
Salt to taste
1 teaspoon turmeric powder
2 tablespoons vegetable oil
1 teaspoon mustard seeds

1 dried red cayenne, serrano, or Thai chili, halved
12 to 15 fresh curry leaves

Peel off the thick green skin from the plantains, and cut them in half lengthwise. Slice each half lengthwise again, and then cut them into small pieces. Wash the plantain slices to remove any dark stains from the outside, then transfer them to a saucepan. Add the cut black-eyed peas in pods, salt, turmeric, and just enough water to cover. Cook over medium heat until the vegetables are soft and almost all the water has evaporated, about ten to twelve minutes. If there is still excess water in the pot, drain the vegetables in a colander.

Heat oil in a large, heavy skillet, and add the mustard seeds. When the mustard seeds start sputtering, add the halved red chili pepper and the curry leaves. Transfer the cooked vegetables to the skillet, and panfry over low heat for half an hour, stirring occasionally. Serve warm, along with rice and curries.

Makes 4 to 6 servings.

Chena Mezukkupuratti: Telinga Potatoes Panfried with Mustard Seeds and Curry Leaves

This root vegetable has an assertive, earthy flavor and a texture that stands up to long low-heat cooking. It melds beautifully with various spices and oil to produce fragrant curries. During monsoon months, this staple root vegetable arrives at our dinner table in many different shapes and forms. In this simple rendition, cubes of it are cooked with turmeric and salt and panfried over low heat until a delicate but crispy crust envelops the soft, light interior.

4 cups telinga potato *(suran)*, peeled and cut into cubes*
Salt to taste
½ teaspoon turmeric powder
2 tablespoons vegetable oil
1 teaspoon mustard seeds
1 dried red cayenne, serrano, or Thai chili, halved
12 to 15 fresh curry leaves

Wash the cut vegetable cubes under running water, place them in a large saucepan, and add just enough water to cover. Add salt and turmeric powder, and cook over medium heat until the vegetable cubes are soft and all the water has evaporated, about twelve to fifteen minutes. If there is still excess water in the pot, drain the vegetables in a colander.

Heat oil in a skillet, and add the mustard seeds. When the mustard seeds start sputtering, add the halved red chili pepper and the curry leaves. Transfer the cooked vegetables to the skillet, and panfry over low heat for half an hour, stirring occasionally. Serve warm, along with rice and curries.

Makes 4 to 6 servings.

*Telinga potato is a large tropical yam. Canned as well as frozen pieces of this yam (called *suran*) is available from Indian grocers. During the summer, it is available fresh from some Indian grocers. If you are using the canned variety, first drain the vegetables. Rinse them under warm running water, and drain them again. Simmer these pieces with salt and turmeric for four to five minutes, and proceed with the remaining steps of the recipe.

Variations:

Chena and *kaya mezukkupuratti:* Instead of just plantains or other types of cooking bananas, a combination of banana and telinga potato pieces are cooked, following the recipe above.

Chena and *chakkakkuru mezukkupuratti:* Seeds of jackfruit go well with this root vegetable. Remove the skin from the jackfruit seeds, and cut them into cubes. Cook them along with the telinga potato cubes. Continue with the above recipe. Frozen jackfruit seeds are also available from Indian grocers in the United States.

Koorka mezukkupuratti: Koorka is another tropical root vegetable. They are available peeled and frozen, and sometimes fresh, from Indian grocers in the United States. Unlike the huge telinga potatoes, *koorka* is a very tiny root vegetable and doesn't have to be cut into pieces. Far from bland, these tiny tubers have a hint of a nutty flavor and a soft texture. Follow the recipe above to make *mezukkupuratti.*

Vellapayaru Mezukkupuratti: Red Beans Panfried with Curry Leaves and Mustard

Refried beans, South Indian style! This is another satisfying staple during the monsoon season. Panfrying cooked beans over low heat allows them to absorb the fragrance of the curry leaves.

2 cups dried red beans
½ teaspoon turmeric
Salt to taste
2 tablespoons vegetable oil
1 teaspoon mustard seeds
2 dried red cayenne, serrano, or Thai chilies, halved
12 to 15 fresh curry leaves

Soak red beans for eight hours (or overnight), and then wash them in several changes of water until the water runs clear. Transfer them to a saucepan, add turmeric and water, and bring it to a boil. Reduce the heat to medium, and cook until the beans are very soft to the touch and can be easily mashed between two fingers (approximately forty to fifty minutes). If necessary, add more water and continue cooking until they are soft. Most of the water should be absorbed by the time the beans are well cooked. Drain any remaining water. Alternatively, the beans may be cooked in a pressure cooker (following the manufacturer's directions) for six to eight minutes. Return them to the saucepan, and season them with salt.

Heat the oil in a large, heavy skillet, and add the mustard seeds. When the mustard seeds start sputtering, add the halved red chili peppers and the curry leaves. Transfer the cooked beans to the skillet, and panfry them over low heat for half an hour, stirring occasionally. Serve warm, along with rice and curries.

Makes 4 to 6 servings.

Vellapayaru and *Kaya Tholi Mezukkupuratti:* Panfried Red Beans and Plantain Skins

When green plantains are peeled for frying or to make other dishes, there will be plenty of thick plantain skins left over. They add texture to this otherwise soft bean dish.

2 cups dry red beans
2 cups fresh green plantain skins, thinly chopped
½ teaspoon turmeric powder
Salt to taste
2 tablespoons vegetable oil
1 teaspoon mustard seeds
1 dried red cayenne, serrano, or Thai chili, halved
12 to 15 fresh curry leaves

Soak the red beans in water for eight hours (or overnight). Rinse them well, and drain. Transfer them to a saucepan, and add water. Sprinkle on a quarter-teaspoon of turmeric, and bring it to a boil. Reduce the heat to medium, and cook until the beans are very soft to the touch and can be easily mashed between two fingers (about forty to fifty minutes). Most of the water will have evaporated by now. If necessary, add more water and cook until the beans are soft. If any water is remaining after is the beans are well cooked, drain them. Alternatively, the beans may be cooked in a pressure cooker for six to eight minutes (following the manufacturer's directions). Sprinkle salt over the cooked beans, and stir well.

In a saucepan, place the chopped plantain skins along with the salt and a quarter-teaspoon of turmeric powder. Add enough water to cover them. Reduce the heat to medium, and cook until the banana skins are soft. Drain any excess water. Combine the cooked beans and the plantain skins.

Heat oil in a skillet, and add the mustard seeds. When the mustard seeds start sputtering, add the curry leaves and the halved red chili pepper. Transfer the cooked beans and plantain skins to the skillet, and panfry for twenty to twenty-five minutes over low heat, stirring occasionally. Serve warm, along with rice and curries.

Makes 4 to 6 servings.

Muthira Upperi: Horse Gram Beans Panfried with Mustard and Curry Leaves

These tiny, flat, slightly elongated, brown-skinned beans are also known as horse gram beans. They are dark brown in color and are a very rich source of protein. Unlike red beans, they do not become very soft when cooked. This bean dish is usually served with *kanji* (rice soup).

2 cups horse gram beans
½ teaspoon turmeric powder
1 teaspoon dried red cayenne, serrano, or Thai chili powder (less for a milder taste)
2 tablespoons vegetable oil
1 teaspoon mustard seeds
1 dried red cayenne, serrano, or Thai chili, halved
12 to 15 fresh curry leaves
Salt to taste

Soak the horse gram beans for eight hours (or overnight). Wash them, and drain well. Place the beans, turmeric powder, and red chili powder in a saucepan, and add water to cover them. Cook until the beans are soft to the touch. If necessary add more water. When the beans are soft to the touch, stir in the salt, and cook for two more minutes. Most of the water should be absorbed by the time the beans are well cooked. Drain any remaining water. Alternatively, cook the beans in a pressure cooker (following the manufacturer's directions) for six to eight minutes.

Heat the oil in a large skillet, and add the mustard seeds. When the mustard seeds start sputtering, add the halved red chili pepper and the curry leaves. Transfer the cooked beans to the skillet, and panfry over low heat for half an hour, stirring occasionally. Serve warm, along with rice and curries.

Makes 4 to 6 servings.

Paavakka Mezukkupuratti: Bitter Gourd Panfried with Spices

Bitter gourd or bitter melon is a vegetable that has ribbed skin with tubercles. The Chinese variety has softer ribs than the Indian variety. As the name suggests, bitter melons have a strong bitter taste. To mellow this taste, first cook the pieces with salt and turmeric for five minutes, and drain the water.

Bitter melon contains chemicals that help control diabetes. This plant-based cure has no side effects, so diabetic patients in India often consume this vegetable whenever it is available.

In the following recipe, bitter melon is cooked with finely chopped sweet onions, which help to neutralize the bitter taste. An extra dose of red pepper and curry leaves harmonizes the tastes and adds spicy overtones to the dish.

6 medium-sized bitter melons
Salt to taste
½ teaspoon turmeric powder
2 tablespoons vegetable oil
1 medium-sized onion, thinly sliced
12 to 15 fresh curry leaves
2 teaspoons cayenne, serrano, or Thai chili powder **(less** for a milder taste)

Wash and cut the bitter melon into thin pieces. Remove the seeds from the inside. Put it in a saucepan with the salt and turmeric. Cover it with water, and cook for five minutes, and drain. Heat oil in a heavy skillet, and panfry the onion and the curry leaves until the onion is translucent. Transfer the cooked bitter melon pieces to the pan, and sprinkle them with red chili powder. Panfry over low heat while stirring periodically. After twenty to twenty-five minutes, the vegetables will become golden brown and crispy. Remove it from the stove, and serve it warm with rice curries.

Makes 4 to 6 servings.

Masala Niracha Paavakka: Bitter Gourd Stuffed with Spicy Onion

In this recipe, tender, small bitter melons are first blanched and then stuffed, almost to the point of bursting, with thinly sliced, panfried onions and an aromatic spice mix. They are then panfried to a golden-brown color, resulting in a texture that is on the cusp of crunchy and tender.

6 small bitter melons
Salt to taste
½ teaspoon turmeric powder
2 cups vegetable oil
1 tablespoon *urad* dal
1 tablespoon coriander seeds
6 dried red cayenne, serrano, or Thai chili peppers (less for a milder taste)
¼ teaspoon tamarind concentrate
2 medium-sized onions, thinly sliced
6 pieces of twine for tying stuffed vegetables

Wash and clean the bitter melons. In a saucepan, bring six to eight cups of water to a boil. Add the bitter melons, salt, and turmeric, and cook for three minutes. Remove it from the stove, and drain. Using a paring knife, make a slit in the middle of each bitter melon, without completely opening it. Scoop out the seeds, and drain the melons on paper towels, with the slits facing down.

In a heavy skillet, heat a half-tablespoon of oil over medium heat, and fry the *urad* dal and the coriander seeds. When the dal turns golden, add the red chili pepper, and fry for one minute. Remove it from the stove, and let it cool. Mix the tamarind and spices, and grind it into a thick puree.

In a large skillet, heat a tablespoon of oil, and fry the chopped onions until they are slightly browned. Remove them from the stove. Combine the fried onions and spices, and stir well. Stuff spiced onions into a melon through the slit, and tie the melon tightly with a piece of twine. Repeat the process with the remaining bitter melons. Heat the remaining oil in a heavy skillet, and panfry the stuffed bitter melons. Keep turning them after a couple of minutes so that they are browned on all sides. Drain them on paper towels. Serve hot.

Makes 4 to 6 servings.

Kadachakka Mezukkupuratti: Breadfruit Panfried with Curry Leaves

Breadfruit is a very starchy vegetable with a white, somewhat fibrous pulp. Although its name ends in "fruit," it is in essence a very starchy tropical vegetable. When cooked, it has almost the consistency of mashed potatoes or yucca. When mildly spiced with turmeric and curry leaves, breadfruit has a very pleasant aroma and taste.

2 firm green breadfruit
½ teaspoon turmeric powder
Salt to taste
2 tablespoons vegetable oil
12 to 15 fresh curry leaves

Peel the thick green skin and cut the breadfruit in half. Cut the segments into half-inch cubes. Place the cubes in a heavy saucepan, pour in enough water to cover, and stir in the turmeric and salt. Cook over medium heat until the vegetable is tender and all the water has evaporated. Stir periodically so that the breadfruit does not stick to the saucepan. Heat the oil in a heavy, large skillet, and fry the curry leaves. Transfer the cooked vegetables to the skillet, and panfry over low heat for twelve to fifteen minutes, stirring occasionally. Serve warm with rice and curries.

Makes 4 to 6 servings.

Beans *Thoran:* Panfried Green Beans with Fresh Coconut and Mustard Seeds

Thoran is a variation of mezukkupuratti. In this recipe, cooked green beans are panfried over low heat with subtle seasonings and garnished with freshly grated coconut flakes. Thoran can be prepared with a variety of vegetables, including green beans, cabbage, tender jackfruit, zucchini, and potatoes.

1 pound fresh string beans
Salt to taste
½ teaspoon turmeric
1 tablespoon vegetable oil
1 teaspoon mustard seeds
2 teaspoons *urad* dal
1 dried red cayenne, serrano, or Thai chili, halved
12 to 15 fresh curry leaves
2 fresh green chilies (serrano or Thai), finely chopped (less for a milder taste)
6 tablespoons freshly grated coconut

Trim the ends off the string beans, and chop them fine. Cook the beans in a saucepan with salt and the turmeric and just enough water to cover, until they are soft. Most of the water should evaporate by the time the beans are cooked. If there is excess water, drain the beans in a colander.

Heat oil in a heavy skillet, and add the mustard seeds. When the mustard seeds start sputtering, add the *urad* dal, halved red chili pepper, and curry leaves, and fry until the dal turns golden. Transfer the cooked beans to the skillet, stir, and reduce heat. Combine the green chilies with the freshly grated coconut, and sprinkle this mixture over the beans. Panfry over low heat for six to eight minutes. Serve warm, with rice and curries.

Makes 4 to 6 servings.

Mottakoozu Thoran: Cabbage Panfried with Green Chilies and Coconut

Cabbage is not by any means a tropical vegetable. In fact, my mother called it "English vegetable." While its origins may be western, these pale green leaves blend perfectly with tropical ingredients and make a good side dish for rice and curries. Here is a recipe for coleslaw, South Indian style.

1 small green cabbage
4 fresh green chilies (serrano or Thai) (less for a milder taste)
Salt to taste
½ teaspoon turmeric
1 tablespoon vegetable oil
1 teaspoon mustard seeds
1 teaspoon each *urad* dal and *chana* dal
1 dried red cayenne, serrano, or Thai chili, halved

12 to 15 fresh curry leaves
¾ cup freshly grated coconut

Cut the cabbage in half, and cut out the thick core in the middle. Shred the leaves as you would for coleslaw. A food processor will do this job very well. Place the shredded cabbage in a colander, and wash it under running water, then drain. Cut the green chilies into thin strips, and combine them with the cabbage. Sprinkle salt and the turmeric over the shredded cabbage, and mix well.

Heat oil in a heavy, large skillet and add the mustard seeds. When the mustard seeds start sputtering, add the dal, halved red chili pepper, and curry leaves, and fry until the dal turns golden. Add the cabbage to the skillet. Mix well, and reduce the heat to low. Sprinkle a tablespoon of water over the cabbage, and cover the skillet. Remove the cover after two minutes, and stir gently. Cook the cabbage for five to eight minutes, stirring occasionally. When the cabbage is well cooked, sprinkle grated coconut on top and stir gently. Serve warm, with rice and curries.

Makes 4 to 6 servings.

Urulakizzangu Thoran: Potatoes Panfried with Green Chilies and Coconut

Here is our hot potato salad, spiced and garnished with—what else?—fresh green chilies and coconut. It tastes good either hot or cold. As there is no mayonnaise in this dish, it stays fresh at room temperature for a whole day. A garnish of toasted dal imparts crunchiness to this salad.

5 medium or 2 large Idaho potatoes
Salt to taste
4 fresh green chilies (serrano or Thai) (less for a milder taste)
1 cup freshly grated coconut
2 tablespoons vegetable oil
½ teaspoon mustard seeds
1 tablespoon each *urad* dal and *chana* dal
1 dried red cayenne, serrano, or Thai chili, halved
12 to 15 fresh curry leaves

Peel the potatoes, and cut them into large cubes. Place them in a heavy saucepan and pour in enough water to cover them. Add salt, and simmer for eight to ten minutes, until they are fork tender. Drain them, and set them aside.

With a mortar and pestle or in a food processor, roughly chop the green chilies. Add the grated coconut, and mix well. Heat oil in a heavy skillet, and add the mustard seeds. When the mustard seeds start sputtering, add the dal, halved red chili pepper, and curry leaves, and fry until the dal turns golden. Reduce the heat to low, add the green chilies and coconut, and fry for a minute or two. Roughly mash the cooked potatoes and add them to the pan. Stir well to combine, and panfry for another five to six minutes over low heat. Serve warm with rice and curries. This dish may also be served at room temperature as a salad.

Makes 4 to 6 servings.

Variation: Thinly slice a few shallots or a medium onion, panfry in two teaspoons of oil, and add to the potatoes.

Idichakka Thoran: **Tender Jackfruit Seasoned with Green Chilies, Mustard Seeds, and Coconut**

During early summer, jackfruit trees are full of tender small jackfruit. By the time it ripens, jackfruit grows up to two feet in length and weighs up to forty pounds. The jackfruit used for this dish is very tender and raw, and the seeds will not have formed at this stage. In the United States, some farmers in Florida grow this crop, and during the season, it is available in Indian grocery stores. It is readily available canned at Indian and Thai grocery stores.

4 cups tender raw jackfruit cubes (fresh or canned)*
Salt to taste
½ teaspoon turmeric powder
2 tablespoons vegetable oil
1 teaspoon mustard seeds
2 teaspoons *urad* dal
1 dried cayenne, serrano, or Thai chili pepper, halved
12 to 15 fresh curry leaves
4 fresh green chilies (serrano or Thai), thinly sliced (less for a milder taste)
1½ cups freshly grated coconut

Bring six cups of water to a boil in a saucepan, and add the jackfruit. Add the salt and turmeric, and cook for ten to twelve minutes, until it is fork tender. Drain and set aside. When it has cooled, chop it finely.

Heat oil in a heavy, large skillet, and add the mustard seeds. When the mustard seeds start sputtering, add the *urad* dal, halved red chili pepper, and curry leaves, and fry until the dal turns golden. Add the chopped jackfruit to the pan, reduce heat to low, and mix well. Panfry for six to eight minutes, stirring occasionally. Sprinkle chopped green chilies and grated coconut on top, and mix well.

Makes 4 to 6 Servings.

*When using canned jackfruit, drain it, then rinse it under running water and drain it in a colander. Canned jackfruit is already skinned and cut into large pieces. Chop it into very thin pieces, and sprinkle them with salt and turmeric. There is no need to cook it further. Follow the remaining steps of the recipe above.

Chapter Six
Chutneys and Pickles

Chutneys

Hotter than blazes or ingratiatingly sweet or sour, chutneys add an astonishing diversity of flavors to a meal. Chutneys have a position of prominence in the food of any part of India, and they are prepared with a limitless variety of ingredients. Though the appeal of chutney is global, Indian chutney has no true equivalent condiment in any other cuisine.

There are three varieties of chutney: fresh chutneys, cooked chutneys, and dry chutneys. Fresh South Indian chutneys are smooth, uncooked purees seasoned with fried mustard seeds, dal, and curry leaves. They are best when freshly made, but they will stay good for a couple of days if refrigerated. Cooked chutneys are soft and pulpy mixtures of cooked ingredients, again seasoned with fried mustard seeds, dal, and curry leaves. These chutneys have a longer shelf life. Leftover chutney may be refrigerated or frozen to be used at a later time as required. Remember to thaw only what is needed, and do not refreeze it. Dry chutneys are prepared with toasted coconut, sesame seeds, and dal. They remain fresh for a longer time at cool room temperature.

A few readily available, fresh ingredients and a solid blender are all you need to prepare fresh chutneys. These simple condiments taste good with Indian food, and they also make excellent dips with a variety of Indian and western appetizers. If you enjoy serving a variety of dishes at your parties, serve appetizers along with Indian chutneys. Your guests will certainly come back for seconds.

Naalikera Chutney: Coconut Chutney

This spicy, hot chutney is an indispensable condiment with our savory breakfast pancakes and steamed dumplings. When making this traditional favorite, using fresh coconut is crucial; this gives it the authentic taste.

2 cups freshly grated coconut
5 fresh green chilies (serrano or Thai) (less for a milder taste)
1 tablespoon freshly grated ginger
Salt to taste
1 tablespoon vegetable oil
½ teaspoon mustard seeds
½ teaspoon *urad* dal
1 dried red cayenne, serrano, or Thai chili, halved
12 to 15 fresh curry leaves

In a blender, grind the coconut, green chilies, ginger, and salt with just enough water to make a smooth, thick puree.

In a small skillet, heat the oil over medium heat, and add the mustard seeds. When the mustard seeds start sputtering, add the *urad* dal, halved red chili pepper, and curry leaves, and fry until the dal turns golden. Remove it from the stove, and stir it into the coconut puree. Serve at room temperature.

Makes 6 to 8 servings.

For a slightly tart taste, add a couple of tablespoons of yogurt to the chutney and stir well. Substitute with jalapeños or dried cayenne peppers when green serrano or Thai chilies are not available.

Variations:

Coconut Cilantro Chutney: Grind half a cup of cilantro leaves along with the coconut in the above recipe. Cilantro will impart herbal overtones and a greenish color to the chutney.

Chutta Chammanthi: This chutney, prepared with fire-roasted coconut pieces, is served as the perfect accompaniment to warm bowls of rice *kanji* (soup) during the monsoon season.

1½ tablespoon coconut oil (or other vegetable oil)
1½ teaspoon *urad* dal
4 dried red cayenne, serrano, or Thai chili peppers
¼ teaspoon asafetida (optional)
1 cup freshly grated coconut

Salt to taste
½ teaspoon tamarind concentrate
12 to 15 fresh curry leaves

Heat a half-tablespoon of oil in a small skillet over medium heat, and add the *urad* dal and chili peppers. Panfry until the dal turns golden brown in color. Stir in the asafetida powder, and remove the pan from the stove. Let it cool down to room temperature. In a skillet, heat a half-tablespoon of oil, and toast the coconut flakes in it until they turn golden brown in color. Remove it from the stove, and stir in the toasted dal and chili peppers. Let it cool to room temperature.

Puree the mix along with salt, tamarind concentrate, and half a cup of water. The puree should have the consistency of thick pesto. Transfer the chutney to a serving bowl. Heat the remaining oil, fry the fresh curry leaves for a minute, and add them to the chutney. This chutney stays fresh for a week in the refrigerator.

Instead of panfrying, the coconut may be toasted in the oven at medium heat. In the traditional recipe, chunks of fresh coconut are wrapped in banana leaves and fire-roasted over the embers in a wood-burning stove.

Almond Chutney: I was really amazed when I discovered that almonds are a good substitute for fresh coconut. I admit it's not authentic; however, the taste is incredibly similar.

Grind a cup of almonds with five or six dried serrano or Thai chili peppers (less for a milder taste), salt, water, and a half cup of curry leaves. You may prepare this chutney without curry leaves, but it will lack the fragrance of these aromatic leaves.

In a small skillet, heat one tablespoon of oil over medium heat, and add a half-teaspoon of mustard seeds. When the mustard seeds start sputtering, add a half-teaspoon of *urad* dal, one halved red chili pepper, and six to eight curry leaves, and fry until the dal turns golden. Add the ground almond puree to the skillet, and stir. Remove from the stove, and serve at room temperature.

Ulli Chammanthi: Shallot Chutney

This fiery hot chutney makes a perfect accompaniment to salty breakfast dishes. The traditional recipe uses hot cayenne peppers. If you prefer a milder taste, reduce the quantity of peppers or substitute with the mildly hot red pepper flakes available in any supermarket. This spicy relish also makes a perfect accompaniment to mellow dishes containing yogurt or cream.

2 tablespoons vegetable oil
2 cups thinly sliced shallots
½ cup dried red cayenne, serrano, or Thai chili peppers (or less for a milder taste)
Salt to taste

Heat oil in a skillet over medium heat, and add the sliced shallots. Fry the shallots until they start browning at the edges. Add the red chili peppers, and fry for two more minutes. Remove it from the stove, sprinkle with salt, and let it cool down to room temperature. Grind into a thick puree. Add a few teaspoons of water if necessary to blend it into a thick, smooth puree.

Makes 4 to 6 servings.

Variation: Onions may be substituted for shallots.

Maanga Chammanthi: Fresh Mango Chutney

During the summer months when fresh mangoes are readily available, mango chutney is standard fare at breakfast, lunch, and supper. It also makes a great dip.

2 medium-sized, unripe, green mangoes
2 cups freshly grated coconut
6 to 8 fresh green chilies (serrano or Thai) (or less for a milder taste)
Salt to taste

Wash and rinse the mangoes, and peel off the skin. Cut them into small pieces. In a blender, combine the mango pieces, grated coconut, chili peppers, and salt with just enough water to grind it into a thick puree. This chutney makes a perfect substitute for coconut chutney.

Makes 4 to 6 servings.

Adamaanga Chutney: Mango Chutney with Dried Spiced Mangoes

It is only possible to make fresh mango chutney during the two- to three-month-long mango season. The following mango chutney recipe may be prepared any time of the year. It is prepared with spiced and dried mango pieces called *adamaanga* (The recipe for *adamaanga* is to be found in the section on sun-dried preserves).

½ cup *adamaanga*
2 cups fresh grated coconut
2 or 3 fresh green chilies (serrano or Thai), or less for a milder taste
1 cup plain yogurt
1 tablespoon vegetable oil
1 teaspoon mustard seeds
1 dried red cayenne, serrano, or Thai chili, halved
12 to 15 fresh curry leaves

Soak the *adamaanga* in a cup of warm water for an hour. In a blender, grind together the soaked *adamaanga,* grated coconut, and green chilies to a thick, smooth puree. Pour the yogurt into the blender, and blend well. Transfer the contents to a saucepan, and cook over medium heat just until bubbling. Remove it from the stove, and set it aside.

In a small frying pan, heat the oil over medium heat, and add the mustard seeds. When the mustard seeds start sputtering, add the halved cayenne pepper and the curry leaves. Remove from the stove, pour the contents over the chutney, and stir well. *Adamaanga* is quite salty, so taste the chutney before adding any additional salt.

Makes 6 to 8 servings.

Thakkali Chutney: **Fresh Tomato Chutney**

It is amazing how a few simple ingredients, when combined in the appropriate manner, can yield such a medley of complex flavors. Chechi, my cousin, prepares this excellent chutney with fresh tomatoes. It's great with both appetizers and breakfast dishes.

6 to 8 ripe tomatoes
Salt to taste
½ teaspoon turmeric powder
2 tablespoons vegetable oil
½ teaspoon mustard seeds
3 teaspoons cumin powder
2 teaspoons powdered fenugreek seeds
4 teaspoons of cayenne or serrano chili powder (or less if you prefer a milder taste)

¼ teaspoon asafetida powder (optional)
12 to 15 fresh curry leaves

Score an *X* at the stem end of each tomato, and drop them in boiling water for thirty seconds. Remove them, and drop them into cool water. It will be easy to peel off the skin. Cut the peeled tomatoes in half, remove the seeds, and slice the tomatoes into thin pieces. In a saucepan, cook the tomatoes and two tablespoons of water along with salt and the turmeric powder. Remove from the stove, mash well, and set aside. This should yield a thick puree.

In a small skillet, heat the oil, and add the mustard seeds. When the mustard seeds start sputtering, add the cumin, fenugreek, cayenne, asafetida, and curry leaves, and fry for a minute. Remove from the stove. (If left on the stove any longer, fenugreek powder will burn and taste bitter.)

Combine the cooked tomatoes with the spices, and mix well. To make the chutney hotter, increase the amount of cayenne. This chutney will keep well in the refrigerator for two weeks.

I also make this chutney with canned tomatoes. Bottled or canned Italian San Marzano tomatoes have the right degree of acidity and blends very well with the spice mixture. In the absence of Italian tomatoes, substitute any readily available canned tomatoes. If you are using canned tomatoes, mix it with about a half-cup of water, salt, and turmeric powder, and cook until the mixture has thickened. Follow the remaining steps of the recipe above.

Makes 2 cups of chutney.

Puliingi: Ginger and Green Chilies in a Tamarind Sauce

This chutney made with fresh ginger and green chilies is a must at any traditional festive meal. The characteristic balance of sweet, salty, hot, and sour elements is accomplished by a combination of fresh green chilies, ginger, tamarind, and brown sugar. Surprisingly, it also tastes great as a dip.

2 tablespoons sesame oil
1 teaspoon mustard seeds
1 dried red cayenne, serrano, or Thai chili, halved
½ cup finely chopped fresh ginger
8 fresh green chilies (Thai or serrano), finely chopped (less for a milder taste)
12 to 15 fresh curry leaves
3 teaspoons tamarind concentrate dissolved in 2 cups of water
½ teaspoon turmeric powder

Salt to taste
2 tablespoons powdered jaggery or brown sugar

Heat the oil in a large, heavy skillet, and add the mustard seeds. When the mustard seeds start sputtering, add the halved red pepper, ginger, green chilies, and curry leaves, and panfry until the green chilies start browning at the edges. Add the tamarind liquid to the frying pan. Sprinkle with turmeric and salt, and simmer until some of the liquid has evaporated and the sauce has thickened (six to eight minutes). Remove from the stove, and stir in the jaggery or brown sugar. *Puliingi* keeps well in the refrigerator for up to two weeks.

Makes 2 cups.

Mulagu Pachadi: Green Chilies in a Spicy Tamarind and Brown Sugar Sauce

Mulagu pachadi, hot and sour cooked chutney with a touch of sweetness, is a specialty of the Paalakkad region in Kerala. Sesame seeds and sesame oil impart a nutty fragrance to it. Although it is a traditional accompaniment to vegetarian lunch or supper, it is equally good with snacks. It makes an unusual and tasty dip for chips and vegetable fritters. Use serrano peppers for a moderately hot sauce. Sesame oil may be substituted with vegetable oil.

3 tablespoons sesame oil
1 teaspoon mustard seeds
1 dried red cayenne, serrano, or Thai chili, halved
12 to 15 fresh curry leaves
2 cups fresh green chilies (serrano or Thai), thinly sliced lengthwise
2 level teaspoons tamarind concentrate blended into 3 cups water
Salt to taste
½ teaspoon turmeric powder
4 tablespoons sesame seeds (preferably black or brown)
3 tablespoons jaggery or brown sugar

Heat the oil in a heavy skillet over medium heat for two minutes, and add the mustard seeds. When the mustard seeds start sputtering, add the halved red chili pepper, curry leaves, and sliced green chilies. Panfry over medium heat until the chilies are slightly browned. Combine the diluted tamarind concentrate, salt, and turmeric powder, and add them to the skillet. Simmer over low to medium heat for ten to twelve minutes, stirring occasionally. Cook and reduce the tamarind mixture until it thickens. Remove from the stove.

In a dry skillet, toast the sesame seeds. When they start popping, remove them from the stove, and let them cool. Using a spice mill or a coffee grinder, grind the toasted sesame seeds to a fine powder. Combine them with the jaggery or brown sugar, sprinkle them over the cooked chutney, and stir well. Transfer to a serving bowl.

Makes 2 to 2 ½ cups.

Kothamallipodi: Spicy Fresh Coriander Chutney Powder

The enticing aroma of fragile green coriander leaves is enjoyed all over India. Its hardy taste is both refreshing and appetizing. Fresh cilantro chutney powder gets a nutty flavor from toasted *urad* dal, while tamarind adds a piquant, sour twist. If you wish to prepare this chutney as a dip, add half a cup of water while blending the ingredients. It makes a good dip.

1 tablespoon vegetable oil
½ cup *urad* dal
⅓ cup *chana* dal
½ cup dried red cayenne, serrano, or Thai chili peppers (less for a milder taste)
12 to 15 fresh curry leaves
¼ teaspoon asafetida powder (optional)
2 cups fresh cilantro leaves
½ tablespoon tamarind concentrate
Salt to taste

Heat the oil in a skillet, and fry the dal. When it starts turning golden brown, add the cayenne peppers, curry leaves, and asafetida, and fry for another minute. Remove from the stove, and let it cool. Process the cilantro leaves, tamarind concentrate, salt, and the fried spices together in a food processor until blended thoroughly. Remove from the processor, and store in an airtight container. Since fresh cilantro leaves are used, this dry chutney has a comparatively short shelf life. It stays fresh for up to two weeks when refrigerated.

Makes 2 to 2 ½ cups.

Chammanthipodi: Spicy Coconut Chutney Powder

Every family has certain favorite dishes that are so satisfying that they never get tired of making it. In our family, one such dish is *chammanthipodi*. This hot, sweet, and sour condiment is traditionally served with rice and curries. However, *chammanthipodi* has surfaced in many different forms in my American kitchen. My husband loves it with *kanji* (rice soup). My younger son thinks it makes a great sandwich spread; his recipe for a *chammanthipodi* sandwich is toasted bread slices with a liberal spread of ghee and a couple of teaspoons of *chammanthipodi* on top. One of our friends insists that his toast needs a light spread of orange marmalade to enhance the taste of *chammanthipodi*, while others think it tastes great sprinkled on top of margherita pizza (of course my Italian friends totally disagree). Sprinkle it on top of tortilla chips brushed with melted butter or warm oil (so that the powder sticks to the chips) for a different and delicious taste.

2 tablespoons vegetable oil
½ cup *urad* dal
1½ cups dried red cayenne, serrano, or Thai chili peppers (less for a milder taste)
3 tablespoons coriander seeds
½ teaspoon fenugreek seeds
½ teaspoon asafetida (optional)
4 cups freshly grated coconut
Salt to taste
½ cup jaggery or brown sugar
2 tablespoons tamarind concentrate

Heat half a tablespoon of oil in a skillet over medium heat, and fry the *urad* dal. When the dal start turning golden brown, add the cayenne pepper and coriander seeds, and fry for another three to four minutes until well toasted. Stir in the fenugreek seeds and asafetida, remove it from the stove, and set it aside. (Overtoasting fenugreek will result a bitter taste.) Heat the remaining oil in a skillet, and panfry the grated coconut over medium heat until it turns golden brown. Let it cool to room temperature. Combine the coconut and fried spices, salt, jaggery (or brown sugar), and tamarind concentrate, and process them in a food processor or a blender to a coarse, grainy powder. It will be dark brown in color and taste sweet, salty, hot, and sour—all at the same time. Store it in airtight jars. It stays fresh for up to three weeks in the refrigerator.

Makes 2 cups.

Podi: Spice Powder Served with *Dosa* and *Idli*

Podi (the Malayalam word for powder) is an old favorite at our breakfast table. It is a dry and spicy hot chutney that is served with a few drops of oil or ghee with most breakfast dishes. Since the ingredients are dry roasted and powdered, it has a longer shelf life.

1 cup *urad* dal
½ cup dried red cayenne, serrano, or Thai chilies (less for a milder taste)
2 tablespoons black sesame seeds
¼ teaspoon asafetida powder
Salt to taste

Wash the *urad* dal, and drain. Spread it on a paper towel to dry thoroughly. In a heavy skillet, dry roast the dal over medium heat until it is golden brown in color. Keep stirring continually so that it is evenly browned. Add the red chili peppers and sesame seeds to the *urad* dal, and keep stirring. The sesame seeds will start popping in a couple of minutes. Add the asafetida powder, stir well, and remove it from the stove. Add salt, and let it cool to room temperature. Using a coffee grinder, process the roasted dal and spices to a fine powder. *Podi* is served along with *dosas* and *idlis*.

Makes 1 to 1½ cups.

Variations: Adding two teaspoons of cumin seeds with the sesame seeds while roasting will give it a different fragrance. Another variation is to use a half-cup of dal and a half-cup of parboiled rice. Dry roast them separately before powdering. When parboiled rice is dry roasted, it will puff up slightly and acquire a golden color.

Veppilakatti: Spicy Lemon Leaf Chutney Powder

The delicate fragrance of fresh lemon leaves gives a subtle dimension to this dry chutney. Although they are not found in supermarkets, fresh lemon leaves are available in regions where lemon trees grow.

½ cup dried red cayenne, serrano, or Thai chili peppers (less for a milder taste)
1 teaspoon sesame oil
¼ teaspoon asafetida powder
7 cups fresh leaves from a lemon tree

1 cup fresh curry leaves
Salt to taste
1½ tablespoons tamarind concentrate
1 tablespoon sesame oil

Panfry the cayenne peppers in oil. Stir in the asafetida powder, and remove from the stove. Let it cool down to room temperature. Wash the lemon leaves and curry leaves under running water, and drain. Remove the veins from the lemon leaves. Spread the washed leaves on paper towels to dry thoroughly. Grind the leaves along with the toasted spices, salt, tamarind, and oil in a blender or a food processor to a coarse, grainy powder. If the ingredients start sticking to the sides, add a few more drops of oil and continue to grind. Store the *veppilakatti* in airtight glass jars. It stays fresh for several weeks in the refrigerator.

Makes 3 cups.

Pickles

"Pickle" is quite a misleading term when it comes to Indian pickles. South Indian pickles are as fiery as the prevailing temperatures—the hotter, the better. They also tend to be very salty, as salt is the main preservative ingredient. When traditional meals are served on banana leaves, one or two pickles are served at the tapering end of the leaf. In any South Indian pantry, you will find several jars of spicy hot pickles. Most pickles keep for a few months; some like *kadumaanga* and *ennamaanga* keep for years.

Summer in Kerala is known for its humidity, with mercury levels climbing to new heights. Summer is also the time for pickling and sun-drying a variety of fruits and vegetables. In times past, the scorching heat of summer never dissuaded families from their pickling and sun-drying rituals. They were family projects, and everyone chipped in to help. The delicious aroma of raw mangoes, lemons, gooseberries, green chilies, ginger, sesame oil, cayenne pepper, and a variety of spices lingered in the air on pickling days. I can still hear, across the decades, the rhythmic clang of *ulakka* (heavy iron poles) pulverizing the spices in the cavity of the *ural* (stone trough) through the silence of hot summer afternoons. My mother insisted that hand pounding spices made a world of difference in the taste of her pickles, because it brought out the best flavors of the spices. In her opinion, machine grinding always unnecessarily heated the spices and took away some of the essential flavors. In the old days, pickles were stored in huge ceramic jars called *bharani*, and after filling a jar with fresh pickles, a clean piece of cloth soaked in sesame oil was laid on top. The lid was placed on top of it and then sealed tight with wet clay. When the clay dried, it became airtight. The jars were moved to a corner of the *kalavara* (pantry), where it stayed for months, undisturbed. The preparation, storage—and months later, the opening of the sealed ceramic jars of pickles—was all like a ritual.

Pickles are made with mangoes, lemon, bitter lemon, gooseberry, green chilies, bitter gourd, and ginger. The selection of fruits and vegetables, chili powder, oil, mustard powder, and salt, and the mixing of these ingredients in the proper way, all contribute to the taste of the pickle. The real secret of spicing and seasoning pickles is not only which spices to use, but also how you use them—whether raw or roasted, whole or ground.

An important thing in making homemade pickles is to use clean, dry, airtight jars for storing. If you want to try a hot pickle before preparing a whole batch, you can always pick up a jar at an Indian grocery. There are some very good brands of South Indian pickles available in the U.S. market; Priya, M.T.R., and Narasu's are my personal favorites. They are fairly inexpensive, and a bottle will last a long time. After use, refrigerate the pickle bottle.

Naranga Curry: Lemon Pickle

Traditionally, lemon pickle is made with thin-skinned Indian sweet lime. Meyer lemons make an ideal substitute. Fresh, hot, and spicy lemon pickle is a must at the festival of Onam. This pickle has a short shelf life, but it will keep for a few weeks in the refrigerator.

6 lemons
¼ cup plus 3 tablespoons sesame oil
1 teaspoon turmeric powder
Salt to taste
1 teaspoon mustard seeds
2 to 3 tablespoons dried red cayenne, serrano or Thai chili powder (less for a milder taste)
1 teaspoon fenugreek seeds, lightly toasted and powdered
¼ teaspoon asafetida powder (optional)

Wash and dry the lemons. Heat a quarter-cup of oil in a skillet, and panfry the lemons over medium heat until their skins turn light brown. Remove from the stove, and when they are cool enough to touch, cut the lemons into small pieces, and discard the seeds. Sprinkle turmeric and salt over the lemon slices, and mix well. Heat the remaining oil in a large skillet, and add the mustard seeds. When the mustard seeds start sputtering, add the cayenne, fenugreek, and asafetida, and fry for another minute. Add the lemon pieces, mix well, and remove it from the stove. If there is not enough oil to coat the entire mixture, add a few more teaspoons of oil and stir. Cool to room temperature, and store in a jar with a tight-fitting lid. It takes one day for the lemon slices to absorb the spices. Refrigerate after the first day.

Makes 2 to 2½ cups.

Vadugappuli Naranga Curry: Bitter Lemon Pickle

Bitter lemons have a very strong tangy, bitter taste. These preserved lemons shock the palate with an assertive sourness along with a hint of bitterness. Back home, those who enjoy this taste often pickle them with just salt. When combined with cayenne pepper and asafetida, the bitterness is mellowed and it becomes a zesty pickle.

8 bitter lemons
1 cup sesame oil
1 teaspoon mustard seeds
1 dried red cayenne, serrano, or Thai chili, halved
¼ teaspoon asafetida powder
10 to 12 fresh curry leaves
Salt to taste
½ cup dried red cayenne, serrano, or Thai chili pepper, powdered

Wash the bitter lemons. Place them in a saucepan with enough water to cover, and bring it to a boil. Reduce the heat, and cook for six to eight minutes. This will help reduce the bitterness of the lemon skins. Drain and cool the cooked lemons. Cut the lemons in half, and remove all seeds. Then cut the lemons into very small pieces.

Heat the sesame oil in a large, heavy skillet, and add the mustard seeds. When the mustard seeds start sputtering, add the halved red chili pepper, asafetida powder, curry leaves, salt, and cayenne pepper powder. Remove from the stove, and stir in the cut lemon pieces. Fold gently to mix well. Store the pickle in an airtight glass container. This pickle will be ready to serve in a couple of days.

Makes 1½ cups.

Nellikkakari: Gooseberry Pickle

Nellikka is the small Indian gooseberry with a sweet and sour taste. There are two types of *nellikka:* the tiny one with ridges and the slightly larger and smoother variety. The tiny gooseberry is used in this pickle. Gooseberries are available at some farmers' markets and specialty produce shops from middle to late summer. Occasionally, fresh gooseberries are available in Indian grocery stores.

1 pound gooseberries
6 tablespoons sesame oil
Salt to taste
6 tablespoons dried red cayenne, serrano, or Thai chili powder
1 teaspoon mustard seeds
1 teaspoon dry roasted and powdered fenugreek seeds
¼ teaspoon asafetida powder
12 to 15 fresh curry leaves

Wash and dry the gooseberries. Heat three tablespoons of oil in a large heavy skillet over medium heat, and panfry the gooseberries. Keep stirring the gooseberries to fry them evenly. After ten to twelve minutes, remove from the stove, and let them cool to room temperature. When they are cool enough to touch, cut the gooseberries into small pieces, and remove the seeds in the middle. Mix the cut berries with salt and cayenne pepper powder, and set aside for at least half an hour, so that the spices have a chance to blend with the berries. Heat the remaining oil, and fry the mustard seeds. When the mustard seeds start spluttering, add the fenugreek powder, asafetida powder, and curry leaves to the oil. Remove it from the stove, and after a minute, pour it over the gooseberries. Mix thoroughly. Cover and store in the refrigerator. The pickle will be ready to serve in two days.

Makes 2 to 2 ½ cups.

Vedinellikka: Dry Gooseberry Pickle

This is a dry pickle made with the large, smooth-skinned gooseberries. This variety has translucent flesh and pale veins that streak from top to bottom. Most gooseberries are tart, but the red-hued ones tend to be somewhat sweeter. Their tartness is mellowed when combined with a sesame oil and spice blend.

1 cup dried red cayenne, serrano, or Thai chili peppers
2 cups and 2 tablespoons sesame oil
Salt to taste
¼ teaspoon asafetida powder
1 pound gooseberries

In a heavy skillet, panfry the cayenne peppers along with two tablespoons of sesame oil for three to four minutes. Remove it from the stove, and let it cool. Using a spice mill or coffee grinder, powder the toasted peppers along with the salt and asafetida. Wash and dry the gooseberries. In a heavy skillet, heat two cups of sesame oil over medium heat, and add the gooseberries. Panfry the berries in oil until they lose their green color and start turning white. Remove them from the stove, sprinkle with the prepared spice blend, and stir well. The spice blend will absorb any remaining oil in the skillet. When it has cooled down to room temperature, transfer it to a jar with a tight-fitting lid. It will be ready to serve in a day or two. It stays fresh at room temperature for four to five days and for a couple of weeks in the refrigerator.

Makes 3 to 3 ½ cups.

A Medley of Mango Pickles

The month of Meenam (mid-March through mid-April) marks the beginning of the much-awaited mango season in Kerala. It lasts from April until the monsoonal rains break in the middle of June. There are several different kinds of mangoes in our region, from the plump and golden *ottumanga* to the slender, green, and incredibly sweet and juicy *chandrakkaran*. *Chandrakkaran* is a special variety of mango that is commonly eaten without cutting. The fruit is gently squeezed to liquefy the pulp. A hole is made at the top of the fruit by biting off a small portion at the tip, and the pulp and juice are sucked out.

No other fruit evokes more passionate regional loyalties than does the mango in India. Schools close for summer vacation by the end of March. Thoughts of hot, windy summers with plenty of mangoes from the backyard trees bring back many fond memories. During the lazy summer afternoons, young boys would climb the branches of gomango trees (a variety of mango tree brought by the Portuguese), while the adults dozed. They would bring back firm, green-skinned mangoes. The children loved sitting in the shade of the mango tree and eating them with rock salt and crushed cayenne pepper wetted with a few drops of oil.

As the weeks passed, the trees would become filled with ripe, golden mangoes, fragrant and intensely sweet, but with a tinge of balancing acidity. In the morning, the ground under the mango trees would be scattered with ripe fruit that had fallen off the tree during the night. Fruit vendors sold a wide variety of mangoes, and practically every meal during this season contained at least one dish made with mangoes. Everyone would be busy processing and preserving the mangoes before the torrential rains of the monsoon season arrived.

I admit that my opinion may be very subjective, but I believe that mangoes get the real royal treatment at the *kovilakams* (palaces) of Kochi. The various mango pickles and preserves they prepare are the very best I have ever tasted. This collection of mango pickle recipes includes preparations from the royal family of Kochi. I am deeply indebted to them for sharing these ancient family recipes with me.

The following recipes are for a variety of mango pickles and preserves. While the first recipe in this collection, *chethumaangakari*, is a fresh pickle with a short shelf life, the others are essentially spicy preserves, and traditionally, a large quantity of ingredients is used. They may also be prepared with a lesser number of mangoes. Adjust the spices accordingly.

Chethumaangakari: Green Mango Pickle

Childhood memories of the bright sunny days of Kerala summers come flooding back when I make this pickle. The taste of fresh, tart mangoes is simply divine. *Chethumaangakari* is a simple mango pickle with a short shelf life, but it is so tasty that there will be nothing left to store after a couple of days. It stays fresh for a week if refrigerated. During the summer months, it is always served at weddings and birthday feasts. If you like your food spicy, try it as a relish. It also pairs very well with Mexican and Southwestern dishes.

2 medium-sized firm green mangoes
Salt to taste
¼ cup vegetable oil
1 teaspoon mustard seeds
½ cup dried red cayenne, serrano, or Thai chili powder (less for a milder taste)
2 tablespoons fenugreek seeds, lightly toasted and powdered
¼ teaspoon asafetida powder (optional)
8 to 10 fresh curry leaves

Wash the mangoes, and cut them into small, thin slices. Sprinkle them with salt, and keep them covered as you assemble the other ingredients. In a skillet, heat the oil, and add the mustard seeds. When the mustard seeds start sputtering, add the cayenne, fenugreek, asafetida, and curry leaves. Reduce the heat to low, add the salted mango pieces, and mix well. Remove from the stove, and let it cool. Store it in glass bottles in the refrigerator. It tastes best the second day, after the mango pieces have absorbed the spices. Reduce the amount of cayenne if you prefer a less spicy pickle.

Makes 2 to 2½ cups.

Variation: Tart and crunchy green Granny Smith apples make an excellent substitute for mangoes. Core but do not peel two apples, and slice them exactly like the mangoes. Sprinkle them with salt and a tablespoon of fresh lemon juice per apple, and let them rest for a few minutes while you prepare the spice mix. Follow the mango pickle recipe above. This pickle stays fresh in the refrigerator for a week.

Uluva Maanga Curry: Mango Pickle with Fenugreek and Cayenne Pepper

This spicy mango preserve takes a couple of months to reach its full potential, but it is certainly well worth the long wait. The tender, tart mangoes absorb the spices and become very soft after a couple of months. What is amazing is that only salt and oil are used as preservatives, and the pickle stays fresh for months without refrigeration.

30 small, tender green mangoes (1 to 2 inches long)
¼ cup fenugreek seeds
1 cup salt
1 cup dried red cayenne, serrano, or Thai chili pepper powder
1 piece of cheesecloth
1 cup sesame oil

Wash the mangoes. Dry roast the fenugreek seeds in a skillet for one or two minutes, let them cool, and grind them into a fine powder. Combine the salt, cayenne pepper powder, and fenugreek powder, and stir well. In a large mixing bowl, combine the mangoes and about one-third of the spice mix, and toss well. Sprinkle a couple of spoonfuls of the spice blend at the bottom of a glass or ceramic jar with a tight-fitting lid. Add a thick layer of lightly spiced mangoes on top. Sprinkle a layer of spice mix on top of the mangoes. Repeat the process until all the mangoes and spices are used up. Cover the jar with the lid, and set it aside. Every day, open the jar, stir with a dry spoon, close the lid tightly, and set it aside. After one week, take a clean, large piece of cheesecloth and fold it to fit the mouth of the jar. Put the folded cloth in a small skillet, and pour in a cup of oil. Let the cloth soak up the oil. Open the jar, stir the mangoes, and place the oil-soaked cloth on top. Cover the lid tightly and store. The preserve will be ready to use in two months. At that time, the mangoes will have absorbed all the spices and oil and they will be very soft.

Ennamaanga: Deep-fried Mangoes with Spices in Sesame Oil

Unlike the previous recipe, here the mango is deep-fried before mixing it with spices. The crispy slices are layered with a hot and spicy blend of spices and stored in an airtight container for several days. The mango slices will absorb the spices and become very soft in a couple of weeks.

50 small, firm green mangoes
8 cups and 3 tablespoons sesame oil
1 cup cayenne, serrano, or Thai chilies, dry roasted and powdered
½ cup fenugreek seeds, dry roasted and powdered
1½ cups sea salt
1 small piece cotton cloth or cheesecloth

Wash and drain the mangoes. Cut then up into thin, long pieces. If the pieces are very fleshy, spread them on a tray, and dry them in the sun for a day or two. Heat seven cups of oil in a heavy pot to 360°F. Deep-fry the mango pieces until crispy. Remove them from the oil, and drain. Combine the cayenne pepper powder and fenugreek powder, and mix well. Spread a layer of fried mangoes in a ceramic or glass pickling jar, sprinkle with salt, and stir well. Sprinkle a tablespoon of the blended spices over them. Spread another layer of mangoes, salt, and spices. Repeat the process until all of the fried mango pieces and spices are used. Pour the remaining cup of oil on top. Take a clean piece of cotton cloth or cheesecloth and fold it approximately to fit the mouth of the pickling jar. Pour three tablespoons of oil on this cloth, and spread it over the mangoes. Place the lid over this and cover it tightly. It takes a couple of weeks for the mango pieces to absorb the salt and spices and become tender.

Uppumaanga: Mangoes in Brine

In times past, this simple condiment—tart green mangos preserved in salt—was a staple in our pantries. It was a permanent standby during monsoon seasons. Fascinating grandmother tales about *uppumaanga* are often retold to children in Kerala.

One such story is that even Lord Guruvayoorappan, the presiding deity of the famous temple in Kerala, was tempted to finish his meal when it was served with *uppumaanga*. The story goes that once, the *mesanthi* (chief priest) of the temple was ill and asked his young son to perform the *uccha pooja* (noontime service) at the temple. The young boy cooked rice in a bell-metal pot and took it inside the shrine. After making the offering according to his father's instructions, the boy closed his eyes and prayed. When he opened his eyes, all of the rice was still in the pot. His eyes welled up with tears, and he pleaded, "O lord, please partake of this humble offering. My father will be furious if you do not eat what I have cooked. I will go home and get some *uppumaanga*. Then will you please finish your meals?" Closing the shrine doors behind him, he ran home and came back with a small bowl of *uppumaanga*. Legend has it that, touched by the little boy's innocence, Lord Guruvayoorappan appeared before him as a little boy and devoured the rice with *uppumaanga*.

When the little boy opened the doors and came out with an empty pot, the temple workers were furious; they thought the boy had finished off their share of the rice, and they complained to his father. Little did the boy know that the food offering was always distributed to the temple workers after the ceremonial offering. When questioned by his angry father, the boy kept repeating that the lord ate all of the rice. That night, when the father was asleep, the lord came to him in a dream and explained that he did indeed consume the rice when the boy pleaded with such innocence and tempted him with such tasty *uppumaanga*.

100 tender mangoes
1 cup sea salt

Chandrakkaran mangoes are used in the traditional recipe. Any other very small mangoes, approximately three-quarters of an inch to one inch long, may be used. Wash the mangoes, and leave a small piece of stem on top. Put the mangoes in a *bharani* (ceramic jar) or glass jar with a tight lid, sprinkle with salt, and stir well. Stir the mangoes twice daily, and set aside. The *uppumaanga* will be ready to serve in a week.

Kadumaanga: Tender Mango Pickle

One of the great combinations of tropical ingredients is mango and cayenne pepper. The acidity of the tender green mango is balanced with the spiciness of cayenne pepper in this pickle. *Kadumaanga* is a very tasty mango pickle traditionally made with small *chandrakkaran* mangoes plucked off the tree before their seeds begin to harden. These mangoes are less than an inch in length and are very tender. Any other variety of small mangoes may be substituted in this recipe. The mangoes are preserved in salt first, and later the spices are added.

100 tender green mangoes
1 cup sea salt
3 cups cayenne, serrano, or Thai chilies, dry roasted and powdered
1¼ cup mustard seeds, powdered
A piece of cotton cloth or cheesecloth for covering the jar
3 tablespoons sesame oil

Wash the mangoes, and drain well. Leaving about a quarter-inch of stem intact, cut off the remaining stem. Put the mangoes in a ceramic or glass pickling jar, and sprinkle with salt. Stir well, cover tightly, and set aside for four to five days. Open the jar a couple of times a day, and stir the mangoes with a dry spoon. After five days, the mangoes will have absorbed the salt and shrunk in size. Combine the cayenne pepper powder and mustard seed powder, and sprinkle over the mangoes. Stir well to coat all of the mangoes. Take a clean piece of cotton cloth or cheesecloth and fold it to fit the mouth of the pickling jar. Pour sesame oil on this cloth, and place it on top of the mangoes. Place the lid over this, and close it tightly. Allow the pickle to absorb all the seasonings for at least a couple of weeks before serving.

In the old days, *kadumaanga* was always prepared in ceramic jars called *bharani*. A *bharani* lid is not tight fitting. To close it tightly, they sealed it with wet clay. As the clay hardened, the jar would become airtight.

Adamaanga: Dried, Spiced Mango Pieces

In India, pickle recipes are passed from one generation to another. This recipe is from my cousin Usha, who got it from her mother-in-law, Kunjipilla Thampuran. *Adamaanga* is a sweet and hot dried mango preserve, a staple in the *kalavaras* (pantries) of *kovilakams* (royal palaces). Its combination of sweet, acidic, and spicy flavors gives it a distinctly southern flavor. *Adamaanga* tastes great just by itself; a cup of boiled rice with some yogurt and a few pieces of *adamaanga* makes a sumptuous light supper. *Adamaanga* is also used in preparing a very tasty chutney.

50 *moovandan* mangoes that are on the verge of ripeness*
1½ cups sea salt
1 cup cayenne, serrano, or Thai chilies, dry roasted and powdered
¼ cup fenugreek seeds, dry roasted and powdered
2 pounds of jaggery or brown sugar

Wash the mangoes, and slice them into long pieces with the skin intact. Place the mango pieces in a glass or ceramic jar, and sprinkle them with salt. Stir well to coat all of the pieces. Cover and set aside for twenty-four hours. The salt will liquefy. The next morning, take out the mango pieces and spread them on a mat (or tray) to dry in the sun. When the sun sets, put the mango pieces back into the salt solution in the jar, and cover it. Follow these steps for two days. On the third day, add the cayenne pepper powder, fenugreek powder, and brown sugar, and stir well. Keep the jar covered for the next two days. On the third day, take out the mango slices, and dry them in the hot sun. After sunset, put them back into the spice mix in the jar, cover, and set aside. Continue this process for a week to ten days, until the mango pieces are completely dry and have absorbed all the spices in the jar. They should be dark brown in color and taste sweet, salty, hot, and sour—all at the same time. Store dried *adamaanga* in airtight jars. This preserve lasts a long time, if only you can keep from eating it.

> **Usha's *adamaanga* memories:**
> My mother used to take me with her while she visited a lady from the royal family. And always, as we took our leave, she would ask me, "Do you like *thera* (dried ripe mango preserve) or *adamaanga*?" I would answer *"Thera"* and gladly pocket a small package she would give me. Once, my brother asked me why she gave me only *thera*. I replied that I always opted for it because I preferred it over *adamaanga*. My brother mulled over it as he relished his share of the *thera*, then suggested that the next time she asked the question, I should answer that I liked both. So I took his advice, and I was pleasantly surprised to get both from her. Years later, I married her son and moved to the United States. Every time I visit her, she gives me two small packages that she has thoughtfully saved from the mango season.

Moovandan is the variety traditionally used in making this preserve. Any lightly tart green mango may be substituted.

Since it is not possible to get *moovandan* mangoes in the United States, I tried this recipe with medium-sized supermarket-variety mangoes, on a much smaller scale. The result was pretty good, thanks to two rainless weeks in Texas.

3 medium-sized raw green mangoes
3 tablespoons salt
4 tablespoons serrano chilies, dry roasted and powdered
1 tablespoon fenugreek seeds, dry roasted and powdered
8 tablespoons powdered jaggery

It took three sunny days to dry the salted mangoes. I mixed the dried mango with spice blend and jaggery and kept it covered for another day. Six more days of drying, and the *adamaanga* was ready. If it is not practical to dry the mangoes in the sun, they may be dried in a dehydrator.

Chapter Seven
Accompaniments and Sun-Dried Preserves

In every cuisine, there are certain dishes that make each menu more complete and more festive. They might not have the status of a course in and of themselves, but without them, the meal would lose some of its appeal. What would American Thanksgiving be without cranberry sauce, for example, or a Mexican dinner without a spicy salsa? In the vegetarian cuisine of Kerala, these palate teasers take on many different forms: salty plantain, jackfruit, or breadfruit chips; steamed plantains; crisp, puffy wafers called *pappadams;* golden, smooth ghee; and tangy buttermilk.

Not all of them are served only with main meals. Crunchy chips are often served as snacks. Making deep-fried chips at home is not a difficult task, and their taste is far superior to store-bought chips. Thanks to food processors, slicing is a breeze. It is important to use oil that can be heated to high temperatures. The oil must be well heated before adding the sliced vegetables for frying, otherwise oil seeps into the food and will make it soggy. Hot oil sears the surface to a firm crispiness.

Ghee is served at the beginning of the meal, and it is also used in making almost all desserts. Tangy buttermilk comes as a palate cleanser toward the end of the meal. During sultry, hot summer afternoons, a cool glass of *sambharam* makes a refreshing drink. We also have a wide array of sun-dried preserves called *kondattam;* they come in handy both as a quick snack and as a pleasant accompaniment to meals. During the summer months, spiced and cooked rice dough, as well as a variety of vegetables, are dried in the sun for several days until they are completely dry.

The practice of spicing and sun-drying rice, vegetables, and fruit goes back several centuries. Cookbooks dating as far back as 1200 AD mention these preserves. My region of India receives hardly any rain during the summer months, so the climate is ideal for processing and preserving summer's bounty before the monsoon season's torrential rains arrive. Back home, there is a saying that the taste of the *kondattam* reflects the efficiency of the hands that made it. In the case of *ari kondattam* and *ari pappadam* (rice crisps and rice wafers), the quality of rice used, the consistency of the rice batter, the degree of spicing, and the shape of the hand press varies from family to family. Once they are completely dry, they are deep-fried in oil before serving. While fried rice crisps make excellent snack food, vegetable crisps are typically served with meals. Drying spiced mango pulp to make *maangaathera* is another summer activity.

In the sunniest regions of the United States, such as the Southwest, these preserves can be prepared in the traditional manner; good results can also be achieved by using a dehydrator or an oven set on low heat.

Varuthupperi: Green Plantain Chips

Deep-fried, crisp, golden yellow plantain chips are a must at feasts. These chips are very popular all over South India. Plantains are cut in three different shapes for frying. For serving at feasts, they are generally quartered lengthwise and then cut crosswise into thin triangular slices. To serve as a snack, they are cut either as full rounds or as half rounds. But no matter what the shape, these crunchy morsels taste simply delicious.

My father was a *varuthupperi* fanatic. For him, plantain chips were definitely not an accompaniment—they were a must with breakfast, lunch, snacks, and dinner. He was also particular about the shape. For breakfast, he preferred the half-moon shape. At lunch and dinner, he wanted them sliced into thin triangles. And for a snack, they had to be perfect thin rounds. Thankfully, Mom had both the resources and the patience to produce them every single day.

6 firm green plantains
6 cups vegetable oil
½ cup concentrated salt water*

Peel off the thick green skins from the plantains, and wash it to remove any dark stain from the outside. Pat them dry with paper towels. When making the smaller, triangular chips, halve the plantain lengthwise, and cut each piece lengthwise again. Then cut each piece crosswise into thin slices. For the half-moon shape, halve the plantains lengthwise, and then cut them crosswise into thin slices. For the round chips, cut the whole plantain crosswise into thin rounds. A food processor comes in handy for cutting them into thin rounds. Fit the processor with the 2mm blade and slowly feed the peeled plantains through the top. This blade cuts the plantains evenly.

Heat the oil in a heavy wok or deep-frying pan to 365°F. When the oil is hot, spread the plantain pieces evenly in the oil, and deep-fry until they are golden and crisp, about five minutes. Add a teaspoon of concentrated salt water to the oil, and cover the pan with a splatter screen. The water will really splatter and make a lot of noise. In a minute or so, when the water has stopped sputtering, remove the cover. By now, all the water should have evaporated, and the crispy fries will be golden and evenly salted. Drain well, and store in airtight containers.

The best way to drain deep-fried plantains is to use a cake cooling rack placed over a cookie tray. The excess oil will drip through the cooling rack and fall onto the cookie tray.

Makes 8 to 12 Servings

*Add one tablespoon of salt to a half-cup of water, and stir well. If there is no salt sediment at the bottom, add more salt, and stir until there is some salt residue left at the bottom and the water is saturated with salt.

Sarkara Upperi: Sweet Plantain Chips

Sarkara upperi is the sweet version of *varuthupperi*. Both of these chips are served at feasts. My mother always added a touch of ghee to these sweet chips, which made them taste just perfect.

6 firm green plantains
6 cups vegetable oil
2 cups jaggery or brown sugar
½ cup water
3 tablespoons ghee
1 teaspoon cardamom **or** 1 teaspoon dried ginger

Peel off the thick green skin, and cut the plantains in half, lengthwise. Cut these long pieces into quarter-inch thick slices. Heat the oil in a heavy wok or deep-frying pan to 365°F. Fry the plantain chips until they are golden and crisp, about six to seven minutes. Remove them from the oil with a slotted spoon, and drain them on a cake cooling rack placed over a cookie tray. Excess oil will drip through the cooling rack and fall onto the cookie tray.

Combine the jaggery (or brown sugar) and water in a heavy skillet, and bring it to a boil. Reduce the heat to medium, and cook until it forms a syrup (215°F to 220°F on a candy thermometer). The syrup should form a single long string when dropped from a spoon. Remove the syrup from the heat and stir in the fried plantain pieces. Stir well to coat. Pour in the ghee, sprinkle with cardamom, and stir well. The syrup will coat the chips evenly and harden in a few minutes. Let them cool, and store them in an airtight container. Serve at room temperature.

Makes 8 to 12 servings.

Chena Varuthathu: Telinga Potato Chips

Deep-fried telinga potato chips are another must at *sadyas*. They are cut into small chunks and deep-fried. These dark-brown fries are never as crispy as banana chips.

1 pound telinga potatoes *(suran)*
6 cups vegetable oil
½ cup concentrated salt water*

Peel off the dark skin of the telinga potatoes, then wash and dry the potatoes. This vegetable has a pinkish color. Cut them into thin strips of approximately one inch in length. In a heavy wok or deep-frying pan, heat the oil to 365°F. Deep-fry the pieces until they are brown and crisp. Add a teaspoon of concentrated salt water to the oil, and cover with a splatter screen. After the water has stopped sputtering, remove the cover. By now, all the water should have evaporated, and the chips will be brown and evenly salted. Drain them on paper towels. Store in airtight containers.

*Add one tablespoon of salt to a half-cup of water, and stir well. If there is no salt sediment at the bottom, add more salt, and stir until there is some salt residue left at the bottom and the water is saturated with salt.

Makes 8 to 12 servings.

Pappadams: Fried *Urad* Dal Wafers

Pappadams are a good accompaniment to any meal. Kerala *pappadams* are different from the *pappadams* usually found in Indian restaurants and food stores. They are made with *urad* flour and a domestic baking powder called *pappadakkaram* and seasoned with cumin and asafetida. Unfortunately, they are not readily available in U.S. markets. They have a very short shelf life if kept outside. *Appalams,* which are available in Indian grocery stores, are a good substitute.

4 cups vegetable oil for deep-frying
8 to 10 *appalams*

In a heavy wok or deep-frying pan, heat the oil to 365°F. Slowly slide an *appalam* into the hot oil. Turn it over immediately with a pair of tongs. Fry for thirty to forty seconds. Remove it from oil, and drain it on paper towels. *Pappadams* may also be roasted over a gas flame or heated in a microwave oven.

Makes 4 to 6 servings.

Chakka Varuthathu: Jackfruit Chips

During the summer months, there is plenty of jackfruit in Kerala. In the United States, it is grown in Hawaii and southern Florida. Inside the thorny, dark green skin, there are several fig-like fruits, each covering a hard seed. As the jackfruit grows to its full size, the seeds and the pods are fully formed. The pods inside are pale yellow, and the raw pods are firm to the touch. At this stage, just like green plantains, the jackfruit is not sweet, and it is used as a vegetable. Jackfruit chips are a must at Vishu celebrations.

1 small green jackfruit
10 cups vegetable oil for frying
½ cup concentrated salt water*

Jackfruit used for frying should be fully grown but not ripe. They will be very firm to the touch, and the pods inside will be pale yellow. Cut the unripe jackfruit in half and remove the tick, thorny green skin. Cut it into segments, and remove the seeds. The seeds are covered with jackfruit pods. Since this vegetable has a tendency to be sticky, smear some oil on your hands before pulling out the seeds. Pull off the pods around the seeds, wash them, and cut them into slices similar to those for shoestring potatoes.

In a heavy wok or a deep-frying pan, heat oil to 365°F. Fry the jackfruit pieces until they are golden and crisp. Add a teaspoon of the concentrated salt water to the oil, and cover with a splatter screen. The water on hot oil will really splatter and make a lot of noise. In a minute or so, when the water has stopped sputtering, remove the cover. By now, all the water should have evaporated, and the crispy chips will be golden brown and evenly salted. Drain them on a cake cooling rack placed over a cookie tray. The excess oil will drip through the cooling rack and fall onto the cookie tray. Store chips in airtight containers.

Makes 15 to 20 servings.

*Add one tablespoon of salt to a half-cup of water, and stir well. If there is no salt sediment at the bottom, add more salt, and stir until there is some salt residue left at the bottom and the water is saturated with salt.

Kadachakka Varuthathu: Breadfruit Chips

Breadfruit is a starchy vegetable that was brought to us by Portuguese explorers. It grows in clusters of two or three and is rounded to cylindrical in shape, with green skin and a white, somewhat fibrous pulp. The green skin is peeled off, and the white, firm flesh is thinly sliced and deep-fried. Because of the shape of the breadfruit, these chips look like little fans.

2 firm breadfruit
6 cups vegetable oil for frying
½ cup concentrated salt water

Peel the thick green skin off the breadfruit, and cut it in half. Cut it into segments, and slice it thin.

In a heavy wok or a deep-frying pan, heat oil to 365°F. Fry the breadfruit pieces until they are golden and crisp. Add a teaspoon of the concentrated salt water to the oil, and cover with a splatter screen. The water on hot oil will really splatter and make a lot of noise. In a minute or so, when the water has stopped sputtering, remove the cover. By now, all the water should have evaporated, and the crispy fries will be golden brown and evenly salted. Drain on a cake cooling rack placed over a cookie tray. The excess oil will drip through the cooling rack and fall onto the cookie tray. Store chips in airtight containers.

Makes 8 to 12 servings.

*Add one tablespoon of salt to a half-cup of water and stir well. If there is no salt sediment at the bottom, add more salt, and stir until there is some salt residue left at the bottom and the water is saturated with salt.

Pazzam Nurukku: Steamed Ripe Plantains

Steamed ripe plantains, a must at Onam feast, add a mild sweetness to any meal. They also make a healthy snack or brunch dish.

4 ripe plantains (the skin may have black spots)
1½ tablespoons ghee
½ cup jaggery or brown sugar

Wash the plantains and trim off their ends. Cut them into two-inch long pieces with the skin intact. Heat water in a steamer. Place the steamer insert over the pot, and place the plantain pieces in the steamer, standing on end. Dot the tops of the pieces with the ghee, and sprinkle them with jaggery or brown sugar. Cover and steam until the fruit is cooked through, approximately ten to twelve minutes. As they are steamed, the plantains will absorb the melted brown sugar and ghee. Serve them warm or cold. Ripe plantains may also be steamed without ghee and jaggery or brown sugar.

Makes 8 to 12 servings.

Neyyu: Ghee or Clarified Butter

This thick, golden liquid with an enticing aroma is a must for making sweets. Ghee is excellent for frying, since it has a higher smoking point than regular butter. Ghee imparts a pleasant aroma to dishes. Ghee is often served with rice and is also used in making most desserts.

One pound of unsalted butter

Melt the butter in a heavy saucepan over medium heat. Melting butter makes a crackling sound while it simmers. When the moisture has evaporated and the milk solids have finally separated, the clear, golden ghee bubbles and rises to the top. At this point, remove the pan from the stove, and let it cool. Strain through a fine mesh strainer to remove the milk solids. The liquid will be golden in color. It will solidify in cooler temperatures but will become clear when heated. Unlike butter, ghee can be stored at room temperature for several weeks and in the refrigerator or freezer for even longer periods.

Makes approximately 1½ cups.

Thayir, Mooru, and *Sambharam*: Yogurt, Buttermilk, and Spicy Yogurt Drink

Homemade yogurt and buttermilk always taste fresher. They do not contain any thickeners or preservatives. Making yogurt at home is a simple process. It is not necessary to buy expensive yogurt makers or thermometers to measure the right temperature. Yogurt can be made at home with either whole milk or reduced-fat milk. Whole-milk yogurt will be thicker in consistency. Store-bought plain yogurt may be substituted for homemade yogurt.

½ gallon milk
½ cup store-bought premium yogurt **or** yogurt culture

Heat the milk in a saucepan over medium heat, and bring it to a boil. Reduce the heat, and simmer for three to four minutes. Remove it from the stove; keep it covered, otherwise a thin film will form on the top. Smear a tablespoon of yogurt culture inside a glass or stainless-steel bowl. Pour slightly warm milk in a thin stream into this bowl. Add the remaining yogurt culture, and stir gently. Cover and keep in a dry, warm place for fermentation. During summer months, yogurt may be left on the kitchen counter to set. In colder months, keep the bowl near a heating unit or inside the oven with the pilot light on. Covering the bowl with a folded towel will also help speed up the process. The yogurt will set in four to six hours.

When yogurt is churned to separate the butterfat, the remaining thin and slightly sour liquid, buttermilk, is produced. Buttermilk or yogurt is used as a souring agent in several coconut-based curries.

Sambharam is a spicy, yogurt-based drink. Back home, it is prepared with slightly sour buttermilk. Plain yogurt also makes good *sambharam*. During hot summer afternoons, it makes a great thirst quencher. In the old days, *thanneer panthals* (small huts serving *sambharam*) were set up along major roadways in Kerala to serve cold drinks to weary travelers on foot.

2 cups plain yogurt **or** 3 cups buttermilk
Salt to taste

4 cups ice-cold water
2 or 3 fresh green chilies (serrano or Thai) (less for a milder taste)
3 tablespoons fresh lemon or lime leaves, thinly sliced (if available)
½ cup fresh curry leaves
1 teaspoon fresh ginger, grated

Combine the yogurt, salt, and water in a blender, and mix well. If using buttermilk, reduce the quantity of water by half. Pour it into a pitcher. Cut the green chilies lengthwise and then into thin strips. (If you prefer the drink mild, reduce or eliminate the green chilies.) Stir in the green chilies, lime or lemon leaves, curry leaves, and grated ginger. Refrigerate for an hour before serving.

Makes 6 servings.

Decoction Coffee: South Indian Coffee

Traditional South Indian coffee is not any special brand of coffee, and it does not require any special equipment to prepare. It is almost like Italian latte, but with sugar already added. The caramelized taste of our coffee comes from boiled milk mixed with sugar.

8 teaspoons very finely ground coffee
2 cups boiling water
2 cups whole milk
3 to 4 teaspoons sugar (according to taste)

The authentic equipment for preparing this coffee is called a decoction pot. A decoction pot is a cylindrical pot with two compartments. The bottom part collects the dripping coffee; it is about the size of a six- or eight-ounce glass. The second part, which fits tightly over the bottom part, has several tiny holes at the bottom. The third piece is a perforated disk with a metal handle attached at the center. To make decoction coffee, place the upper compartment over the bottom one. Add coffee powder to the top compartment, and place the perforated disk on top. Push down slightly, tightly packing the coffee. Pour boiling water over the disk until the top compartment is full. Cover and set aside. Since the coffee grounds are very fine, it will take a few minutes for the water to drip down. The coffee collected in the bottom half will be strong and flavorful.

While the coffee is dripping, place milk in a heavy saucepan, and bring it to a boil. When the milk starts bubbling and rises to the top, remove it from the stove. Stir in sugar. Pour the coffee over the hot milk, and stir. Your coffee is ready to enjoy. If you like a foamy top, froth the milk with a milk frother, or hold the pot about a foot above the coffee cup, and pour it slowly into the cup.

But you don't have to run out and get a decoction pot to make this coffee. A French coffee press is one alternative to a decoction pot; otherwise, use a regular coffee pot. If you are using a regular filter coffee pot, place the coffee filter over the pot, and add finely ground coffee. With the back of a spoon, press it down so that the coffee is packed tightly. Pour in one cup of boiling water, and let it drip. Repeat with the remaining cup of hot water. By pouring in only one cup at a time, the water drips slowly and absorbs the full flavor of the coffee.

Makes 4 cups of coffee.

Sun-Dried Preserves

Summer is the time of the year for processing and preserving vegetables and fruits before the torrential rains of monsoon. Okra, bitter gourd, green chili peppers, tender black-eyed peas in pods, snake gourd, lotus stems, and bitter-tasting *chundanga* and *manathankali* for drying; ripe mangoes for sun-dried mango preserve; and green jackfruit for *pappadams*—the list goes on. Sun-dried preserves are also made with cooked and spiced rice batter. Since these preserves are always made in large quantities and stored, I have not included a number of servings after each of these recipes.

A favorite preserve of mine is *maangaathera,* a sun-dried mango preserve that bursts with the tropical flavors of sweet mangoes, spicy hot cayenne peppers, and sugar. It is very similar to Fruit Roll-Ups, but with a shocking bite of cayenne pepper.

Arikondattam: Spicy Rice Crisps

Deep-fried spicy rice crisps make a quick and easy snack. Although they are traditionally served with rice soup or a simple meal of rice and a curry, they make an excellent companion to a glass of ice-cold beer! Mildly fermented rice batter is combined with a few spices and cooked to a thick consistency. Using a snack press, it is then pressed into thin strands onto a large tray covered with a piece of cheesecloth. It is dried in the sun until very dry.

4 cups long-grain rice
Salt to taste
½ teaspoon ground cayenne pepper
¼ teaspoon asafetida powder

2 tablespoons black sesame seeds
2 tablespoons cumin seeds
4 cups vegetable oil

Soak the rice in water for four to six hours. Rinse in several changes of water until the water runs clear, and drain. In a blender, grind the rice with just enough water to make a very fine, thin batter. Add salt to taste, and stir well. Cover and leave overnight at room temperature to ferment. The next morning, mix the cayenne powder, asafetida, sesame seeds, and cumin seeds into the batter, and stir well. Pour enough water to make a thin batter. Cook the batter in a heavy saucepan over medium heat, stirring constantly, until it thickens and forms a soft dough (about the consistency of mashed potatoes). Remove it from the heat, and let it cool.

Spread a piece of cheesecloth or a clean kitchen towel over a large tray. Fit the snack press with the three-star disk, and fill it with dough. Press thick strands of dough onto the cheesecloth. Dry the strands in direct sunlight until the *arikondattam* is completely dry. This may take a couple of days. Alternatively, they may be dried in a dehydrating unit. Store in airtight containers.

When you are ready to use them, heat oil in a heavy saucepan or a wok to 375°F. Sprinkle a handful of crisps into the oil, and stir. When deep-fried, they will puff up and become very crunchy and delicious. Remove them with a slotted spoon, and drain.

Variation: *Unnithandu* (plantain stems) add a crunchy texture to rice crisps. After the bananas are harvested, the plant is usually cut down. Peel off the green outer skin of the trunk. The white stem inside will be about four to five inches in diameter. Finely chop the plantain-stem pieces and stir them into the dough. Shape the dough into small balls, and sun-dry them for a few days until they are completely dry. Deep-fry before serving.

Ari Pappadams: Rice Wafers

When deep-fried in oil, this thin rice wafer literally expands to twice its size. These crispy wafers have the nutty fragrance of sesame seeds.

2 cups long-grain rice
Salt to taste
¼ teaspoon asafetida powder
1 tablespoon black or brown sesame seeds

1 tablespoon cumin seeds
30 to 40 pieces of banana leaves **or** parchment paper cut into four-inch squares

Soak rice in water for four to six hours. Rinse it in several changes of water until the water runs clear, and drain. In a blender, grind the rice with just enough water to make a very fine, thin batter. Remove it from the blender and stir in salt, asafetida powder, sesame seeds, and cumin seeds. Add enough water to make a fine batter (the consistency of crepe batter). Keep it covered overnight while fermenting.

Traditionally, the batter is spread on the round, flat leaves of a tropical plant or banana leaves and steamed in an *idli* steamer. You can also line a stack of *idli* plates with small squares of parchment paper or cheesecloth.

Spread a tablespoon of batter thinly on each piece. Meanwhile, boil three cups of water in a large saucepan. Stack the plates, and place them inside the pot, cover, and steam for ten to twelve minutes. Remove the stacks, and let it cool. When they have cooled to room temperature, peel the *ari pappadams* from the leaves, paper, or cloth, set them on a clean tray, and dry them in the sun until they are dry and crisp. When they are completely dry, store them in airtight containers.

When you are ready to use them, heat oil in a wok or frying pan to 365°F and deep-fry the *pappadams.* They will puff up and become very crunchy and delicious. Remove them with a slotted spoon, and drain.

Vendakka Kondattam: Okra Crisps

When okra is in abundance, it is dried and preserved as okra crisps. When deep-fried in oil, these crisps have the fragrance of crispy panfried okra.

3 pounds fresh okra
1 teaspoon turmeric powder
Salt to taste

Wash the okra, and drain it until it is completely dry. Cut it into thin slices approximately one-eighth inch thick. Spread them evenly in a single layer on a large tray, and dry them in the sun. After two days of drying, it is time to salt the okra. Bring water to a boil in a large saucepan. Stir in salt and turmeric powder. When the water starts bubbling, reduce the heat, and add the okra pieces. Blanch them for about one minute, and drain them well.

Spread the okra pieces in a single layer on large trays, and dry them in the sun until they are completely dry. This will take two to three days. They may also be dried in a dehydrator. Store dried okra in airtight containers.

When you are ready to use them, heat oil in a wok or frying pan to 365°F, and deep-fry the okra pieces. They will puff up and become very crunchy. Remove them with a slotted spoon, and drain.

Paavakka Kondattam: Spicy Bitter-Gourd Crisps

Bitter melon is another vegetable that is sun-dried during the summer. The bitterness of the vegetable is tamed by blanching it along with salt and turmeric before drying it in the sun. Bitter melons are readily available in Indian stores as well as Chinese and Mexican markets.

3 to 4 pounds fresh bitter melons
1 teaspoon turmeric powder
2 teaspoons cayenne powder
Salt to taste

Wash the bitter melons, and drain them. Cut them into thin slices approximately an eighth-inch thick. Bring water to a boil in a large saucepan. Stir in salt and turmeric. When the water starts boiling, reduce the heat, and add the pieces of bitter melon. Blanch them for two minutes, and drain well. Sprinkle on cayenne powder, and stir. Spread them on one or two large trays in a single layer, and dry them in the sun until they are completely dry. This may take two to three days. They may also be dried in a dehydrator. Store in airtight containers.

When you are ready to use them, heat oil in a wok or frying pan to 365°F, and deep-fry the melon pieces. They will puff up and become very crunchy and delicious. Remove them with a slotted spoon, and drain.

Variations:

Thamaravalayam Kondattam (**Lotus Stem Crisps**): The stem of the lotus plant is another vegetable that is blanched along with red pepper and turmeric and sun-dried. Lotus stems are sometimes available in Chinese markets. Wash the lotus stems thoroughly under running water. Cut two to three pounds of lotus stems into quarter-inch slices, and cook them in plenty of water along with salt and one teaspoon of turmeric powder. Drain them after three minutes.

Sprinkle them with cayenne pepper, and mix well. Spread them in a single layer on trays, and dry them in the sun or in a dehydrator.

When you are ready to use them, heat oil in a wok or frying pan to 365°F, and deep-fry them. They will puff up and become very crunchy and delicious. Remove them with a slotted spoon, and drain.

Payaru Kondattam: **Black-Eyed Pea Crisps:** Tender, fresh black-eyed peas in pods (or long beans) are another vegetable that can be dried in this way. Fresh black-eyed peas are generally available in farmers' markets during the summer. Long beans are readily available in Indian stores as well as Chinese markets. Wash and drain the beans, and cut them into two to two-and-a-half inch pieces. Bring water to a boil in a large saucepan. Stir in salt and turmeric powder. When the water starts bubbling, reduce the heat, and blanch the beans for two minutes, then drain well. Spread them in a single layer on one or two large trays, and dry them in the sun until they are completely dry. They may also be dried in a dehydrator. Store dried black-eyed peas in airtight containers.

When you are ready to use them, heat oil in a wok or frying pan to 365°F, and deep-fry the beans. They will puff up and become very crunchy and delicious. Remove them with a slotted spoon, and drain.

Mulagu Kondattam: Green Chili Crisps

The spicy, hot bite of the green chilies is tamed by soaking them in salted yogurt before they are sun-dried.

40 to 45 fresh green chilies
3 cups yogurt
4 tablespoons salt

Wash and clean the green chilies. Using a toothpick, pierce a hole in the middle of each green chili. Mix the yogurt and salt together in a large bowl, stirring well. Soak the chilies in the salted yogurt overnight. In the morning, using a slotted spoon, remove the green chilies from the liquid, and spread them on a tray to dry in the sun. Keep the remaining yogurt in the refrigerator. In the evening, put the green chilies back into the yogurt, cover, and set aside. Repeat the process until the yogurt is absorbed by the green chilies. After that, store the green chilies overnight on the drying tray itself, and dry them in the sun for another four to five days, until they are completely dry. Store dried chilies in airtight containers.

When you are ready to use them, heat oil in a wok or frying pan to 365°F, and deep-fry the chilies. They will puff up and turn brown. Remove them with a slotted spoon, and drain.

Maangaathera: Dried Ripe Mango Preserve

Maangaathera is a sun-dried mango preserve that bursts with the tropical flavors of sweet mangoes, spicy hot cayenne peppers, and sugar. It takes several days to complete the process, but it certainly is worth the wait. This preserve is a staple in the pantries of the royal family. *Maangaathera* will require six to eight batches of the following ingredients over a period of a week to ten days:

8 cups mango pulp from very sweet mangoes
Salt to taste
2 tablespoons cayenne peppers, panfried and powdered
1 cup jaggery **or** brown sugar

Combine the mango pulp with salt, cayenne pepper, and jaggery or brown sugar, and stir well. Evenly spread the spiced pulp in a thin layer on a clean straw mat, and dry it in the sun. In the evening, bring it inside, and keep it covered with a clean piece of cloth or a kitchen towel. Dry it in the sun again on the second day. By then, the pulp will have hardened. Make another batch of spiced mango pulp, and spread it over the dried pulp. Repeat the process every other day until at least six to eight layers of pulp has been spread and dried. Keep drying it in the sun until it is completely dry. Cut the dried preserve into two- to three-inch wide squares, cover them with plastic wrap, and store them in an airtight jar. They make an excellent snack.

Instead of straw mats, plastic wrap spread on a tray may be used. Also, brown sugar may be substituted with white sugar. Depending on your preference, increase or decrease the quantity of sugar and cayenne pepper added to the pulp.

Chakka Pappadams: Jackfruit Wafers

Green jackfruit pods are cooked and blended with spices to make thin wafers. These spicy wafers have the distinct taste of jackfruit enhanced by the nutty taste of sesame seeds.

10 cups green jackfruit pods, cut into small pieces
Salt to taste
½ teaspoon turmeric powder
3 to 4 tablespoons hot cayenne powder (less for a milder taste)
¼ teaspoon asafetida powder
2 tablespoon black or brown sesame seeds
2 tablespoon cumin seeds

Place the jackfruit pods in a heavy saucepan, and pour in enough water to cover them. Sprinkle them with salt and turmeric, and cook them over medium heat until the pods are well cooked. Remove them from the stove, and drain. Grind the cooked pods along with cayenne pepper into a thick, smooth puree. Remove it from the blender, and stir in the asafetida powder, sesame seeds, and cumin seeds. Spread a tablespoon of this puree in a thin three-inch circle on a piece of parchment paper spread on a tray. Repeat with the remaining batter. Dry it in the sun for a couple of days, until completely dry and crisp. Store the dried wafers in airtight containers.

When you are ready to use them, heat oil in a wok or frying pan to 365°F, and deep-fry the wafers. They will puff up and become golden brown. Remove them with a slotted spoon, and drain.

Makes 30 to 35 wafers.

Chapter Eight
Paayasams (Puddings)

Puddings are among South India's many culinary treasures that are practically unknown to the rest of India, let alone the western world. You will never find most of them on an Indian restaurant menu; the only variety of *paayasam* you will find in a restaurant in the United States is *gheer,* the North Indian rice pudding. A few restaurants may also serve *semiya paayasam.*

These puddings are made with either rice, tropical fruit, or dal and cooked in milk or coconut milk. The velvety-smooth homemade tropical fruit jams and coconut milk impart a delicately sweet creaminess to the fruit-based *paayasams.* The creaminess of the puddings is accented with toasted coconut, raisins, and cashews. Our jams of sweetened, preserved tropical fruit require no hot-water baths or sterilized jars—just ripe fruit, ghee (preferably homemade), brown sugar, and less than an hour in the kitchen.

It is only human that we believe God's favorite food is dessert. There are several Hindu temples in Kerala that are famous for their special *paayasams.* The *pantheeraazi paal paayasam* of Poornathrayeesa Temple at Thripunithura and the *neypaayasam* of Chottanikkara Temple are indeed inimitable. *Paal paayasam* is believed to be the favorite dessert of Lord Krishna. On Janmashtami, Lord Krishna's birthday, *paal paayasam* is offered at all Krishna temples across the country. *Neypaayasam* is the offering at the temple of Durga, the goddess of strength. It is so rich with ghee and brown sugar that it stays fresh for several days, even without refrigeration.

The quality of ingredients always makes a great difference in the end product; the rice used for *paayasam* is no different. Back home, hand-pounded *unakkalari,* the aristocrat of rice varieties, is used for making *paayasam.* But like all true aristocrats, it is scarce, and I believe it is never exported abroad. It has a delicate flavor and a consistency that has just the right cling, and it cooks into a perfect *paayasam.* The clinging consistency of the *paayasam* depends on the starchiness of the rice. The rice should possess just enough starch to cling in cooking, but not too much to become gummy.

The authentic pot for cooking *paayasam* is the *uruli*, a heavy and shallow bell-metal pan with a curved interior. A heavy pot that transmits consistent, even heat is a perfect substitute. Do not use parboiled rice for *paayasam*; those grains always stay separate. In the absence of the real stuff, medium-grain or long-grain white rice is the preferred substitute.

Paal Paayasam: Rice Pudding

Much is made of rice in Kerala, and in its best incarnation, it becomes amazingly delicate and creamy, nestled in a pool of slowly simmered, condensed, and sweetened milk. Traditionally, *paayasam* is cooked over a slow-burning wood fire for several hours, so that the milk cooks down and thickens. Once the sugar is added, the rice stops cooking, and the long, slow simmer will not make it into a soggy lump. Instead, the milk will condense and develop a reddish hue. The following is a simpler version of this delicious dessert.

½ cup long-grain rice
½ gallon whole milk
2¼ cups sugar
2 cups heavy cream

Wash and rinse the rice in several changes of water until the water runs clear. Heat the milk in a saucepan over medium heat. When it comes to a boil, add the rice, lower the heat, and cook for fifteen minutes, stirring continually to prevent scorching. To test if the rice is ready, take out some grains with a spoon, and try to mash them. If it is very soft to the touch and easily mashes, it is cooked. If necessary, cook for a few more minutes. Stir in the sugar, and cook for another ten to twelve minutes. Pour in the heavy cream, and bring it to a boil. Reduce the heat, and simmer for twenty-five to thirty minutes, stirring occasionally. Remove the pan from the stove, and keep it covered to prevent the milk from forming a skin. This dessert may be served either warm or cold.

Makes 4 to 6 servings.

Variation: Back in Kerala, rice pudding gets a pinkish color. This is because it is cooked for a longer time, thereby allowing the milk to caramelize. A quick and easy way to get this pinkish color is to use a can of condensed milk in the place of cream and sugar. It will also shorten the cooking time. First, cook the rice in milk. Pour the condensed milk into the pot in a thin stream. Keep stirring continuously, so that the condensed milk is properly incorporated. Simmer for another fifteen minutes. Taste for sweetness, and stir in more sugar if needed.

Neypaayasam: Rice Pudding with Brown Sugar and Ghee

The texture of *neypaayasam* is very similar to that of Italian risotto. Like risotto, it is a creamy and closely bound mass of rice grains; but unlike risotto, *neypaayasam* is very sweet, and it is enriched with ghee, cashew nuts, coconut, and raisins. Being rich with ghee and brown sugar, it remains fresh for several days, even without refrigeration.

2 cups long-grain rice
2½ cups jaggery **or** brown sugar
2 cups of ghee
⅓ cup unsalted cashew nuts, broken into pieces
2 tablespoons fresh coconut, thinly sliced
2 tablespoons seedless raisins
1 teaspoon cardamom seeds, crushed

Rinse the rice in several changes of water until the water runs clear. In a saucepan, bring three and a half cups of water to a boil, and stir in the rice. Cook it over medium heat for fifteen to eighteen minutes, until the rice is well cooked and almost all of the water has evaporated. Once the brown sugar is added, the rice will stop cooking.

Place a heavy skillet over medium heat, and melt the jaggery or brown sugar along with three tablespoons of water. When the sugar has liquefied and has started bubbling, transfer it to the rice pot along with two tablespoons of ghee, and keep stirring gently. Reserve three tablespoons of ghee for frying the garnishes. Keep adding the remaining ghee to the rice, a couple of tablespoons at a time, stirring until the rice absorbs all of it. Cook for fifteen to twenty minutes. When well cooked, the *neypaayasam* will start leaving the sides of the pot as you stir. Remove the pot from the stove.

Heat the remaining ghee in a small skillet over medium heat, and add the cashew nuts. When they start turning golden brown, add the coconut slices and raisins, and keep stirring. The coconut will turn golden brown, and the raisins will become plump as they soak up the ghee. Garnish the *neypaayasam* with toasted nuts, raisins, and ghee. Sprinkle it with crushed cardamom, and stir gently. It tastes heavenly, warm or cold.

Makes 6 to 8 servings.

Idichu Pizinja Paayasam: Rice and Mung Dal Pudding with Coconut Milk

Creaminess is not an attribute that belongs to dairy alone; in the following recipe, coconut milk cooked down over low heat adds a creamy sweetness to the *paayasam*. This *paayasam* is traditionally served as the first course at Puthiri feast to celebrate the cooking of rice from a new harvest.

1 cup long-grain rice
4 tablespoons ghee
⅓ cup mung dal
3½ cups jaggery **or** brown sugar
6 cups fresh coconut milk*
¼ cup coconut, thinly sliced
⅛ teaspoon ginger powder (optional)
2 teaspoons cardamom, crushed
½ cup each honey and ghee (to serve with *paayasam*)

Rinse the rice in several changes of water until water runs clear. Heat one teaspoon of ghee in a heavy saucepan over medium heat. Add the dal, and fry until it is golden brown in color. Keep stirring while frying. Remove the saucepan from the stove, rinse the dal, and leave it in a strainer for a few minutes until it is completely drained. In a heavy saucepan, bring two and a half cups of water to a boil. Stir in the rice and dal, and cook until it is soft to the touch, approximately fifteen to eighteen minutes. Most of the water should have evaporated by now. Stir in the jaggery or brown sugar and two tablespoons of ghee, and cook for another fifteen minutes over medium heat, stirring continually. Pour in the coconut milk and reduce the heat. Avoid boiling—it will result in separated coconut milk. Simmer for twenty minutes while stirring. Remove from the stove. Fry the coconut pieces in the remaining ghee, and add them to the *paayasam*. Sprinkle it with ginger and cardamom, and stir gently. This *paayasam* is usually served with a spoonful each of honey and ghee on top.

Makes 6 to 8 servings.

*Six cups of fresh coconut milk may substituted with six cups of canned coconut milk, or six cups of coconut milk made from coconut-milk powder, or four cups of whole milk mixed with two cups of heavy cream. The last substitution will lack the flavor of coconut milk.

Paal Ada Pradhaman: Rice Pudding with Steamed Rice Flakes

Paal ada pradhaman is the ultimate dessert at Kerala weddings. In this elaborate version of rice pudding, rice grains go through an intricate process and emerge as thin, light flakes. These flakes are then simmered in whole milk and sugar for hours to yield a thick, creamy, and luscious pudding. No intrusive spicing or garnishing is done; you taste only the sweetness and freshness of milk, sugar, and rice. Use a heavy pot for cooking this dessert.

1 cup long-grain rice
Several pieces of banana leaves, approximately six to eight inches long
2 tablespoons ghee
1 gallon whole milk
2 cups heavy cream
4 cups sugar

Soak the rice for four to five hours, and rinse it until the water runs clear. Using a blender, pulverize the rice with just enough water to make a very smooth batter. Add the water slowly to the blender to get the right consistency. The batter should be smooth and thin, but thick enough to coat the back of a spoon.

Rinse the banana leaves, and toast them over the stove for a few seconds, until the color turns dark and they become pliable. Tear thin strips from one piece of leaf to use for tying. Smear a little ghee on each piece of leaf, and spread on a thin layer of rice batter. Roll the leaves into cylinders, and tie them with leaf strips.

Bring water to a boil in a heavy saucepan. When the water starts boiling, add the rolled-up leaf cylinders, and reduce the heat. Cook over medium heat for six to eight minutes. Remove them from the water, and drain. Open the cylinders, and cool to room temperature. When it has cooled down, peel off the *ada* and cut it into thin flakes. Cooked *ada* will not flake into thin pieces by itself, but it can easily be cut into thin pieces.

Ada flakes are cut into very small pieces, approximately one-sixteenth of an inch in length and width. Spread them on a clean towel or paper towels to dry.

In a heavy saucepan, bring milk to a boil, and add the *ada* flakes. Reduce the heat, and simmer for fifteen to twenty minutes, until the flakes are cooked. Keep stirring. Add sugar, and continue stirring. After thirty minutes, pour in heavy cream, and stir well. Simmer for another fifteen minutes. Keep stirring periodically. Remove it from the stove, and keep it covered, otherwise the milk will form a skin on top. It may be served either warm or at room temperature, or, if you prefer, chilled.

Makes 6 to 8 servings.

Variation: Commercially processed rice flakes, available at Indian grocery stores, may be substituted for homemade *ada*. They lack the softness of fresh rice flakes and the fragrance from the fresh banana leaves. However, the time spent in preparing this dish is cut down to a mere thirty minutes.

½ cup dried *ada* flakes
½ gallon whole milk
1 can condensed milk

Soak the *ada* flakes for two hours in hot water, rinse, and drain. In a heavy saucepan, cook the *ada* flakes in milk until they are very soft. These flakes take a longer time to cook than fresh flakes. Pour in the condensed milk, in a thin stream, while stirring continuously, so that it is properly incorporated. Simmer for twenty minutes. Keep stirring while it simmers. Taste for sweetness, and add more sugar if needed. Remove it from the stove, and keep it covered.

Avil Paayasam: Pounded Rice Pudding

In this quick and easy version of rice pudding, long-grain rice is substituted with *avil* (pounded rice), which takes very little time to cook.

1 cup *avil*
½ gallon whole milk
2 cups sugar
1 cup cream
2 tablespoons ghee
10 unsalted cashew nuts, broken into pieces
10 raisins
1 teaspoon cardamom, crushed

Rinse the *avil,* and drain it in a colander. Bring the milk to a rolling boil in a heavy saucepan. Reduce the heat to medium, and stir in the *avil.* When it boils again, add the sugar, and stir. Reduce the heat, and cook for ten minutes, stirring periodically. Pour in the cream, and let it simmer for another fifteen minutes. Stir periodically.

    Heat the ghee in a skillet, and fry the cashew nuts. When they start turning golden brown, add the raisins, and keep stirring until they plump up. Garnish the *paayasam* with ghee, nuts, and raisins. Sprinkle it with cardamom, and stir gently. Serve warm or cold.

Makes 4 to 6 servings.

Gothambu Pradhaman: Wheat Pudding

In one of its rare appearances in our cuisine, Durham wheat is combined with brown sugar and coconut milk and cooked into a delicate pudding. This often appears as a second or third dessert at wedding and birthday feasts.

1 cup cracked wheat
4 tablespoons ghee
2½ cups jaggery **or** brown sugar
6 cups coconut milk*
2 teaspoons cardamom, crushed
1 teaspoon ginger powder

Wash the cracked wheat, and drain. Heat two tablespoons of ghee in a heavy saucepan, and add the cracked wheat. Toast the wheat for two to three minutes, stirring continually. Stir in one and a half cups of water, and bring it to a boil. Reduce the heat, and simmer until the wheat is well cooked, approximately six to seven minutes. Stir periodically to make sure that the grains do not stick to the pot. To test if the wheat is ready, take out some grains with a spoon, and try to mash them. If it is very soft to the touch and easily mashes, the wheat is cooked. Combine the jaggery (or brown sugar) with the cooked wheat, and continue stirring. Once all the brown sugar has melted and become well incorporated, pour in coconut milk in a thin stream, stirring continuously. Cook over medium heat, so that the coconut milk only simmers. Boiling will result in separated coconut milk. Simmer for twenty-five to thirty minutes, stirring periodically, until the coconut milk has thickened. Add the remaining ghee to the pot, and sprinkle it with cardamom and ginger powder. Stir gently, remove it from the stove, and keep it covered (otherwise the coconut milk will form a skin on the top). This dessert may be served either warm or cold.

Makes 4 to 6 servings.

*Six cups of fresh coconut milk may substituted with six cups of canned coconut milk, or six cups of coconut milk made from coconut-milk powder, or four cups of whole milk mixed with two cups of heavy cream. The last substitution will lack the flavor of coconut milk.

Semiya Paayasam: Vermicelli Pudding

One of the rare ways pasta comes to our dinner table is in the form of a creamy sweet pudding. It is made with extremely thin Indian Durham wheat noodles, thinner than angelhair pasta. Two kinds of noodles are available at Indian grocery stores; one is toasted, and the other is not toasted. The toasted noodles have a golden-brown color. They are extremely thin and very easy to break into tiny pieces. Personally, I prefer the toasted noodles.

3 tablespoons ghee
1 cup thin Indian vermicelli *(semiya)*, crushed into tiny pieces
5 cups whole milk
2 cups half-and-half
2 cups sugar
10 unsalted cashew nuts, broken into pieces
1 tablespoon raisins
1 tablespoon cardamom, crushed

Heat one tablespoon of ghee in a heavy skillet, and toast the vermicelli over low heat. Keep stirring until the noodles are toasted to a golden-brown color. If using toasted noodles, just add them to the skillet, and stir well to coat with ghee. This will take only a minute or less. Watch carefully while stirring, so that the noodles do not burn and turn dark brown. Remove the skillet from the heat, and set it aside.

In a heavy saucepan, bring milk to a boil, reduce the heat, and stir in the toasted noodles. Cook over medium heat for ten to twelve minutes, stirring periodically to ensure that the noodles do not stick to the bottom of the pot. Pour half-and-half in a thin stream into the pot while stirring constantly. Add sugar, and continue to simmer for another twenty-five to thirty minutes. Continue to stir the pot every three to five minutes. Do not let the milk boil and rise to the top. After about thirty minutes, the milk should be thick enough to coat the back of a spoon. Remove the pan from the stove, and keep it covered to prevent a skin forming on the top.

Heat the remaining ghee in a skillet, and fry the cashew nuts. When they start turning golden brown, add the raisins, and keep stirring until they plump up. Garnish the *paayasam* with ghee, nuts, and raisins. Sprinkle it with cardamom, and stir gently. Serve warm or cold.

Makes 6 to 8 servings.

Kadala Pradhaman: Chana Dal Pudding with Brown Sugar and Coconut Milk

This rich and flavorful coconut milk *paayasam* is thickened with cooked *chana* dal. While crushed cardamom adds fragrance, ghee-toasted cashews and coconut pieces provide a mild crunch to this creamy pudding.

1 cup *chana* dal
2½ cups jaggery **or** brown sugar
6 cups fresh coconut milk*
1 teaspoon cardamom, crushed
3 tablespoons ghee
¼ cup unsalted cashew nuts, broken into pieces
¼ cup coconut, cut into thin pieces
1 tablespoon raisins

Heat one tablespoon of ghee in a heavy saucepan over medium heat. Add the dal, and fry until it is golden brown in color. Keep stirring while frying. Remove the saucepan from the stove. Rinse the dal, and leave it in a strainer for a few minutes, until it is completely drained. Combine the dal and one and a half cups of water in a heavy saucepan, and cook until the dal is soft to the touch (approximately ten minutes). Most of the water will be absorbed by now. Add the jaggery (or brown sugar) to the dal, and cook it over medium heat for about ten to twelve minutes. Stir gently, so that the dal is not mashed and it does not stick to the pan. Pour in the coconut milk, and cook for another twenty to twenty-five minutes over low to medium heat. Avoid boiling—it will result in separated coconut milk. When it has thickened, remove it from the stove, and sprinkle it with crushed cardamom. Heat the ghee in a skillet, and fry the cashew nuts. When the nuts start turning golden brown, add the coconut slices and raisins, and keep stirring. The coconut will turn golden brown, and the raisins will become plump as they soak up the ghee. Add the fried garnishes to *pradhaman*. Serve warm or cold.

Makes 6 to 8 servings.

*Six cups of fresh coconut milk may substituted with six cups of canned coconut milk, or six cups of coconut milk made from coconut-milk powder, or four cups of whole milk mixed with two cups of cream or half and half. The last substitution will lack the flavor of coconut milk.

Variation: *Parippu Pradhaman* (Mung Dal Pudding with Brown Sugar and Coconut Milk) This is another version of the previous recipe. Here *chana* dal is replaced with pan-roasted mung dal. It tastes great served warm or cold.

1 cup mung dal
3 tablespoons ghee
2½ cups jaggery **or** brown sugar
6 cups fresh coconut milk*
1 teaspoon cardamom, crushed
¼ cup unsalted cashew nuts, broken into pieces
¼ cup fresh coconut, thinly sliced
1 tablespoon raisins

Heat one tablespoon of ghee in a heavy saucepan over medium heat. Add the dal, and fry until it is golden brown in color. Keep stirring while frying. Remove the saucepan from the stove. Rinse the dal, and leave it in a strainer for a few minutes, until it is completely drained. Combine the dal and one and a half cups of water in a saucepan, and cook over medium heat until the dal is soft enough to mash with a spoon (about ten to twelve minutes). Stir periodically to make sure that the dal does not stick to the bottom of the pan. Most of the water will be absorbed by this time. Add the jaggery (or brown sugar), and continue to cook over medium heat for another eight minutes. Stir gently, so that the dal is not totally mashed and does not stick to the pan. Pour in the coconut milk, and cook for twenty to twenty-five more minutes over low heat, stirring occasionally. Do not let the coconut milk come to a boil; boiling will result in separated coconut milk. Remove it from the stove, and sprinkle it with crushed cardamom. Heat the ghee in a skillet, and fry the cashew nuts. When they start turning golden brown, add the coconut slices and raisins, and keep stirring. The coconut will turn golden brown, and the raisins will become plump as they soak up the ghee. Add the fried garnishes to the *pradhaman*. Serve warm or cold.

Makes 6 to 8 servings.

*Six cups of fresh coconut milk may substituted with six cups of canned coconut milk, or six cups of coconut milk made from coconut-milk powder, or four cups of whole milk mixed with two cups of cream or half and half. The last substitution will lack the flavor of coconut milk.

Pazza Pradhaman: Ripe Plantain Pudding

This delicately smooth dessert is made with homemade plantain jam. The jam is prepared by cooking ripe plantains with brown sugar and ghee. With the abundance of ripe plantains in Kerala, this is one of our staple desserts at feasts.

1 cup jaggery **or** brown sugar
¼ cup water
1 cup ripe plantain jam (recipe follows)
6 cups fresh coconut milk
3 tablespoons ghee
1 tablespoon fresh coconut, thinly sliced
2 teaspoons cardamom, crushed

Combine the jaggery (or brown sugar) and water in a heavy saucepan, and place it over medium heat. When it begins to boil, stir in the plantain jam, and mix thoroughly. Slowly stir in the coconut milk, and simmer over low to medium heat for twenty to twenty-five minutes, stirring occasionally. Do not let the coconut milk come to a boil; boiling will result in separated coconut milk. Heat the ghee in a small skillet, and fry the coconut pieces until they are golden brown. Pour the ghee and coconut over the *pradhaman,* and garnish it with crushed cardamom. Remove it from the stove, and keep the pot covered until it is time to serve. Serve either warm or cold. It stays fresh for up to four days in the refrigerator.

Makes 4 to 6 servings.

*Six cups of fresh coconut milk may substituted with six cups of canned coconut milk, or six cups of coconut milk made from coconut-milk powder, or four cups of whole milk mixed with two cups of cream or half and half. The last substitution will lack the flavor of coconut milk.

Pazzam Varattiyathu (Ripe Plantain Jam)

4 ripe plantains
4 cups jaggery **or** brown sugar
1cup ghee

Peel the plantains, cut them into small pieces, and place them in a heavy saucepan. Add just enough water to cover, and cook over medium heat, stirring occasionally, so that the plantains do not stick to the bottom of the pan. Cook for twenty to twenty-five minutes, until it is very soft. Stir in the jaggery (or brown sugar), and mix well. Mash the cooked plantains with a potato masher or a heavy spoon. Stirring continuously, add the ghee, a few tablespoons at a time. After about ten minutes, the jam will thicken and start leaving the sides of the pan as it is stirred. Remove it from the stove and let it cool to room temperature. This jam will keep for several days in a cool, dark place and for up to six months in the refrigerator.

Makes about 3 cups.

Variation: *Maampaza Pradhaman* (Ripe Mango Pudding)

Golden-ripe mango slices, when cooked with brown sugar and ghee, transform into a delicate and flavorful fruit jam. When combined with brown sugar and coconut milk and leisurely simmered, it becomes a dark and creamy mango pudding.

1 cup jaggery **or** brown sugar
¼ cup water
1 cup ripe mango jam (recipe below)
6 cups fresh coconut milk
3 tablespoons ghee
1 tablespoon fresh coconut, thinly sliced
2 teaspoons crushed cardamom

Combine the jaggery (or brown sugar) and water in a heavy saucepan, and place over medium heat. When it begins to boil, stir in the mango jam, and mix thoroughly. Slowly stir in the coconut milk, and simmer over low to medium heat for twenty to twenty-five minutes, stirring occasionally. Do not let the coconut milk come to a boil; boiling will result in separated coconut milk.

Heat the ghee in a skillet, and fry the coconut pieces until they are golden brown. Pour the ghee and coconut over the *pradhaman,* and garnish it with crushed cardamom. Remove it from the stove, and keep the pot covered until it is time to serve. Serve either warm or cold. It stays fresh for up to four days in the refrigerator.

Makes 4 to 6 servings.

*Six cups of fresh coconut milk may substituted with six cups of canned coconut milk, or six cups of coconut milk made from coconut-milk powder, or four cups of whole milk mixed with two cups of cream or half and half. The last substitution will lack the flavor of coconut milk.

Maanga Varattiyathu (Ripe Mango Jam)

4 cups ripe mango pieces, without skin
3 cups jaggery **or** brown sugar
¾ cup ghee

Cut the mangoes into small pieces, and place them in a heavy saucepan. Add just enough water to cover, and cook over medium heat, stirring occasionally so that the mango does not stick to the bottom of the pan. Cook for fifteen to twenty minutes, until it is very soft. Stir in the jaggery (or brown sugar), and mix well. Mash the cooked mangoes with a potato masher or a heavy spoon. Stirring continuously, add the ghee, a few tablespoons at a time. After about ten minutes, the jam will thicken and start leaving the sides of the pan as it is stirred. Remove it from the stove, and cool to room temperature. This jam will keep for several days in a cool, dark place and for up to 6 months in the refrigerator.

Chakka Pradhaman: Jackfruit Pudding

Jackfruit is an acquired taste. The yellow, fig-like fruit pods held inside giant ripe jackfruit have a very distinct tropical aroma. Even those who do not particularly care for this strong-scented fruit in its raw stage love it when it is presented in pudding form. When cooked in ghee and simmered with coconut milk and brown sugar, jackfruit loses its strong aroma and evolves into a delicately creamy dessert that is hard to resist.

¼ cup water
1 cup jaggery **or** brown sugar
1 cup ripe jackfruit jam (recipe below)
6 cups coconut milk
3 tablespoons ghee
1 tablespoon fresh coconut, thinly sliced
2 teaspoons crushed cardamom

Combine the jaggery (or brown sugar) and water in a heavy saucepan, and place it over medium heat. When it begins to boil, stir in the jackfruit jam, and mix thoroughly. Slowly stir in the coconut milk, and simmer over low to medium heat for twenty to twenty-five minutes, stirring occasionally. Do not let the coconut milk come to a boil; boiling will result in separated coconut milk.

Heat the ghee in a skillet, and fry the coconut pieces until they are golden brown. Pour the ghee and coconut over the *pradhaman,* and stir in the crushed cardamom. Remove it from the stove, and keep the pot covered until it is time to serve. Serve either warm or cold. It stays fresh for up to four days in the refrigerator.

Makes 4 to 6 servings.

*Six cups of fresh coconut milk may substituted with six cups of canned coconut milk, or six cups of coconut milk made from coconut-milk powder, or four cups of whole milk mixed with two cups of cream or half and half. The last substitution will lack the flavor of coconut milk.

Chakka Varattiyathu (Jackfruit Jam)

Making jackfruit jam was always a summer project at our house. The cook separated the fleshy yellow pods of jackfruit from the seeds and piled them up in a large bronze *uruli*. After lunch, the jam cooking started. The *uruli* was moved to the wood-burning stove on the lower raised platform. It was easier to stir a large pot when it was placed on the lower platform. Water was poured into the *uruli*—just enough to cover the fruit pods—and few more wood logs were put into the belly of the stove. As the pods simmered in water, an intense smell, sharp and sweet, filled the kitchen.

The cooked fruit was mashed and pureed with a large wooden masher. Chunks of jaggery were put in, and the stirring began. "Keep on stirring continuously, or else it will stick to the pot," Mom repeated every time, and the cook nodded his head in agreement. As he stirred the pot, soon the mix turned golden brown in color and started bubbling. He popped a couple more dry wooden logs into the stove and shook them slightly so that the heat was distributed evenly under the *uruli*. There were no gadgets for controlling and adjusting the temperature. As he continued to stir, Mom poured ladlefuls of golden ghee into the *uruli*. After some time, the jam thickened and began leaving the sides of the *uruli* as he stirred. The jam had a smooth and glistening texture when it was fully cooked. The *uruli* was moved from the stove and covered with a fresh banana leaf. When it cooled to room temperature, it was transferred to a container and moved to a shelf in the *kalavara* (pantry).

4 cups ripe jackfruit segments*
4 cups jaggery **or** brown sugar
1 cup ghee

Remove any remaining seeds from the jackfruit segments, cut them into thin slices, and place them in a heavy-bottomed pot. Pour in just enough water to cover the fruit pieces. Cook over medium heat. Stir occasionally to make sure that it does not stick to the bottom of the pan. In about half an hour, it will be well cooked. Mash the cooked jackfruit with a potato masher or a heavy spoon. Add the jaggery (or brown sugar), and mix well. Cook while stirring continuously and adding ghee, a few tablespoons at a time. After about thirty minutes, the jam will be thick and smooth, and it will start leaving the sides of the pot as you stir. It will be glazed with ghee. Remove it from the stove, and let it cool. This jam stays good for months in a cool, dark place and in a refrigerator for even longer time.

*Frozen or bottled ripe jackfruit segments in sugar syrup are available in Indian grocery stores. Drain the segments, and proceed with the recipe above to make jackfruit jam. These fruit segments will take less time to cook.

Chapter Nine
Breakfasts and Brunches

A South Indian breakfast is anything but sweet; it is delicious, nutritious, and satisfying. Our breakfasts of steamed rice cakes, wafer-thin pancakes, delicate dumplings, and thin, soft rice noodles are a true revelation of the subtle tastes and variety of textures that can be achieved with a few simple ingredients. Although almost all these recipes are prepared with batters or dough made of rice and lentils, variously shaped and spiced, all have their own distinct texture, taste, and appearance. Compare these dishes to croissants, muffins, and breads—all made with the same ingredients, and yet, each one different from the others. The dishes in this chapter are traditionally served with savory chutneys, spicy curries, and various other accompaniments. All of them also make excellent brunch choices.

While the first three of the following recipes are of Kerala origin, the influence of Tamil Nadu cuisine is clearly reflected in the recipes for *dosa, idli* and *vada*. Today, these dishes are as much a part of Kerala cuisine as they are of Tamil Nadu cuisine.

Puttu: Steamed Rice Flour and Fresh Coconut Logs

Log-shaped *puttu* is made by steaming roasted rice flour and fresh coconut in metal tubes. Traditionally, *puttu* was steamed in bamboo logs. This method gave the dish its cylindrical shape and a pleasant fragrance. *Puttu* may also be prepared by steaming the flour-and-coconut mixture in a steamer basket. The dry, flaky *puttu* is traditionally served with *kadala* curry (a spicy curry of brown chickpeas simmered in a sauce of fresh roasted coriander and red chilies, seasoned with curry leaves and cilantro), fried *pappadams,* and finger bananas. Potato stew or brown stew also goes very well with *puttu.*

2 cups rice flour
1½ cups freshly grated coconut
1 tablespoon ghee
Salt to taste

In a heavy skillet, dry roast the rice flour over medium heat, stirring continuously. When the flour starts to turn pinkish in color (after about five minutes), remove it from the stove, and let it cool. After it has cooled, add one cup of the grated coconut and some salt, and mix well. Sprinkle a half-cup of water over the flour, and mix well. It should be wet but not lumpy. Add a few more spoons of water if necessary. Stir in the ghee. Though not called for in the traditional recipe, it adds a flakier texture to *puttu*.

Heat water in a *puttu kudam* or in a pot fitted with a steamer insert. If using the *puttu kudam*, insert the flat disk with holes at the bottom of the tube. Fill half of the tube with the prepared rice flour and coconut mixture. Sprinkle a tablespoon of the remaining coconut on top, and fill the rest of the tube with more rice and coconut mixture. Sprinkle on another tablespoon of grated coconut, cover the tube with the three-holed lid, and attach the tube to the pot of boiling water. Steam for five minutes; when the *puttu* is cooked, steam will start coming through the holes on the lid. Remove the tube from the pot and open the lid. Using the handle of a large spoon, slowly push the *puttu*, and slide it onto a plate. Repeat with the remaining rice flour and coconut mixture and fresh grated coconut.

If using the steamer insert, spread a piece of wet cheesecloth in the insert, and spread the rice flour mixture on top. When using this method, add all the grated coconut to the rice flour. Cover and steam for eight to ten minutes.

Makes 2 logs (2 to 4 servings).

Noolpittu (Idiappam): Fresh Rice Noodles with Coconut Filling

These homemade rice-noodle cakes with fresh coconut filling are traditionally steamed in banana leaves. It imparts a pleasant aroma to the cakes. A piece of cheesecloth or parchment paper may be substituted for banana leaves.

2 cups long-grain rice
2 tablespoons vegetable oil
Salt to taste
1½ cups freshly grated coconut

> Noolpittu was mentioned in ancient Indian literature as far back as the fifth century AD. Surprisingly, the recipe has remained unchanged to this day.

Soak the rice for four to five hours, rinse it in several changes of water until the water runs clear, and drain. Using a blender, grind the rice with just enough water to make a very smooth batter. Heat a heavy skillet over medium heat, and pour in the oil. When it is hot, stir in the batter, add salt, and reduce the heat to medium low. Stirring continuously, cook the batter until it thickens and starts to leave the sides of the pan. At this point, the batter will have changed to a dough-like consistency. Remove it from the stove, and let it cool.

Spoon the dough into a snack press fitted with the thin-holed plate. Heat three inches of water in a saucepan fitted with a steamer insert. While the water is heating, cut banana leaves (if available), parchment paper, or a clean piece of cheesecloth into four- to five-inch squares. If using banana leaves or paper, oil them lightly. If using cheesecloth, wet it. Press a three and a half inch circle of dough onto the leaf, paper, or cloth. Sprinkle on a tablespoon of grated coconut, and press another layer of dough over it. Repeat with the remaining dough. Arrange the noodle cakes in a single layer on the steamer insert, and steam for ten to twelve minutes. Remove them from the stove, let them cool down for a few minutes, and then transfer them to a serving plate. Serve with potato stew, brown stew, or coconut chutney.

Makes 8 to 10.

Variation: Instead of preparing the noodles from scratch, substitute with dehydrated rice noodles, available at Indian grocery stores. These noodles must be soaked in hot water for three to four minutes to make them pliable. Drain them in a colander. Spread two or three tablespoons of wet noodles in a three and a half inch circle on a banana leaf (if available), parchment paper, or a clean piece of wet cheesecloth. Sprinkle on a tablespoon of grated fresh coconut, and cover with another layer of wet noodles. Continue with the recipe as above.

Frozen *idiappam* without coconut filling is available at many Indian grocery stores in the United States.

Vellayappam: Rice and Coconut Milk Pancakes

Vellayappam, with lacy edges and a soft center, is made with a fermented batter of rice flour, coconut milk, and yeast. To get the proper shape, *vellayappam* is traditionally made in *vellayappam* pans. These pans are inexpensive and available at some Indian stores. A small wok or nonstick skillet makes a good substitute. The shape may not be perfect, but the taste certainly will be.

⅓ cup cream of rice or farina*
2 cups rice flour **or** two cups long-grain rice
1 packet dry yeast**
Salt to taste

2 tablespoons sugar
1½ cups coconut milk***
¼ cup vegetable oil (for greasing the pan)****

Cook the cream of rice (or farina) over medium heat with enough water to make a thick porridge. Stir continuously to avoid allowing any lumps to form. Remove it from the stove, and let it cool to room temperature.

If using long-grain rice, soak the rice for four to five hours, rinse and then grind it with one fourth of a cup water into a smooth, thick batter. If using rice flour, mix it with enough water to make a thick, smooth batter. Dissolve the yeast in two tablespoons of warm water, and stir well. Keep it aside for a few minutes, until it is fully dissolved and foamy.

Combine the yeast, salt, cooked cream of rice (or farina), and rice batter. Do not add too much water. When it ferments, the batter will become thin. Cover and set aside for six to eight hours or overnight. The batter will rise and become bubbly.

Just before making the *vellayappam,* add the sugar and one and a quarter cups of coconut milk to the batter, and mix well. The batter should have the consistency of heavy cream. Set aside the remaining quarter-cup of coconut milk to spread over the cooked *vellayappams.*

Heat the *vellayappam* pan over medium heat. To test if the pan is ready, sprinkle a few drops of water on it, and it will start sizzling immediately. Grease the pan with a few drops of oil. Pour a ladleful of batter onto the center of the pan. Lift the pan, and give it a twist, so that the batter swirls to the edges of the pan and retreats to the base, forming a *vellayappam* six to seven inches in diameter. Around the edges, it should be thin and lacy. Cover and cook over low to medium heat for two minutes. These pancakes are not be turned over and cooked. Lift the lid after two minutes, and see if the center has cooked and the edges have begun to turn golden brown. If not, cover and cook for another minute. Remove it from the stove. Run a spatula around it, and slide it onto a plate. Spread a teaspoon of coconut milk over the *vellayappam.* Repeat with the remaining batter.

Always allow each *vellayappam* to cool a little before stacking, because they have a tendency to stick together. Serve with potato stew or brown stew.

*In the traditional recipe, rice is soaked, drained, and pounded to make rice flour. Before pounding it into a fine powder, one-third of a cup of coarse rice powder, similar in consistency to farina, is kept aside for making the porridge.

**Instead of yeast, the traditional recipe uses coconut toddy, or the water from a coconut, fermented overnight.

***Fresh coconut milk may be substituted with coconut milk made from coconut-milk powder, or with canned coconut milk.

****Instead of greasing the pan with oil, spray with Pam, Wesson, or Mazola oil spray.

> Vellayappam is another dish mentioned in ancient Indian literature as far back as the fifth century AD. Surprisingly, this recipe has remained unchanged to this day.

Makes 10 to 12.

Naalikera Dosa: Rice and Coconut Pancakes

Here is a *dosa* made with freshly grated coconut and rice. As this version does not require several hours of soaking and fermenting (as in the traditional recipe), it is an easy alternative to regular rice and *urad* dal *dosa*. Back home, it is a standby when there are unexpected guests for breakfast or evening tea. These *dosas* are soft and do not become very crisp. Serve them with coconut chutney or coconut and cilantro chutney. These may be served either hot or at room temperature.

2 cups long-grain rice
1½ cups freshly grated coconut
Salt to taste
3 or 4 fresh green chilies (serrano or Thai), finely chopped (less for a mild taste)
1 teaspoon fresh ginger, finely grated
6 to 8 curry leaves
¼ cup sesame oil

Soak the rice for one to one and a half hours, rinse it in several changes of water until the water runs clear, and drain. In a blender, grind the rice and coconut together with just enough water to make a medium-thick batter (about the consistency of pancake batter). Remove the batter from the blender, and stir in the salt, green chilies, ginger, and curry leaves. Heat a heavy cast-iron griddle or a nonstick griddle over medium heat. When the griddle is hot, pour a half-cup of the batter onto the middle of the griddle. With quick circular motions, spread the batter evenly into a thin pancake. Pour a teaspoon of the oil around the edges, and cook for a minute or two. The bottom of the *dosa* will begin to turn light brown, and the edges will start to leave the griddle. With a spatula, loosen the sides, and it will come off easily. Flip the *dosa*, and cook the other side for one and a half to two minutes, depending on the thickness of the *dosa* and the heat of the griddle. Remove it to a plate. Before starting the second *dosa*, rub the surface of the griddle with an oily paper towel. Continue until all the batter is used.

Makes approximately 10 to 12.

Dosa: Rice and *Urad* Dal Pancakes

Mention South Indian food, and the first thing that comes to mind are two dishes: *dosa* and *sambar*. This thin and lacy pancake, made with fermented rice and *urad* dal batter, is a favorite breakfast dish all over South India. Fermentation is a key factor in making good *dosa*. It is easy to ferment the batter during summer months. During winter months, either keep the bowl of batter near a heating unit or keep it for a few hours inside an oven with a pilot light. The warmth inside the oven will help speed up the fermentation.

2 cups long-grain rice*
1 cup whole *urad* or *urad* dal*
1 teaspoon fenugreek seeds** (optional)
Salt to taste
⅓ cup sesame oil or vegetable oil

Soak the rice, *urad* dal, and fenugreek seeds separately for five to six hours. Wash the soaked ingredients thoroughly in several changes of water until the water runs clear, and drain. Grind the rice and dal separately along with sufficient water to make a very smooth batter (similar to pancake batter) of pouring consistency. If using fenugreek, grind it along with the *urad* dal. Combine the batters, stir in salt, cover, and set aside for six to eight hours to ferment. Keep the batter in a larger vessel, as the volume of the batter increases with fermentation. Stir the batter thoroughly to make sure that it is of pouring consistency. If it appears to be too thick, add more water, and stir well.

Heat a heavy cast-iron griddle or a nonstick griddle over medium heat. Sprinkle a few drops of water on the griddle, and if it sizzles immediately, the griddle is ready. Lightly brush the surface of the griddle with oil. A small piece of cloth or a paper towel may be used for spreading the oil. When the griddle is hot, pour a half-cup of the batter onto the middle of the griddle. With quick circular motions, spread the batter evenly into a thin pancake. Pour a teaspoon of the oil around the edges, and cook for a minute or two. The bottom of the *dosa* will begin to turn light brown, and the edges will start to leave the griddle. With a spatula, loosen the sides, and it will come off easily. Flip the *dosa,* and cook the second side for one and a half to two minutes, depending on the thickness of the *dosa* and the heat of the griddle. Remove it to a plate. Before starting the second *dosa,* rub the surface of the griddle with an oily paper towel. Continue with the remaining batter.

Any remaining batter can be refrigerated and used later. It stays fresh for four to five days in the refrigerator. Bring the batter to room temperature before proceeding to make *dosas. Dosa* is usually served with *sambar,* chutney or *podi. Dosa* tastes best when it is piping hot.

Makes 20 to 25 dosas.

*Traditionally, the batters for *dosa* and *idli* are prepared with parboiled rice and black-skinned *urad* dal. A smaller quantity of black-skinned *urad* dal is required (one-third cup dal to one cup rice compared to one cup dal to two cups of rice, as in this and the following recipe). Yet it has to be washed several times to remove the skin before grinding—a long and tedious process. The long-grain rice available in U.S. supermarkets makes good batter. Skinned, whole *urad* produces better-quality batter than split *urad* dal.

**Fenugreek is optional. It gives a good golden-brown color to dosa.

> Dosa's recorded history goes back to the sixth century AD. According to Indian culinary historian K. T. Achaya, the early form of *dosa* was a pure rice product, shallow-fried in a pan. The addition of *urad* dal, the fermentation of the batter, and the various fillings for *dosa* are all later developments.

Variations:

Onion *dosa:* Sprinkle thinly chopped onions or shallots over the surface of the dosa while it is cooking. Fold it, and cook for a minute or two more. Pour half a teaspoon of oil over the dosa to make it crispy. Serve with sambar and chutney.

Rava *dosa:* Here is another quick alternative to rice and *urad* dosa. This batter does not require any grinding or fermenting.

2 cups farina or cream of wheat
1 cup all-purpose flour
1 cup plain yogurt
2 teaspoons cumin seeds
1 fresh green chili (serrano or Thai), finely chopped
1 tablespoon ginger, finely grated
12 to 15 fresh curry leaves
2 tablespoons cilantro leaves, roughly chopped
Salt to taste
Water as required
¼ cup vegetable oil

In a medium-sized bowl, mix the farina, all-purpose flour, yogurt, cumin seeds, green chili, ginger, curry leaves, cilantro leaves, and salt. Stirring continually, pour in water a little at a time to make a smooth, thin batter. Cover the bowl, and let the batter rest for approximately one hour. Follow the method described above for making *dosa*. Serve hot with coconut chutney and sambar.

Makes 10 to 12.

Godambu dosa: *Godambu dosa* is a staple on partial-fasting days when eating rice is a taboo. These *dosas* are tasty but quite different from the regular rice-and-*urad dosa*. As the batter does not require any fermentation, this *dosa* can be prepared within a short time.

2 cups finely ground whole-wheat flour
½ cup all-purpose flour
Salt to taste
Water as required
¼ cup ghee or vegetable oil

In a medium-sized bowl, mix the wheat flour, all-purpose flour, and salt. Stirring continually, pour in water a little at a time to make a smooth, thin batter. Cover the bowl, and let the batter rest for approximately half an hour. Follow the method described above for making *dosa*. Serve hot with coconut chutney and sambar.

Makes 8 to 10.

Masala *Dosa*: Rice and *Urad* Dal Pancakes Stuffed with Spicy Potatoes and Onions

Dosa, when filled with a spicy potato and onion masala (dry curry), becomes masala *dosa*. Once you learn to make *dosa*, filling it with the masala is a very easy step. Traditionally, it is served with *sambar* and coconut chutney.

Onion and Potato Masala

3 or 4 medium-sized potatoes
Salt to taste
1 teaspoon turmeric powder
2 tablespoons vegetable oil
1 teaspoon mustard seeds
1 teaspoon *urad* dal
1 teaspoon *chana* dal
1 dried red cayenne, serrano, or Thai chili, halved
1 teaspoon fresh ginger, finely grated
2 fresh green chilies (serrano or Thai), thinly sliced (less for a milder taste)
12 to 15 fresh curry leaves
2 medium-sized onions thinly sliced
2 tablespoons cilantro leaves, finely chopped
8 cups *dosa* batter

Peel and cut the potatoes into small cubes. Cook with salt, turmeric, and just enough water to cover, until they are soft and fork tender. Most of the water should have evaporated by now. Heat the oil in a heavy skillet, and add the mustard seeds. When the mustard seeds start sputtering, add the dals and the halved red chili pepper. Panfry them until the dal turns golden brown. Stir in the ginger, green chilies, curry leaves, and onions. Fry until the onion is golden brown in color. Pour the contents of the skillet over the cooked potatoes, and stir well. Garnish with cilantro leaves. The potato masala should be very thick in texture.

Make *dosas* with a little extra oil, and when both sides are cooked, place three to four tablespoons of masala in the middle of the *dosa*. Fold both sides over to cover (similar to an enchilada). Turn it over, and serve hot with sambar and chutney.

Makes 10 masala *dosas*.

Idli: Steamed Rice and *Urad* Dal Cakes

Idli is a staple breakfast dish all over South India. These soft, round, steamed cakes made with fermented rice and *urad* dal batter are spongy and moist, grayish-white in color, and taste salty and mildly sour. Traditionally, they are steamed in *idli* steamers. A stack of *idli* plates can be purchased separately from Indian grocers. They are inexpensive and fit inside a four- or six-quart pot. As an easier alternative, you may use an egg poacher.

2 cups long-grain rice
1 cup whole skinned *urad* or *urad* dal
Salt to taste
2 tablespoons oil or ghee (for greasing the *idli* plates)

Soak rice and dal separately in water. Rinse both ingredients in several changes of water until the water runs clear, and drain well. First, grind the dal in a blender with just enough water to make a very smooth, thick batter. Remove it from the blender, and grind the rice with just enough water to make a thick, coarse batter. Combine the two batters, add salt, and stir well. Cover and set aside to ferment for eight to ten hours or overnight. *Idli* batter should be thicker than the *dosa* batter in the previous recipe. Gently fold the batter before making the *idlis*. Do not stir; it is the trapped air in the fermented batter that makes the *idlis* soft and fluffy.

Fill the bottom of an *idli* steamer (or a large saucepan, or an egg poacher) with water, about two inches high, and bring it to a boil. The water level should be just below the *idli* stacks. Oil the *idli* plates or egg-poacher cups, and pour a small ladleful of batter into each one. Stack the plates inside the steamer, and steam the *idlis* for fifteen to twenty minutes. Remove the *idli* plate stack from the steamer, and let it cool for five minutes. To remove *idlis,* run a butter knife around each *idli,* and slide it out. Serve with *sambar,* chutney, or *podi. Idlis* are good either warm or cold. An egg poacher would make four *idlis* at a time.

Makes approximately 32 *idlis.*

Since ancient times, maritime trade existed between South Indian kingdoms and Southeast Asia. With the settlement of Indian traders by the sixth century AD, Southeast Asia underwent a gradual period of Indianization. Peacefully and gradually, the Hindu religion spread throughout the archipelago. These Hindu kingdoms had religious, cultural, trade, and diplomatic relations with South India. It is believed that from the eighth through the twelfth century AD, some of the Indonesian Hindu kings often visited India in search of suitable brides. A contingent of cooks accompanied them, and they are believed to have introduced fermentation techniques and steam cooking to South Indian cuisine.

A Chinese traveler of the seventh century wrote that at the time of his visit, Indians did not use steam cooking methods, which were popular in China. According to Indian food historian K. T. Achaya, the *idli* made it into ancient Indian literature by the tenth century AD. It was considered one of the eighteen dishes a lady should serve her guests. The earlier *idlis* were made with *urad* dal only. By the fifteenth century, rice was in use in the preparation of *idli*.

In certain parts of South India, *idli* batter is blended with various spices before steaming. Giant *idlis*, weighing almost two or three pounds, made with two kinds of dal and flavored with various spices, are prepared as offerings at the Vishnu temple at Kancheepuram, Tamil Nadu.

Note: *Idlis* freeze very well for up to four months. After making *idlis,* remove them from plates, and cool to room temperature. Pack them in freezer bags or containers, and freeze. To defrost *idlis,* remove them from the containers to a plate, cover with a paper towel, and place in the microwave oven. Sprinkle a few drops of water on the paper towel, and place a small bowl of water next to the plate. Heat on low power for four to five minutes, then check them. If necessary, heat two to three minutes longer, until the *idlis* are warm and ready to serve.

Raamasseri idli: Feather-light, flat *idlis* are a specialty of Raamasseri village, near my hometown, Chittur. Raamasseri *idli* makers steam their *idli* in clay pots. These pots have hollow bottoms that are tightly strung with twine, almost like tennis racquets. A piece of cotton cloth is spread over these strings before pouring the *idli* batter. Four of them are stacked, one over the other, and placed inside an unglazed clay pot of boiling water. It is then covered with another clay pot. When the *idlis* are cooked, a large, flat jackfruit tree leaf is placed over each clay container, and it is slowly turned upside down. They are then transferred to a rattan tray lined with fresh banana leaves. These *idlis* have an earthy aroma of clay pots and banana leaves.

Idli Uppuma: Idli Panfried with Green Chilies, Curry Leaves, and Mustard Seeds

In my childhood, leftover *idli* from breakfast often appeared as *idli uppuma* for an afternoon snack. It is a healthy snack that is quick and easy to make.

6 to 8 *idli*
2 tablespoons vegetable oil
1 teaspoon mustard seeds
1 teaspoon *urad* dal
1 teaspoon *chana* dal
2 or 3 fresh green chilies (serrano or Thai), finely chopped (less for a mild taste)
1 tablespoon fresh ginger, finely grated
6 to 8 curry leaves, finely chopped

Cut the *idli* into small cubes, and set aside. Heat the oil in a heavy skillet, and add the mustard seeds. When the mustard seeds start sputtering, add the *urad* and *chana* dal, and fry until they turn golden brown. Stir in the green chilies, ginger, and curry leaves, and fry for a couple of minutes. Add the *idli* pieces, and gently toss the ingredients together. Remove from the stove. *Idli uppuma* is served as is, or with coconut chutney.

Makes 4 to 5 servings.

Oothappam: Spicy Pancakes

These spicy pancakes are a quick way to use up leftover *idli* batter.

4 cups *idli* batter (recipe above)
1 cup water
1 tablespoon fresh ginger, finely grated
6 to 8 curry leaves, finely chopped
2 or 3 fresh green chilies (serrano or Thai), finely chopped (less for a mild taste)
2 cups shallots or onions, finely chopped
½ cup vegetable oil

Pour water, a little at a time, into the *idli* batter, and stir well to make a thick but spreadable batter. Stir in the ginger and the curry leaves. Combine the chopped onions and green chilies in a bowl.

Heat a heavy cast-iron griddle or a nonstick griddle over medium heat. Lightly oil the surface of the griddle, using a piece of cloth or paper towel dipped in oil, and set aside the towel for use between each *oothappam*. When the griddle is hot, pour a half-cup of batter onto the middle of the griddle. With quick circular motions, spread the batter evenly into a thick pancake. Pour a teaspoon of the oil around the edges, sprinkle on a few tablespoons of the onion and chili mixture, and spread another teaspoon of oil on top. Cook for a minute or two. The bottom of the *oothappam* will begin to turn light brown, and the edges will start to leave the griddle. With a spatula, loosen the sides, and it will come off easily. Flip it, and cook the second side for about two minutes, depending on the thickness of the pancake and the heat of the griddle. Remove it to a plate. Before starting the second one, rub the surface of the griddle with an oil-dipped paper towel. Continue until all of the batter is used. Serve hot, with *sambar* and coconut chutney.

Makes 10 to 12.

Ada: Thick Pancakes with Rice and a Mix of Dal

These spicy, flat cakes, made with a thick, coarse batter of rice and two kinds of dal, require no fermentation. *Ada* is thick and crispy and very filling. It makes a good brunch dish.

2 cups long-grain rice
1 cup *tuvar* dal
1 cup *urad* dal
Salt to taste
½ teaspoon black pepper, coarsely crushed
½ tablespoon dried red cayenne, serrano, or Thai chili powder (less for a milder taste)
¼ teaspoon asafetida powder (optional)
12 to 15 fresh curry leaves
½ cup sesame oil (or vegetable oil)

Soak rice and dal separately for four to five hours. Rinse them in several changes of water until the water runs clear. Drain, and grind them together in a blender with just enough water to make a thick and grainy batter. Remove it from the blender, and stir in salt, black pepper, chili pepper powder, asafetida, and curry leaves.

Heat a large cast-iron griddle or a nonstick skillet over medium-high heat. Lightly oil the surface of the griddle, using a paper towel dipped in oil, and reserve the towel for use between each *ada*. When the griddle is hot, pour a half-cup of the batter onto the middle of the griddle. With quick circular motions, spread the batter evenly into a thick, flat cake. Pour a teaspoon of oil around the edges, and cook for two to three minutes. The bottom of the *ada* will become a golden color, and the edges will start leaving the griddle. With a spatula, loosen the sides, and it will come off easily. Flip it over, and cook the second side for one and a half to two minutes, depending on the thickness of the *ada* and the heat of the griddle. Remove it to a plate. Repeat with the remaining batter. Serve hot with coconut chutney.

Makes 10 to 12.

Uzunnu Vada: Deep-Fried *Urad* Dal Fritters

Light and fluffy *uzunnu vada* has a texture that is somewhere between crunchy and tender. Take a bite of this little doughnut-shaped snack, and a burst of flavor explodes in the mouth—the intense flavors of ginger, cilantro, and curry leaves; the bright spark of black pepper; and the fiery bite of green chili. *Uzunnu vada* is served with a couple of spicy chutneys or *sambar*. When soaked in *tuvar* dal and tomato soup *(rasam)*, it becomes *rasavada*.

1 cup skinless whole or split *urad* dal
¼ teaspoon asafetida powder (optional)
Salt to taste
1 teaspoon whole black peppercorns
4 or 5 green chilies (serrano or Thai), finely chopped (less for a milder taste)
12 to 15 fresh curry leaves
1 tablespoon fresh cilantro leaves, chopped
1 tablespoon fresh ginger, grated
6 cups vegetable oil (for deep-frying)

Soak the *urad* dal in water for three to four hours, wash it in several changes of water until the water runs clear, and drain. In a food processor, combine the *urad* dal, asafetida powder, and salt, and process them into a thick, smooth dough. Since the dal absorbs water while soaking, there is no need for extra water while processing. Remove the dough from the processor, add black peppercorns, green chilies, curry leaves, cilantro leaves, and grated ginger, and mix well.

Heat the oil in a heavy frying pan or wok to 365°F. When the oil is hot, wet the palms of your hands, and shape about two tablespoons of dough into a thick disk. With a wet index finger, make a hole in the middle, then slowly slide the *vada* into the hot oil. Turn the *vada* with a slotted spoon, and cook on both sides. Repeat with the remaining dough. Fry the *vadas* until they are golden brown, approximately four to six minutes. Remove them from the oil, and drain. (Use a cake cooling rack placed over a cookie tray to drain them. Excess oil will drip through the cooling rack and fall on the cookie tray.) Serve hot, with coconut chutney and/or *sambar*.

Makes 20 to 22 medium-sized *vadas*.

Tayir Vada: Vada in Spicy Yogurt Sauce

Vadas made with different types of dal and soaked in spicy yogurt sauce are a favorite snack all over India. In our home, we thicken the yogurt sauce with coconut and green chilies. *Thayir vada* makes an excellent brunch dish.

1 cup freshly grated coconut
4 or 5 fresh green chilies (serrano or Thai), finely chopped (less for a milder taste)
3 cups plain yogurt
Salt to taste
1 tablespoon vegetable oil
1 teaspoon mustard seeds
1 teaspoon *urad* dal
1 teaspoon *chana* dal
1 dried red cayenne, serrano, or Thai chili, halved
12 to 15 fresh curry leaves
15 to 20 *urad vadas* (prepared following the recipe above)
2 tablespoons fresh cilantro leaves, thinly chopped

Grind the grated coconut, green chilies, and one cup of the yogurt into a fine puree. Remove it from the blender, and stir in the remaining yogurt and salt. Heat the oil in a heavy skillet, and add the mustard seeds. When the mustard seeds start sputtering, add the *urad* and *chana* dal, and fry until they turn golden brown. Add the red chili pepper and curry leaves. Remove the spice mixture from the stove, add it to the coconut yogurt sauce, and stir well. Add the *vadas* to the yogurt sauce, and soak them for at least an hour before serving. Sprinkle with cilantro leaves and serve.

Makes 15 to 20 *thayir vadas*.

Uppuma: Farina Spiced with Green Chilies, Ginger, and Curry Leaves

Farina, the base for the sweet and hardy western porridge, has a whole new spicy twist in this simple breakfast dish. It tastes good either warm or at room temperature. Back home, this is another favorite breakfast dish on partial-fasting days. When packed in toasted banana leaves, *uppuma* absorbs the fragrance of the leaves. It is often packed this way when taking it as a school lunch or as a snack on a long train journey. As the cooked grains of farina hold together, it is easy to mold this dish into any shape.

2 cups *rava* or farina
2 tablespoon vegetable oil
1 teaspoon mustard seeds
½ teaspoon *urad* dal
½ teaspoon *chana* dal
1 dried red cayenne, serrano, or Thai chili, halved
12 to 15 fresh curry leaves
2 teaspoons freshly grated ginger
4 fresh green chilies (serrano or Thai), thinly sliced (less for a milder taste)
4 cups water
Salt to taste
1 tablespoon ghee **or** coconut oil
1 tablespoon toasted cashew nut pieces
1 cup freshly grated coconut (optional)

In a heavy skillet, dry roast the farina until it turns light pink in color, and set it aside. Heat the oil in another skillet, and add the mustard seeds. When the mustard seeds start sputtering, add the *urad* dal and *chana* dal, and fry until they turn golden brown. Add the halved red chili pepper, curry leaves, ginger, and green chilies. Fry for two to three minutes, stirring continuously. Pour the water into the skillet, and bring it to a boil. Stir in salt, and add the farina in a thin stream. Keep stirring so that no lumps form. In a few minutes, the *uppuma* will thicken. Stir in the ghee (or coconut oil), and mix well. Remove it to a serving bowl or platter, and garnish it with cashew nuts and fresh coconut. Serve with coconut chutney.

The grains of farina are small, like the Indian *rava*. Cream of wheat may be substituted for farina.

Serves 4 to 6.

Variations:

Cracked-Wheat *Uppuma:* *Uppuma* may also be made with cracked wheat. It takes a little more time to cook cracked wheat. For two cups of cracked wheat, use six cups of water. All other ingredients remain the same. Follow the recipe for farina *uppuma*.

Semiya *Uppuma:* This dish is prepared with extra-thin Indian wheat noodles called *semiya*. Crush the noodles to half-inch pieces, and follow the recipe for farina *uppuma*.

Mixed Vegetable *Uppuma:* Spicy Farina with Mixed Vegetables

Here is a colorful version of the simple *uppuma* in which a variety of vegetables add texture, taste, and flavor to the dish. It may be prepared with either farina or *semiya*.

2 cups *rava* or farina or *semiya*
2 tablespoon vegetable oil
1 teaspoon mustard seeds
½ teaspoon each *urad* dal and *chana* dal
1 dried red cayenne, serrano, or Thai chili, halved
12 to 15 fresh curry leaves
2 teaspoons freshly grated ginger
4 fresh green chilies (serrano or Thai), thinly sliced (less for a milder taste)
2 small onions, finely chopped
6 cups water
Salt to taste
¼ cup shelled or frozen green peas
1 medium-sized potato, peeled and cut into small cubes
1 small carrot, peeled and cut into small pieces
1 tablespoon ghee **or** coconut oil
1 tablespoon toasted cashew nut pieces
2 tablespoons chopped cilantro leaves

In a heavy skillet, dry roast the farina or *semiya* until it turns light pink in color, and set it aside. Heat the oil in another skillet, and add the mustard seeds. When the mustard seeds start sputtering, add the *urad* dal and *chana* dal, and fry until they turn golden brown. Add the halved red chili pepper, curry leaves, ginger, green chilies, and onion. Fry for two to three minutes, stirring continuously, until the onions are fried. Add the water and salt to the skillet, and bring it to a boil. Stir in the vegetables, cover, and cook over medium heat until the vegetables are tender. Add the farina (or *semiya*) in a thin stream, and keep stirring so that no lumps form. In a few minutes, the *uppuma* will be dry. Add the ghee or coconut oil, and mix well. Remove it to a serving bowl or platter, and garnish it with cashew nuts and chopped cilantro leaves. Serve with coconut chutney. The grains of farina are small like the Indian *rava*. If both of these are unavailable, cream of wheat may be substituted.

Serves 4 to 6.

Kozhukkatta: Steamed Rice and Fresh Coconut Balls

A unique feature of our cuisine is the myriad ways in which rice and coconut are combined to make dishes that are entirely different in taste and texture. These mildly spiced and steam-cooked balls made of rice and fresh coconut are fluffy and flavorful.

2 cups long-grain rice
1½ cups freshly grated coconut
Salt to taste
2 tablespoons vegetable oil
1 teaspoon mustard seeds
1 teaspoon *urad* dal
1 teaspoon *chana* dal
3 dried red cayenne, serrano, or Thai chilies, broken into pieces (less for a milder taste)
12 to 15 fresh curry leaves
¼ teaspoon asafetida powder

Soak rice for three to four hours, rinse it in several changes of water until the water runs clear, and drain. Combine the rice, grated coconut, and salt in a food processor with just enough water to grind it into a grainy, coarse, thick dough. Heat the oil in a heavy skillet, and add the mustard seeds. When the mustard seeds start sputtering, add the *urad* dal and *chana* dal, and fry until they turn golden brown. Add the red chili peppers, curry leaves, and asafetida. Stir in the rice-coconut dough along with a ladleful of water, and cook over low heat, stirring continuously, until it thickens and leaves the sides of the skillet. Remove it from the stove, and let it cool. When it is cool enough to touch, shape the dough into small balls about the size of a lemon. Boil water in a saucepan, and place a steamer insert on top. Spread a small piece of wet cheesecloth over the insert, and arrange the *khozukkatta* on it in a single layer. Cover and steam for ten to fifteen minutes. Serve with *sambar* or coconut chutney.

Serves 4 to 6.

Variation:

Uppuma Khozukkatta: In this version, the *khozukkatta* dough is combined with soaked *tuvar* dal. Instead of regular rice, this dish uses steamed cream of rice. Grits make an excellent substitute.

2 cups cream of rice or grits
Salt to taste
1 cup freshly grated coconut
½ cup *tuvar* dal, soaked for four to five hours, washed, and drained
2 tablespoons vegetable oil
1 teaspoon mustard seeds
1 teaspoon *urad* dal
1 teaspoon *chana* dal
3 dried red cayenne, serrano, or Thai chilies, broken into pieces (less for a milder taste)
10 to 12 fresh curry leaves
¼ teaspoon asafetida powder

Boil water in a saucepan with a steamer insert. Spread a piece of cheesecloth over the steamer insert, spread the cream of rice (or grits) on it, and sprinkle a few drops of water on top. Cover and steam for eight to ten minutes. Remove it from the stove, and spread on a platter. When it is cool enough to touch, add salt, grated coconut, and the soaked *tuvar* dal, and mix well. Heat the oil in a heavy skillet, and add the mustard seeds. When the mustard seeds start sputtering, add the dals, and fry until they turn golden brown. Add the red chili peppers, curry leaves, and asafetida. Stir in the steamed cream of rice (or grits) and coconut. Remove it from the stove, and let it cool. If the mix is dry, sprinkle on a couple spoonfuls of water, and mix well.

When it is cool enough to touch, shape the dough into small balls about the size of a lemon. Boil water in a saucepan, and place the steamer insert in it. Spread a small piece of wet cheesecloth over the insert, and arrange the *khozukkatta* on it in a single layer. Cover and steam for ten to fifteen minutes. Serve with *sambar* or coconut chutney.

Serves 4 to 6.

Chapter Ten
Savory Snacks

The Western menu, based on an appetizer, a salad, a main course, and dessert, does not exist in the traditional South Indian meal. Rather, we offer several dishes at the same time, arranged around a large portion of rice. In fact, there is no word in our language, Malayalam, that is the equivalent of "appetizer." The simple theory is that there is no need to stimulate an appetite for rice; in fact, eating before a meal is often discouraged. While growing up in Kerala, during evening hours, if we ever tried to raid the pantry for snacks, one of the adults in the family would shout from behind, "It is almost time for supper. Don't ruin your appetite for rice!"

But when guests drop in during the course of a day—more often than not, unannounced—they are always entertained with an enticing array of snacks. Snacks are also served with afternoon tea. There are two types of snacks: those that can be prepared almost a week ahead, and those that taste best when served hot off the stove. Although these are not considered appetizers, I have had great success serving them as such. Practically none of them are very difficult or time-consuming to prepare, and many can be prepared in advance and either reheated or served at room temperature.

Murukku: Rice and *Urad* Dal Pretzel

Whenever *murukku* was made at home, Mom always sought the help of our neighbor Janu Ammiyaar, the undisputed expert of *murukku* making in our hometown. She sat on the floor under the whirling ceiling fan and mixed rice and *urad* flours, cumin, sesame, salt, and water in a large stainless-steel bowl. A chunk of dark-brown asafetida soaked in a small bowl of water. She gently rolled it with her index finger, and the water turned cloudy. She sprinkled the spicy liquid on the dough and kneaded some more. As she inhaled the fragrance of asafetida, she remarked, "This is real *perumkaayam*. I don't like those fragrance-free powders from a box," referring to the bottled, less flavorful asafetida.

After several minutes of pounding and kneading, a silky-smooth ball of dough emerged. She pinched a tiny piece of dough and made it into a small pyramid, and placed it at one end of the cotton cloth spread on the floor. She closed her eyes and murmured a prayer in Tamil, her mother tongue; that was how she paid homage to Lord Ganapathi, destroyer of all evils. Now she was confident that her *murukku* was going to turn out perfect. She oiled her palm with coconut oil and took a lemon-sized piece of dough, and twisted it into wavy *murukku* curls on the white cotton cloth. Watching her effortlessly turn out thin, multi-layered circles of curly spirals, with just her index finger and thumb, was fascinating and dissuading at the same time.

Balan, our cook, put a couple of tamarind logs into the belly of the *aduppu* (wood-burning stove) and blew through a hollow iron rod. Then he placed a large bronze *uruli* on the stove top and poured coconut oil into it. The logs flickered as they burned under the *uruli*. When she finished twisting the *murukku*, Janu Ammiyaar called out, "*Baalaa, enna moothaacha?*" ("Balan, is the oil hot enough?") She transferred the *murukku* to a large plate and took it into the kitchen. She gently dropped the circlets into the oil in batches. As they turned golden brown and floated up, she removed them from the oil and spread them on a large plate covered with an old newspaper. Deep-fried to crunchy perfection, her *murukku* literally melted in the mouth.

Making this snack by hand is rather tricky and time-consuming, but using a metal snack press is an easy alternative. This recipe makes enough to fill a four-quart bowl. It is a great snack with a cold glass of beer.

3 cups rice flour
1 cup *urad* flour
Salt to taste
1 tablespoon cumin seeds
2 teaspoons sesame seeds (preferably brown or black)
¼ teaspoon asafetida powder
6 to 8 cups vegetable oil (for deep-frying)

Combine rice flour, *urad* flour, salt, cumin seeds, sesame seeds, and asafetida, and mix thoroughly. Using just enough water, make a soft dough. Knead well. Heat the oil to 365°F in a heavy saucepan or a wok. Fit the metal snack press with a five-holed disk, and fill with dough. Press the dough directly into the oil. As the dough falls, move the press around in a circular motion so that it is distributed evenly in the oil. Deep-fry until the *murukku* is golden and crispy. Remove it from the oil, and drain. Repeat with the remaining dough. Let it cool to room temperature. Store *murukku* in airtight containers.

This recipe makes enough to fill a four-quart bowl.

Variations

Steamed all-purpose flour may be used as a substitute for rice flour. Spread a clean, dry cheesecloth in a steamer insert and spread the all-purpose flour over it. Heat water in a saucepan, and place the steamer insert on top. Cover tightly, and stream the flour for five minutes. Remove it from the stove, and let it cool to room temperature. Follow the remaining steps to make murukku.

Girija's *Cheruparippu Murukku*

My sister Girija makes crispy *murukku* with rice flour and mung dal. Here is her recipe.

1 cup mung dal
4 cups rice flour
Salt to taste
2 tablespoon cumin seeds
2 teaspoons sesame seeds (preferably brown or black)
¼ teaspoon asafetida powder
6 to 8 cups vegetable oil (for deep-frying)

Wash and clean the mung dal in several changes of water until the water runs clear, and drain. In a saucepan, cook the mung dal along with one and a half cups of water over medium heat. Add more water if necessary, but allow almost all of the water to evaporate. Remove it from the stove, let it cool to room temperature, and then mash it. Combine the dal, rice flour, salt, cumin seeds, sesame seeds, and asafetida with just enough water to form a soft dough, and knead well. Follow the steps for making *murukku*.

Cheeda: Fried Spicy Rice and *Urad* Dal Balls

These crispy and crunchy marbles are a delight to pop into the mouth. *Cheeda* gets its flavor from a variety of complementary ingredients: cumin, black pepper, sesame seeds, and ghee. It is a must for Janmashtami (Lord Krishna's birthday) celebrations.

1½ tablespoons crushed black pepper
1 tablespoon cumin seeds
3 cups rice flour
1 cup *urad* flour
¼ teaspoon asafetida powder
2 teaspoons sesame seeds (preferably black sesame seeds)
Salt to taste
4 tablespoons ghee
Six to eight cups vegetable oil (for deep-frying)

Grind the black pepper and cumin into a coarse powder using a coffee mill or blender. In a large bowl, combine the spice powder with both flours, asafetida, sesame seeds, salt, and ghee. Add just enough water to make a thick dough, and knead. Take a large pinch of the dough in the palm of your hand, and roll it into large marble-sized balls. Repeat with the remaining dough. Spread the balls on a cheesecloth, a clean and smooth kitchen towel, or a paper towel to dry for five minutes.

Heat the oil to 365°F in a heavy saucepan or a wok, and fry a few *cheedas* at a time. Fry until the *cheedas* are golden and crispy. Remove them from the oil, and drain. Store them in airtight containers. They stay fresh for a week.

This recipe makes enough to fill a three-quart bowl.

Omappodi: Deep-fried *Besan* Strings

Here the quintessential Indian snack, *sev* noodles, is spiced with ajowan. These thin noodles are shaped with a metal snack press fitted with a fine-holed disk. A potato ricer also comes in handy as a appliance for making these crispy, thin noodles.

1 teaspoon ajowan
3 cups *besan (chana* dal flour)
1 tablespoon rice flour
2 tablespoons butter (at room temperature)
Salt to taste
6 cups vegetable oil (for frying)

Clean the ajowan seeds, and powder them. Combine the *besan,* rice flour, powdered ajowan, butter, and salt with just enough water to make a soft dough. Heat the oil in a heavy saucepan or wok to 365°F. Fit the snack press with the thin-holed disk, fill it with the dough, and press it directly into the hot oil. As the noodles fall, move the press around in circular motion so that they are distributed evenly in the oil. Fry until the top side is golden and crispy, approximately one and a half minutes. Using a spatula, turn over the noodles, and fry for another minute. Remove them from the oil, and drain. Repeat the process with the remaining dough. Each batch of noodles will come out as a large circle. After it has cooled to room temperature, break it into pieces, and store them in an airtight container.

This recipe makes enough to fill a four-quart bowl.

Kara Mixture: Spicy, Crunchy Mix

Kara mixture is the South Indian version of the popular Indian snack *chiwda.* Every region in India has its own version of this snack, made with slight variations in ingredients and spicing. This light and flavorful snack is literally a mixture of colors, flavors, and textures. *Kara* means "hot" and tastes just as the name suggests. *Kara* mixture does not contain any of the raisins or dates you would find in *chiwda.* Though the preparation is a bit time-consuming, it is not very difficult to make.

In the following traditional recipe, crunchy, yellow, deep-fried *chana* flour stings and tiny balls are combined with toasted peanuts, cashews, deep-fried pounded rice, and puffed rice. The mixture is seasoned with red pepper, asafetida and curry leaves.

4 cups *besan (chana* dal flour)
Salt to taste
8 cups vegetable oil (for frying)
1 cup pounded rice
1 cup puffed rice
½ cup peanuts
20 to 25 cashew nuts, cut into small pieces
¼ teaspoon asafetida powder
1 teaspoon dried red cayenne, serrano, or Thai chili powder (less for a milder taste)
12 to 15 fresh curry leaves

Combine two cups of *besan*, salt, and enough water to make a thin batter. Heat the oil in a heavy saucepan or wok to 365°F. Pour a cup of the batter at a time into the hot oil through a slotted spoon with round holes or, if possible, a *laddu* sieve (a large metal plate with round holes and a handle). The batter will form small beads called *boondi*. Stir and fry until they are crispy and golden. Remove the beads with a slotted spoon, and drain. Repeat with the remaining batter.

Combine the remaining *besan* flour with salt and just enough water to make a soft dough. Fit the snack press with the thin-holed disk, and fill it with the dough. Squeeze the dough through the press directly into the hot oil. The dough will come out of the press in thin strings. As they fall, move the press around in a circular motion so that they are distributed evenly in the oil. Cook the noodles over medium heat until they are golden and crispy. Remove them from oil, and drain. Repeat with the remaining dough. When they are cool, crush the noodles into thin pieces, and combine them with the *boondi*.

Clean the pounded rice and the puffed rice. Deep-fry the pounded rice until it is crispy, and drain. Heat one tablespoon of oil in a large skillet, and fry the nuts. When the nuts are slightly browned, add the red chili powder, asafetida, and curry leaves to the skillet, and stir well. Add the puffed rice and salt to the skillet, and stir. Mix together the *boondi*, *sev*, and fried pounded rice, add them to the skillet, and remove it from the stove. Using a salad spoon and fork, toss well. Cool it to room temperature, and store it in airtight containers.

This recipe makes enough to fill a four-quart bowl.

Quick and easy versions: Substitute deep-fried pounded rice and puffed rice with Rice Krispies cereal and Puffed Rice cereal. Deep-fried *besan* strings and balls (called *sev* and *boondi*) are available from Indian grocers. The asafetida may be skipped altogether. Heat a tablespoon of oil in a large skillet, and fry the nuts. When they start browning, add red pepper flakes and curry leaves, and stir well. Turn off the heat. Add two cups each of Rice Krispies cereal and Puffed Rice cereal to the skillet, and sprinkle with salt. Add two cups each of store-bought *sev* and *boondi*. Toss well to combine. Heat the oven to 300°F. Spread the mixture in a large baking dish, and place it inside the oven. Toast for five to eight minutes, until the cereals have heated through. Remove it from the oven, and let it cool to room temperature. Store the mixture in an airtight container. Even *boondi* and *sev* may be substituted with Corn Chex and Rice Chex cereals.

Pappadavada (Thatta): Deep-Fried Spicy Rice and *Urad* Dal Disks

These spicy, golden, thin crackers studded with *tuvar* dal and curry leaves are an absolute delight to munch. They stay fresh for over a week when stored in airtight containers.

3 cups rice flour
½ cup *urad* dal flour
2 tablespoons *tuvar* dal, cleaned and soaked for two to three hours and drained
1 tablespoon dried red cayenne, serrano, or Thai chili powder (less for a milder taste)
¼ teaspoon asafetida powder
1 teaspoon cumin powder
12 to 15 fresh curry leaves
Salt to taste
1 tablespoon ghee or oil
4 cups vegetable oil (for frying)

Combine the rice flour, *urad* flour, soaked *tuvar* dal, cayenne powder, asafetida, cumin seeds, curry leaves, salt, and ghee in a large mixing bowl. Pour in just enough water to form a medium-soft dough, and knead with your hand. Roll the dough into small, lime-sized balls. Spread a large piece of cheesecloth or a smooth, clean kitchen towel on the countertop. Place the balls on the kitchen towel. Wet your fingers with water, and flatten each ball into a disk, two to two and a half inches in diameter. With your index finger, make an indentation at the center of each disk. Let them dry for half an hour. The cloth will absorb some of the water from the dough and make it easier to fry. Heat the oil in a heavy saucepan or wok to 365°F, and deep-fry the disks until they are golden, approximately four to five minutes. Remove them from the oil with a slotted spoon, and drain. (Use a cake cooling rack placed over a cookie tray to drain them. Excess oil will drip through the cooling rack and fall on the cookie tray.) Store them in airtight containers. They will keep fresh for a week.

Makes approximately 25.

Variation: To serve as a party snack, make small rounds, the size of round tortilla chips.

Thengavada: Deep-Fried Spicy Rice and Coconut Disks

These salty, crunchy coconut rice crackers are laced with crushed black pepper. They stay fresh for a week if stored in airtight containers.

1 cup long-grain rice
1 cup fresh coconut, finely grated
Salt to taste
½ teaspoon turmeric powder
½ tablespoon crushed black pepper
1 tablespoon ghee **or** oil
4 cups vegetable oil for deep-frying

Soak the rice in water for one to one and a half hours, rinse it in several changes of water until the water runs clear, and drain. In a food processor, combine the rice, coconut, and salt, and process them into a very thick, coarse, grainy dough. Remove the dough from the processor, and sprinkle it with turmeric and crushed black pepper. Add the ghee to the dough, and knead well. Spread a large piece of cheesecloth or a smooth, clean kitchen towel on the countertop. Break off pieces of the dough, and roll them into small, lime-sized balls. Place the balls on the kitchen towel. Wet your fingers with water, and flatten each ball into a disk, two to two and a half inches in diameter. With your index finger, make an indentation at the center of each disk. Let them dry for half an hour. The cloth will absorb some of the water from the dough and make it easier to fry. Heat the oil in a heavy saucepan or wok to 365°F, and deep-fry the disks until they are golden, approximately five to six minutes. Remove them from the oil with a slotted spoon, and drain. (Use a cake cooling rack placed over a cookie tray to drain. Excess oil will drip through the cooling rack and fall on the cookie tray.) Store them in airtight containers. They will keep fresh for a week.

Makes approximately 20.

Ribbon *Pokavada:* Spicy Rice and *Besan* Ribbons

These crunchy, golden ribbons, flavored with cayenne pepper, cumin, and asafetida, are made with the snack press. When broken into pieces, they look almost like corn chips.

1 cup *chana* dal flour *(besan)*
3 cups rice flour
¾ tablespoon dried red cayenne, serrano, or Thai chili powder (less for a milder taste)
¼ teaspoon asafetida powder (optional)
1 tablespoon crushed cumin seeds
Salt to taste
6 cups vegetable oil (for deep-frying)

In a mixing bowl, combine all of the ingredients except the oil. Add water, a few tablespoons at a time, and mix well to make a soft dough. Heat the oil in a heavy saucepan or wok to 365°F. Spoon the dough into a snack press fitted with the *pokavada* plate, the one with two long, rectangular slits in the middle. Squeeze the dough through the press directly into the hot oil. The dough will come out of the press in the shape of ribbons three-quarters of an inch wide. As the ribbons fall, move the press around in a circular motion so that they are distributed evenly in the oil.

When the ribbons are crisp and golden (approximately four to five minutes), remove them from the oil with a slotted spoon, and drain. (Use a cake cooling rack placed over a cookie tray to drain. Excess oil will drip through the cooling rack and fall on the cookie tray.) Repeat the process with the remaining dough. Stored in airtight containers, this snack stays fresh for a week.

This recipe makes enough to fill a four-quart bowl.

Urulakkizangu Bondas: Spicy Potato Fritters

Bondas are spicy little potato balls encased in a golden-yellow *besan* crust. When served with tomato chutney, these fritters make a great brunch dish.

For the filling:
3 large russet potatoes, peeled and cut in one-inch pieces
½ teaspoon turmeric powder
Salt to taste
1 tablespoon vegetable oil
1½ teaspoon mustard seeds
1 teaspoon *urad* dal
1 teaspoon *chana* dal
1 dried hot red chili, broken into pieces, **or** ½ teaspoon red pepper flakes
6 to 8 fresh curry leaves
4 to 5 fresh green chilies (serrano or Thai), finely chopped (less for a milder taste)

For the batter:
2 cups *besan* flour (chickpea flour)
1 teaspoon dried red cayenne, serrano, or Thai chili powder (less for a milder taste)
¼ teaspoon asafetida powder (optional)
Salt to taste
6 cups vegetable oil (for deep-frying)

Place the potatoes in a large saucepan, and cover with water. Add the turmeric and salt, and bring it to a boil. Reduce heat to medium-low, cover, and cook for about ten minutes or until tender. Drain the potatoes, and mash them coarsely with the back of a spoon. Set aside.

Heat two tablespoons of oil in a large skillet over medium heat, and add the mustard seeds. When the mustard seeds start sputtering add the *chana* dal and *urad* dal, and fry them until they turn light brown. Stir in the red chili pepper, curry leaves, and green chilies. Fry for two to three minutes, then stir in the mashed potatoes, and mix well. Remove it from heat, and set aside. Shape the cooled mixture into one-inch balls, and set them on a plate. This part of the recipe can be completed a day ahead, covered, and refrigerated.

To make the batter, combine the *besan,* cayenne pepper, asafetida, and salt in a bowl, and mix well. Add just enough water to make a thin batter (about the consistency of pancake batter). Heat oil in a heavy pan or wok to 365°F. Dip the balls into the batter, then carefully slide them into the hot oil, and deep-fry until golden (about four to five minutes). Remove the *bondas* from the oil, and drain them on a cooling rack placed over a cookie tray. Serve hot, with fresh tomato chutney.

Makes approximately 20.

Both the filling and the batter may be prepared ahead of time. Fried *bondas* reheat well in a microwave or a conventional oven. If using a microwave, cover a plate of *bondas* with a paper towel sprinkled with water. Place a small bowl of water in the microwave. Cook on medium setting for about two to three minutes. If you are using a conventional oven, preheat it to 275°F, and warm the *bondas* for five to seven minutes. Fresh ones, of course, taste better.

Variations

Mixed Vegetable *Bondas:* Although *bondas* are traditionally made with potatoes, they can also be made with mixed vegetables. Follow the recipe above, but use only two potatoes and add a half-cup of cooked green peas and a half-cup of cooked carrot pieces to the skillet with the potatoes. Roughly mash all ingredients together, and form them into one-inch balls. Dip the balls in the batter, and deep-fry as directed above.

Instant *Bondas:* If you don't have the time to boil potatoes, instant mashed potatoes come in handy as a substitute. Prepare the mustard-dal-curry leaf-green chili mixture as directed above, and cook two minutes. Reduce heat, and add a half-teaspoon of turmeric powder, salt, and one cup of water to the pan. Bring the water to a boil, and gradually add one and a half cups of instant mashed potatoes, stirring continuously. Remove it from the heat, and let the mixture cool. The consistency should be thicker than regular mashed potatoes, so that it can be rolled into balls. Adjust the amount of water and instant mashed potatoes to obtain this consistency. Dip the balls in the batter, and deep-fry as directed above.

Tex-Mex *Bondas:* To give the recipe a Tex-Mex accent, combine half the quantity of mashed potatoes with one cup of cooked and drained corn kernels, a quarter-cup of chopped onion, one tablespoon of chopped cilantro, one teaspoon of finely chopped green chili, and one and a half cups of well-drained cottage cheese. Sprinkle a half-cup of *besan* on top, and mix well. Shape into one-inch balls, dip them in batter, and deep-fry as directed above.

Bajji or *Pokavadas:* Vegetable Fritters

Chewy, crunchy deep-fried *pokavadas* make great appetizers when served with a spicy chutney or salsa. They can be prepared with a variety of vegetables. Cauliflower, eggplant, green plantain slices, onion, potato, and spinach leaves are some of the vegetables used in making *pokavadas*. To save time, assemble the batter and vegetable slices ahead, and deep-fry them just before serving.

For the batter:
3 cups *chana* flour *(besan)*
3 tablespoons rice flour
¼ teaspoon asafetida powder (optional)
1 to 2 teaspoons dried red cayenne, serrano, or Thai chili powder (less for a milder taste)
Salt to taste

Vegetables for pokavada:
1 medium-sized potato, peeled and cut into thin rounds

1 medium-sized onion, peeled and cut into thin rounds
1 cup cauliflower florets
1 small eggplant, cut into thin rounds
1 green plantain, peeled and cut into thin pieces
A few spinach leaves
6 cups oil (for frying)

Combine all the ingredients for the batter in a large mixing bowl, and pour in water slowly while beating with a whisk. The mixture should have the consistency of pancake batter, so that it will leave a thin coating on the vegetable slices.

Heat the oil in a heavy saucepan or wok to 365°F. Dip the vegetable slices in the batter, slide them into the hot oil, and deep-fry them until they are golden and crisp. Remove them from the oil, and drain. Serve hot with chutneys. Unlike *bondas,* these fritters do not reheat well in the oven. It is better to serve them hot off the stove.

This recipe makes enough to fill a four-quart bowl.

Parippu Vadas: Deep-Fried Spicy *Tuvar* Dal Fritters

These deep-fried, flat, round legume fritters have a crunchy crust. They may be served soaked in *rasam* (tomato and *tuvar* dal soup) as a first course. Or, for a cool refreshing twist, serve them soaked in lightly spiced yogurt. Traditionally, *parippu vadas* are prepared with *tuvar* dal. It may be substituted with either *chana* dal or the dried yellow split peas that are readily available in any U.S. supermarket.

1 cup *tuvar* dal or yellow split peas
¼ teaspoon asafetida powder (optional)
Salt to taste
1 tablespoon chopped fresh cilantro leaves
1 medium-sized onion, thinly chopped
4 or 5 fresh green chilies (serrano or Thai), finely chopped (less for a milder taste)
1 tablespoon grated fresh ginger
12 to 15 fresh curry leaves
6 cups vegetable oil (for deep-frying)

Soak the *tuvar* dal in water for three to four hours, rinse it in several changes of water until the water runs clear, and then drain. In a food processor, combine three tablespoons of the soaked *tuvar* dal, asafetida, and salt, and process to a thick dough. Add the remaining soaked *tuvar* dal, and grind coarsely. Since the dal absorbs water during soaking, there is no need to add extra water when processing. The ground dough should be very thick, so that it can be shaped into small disks. Remove it from the processor, sprinkle it with chopped cilantro leaves, onion, green chilies, ginger, and curry leaves, and mix well. Heat the oil in a heavy pan or wok over medium heat to 365°F. When the oil is hot, wet the palms of your hands, and shape two tablespoons of the dough into a disk one and a half to two inches in diameter. Slide the *vada* gently into the hot oil. Turn it around with a slotted spoon, and cook both sides. Repeat with the remaining dough. Fry the *vadas* until they are golden and crisp, approximately four to six minutes. Remove them from the oil, and drain. (Use a cake cooling rack placed over a cookie tray to drain. Excess oil will drip through the cooling rack and fall on the cookie tray.) Serve hot, with coconut chutney or tomato chutney.

Makes 20 to 22 *vadas*.

Sevaka: Panfried Spicy Rice Noodles

Sevaka is seasoned rice noodles, South Indian style. In Kerala, it is often served as an afternoon snack. It also makes a good brunch dish.

2 cups long-grain rice
2 tablespoons sesame oil* (or vegetable oil)
Salt to taste
1 teaspoon mustard seeds
1 teaspoon *urad* dal
1 teaspoon *chana* dal
1 fresh green chili (serrano or Thai), thinly sliced
1 or 2 hot red chili peppers, broken into pieces, **or** ½ teaspoon crushed red pepper
1 teaspoon fresh grated ginger
A few curry leaves
1 tablespoon toasted cashew nut pieces (or peanuts)
1 tablespoon chopped cilantro leaves

Soak the rice for four to five hours. Rinse it in several changes of water until the water runs clear, and drain. Using a blender, grind the rice with just enough water to make a very smooth batter. Heat a heavy skillet over medium heat, and pour in two tablespoons of oil. When it is hot, stir in the batter, add salt, and reduce the heat to low. Stirring continuously, cook the batter until it thickens and starts to leave the sides of the pan. At this point, it will have a dough-like consistency. Remove it from the stove, and let it cool.

Spoon the dough into a snack press fitted with the thin-holed plate. Heat three inches of water in a saucepan fitted with a steamer insert. Line the steamer insert with a cheesecloth or a clean, thin towel. Press the dough onto the cheesecloth in the steamer insert, moving the press around in a circular motion over the cloth so that the noodles are distributed evenly. Cover and steam for ten to twelve minutes over medium heat, until the noodles are cooked. Remove them from the heat, and let them cool. With a spoon, break the cooked noodles into quarter-inch to half-inch pieces.

In a heavy skillet, heat the remaining oil, and add the mustard seeds. When the mustard seeds start sputtering, add the dal, and fry for about a minute until they are golden brown. Add the green and red chilies, ginger, and curry leaves, and fry for a minute. Reduce the heat to low, add the broken noodles along with toasted nuts, and mix well. Remove it from the stove, and sprinkle with cilantro leaves. Serve with coconut chutney.

Makes 6 servings.

*Sesame oil is used in the traditional recipe.

Dehydrated rice noodles, available in Indian and other Asian grocery stores, may be substituted for noodles made from scratch. Dehydrated noodles must be soaked in hot water for three to four minutes to make them pliable. Then steam them for ten to twelve minutes before proceeding with the remaining steps of the recipe. Frozen *idiappam,* available at many Indian grocery stores in the United States, is another alternative. Defrost it and break it into small pieces before proceeding with the recipe above.

Variations

Thayir Sevaka: Prepare four cups of *sevaka,* following the above recipe. Mix the *sevaka* with a cup of thick yogurt, and stir well.

Puli Sevaka: Combine a tablespoon of tamarind concentrate with one cup of water and salt to taste, and boil the mixture until it is reduced to a half-cup. Add three cups of *sevaka* (prepared following the above recipe), and mix well. Panfry over medium heat until all the water has evaporated.

Puli Avil: Pounded Rice Spiced with Tamarind and Mustard Seeds

Here is a spicy snack that can be prepared in less than thirty minutes. Just like rice noodles, pounded rice is seasoned with a tangy tamarind sauce.

2 cups pounded rice
1 tablespoon sesame oil (or vegetable oil)
½ teaspoon mustard seeds
1 dried red cayenne, serrano, or Thai chili, broken into pieces, **or** ½ teaspoon crushed red pepper
2 fresh green chilies (serrano or Thai), cut into thin slices (less for a milder taste)
1 teaspoon grated fresh ginger
10 to12 fresh curry leaves
½ teaspoon tamarind concentrate
¼ teaspoon turmeric
Salt to taste
1 tablespoon chopped cilantro

Rinse the pounded rice in a colander under running tap water, and drain. Heat the oil in a heavy skillet, and add the mustard seeds. When the mustard seeds start sputtering, add the red chili pepper, green chilies, ginger, and curry leaves, and fry for a couple of minutes. Reduce the heat, and stir in the tamarind concentrate along with one cup of water. Add turmeric and salt, and cook for five minutes over medium heat. Add the drained pounded rice, and stir well. Cook until all of the liquid is absorbed. Remove it to a serving bowl, and garnish with cilantro leaves.

Makes 4 to 6 servings.

Kannanaadan: Semi-Ripe Plantains Panfried with Mustard Seeds and Curry Leaves

This is an easy-to-prepare dish that is often served as a healthy after-school snack. It is made with semi-ripe plantains and served with *puliingi,* ginger, and green chili pickle. (A recipe for *puliingi* can be found in the chapter on chutneys and pickles.)

2 just-ripening plantains
Salt to taste
¼ teaspoon turmeric powder
1½ tablespoons vegetable oil
½ teaspoon mustard seeds
½ teaspoon *urad* dal
1 dry red cayenne, serrano, or Thai chili, broken into pieces, **or** ½ teaspoon crushed red pepper
12 to 15 fresh curry leaves

Peel the plantains, and cut them lengthwise down the middle. Cut these long pieces into quarter-inch thick pieces. In a skillet, cook these pieces along with salt, turmeric powder, and half a cup of water over medium heat. When the plantain pieces are cooked, almost all of the water should have evaporated. Stir gently so that the pieces do not stick to the pan. Remove them from the stove, and set aside. Heat the oil in a small skillet, and add the mustard seeds. When the mustard seeds start sputtering, add the *urad* dal, red chili pepper, and curry leaves, and fry until the dal turns golden brown. Remove it from the stove, pour it over the cooked plantains, and stir gently. Serve with *puliingi*.

Makes 3 to 4 servings.

Chapter Eleven
Desserts: Sweet Treats

Indian desserts unfortunately have received a cool reception in the West—they are often considered just too sweet. Sadly, this reputation was created by Indian restaurants that serve only the most sugary of sweets. In South India, desserts are generally a part of festive occasions, not everyday meals. And on these occasions, *paayasam* (pudding) is the traditional dessert. Although we have a wide range of sweets, they are prepared at festivals and most frequently served with tea or coffee.

Not all of our desserts are very sweet; several of them are only mildly sweet. I call them sweet treats because they are a feast for both the eyes and the mouth. During holidays and temple festival days, most homes will have a good supply of these sweets. Some of these sweets are prepared at our temples as offerings. Brown-sugar sweets have a rustic look and a homemade taste, and they make a healthy snack food. Sweets prepared with refined sugar are delicate, vibrant, and bursting with the flavors of cardamom and ghee, and they make excellent desserts.

The major ingredients used in making these sweets are white and brown sugar, ghee, *besan* flour, and cardamom. *Besan* flour is made from hulled Indian brown chickpeas *(chana* dal). It is very fine in texture and pale yellow in color. Indian grocery stores sell two kinds of *besan* flour: one is extra fine, and the other is slightly coarse. Use the extra-fine variety for sweets. It is also available in gourmet and specialty food stores. My personal favorite brands of these ingredients are Imperial brand pure cane sugar, Land O'Lakes brand unsalted butter, and Laxmi brand *besan* flour. All of these sweets are stove-top preparations, and they are not very complicated or time consuming.

Festivals and Sweets

Navarathri

The festival of nine nights is one of the biggest and most colorful of Hindu festivals. It is a celebration of life, culture, popular customs, and traditions. It is also a time for reunion. Navarathri means different things to different communities or even generations; it is a kaleidoscope of beliefs and traditions. Navarathri is celebrated with intense fervor and zest as Durga Puja in West Bengal. In Punjab, Navarathri is a period of fasting. In Gujarat, the evenings and nights are occasions for the fascinating Garba dance. In northern India, the festival wears the colorful attire of Ramlila, and various incidents from Lord Rama's life are enacted. The Dasara of Mysore is famous for its caparisoned elephants that lead a colorful procession through the streets of the city. In most parts of southern India, the tradition is to set up *kolu*—beautiful and elaborate displays of colorful dolls in the shapes of the many gods and goddesses of the Hindu pantheon. The last three days are especially devoted to celebrating the three aspects of the mother goddess: Durga, the divine protector; Lakshmi, who bestows peace and prosperity; and Saraswathi, who blesses with knowledge.

The *kolu* doll collections are handed down from one generation to the next. These dolls, made of mud or carved in wood, are painted in various colors and embellished with jewelry. More than a religious festival, Navarathri is also an expression of creativity. The potter shows his skill in making images, the painter in drawing pictures, the musician in playing his instrument, and the priest in reciting the sacred books.

Navarathri was celebrated in my hometown with much fanfare for the full nine days. *Kolu* was so much fun in our joint family! A week before the holiday, we prepared the *kolu* room, assembling tiers of steps from the ceiling to the floor and decorating it with bright-colored fabrics, gilded paper, and colorful lights. The doll boxes were brought down from the attic, and we sat around on the floor, taking them out one by one from their packaging.

My cousin climbed up and placed an image of Lord Ganapathi, the one who removes all obstacles, at the center of the top tier. To his right side, we lined up Siva, clad in tiger skin; Parvathi, in her beautiful green sari and gold jewelry; and Subrahmanya, seated on a peacock. Then, to the left, we placed Lakshmi, adorned in beautiful red silk and seated on a large, pink lotus flower. Next to her was the gorgeous image of Saraswathi in her gossamer-thin white sari with gold borders, holding her favorite musical instrument, the *veena*. The next tier held images of the mother goddess in her various incarnations.

Then there were tiers dedicated to the great Hindu epics, *Ramayana* and *Mahabharata*. For the *Ramayana*, there was Rama, his wife Seetha, and Hanuman (the monkey-faced son of the god of the wind); and another set of Rama with his wife and brothers Lakshmana, Bharatha, and Sathrughna. Then, representing the *Mahabharata*, there was the large statue of Pandavas and Kauravas playing chess, another of Geethopadesa (Krishna advising Arjuna), and one of Paanchali crying out to Krishna as Dussasana rips off her sari. There was a whole array of Krishna dolls on the tier below: Krishna sneaking butter from an earthenware pot; Krishna opening his baby mouth and showing his foster mother, Yasoda, the entire universe inside; Krishna dancing on top of the serpent Kaliya; Krishna dancing with the Gopis, and Krishna with his favorite, Radha.

At Navarathri, in South India, we also thank the mother goddess for the bounty of the pulse harvest. October is the beginning of our mild autumn, and it is the harvest time for various pulses—chickpeas, black-eyed peas, *urad* beans, *tuvar* beans, and mung beans—a major source of protein in our vegetarian diet. Harvests are always celebrated with pageantry and ritual; pulse seeds are sown, sprouting is watched, and offerings are made with different pulses during the nine days of festivities. At the bottom tier of the *kolu* display, we made a little pond out of a large clear bowl, filled with water and set in mud spread on a wooden tray. We sowed pulse seeds around the miniature pond and watered them every day. In a few days, the pulses sprouted and made a miniature garden around the little pond.

It is a fun festival for children: nine days of exuberance and extravagance, a profusion of favorite sweets and snacks, and a three-day holiday from school and homework. The women of the house invited their friends and neighbors to view their *kolu* display. They also visited relatives' and friends' houses, and everyone returned home with little packets of snacks and sweets—most importantly, *sundal,* a delicious and spicy bean salad prepared as *prasadam* (offering) for the day. Various desserts and snacks were prepared every day as offerings, and their number and variety kept increasing as the days passed. Every day, at least one new dish was added to the menu, but most often, two or three new dishes were added. Often, all of the accumulated dishes were cooked every day. (This has a distant similarity to the Christmas song "The Twelve Days of Christmas," in which gifts to the lady keep growing in number.) By the ninth day, a minimum of nine dishes would be prepared.

Each evening, we went to the temple, dressed in festive clothes. Flower vendors sold fragrant jasmine and other flower garlands at the temple gate. Classical music and dance performances went on at the Navarathri *mandapam* (podium). At dusk, the many bronze oil lamps around the temple were lit, and the idol of the goddess was decorated with fragrant flowers and sandalwood paste. *Chenda* drums, accompanied by a heavy brass chimes, ushered in people for evening prayers. (The *chenda*, played during prayers, is one of the traditional temple instruments of Kerala.) The priest entered the *sreekovil* (sanctum sanctorum) with the *nivedyam* (food offering) and closed the thick wooden door behind him. After several minutes, he pulled open the wooden door, and the chimes of many bronze bells surrounding its spire drifted through the air and mixed in gentle harmony with hushed and reverential whispers. The priest concluded the formal offering with lighted oil lamps and the burning of camphor cubes. Later, we lined up with cupped right palms outstretched to receive a small serving of the *nivedyam* offered at the temple.

On Durgashtami, the ritual offering *Poojavaipu* was performed in the evening. Both prayer books and schoolbooks were bundled up in a piece of cloth and placed in front of the *kolu* display, either at home or at the temple. Also on this day, agricultural implements and artists' instruments were placed before the idol of Saraswathi to invoke the divine blessings of the goddess of learning. For the next three days, everyone refrained from reading, writing, and any kind of work. Schools and offices were closed, and it was a time for prayer and feasting.

On the eighth and ninth days, the celebrations reached a fever pitch. The grand finale on Vijayadasami is believed to be the most auspicious time for all new ventures. Book bundles were taken out in a ceremony called *Poojayeduppu*. It was time for *Vidyarambham,* which literally translates to "propitious beginning of education"—both writing and reading. After writing the auspicious words HARI SRI and the alphabets on sand spread in front of us, we read a few paragraphs from the prayer book and then from our school texts. In temples dedicated to the divine mother, on this day, little children were initiated into the world of letters. The children were seated on the lap of their uncle or father. The adult wrote the auspicious words HARI SRI in Malayalam on the child's little tongue with a gold ring, praying for the divine mother to bless him or her with the skills for reading and writing. They held their little fingers and helped the children write the same words on raw rice spread in front them.

Today, changed lifestyles—nuclear families, working women, and homework-laden children—have naturally changed the way Navarathri is celebrated. In our own family, the beautiful doll collection remains covered in clothes and stored in our attic. With our family scattered around the world, there are no youngsters to set up a *kolu* display at home. Most religious rites are performed at our temple, but within prescribed parameters of time.

Deepavali

Like Navarathri, Deepavali (Diwali) means different things to different communities. In many states, it is also the New Year. In some other parts, it is celebrated to commemorate Lord Rama's return from exile. In southern and western India, Deepavali ("Festival of Lights") celebrates the blessing Lord Krishna bestowed on the demon king Narakasura. He was a powerful and arrogant king who began abusing the world. The tormented sages appealed to Lord Krishna to protect the world. During a fierce battle with the demon king, Krishna cast his ultimate weapon, *sudarsana chakra*, at the demon and killed him. Before he died, Narakasura realized his mistake and pleaded for Krishna's forgiveness. Krishna forgave him and granted his dying wish that all those who take an oil bath on the anniversary of that day will be saved from all evil. Therefore, the death of Narakasura is celebrated by taking oil baths, wearing festive new clothes, and lighting rows of lamps, symbolizing the removal of darkness and ignorance from the mind and unveiling the light of knowledge. The celebration of Deepavali is marked by the lighting of innumerable lamps in every courtyard and the bursting of crackers. Sweets and new clothes are part of the festivities, as in other festivals.

In Kerala, Deepavali celebrations are not very elaborate. After a predawn oil bath (in which the hair is massaged with plenty of coconut oil before a shower), we were always served something sweet to eat. A day beginning with a dessert! Then children lit fireworks. Gift giving was again a part of the festivities. In the old days, as with the Onam festival, the farmer tenants leasing our land for cultivation brought us green and ripe plantains, vegetables, and *avil* (pounded rice), and our uncle presented them each with a set of cotton clothes.

Sweets are divided into two categories: sweets prepared with jaggery or brown sugar, and sweets made with refined white sugar. The recipes for savory snacks prepared at these occasions are included in an earlier chapter. As ovens were not used in India until very recently, all of these sweets are prepared on the stove top. They often require constant attention and continuous stirring.

Sweets with Jaggery or Brown Sugar

Manoharam: Fried Rice and *Urad* Dal Strings Sweetened with Brown Sugar

A combination of the same two ingredients that make fluffy *idlis* and crispy *dosas*, when combined with brown sugar and ghee, emerge as a totally different sweet and crunchy snack. *Manoharam* strings are pressed through a metal snack press, similar to a cookie press, directly into hot oil.

½ cup cleaned *urad* dal
2 cups rice flour
4 tablespoons ghee
6 cups vegetable oil (for deep-frying)
2 tablespoons coconut pieces, finely chopped
2 cups jaggery **or** brown sugar

Dry roast the *urad* dal in a skillet over medium heat until it turns light brown in color. Let it cool to room temperature. With a grinder or coffee mill, grind the roasted dal into a fine flour. Combine the rice flour, *urad* flour, and three tablespoons of ghee. Add a few sprinkles of water, and knead it into a soft dough. Continue kneading the dough until it is very soft. A food processor works great for these steps.

Heat the oil in a heavy skillet or a wok to 365°F. Fit the metal snack press with the three-holed disk, and fill it with dough. Press the dough directly into the oil. As the dough falls, move the press around in a circular motion so that it is distributed evenly in the oil. Cook until the dough strings are golden and crispy. Remove them from the oil, and drain. Break the fried strings into pieces approximately half an inch long. Heat the remaining ghee, and fry the coconut pieces until they are browned.

In a heavy skillet, mix the jaggery (or brown sugar) with a couple of tablespoons of water, and cook over medium heat to make a syrup (approximately 245°F to 250°F degrees on a candy thermometer). To test the syrup, drop half a spoonful of the syrup into a cup of cold water. The syrup forms a firm ball when dropped in water. It will not flatten when removed from the water but remains malleable and will flatten when squeezed. Add the fried strings and coconut pieces, along with the ghee, to the syrup, and stir. Cool it, and store it in airtight containers.

Makes 18 to 20 servings.

Vellacheeda: Rice, Dal, and Brown Sugar Balls with Cardamom and Sesame Seeds

Another incarnation of the incredible combination of rice and *urad* dal is sweetened with brown sugar and gently spiced with cardamom and sesame seeds. Large, dark, marble-sized *vellacheeda* is a crunchy, sweet snack.

¼ cup cleaned *urad* dal
2 cups rice flour

2 cups jaggery **or** brown sugar
2 tablespoons ghee
1 teaspoon crushed cardamom
1 tablespoon black sesame seeds
1 tablespoon thinly chopped fresh coconut pieces (optional)
6 cups vegetable oil (for deep-frying)

Dry roast the *urad* dal in a skillet over medium heat until it turns light brown in color. Let it cool to room temperature. With a grinder or coffee mill, grind the roasted dal into a fine flour. In a heavy skillet, dry roast the rice flour separately for three to four minutes while stirring continuously. Do not allow the rice flour to turn pale brown in color. Let it cool, combine it with the *urad* dal flour, and mix thoroughly.

Heat two and a half cups of water in a skillet, add the jaggery (or brown sugar), and bring it to a boil. Reduce the heat, and keep stirring. Pour in the ghee, and add the flour mixture in a thin steam. Stirring continuously, cook over medium heat for five to six minutes, until it reaches a dough-like consistency. Remove it from the stove, and let it cool. Add the cardamom, sesame seeds, and coconut pieces to the dough, and knead well. Shape it into large marble-sized balls, and spread them on a clean kitchen towel to dry. Heat oil in a heavy pan or a wok to 365°F, and deep-fry them until they are brown in color. Drain them, and store them in airtight containers.

Makes 25 to 30.

Cheruparippu Poornam: Mung Dal Fudge

Dal not only thickens our curries and provides the protein component to our vegetarian diet, it also makes excellent puddings and sweets. When combined with cardamom and ghee, it has a totally different taste.

2 cups mung dal
1½ cups jaggery **or** brown sugar
1 tablespoon crushed cardamom
¾ cup ghee

Rinse the mung dal in several changes of water until the water runs clear. Transfer it to a saucepan, and add just enough water to cover. Cook over medium heat while stirring periodically so that it does not stick to the pot. If necessary, add more water, one tablespoon at a time. Allow almost all of the water to evaporate, and mash well. It must have the consistency of mashed potatoes.

In a large, heavy skillet, melt the jaggery (or brown sugar) along with a tablespoon of water. Stir in the cooked dal, sprinkle with crushed cardamom, and pour in the ghee, a couple of tablespoons at a time. Cook over low heat, stirring continuously. After the ghee is absorbed, add more, a few spoons at a time, until all of it is used up. Cook until it becomes thick and starts leaving the sides of the pan as you stir. Cool and serve.

Makes 2½ cups.

Ubbidu: Sweet Wheat-Flour Flatbread

This light, sweet flatbread makes an ideal breakfast or brunch dish. Silky-soft flour dough is stuffed with a sweet coconut and *chana* dal mixture seasoned with cardamom. It is then rolled out into thin rounds and cooked on a hot griddle with a touch of ghee.

1 cup whole-wheat flour
1 cup all-purpose flour
½ teaspoon turmeric powder
½ cup vegetable oil
1 cup *chana* dal
2 cups freshly grated coconut
½ cup and 3 tablespoons ghee
2 cups jaggery **or** brown sugar
2 teaspoons cardamom powder

Combine the whole-wheat and all-purpose flour, a quarter-teaspoon of turmeric powder, and the oil with just enough water to make a very soft dough. Cover it with plastic wrap, and let it rest.

Wash and rinse the *chana* dal in several changes of water until the water runs clear. Transfer it to a saucepan, and add the remaining turmeric powder and just enough water to cover. Cook over medium heat until it is very soft, while stirring periodically. If there is excess water, drain it. Grind the cooked dal and the grated coconut into a fine and very thick puree.

Heat a half-cup of ghee in a heavy skillet, and add the jaggery (or brown sugar), cardamom, and the coconut and *chana* dal puree. Cook over medium heat, stirring continuously, until the contents start leaving the sides of the pan as you stir. Spread it on a large plate, and let it cool.

Make lemon-sized balls with both the dough and the cooked dal and coconut mixture. Roll out the dough into a four-inch circle, and place a dal and coconut ball in the middle. Gather the dough around it, and close. Repeat the process with the remaining dough and filling. Flatten the filled dough balls into circles of about five to six inches in diameter. A tortilla press would work perfectly for this task.

Cook the disks on a heated griddle for a minute or so, then turn them over and cook the other sides. Remove them from the griddle, and brush them with ghee. Serve warm or at room temperature.

Makes 20 to 25.

Avil Nanachathu: Pounded Rice Sweetened with Brown Sugar and Fresh Coconut

During my childhood, there was always plenty of *avil* in the house during two holidays: Puthiri and Deepavali. Needless to say, it appeared in several different combinations at various meals. This sweet and mildly seasoned version makes a perfect snack.

2 cups *avil* (cleaned)
1 cup jaggery **or** brown sugar
2 tablespoons ghee
1 teaspoon cardamom powder
1 cup freshly grated coconut

Rinse the *avil,* and drain it in a colander. In a heavy skillet, mix the jaggery (or brown sugar) with three tablespoons of water, and cook it over medium heat to make a syrup (approximately 245°F to 250°F degrees on a candy thermometer). To test the syrup, drop half a spoonful of the syrup into a cup of cold water. The syrup forms a firm ball when dropped in water. It will not flatten when removed from the water but remains malleable and will flatten when squeezed. Add the *avil* to the syrup along with the ghee and cardamom powder, and cook it over medium heat, stirring continuously, until it is dry. Remove it from the stove, sprinkle it with grated coconut, and stir.

Makes 2½ cups.

Pazza Palahaaram: Banana Pancakes

This is a vegetarian version of banana pancakes, made without eggs. Though they are traditionally served as a snack, they also make great breakfast pancakes when sprinkled with powdered sugar and served with honey or maple syrup.

1½ cups long-grain rice
6 ripe bananas
1 cup jaggery **or** brown sugar
½ cup ghee

Soak the rice for three to four hours. Rinse it in several changes of water until the water runs clear, and drain. Peel the bananas, and cut them into small pieces. Combine the rice, banana, and half a cup of water in a blender, and grind them into a smooth batter. Add the jaggery or brown sugar, and grind again. Add a few more teaspoons of water, if necessary. The batter should have the consistency of pancake batter.

Heat a heavy cast-iron griddle or nonstick griddle over medium heat. Sprinkle a few drops of water on the griddle, and if it sizzles immediately, the griddle is ready. Smear the griddle surface with a quarter-teaspoon of ghee. (Too much ghee will make the *pazza palahaaram* stick to the griddle.) Pour a ladleful of batter onto the center of the griddle. With quick circular motions, spread the batter evenly to form a thick pancake. Pour half a teaspoon of ghee around the edges and a few drops inside the pancake. Cook for a minute or two. When the pancake is cooked, the edges will start leaving the griddle. With a spatula, turn over the pancake, and cook for another minute or two, until the second side is also golden in color. Remove it from the griddle, and repeat with the remaining batter. *Pazza palahaaram* is served at room temperature as a snack. For breakfast, serve them hot, sprinkled with powdered sugar and accompanied by honey or maple syrup.

Makes 14 to 16 pancakes.

Oralappam: Rice, Coconut, and Mung Dal Balls

When I want a sweet snack on sultry summer afternoons, I often yearn for my *ammayi*'s (aunt's) *oralappam*. During the summer, my maternal uncle's wife, Kamalam K. Menon, made this tasty snack, which involved very little stove-top cooking. Cooking on a wood-burning stove on a hot summer day was never a pleasant task. She always made sure that the cook dry-roasted rice and mung dal as soon as he finished preparing lunch. Later in the afternoon, she supervised the pounding of ingredients. She sat next to the large *ural* (stone trough) kept at the back veranda, with a bowl of jaggery cubes in her lap.

Our cook poured handfuls of roasted dal and rice into the cavity of the *ural* and pounded it with an *ulakka* (long wooden pole with a metal bottom). *Ammayi* insisted that this made a world of difference, because hand pounding brought out the subtle flavors, something machine grinding never could do. When the grains turned into a coarse powder, she meticulously tested the texture with her fingers. Sometimes she asked the cook to pound some more, until the texture was just right. She directed him to add the grated coconut to the *ural,* and the pounding continued. She put jaggery cubes into the cavity, one at a time, and he kept pounding. The grains, coconut, and jaggery mingled well under the rhythmic pressure of the *ulakka*. When she felt the consistency was just right, she asked him to stop pounding. She scooped out the contents, put them on a large plate, and brought it inside. Sitting at the kitchen table, she smeared her palm with ghee, picked up a handful of the mixture, and rolled it into small lime-sized balls.

Here is an easy-to-prepare recipe for this sweet snack, which is rich in both protein and carbohydrates. I use my trusty food processor to combine the ingredients. I admit the texture is not as perfect as my aunt would have preferred, but the taste very much reminds me of her delicious *oralappam*.

2 cups parboiled rice
1 cup whole mung dal
3 cups freshly grated coconut
1 cup jaggery **or** brown sugar
1 tablespoon ghee

Separately rinse the rice and mung dal in several changes of water until the water runs clear, and drain. Spread them separately on clean kitchen towels and dry well. In a heavy skillet, dry roast them separately, one after the other, over medium heat. The rice grains will puff up slightly and will take on a reddish hue. Combine the rice and the dal, transfer them to a food processor, and grind them into a coarse, grainy powder. Add the grated coconut and jaggery (or brown sugar) and process them using the pulse (on/off) switch. When the ingredients are thoroughly mixed, remove them from the processor to a platter. Smear a little ghee on the palm of your hand, pick up a handful of mixture, and roll it into a ball that is one to one and a half inch in diameter. Repeat with the remaining mixture. Store in airtight containers.

Makes 18 to 20.

Poruvalanga: Rice and Mung Dal Balls

Poruvalanga is another healthy snack made of rice, mung dal, and brown sugar. It stays fresh for a couple of weeks. In the old days, it was a preferred sweet to take while traveling.

My cousin Kamala Menon used to keep a good supply of this sweet snack during summer holidays. We broke them by holding them against the huge hinges of teak doors. As we slowly closed the door, the hard-as-a-rock balls broke into pieces. The timing had to be precise, so as not to let it fall all over the floor; on days when we missed catching the pieces, rows of tiny black ants carried away the crumbs.

In the old days, this sweet snack was made as hard as a rock. By adjusting the consistency of the syrup, I make them softer.

4 cups parboiled rice
1½ cups whole mung
4 cups jaggery **or** brown sugar

Rinse the rice and mung dal separately in several changes of water until the water runs clear, and drain. Spread them separately on clean kitchen towels and dry well. In a heavy skillet, dry roast them separately, one after the other, over medium heat. The rice grains will puff up slightly and take on a reddish hue. Combine the rice and dal, and them grind into a fine powder.

In a heavy skillet, mix the jaggery (or brown sugar) with three tablespoons of water, and cook over medium heat to make a syrup (approximately 235°F to 240°F degrees on a candy thermometer). To test the syrup, drop half a spoonful of the syrup into a cup of cold water. It will form a soft ball, but it will flatten like a pancake after a few moments in your hand.

Reduce the heat to very low, just to keep the syrup warm. Spread a cup of the rice-and-dal powder in a plate, pour a small ladleful of syrup in the middle, then quickly cover it with the powder, and stir well. Wet the palm of your hand in ice-cold water, pick up a handful of the mixture, and roll it into a ball, one to one and a half inch in diameter. Repeat with the remaining powder and syrup. As the syrup is hot, always wet your hand with ice-cold water before picking up the mixture. These balls will harden as they cool. Store them in airtight containers.

Makes 30 to 35.

Kumbilappam: Jackfruit Jam in Rice Cones Steamed in Banana Leaves

I still remember the fragrance of steaming *kumbilappams* that enveloped the whole house during summer holidays. After my mom had finished making jackfruit jam in the huge bell-metal *uruli*, the logs in the wood-burning stove were still red-hot. Transferring the jam into a large stainless-steel container, Mom would leave some of it behind in the *uruli* for making *kumbilappam*. Balan, our cook, scraped every last bit of jam from the *uruli* and mixed it with rice flour, brown sugar, and spices. He then toasted a few banana leaves and made cones with them. Then he filled the cones with the mix of jam, brown sugar, and rice and tied them tightly with a piece of banana leaf. He placed the heavy brass *idli* steamer over the glowing red logs and filled it a quarter of the way with water. He placed the filled cones on *idli* plates and stacked them. Carefully, he then placed them inside the steamer and covered it with a tight lid. The cones were left steaming until he came back to the kitchen to make evening tea. Those slow-cooked, sweet *kumbilappams* were a treat. They had an incredible flavor: a combination of the smoky fragrance of burning wood and the fragrance of toasted banana leaves.

2 cups rice flour
1 cup jackfruit jam*
½ cup and 2 tablespoons ghee
1 teaspoon baking powder
1 cup jaggery **or** brown sugar
1 teaspoon cardamom powder
Several banana leaf pieces, cut into pieces seven to eight inches long
2 tablespoons ghee
A box of small toothpicks

Our *kumbilappams* are cooked in exactly the same way as tamales. Combine the rice flour, jackfruit jam, half a cup of ghee, baking powder, and jaggery (or brown sugar) with just enough water to make a silky-smooth and very thick batter. Add the cardamom powder, and mix well.

With a pair of tongs, pick up a piece of banana leaf and toast it over a medium flame for ten seconds, holding it high and being careful not to burn it. The leaf will become more pliable. Tear thin strips from one piece of leaf, and set them aside to use for tying. Reserve a couple of leaf pieces to spread at the bottom of the steamer insert. Brush the remaining leaves with a little ghee. Make a cone with each piece of leaf, and pin it with small toothpicks. Fill the cones three-fourths full with the prepared batter. Bring the sides of the banana leaf together at the top, twist them, and tie them with the strips.

Fill the bottom half of a steamer pot with three inches of water, and bring it to a boil. Line the steamer insert with the reserved banana leaf pieces, and arrange the *kumbilappams* with their tied sides up. Place the steamer insert over the boiling water, and cover with a tight lid. If the lid is not very tight, cover the insert with a piece of aluminum foil, and then place the lid on top. It is important that no steam escape while cooking. Reduce the heat, and steam for forty-five minutes to an hour over simmering water. Check and add more water to the pot as needed. The *kumbilappams* are done when they feel firm to the touch but are not hard. Insert a toothpick, and if it comes out clean, it is cooked. The cooked dough slides off easily from the leaves. Let them rest for a few minutes before serving.

Makes 16 to 18.

*See the previous chapter on *paayasams* for the jackfruit jam recipe.

White-Sugar Sweets

Sugiyan: Deep-Fried Sweet Mung Dal Balls

These delicious deep-fried dal dumplings, when served as a brunch dish, make a perfect companion to tangy lemon rice.

1 cup mung dal
1½ cups water
1¼ cups sugar
1 teaspoon crushed cardamom
5 cups vegetable oil
3 tablespoons *urad* flour
10 tablespoons rice flour
½ cup hot ghee

Rinse the mung dal in several changes of water until the water runs clear. Transfer it to a saucepan, and add just enough water to cover. Cook over medium heat while stirring periodically so that it does not stick to the pan. If necessary, add more water, one tablespoon at a time. Allow almost all of the water to evaporate. It must have the consistency of mashed potatoes.

Combine the cooked dal with the sugar, and mash thoroughly. Cook the mixture over medium heat, stirring continuously so that the dal will not stick to the skillet. (Or cook it for ten to twelve minutes at high power in a microwave oven; the cooking time will vary depending on the power of the oven.) Sprinkle it with cardamom, and stir well. At this point, the mixture will be soft. Let it cool to room temperature. When cooled, it will be thick in consistency. Refrigerate in order to cool it quickly. Shape it into small balls.

In a heavy skillet, heat the oil to 340°F. In a bowl, combine the *urad* flour and rice flour with just enough water to make a batter. The batter should have the consistency of pancake batter, so that it will leave a coating on the dal balls. Slightly flatten the balls with your fingers, dip them in batter, and deep-fry until they are golden brown and crunchy. Drain them, and serve hot. Before serving, make small hole in the center of each ball with a spoon, and fill it with hot ghee.

Makes 16 to 18.

Mysorepak: *Besan* Fudge

These scrumptious golden-beige squares are deliciously crisp and crumbly. Constant stirring while the *besan* flour is toasting in sugar and ghee creates tiny air pockets in the fudge. It is impossible to believe, from its flavor and fragrance, that *mysorepak* is a combination of just three basic ingredients—flour, sugar, and butter. This confection is a must at weddings as well as at the Navarathri and Deepavali festivals.

1 pound butter (clarified into ghee)
1 cup *besan* (Indian chickpea flour)
2 cups sugar
¾ cup water

It is ideal to use freshly prepared ghee. Start preparing the ghee after you have assembled the other ingredients for *mysorepak*. This will assure that the ghee is still hot when it is added to the flour and sugar mixture.

Melt the butter in a heavy saucepan over medium heat, and let it simmer. Melting butter will make a crackling sound as it simmers. When all of the moisture has evaporated and the milk solids have separated, the crackling sound stops, and clear, golden ghee bubbles and rises to the top. Remove the saucepan from the stove, and strain the ghee through a fine-meshed sieve. This liquid will be golden in color.

Grease a rectangular baking pan with a tablespoon of ghee, and set it aside. Use very fine *besan* flour to make *mysorepak*. Sift the flour, and put it in a large, fine-meshed sieve or flour sifter. Combine the sugar and water in a heavy skillet, and cook it over medium heat until the sugar has completely dissolved. When the sugar has melted, start adding *besan* flour to the syrup by shaking the sieve slowly over the skillet. Sifting the flour directly into the syrup assures that it is evenly distributed. Keep stirring continuously to prevent lumps from forming. After all of the flour is added, pour in the fresh, hot ghee, 1 tablespoon at a time, stirring continuously. (Use a whisk for stirring. It will make more air pockets in the finished product.) By the time all of the ghee is added (approximately ten minutes), the mixture will be bubbly and fluffy and will start leaving the sides of the pan as you stir it. The color will change from light yellow to a slightly darker beige. Remove it from the stove, pour it into the greased baking pan, and spread it evenly by gently shaking the pan. Do not press down with a spoon; that would destroy the trapped air bubbles. After about two minutes, cut the *mysorepak* into squares or diamond shapes. *Mysorepak* hardens quickly. When it is completely cooled, separate the pieces, and remove them from the pan. Store in an airtight container. It stays fresh for about a week, or it can be frozen for up to four months. Defrost it and bring it to room temperature before serving.

Makes 30 to 35 pieces.

Laddu: Sweetened *Besan* Bead Balls with Cashews and Raisins

My mother created an aura of mystique around her fabulous desserts. Her sweets were not everyday fare but were reserved for special occasions. She made *laddu* at home once a year for the Navarathri festival, and then again for family weddings. My mother's recipe for *laddu* included no flavoring agents. According to her, if you do not skimp on good-quality ghee, there is no need for any other flavoring. Some cooks prefer to add a rather strong flavoring called green camphor; others add cardamom or cloves.

My mother and my cousin's wife, Narayani, (we fondly called her *Edathi*) always started making *laddu* when everyone else had gone for a siesta break after lunch. They had the kitchen all to themselves. *Edathi* was the one who always assisted Mom in making *laddu*. "Narayani, where is the *kannappa?*" (ladle with holes) Mom would ask, and *Edathi* produced it instantly. The two of them fed a few tamarind logs into the belly of the wood-burning stove and placed a large bronze *uruli* on top. While Mother prepared the *besan* batter to a perfect consistency, *Edathi* started on the sugar syrup. "Don't forget to clean the sugar," Mom reminded her, and *Edathi* poured half a cup of milk into the bubbling sugar syrup. Dirt rose up to the top, and she skimmed it off with a long ladle. As the syrup began to thicken, they tested it for consistency, colored it with *laddu* coloring, and kept it warm over the stove. Mom heated ghee in another *uruli*. When it was hot enough, she poured a large cup of golden batter though the multi-holed *kannappa*. Tiny beads formed instantly in the ghee, and minutes later, they rose to the top. *Edathi* scooped them out with a small *kannappa* and transferred them to the sugar syrup. And the process continued. When all of the batter was used up, *Edathi* fried cashew nuts and raisins in ghee in a small skillet and poured them over the *besan* beads in syrup. Mom gently stirred it, being careful not to break the sugar-soaked beads. She called out for the cook to move the heavy *uruli* to the dining room, where it sat under a humming ceiling fan. They rested awhile, as the *boondi* (beads) cooled. Half an hour later, they dipped their palms in warm milk, took handfuls of *besan* beads, and shaped them into perfect *laddu*.

2 cups sugar
¾ cup water
A few drops orange food coloring
2 cups *besan*
6 cups ghee **or** oil (for frying)
6 tablespoons ghee for garnish
12 cashew nuts, broken into small pieces
1 tablespoon seedless raisins

In a heavy skillet, combine the sugar with three-quarters of a cup of water and the food coloring, and cook over medium heat to one-string consistency syrup (215°F to 220°F on a candy thermometer). The liquid sugar may be pulled into brittle threads. To test, take a small amount of the syrup in a spoon, and drop it from about two inches above the pot. If it spins a long thread as it drips, it is done. Set it aside.

> *Laddu* is considered the favorite sweet of Lord Venkateswara at the famous Tirupathi Temple in Andhra Pradesh. The *laddus* at this temple are made very large, the size of a baseball, and they are distributed to devotees as *prasadam* (blessing). Some thirty cooks are employed by this temple to make more than seventy thousand *laddus* every day.

In a large bowl, mix the *besan* with enough water to make a batter of pouring consistency (like pancake batter). Heat the ghee (or oil) in a heavy saucepan or a wok to approximately 335°F to 340°F. Pour about a cup of the batter at a time through a slotted spoon with round holes or, if possible, a *laddu* sieve (a large metal plate with round holes and a handle) into the hot fat. The batter will form small beads. Stir and fry until they are crispy and golden. Remove the beads *(boondi)* with a slotted spoon, transfer them directly into the syrup, and stir. Repeat the process with the remaining batter.

If the syrup becomes too thick, add a few drops of boiling water, and stir. Heat six tablespoons of ghee in a small skillet, and add cashew pieces. When they are lightly browned, add the raisins, and remove it from the stove. Stir the nuts and raisins along with ghee into the skillet of sugared *boondi,* and mix well. After the mix has cooled down, shape it into small balls.

Makes 18 to 20.

Gothambu Halvah: Wheat-Flour Fudge with Cashews and Cardamom

The essence of wheat kernels, when combined with sugar, cashews, ghee, and cardamom, emerges as this silky-soft confection. Extracting the very fine paste of wheat kernels is a tedious process, but when you taste this sweet, you will agree that it is well worth the effort.

4 cups whole-wheat flour (preferably the very fine Indian wheat flour)
14 to 16 cups water
½ cup ghee
2 tablespoons slivered cashews
A few drops orange food coloring
3 cups sugar
2 teaspoons cardamom powder

In a large mixing bowl, combine the wheat flour with plenty of water, and stir well. Cover the top of another large, high-sided bowl with two layers of cheesecloth, and tie it tightly. Pour the water mixed with wheat flour carefully through the cheesecloth. After all the liquid has dripped into the bowl, squeeze the cheesecloth, remove it from the bowl, and discard the larger grains of wheat flour collected in it. Keep the bowl covered, and set it aside for four to six hours. The fine wheat flour will settle at the bottom of the bowl, and the water on top will be clear. Slowly tilt the bowl, and discard this water. At the bottom of the bowl, there will be about three cups of thick and very fine wheat paste.

Heat a couple of teaspoons of ghee, and toast the cashews to a golden-brown color. Pour the ghee and cashews into a thirteen-inch long baking pan, and set it aside. In a heavy, large skillet, combine the wheat paste, food coloring, and sugar, and cook over medium heat while stirring continuously. When the liquid starts bubbling and thickening, start adding ghee, one tablespoon at a time. Sprinkle it with cardamom powder, and cook for eight to ten minutes. The halvah will thicken and start leaving the sides of the pan when it is stirred. Remove it from the stove, and pour it over the ghee and cashew pieces in the baking pan. Let it cool. Cut it into the desired shapes, and serve with the cashew side up.

Makes 20 to 22 pieces.

Badusha: Cream and Flour Disks in Sugar Syrup

These mysteriously creamy rounds are sinfully rich with heavy cream, sugar, and butter. When deep-fried and soaked in sugar syrup, they emerge as flat doughnut holes, but ten times richer and softer.

½ cup heavy cream **or** whole milk
1 cup all-purpose flour
½ teaspoon baking powder
¼ pound (one stick) unsalted butter, at room temperature
4 cups oil (for frying)
1 cup sugar
A few drops orange food coloring

In a heavy saucepan, bring the cream to a boil, and set aside. When it is cool, mix the flour, cream, and baking powder, and knead it into a smooth dough. Add the soft butter to the dough, and knead well. (All of this may be done in a food processor.) Roll the dough into one-inch diameter balls. Flatten the balls into one and a half inch rounds, and make a depression in the middle of each by lightly pressing with a finger.

In a large, heavy skillet, heat the oil over low heat until it is 335°F to 340°F. If the oil is very hot, the *badusha* will turn dark on the outside and will not cook on the inside. Fry the rounds until they are golden brown, and drain. In a heavy skillet, combine the sugar with one-third cup of water and the food coloring, and cook over medium heat to one-string consistency syrup (215°F to 220°F on a candy thermometer). The liquid sugar may be pulled into brittle threads. To test, take a small amount of the syrup in a spoon, and drop it from about two inches above the pot. If it spins a long thread as it drips, it is done. Set it aside.

Soak the fried rounds in the syrup, and gently stir with a flat ladle so that they are fully covered with the syrup. Place a cake cooling rack on top of a cookie sheet covered with sheets of paper towels. Using tongs, remove the *badusha* from the syrup and place them on the cooling rack. The syrup will cover the rounds evenly, and any excess syrup will drip down onto the paper towel. Store them in an airtight container.

Makes 20 to 22.

Naalikera Burfi: Fresh Coconut Fudge

In addition to its traditional role in chutneys, curries, and puddings, coconut is also used in making this flaky, chewy fudge.

4 cups freshly grated coconut
2 cups sugar
1 teaspoon crushed cardamom
1 cup ghee

In a food processor, grind the grated coconut into a very coarse puree along with just a sprinkle of water. In a heavy skillet, combine the sugar with three-quarters of a cup of water, and cook over medium heat to one-string consistency syrup (215°F to 220°F on a candy thermometer). The liquid sugar may be pulled into brittle threads. To test, take a small amount of the syrup in a spoon, and drop it from about two inches above the pot. If it spins a long thread as it drips, it is done.

Stir in the ground coconut and crushed cardamom, and cook over medium heat, stirring constantly. Add the ghee, a tablespoon at a time, and keep stirring. When it starts leaving the sides of the pan as you stir it, remove it from the stove, spread it on a well-greased plate or metal tray, and let it cool. It will harden slightly as it cools. Cut it into square or diamond shapes. When it is cool, remove it from the plate, and store in an airtight container.

Makes 20 to 25 pieces.

Paalgova: Milk Fudge

When milk is cooked down over medium-low heat, the sugar in the milk caramelizes and evolves into a creamy, beige fudge. It has the flavor of caramel toffee and a velvety smooth texture. Though it is somewhat time consuming to prepare, the end result is an exquisitely tasty fudge.

2 quarts full-cream whole milk
2 cups heavy cream
2½ cups sugar

Combine the cream and milk in a heavy saucepan, and bring to a rolling boil over medium heat. Reduce the heat, and continue stirring for fifteen minutes. Continued stirring is required because milk, while it is boiling, has a tendency to rise to the top and spill over the rim very quickly. Stir in the sugar, and cook for another fifteen minutes, stirring continuously. Reduce the heat, and cook until it becomes a thick mass. Stir frequently to prevent the fudge from sticking to the bottom of the pan. The *paalgova* will change in color from pure white to deep beige as it cooks down, and it will have the consistency of thick frosting. Remove it from the stove, and spread it on a greased plate to cool. It can be shaped into small balls after it cools. Another alternative is to scoop it up with a large melon scoop, and place it in mini paper muffin cups. Store it in an airtight container.

Makes 20 to 22 pieces.

Rava Laddu: Sweet Semolina Balls with Cardamom and Raisins

This easy version of *laddu* is made with the breakfast cereal farina. It doesn't taste anything like breakfast porridge. The best part is that, from start to finish, it will probably take less than thirty minutes to make.

2 cups farina or cream of wheat
½ cup and 3 tablespoons ghee
10 cashew nuts, broken into pieces
20 raisins
3 cups sugar
A few drops orange food coloring
1 teaspoon cardamom powder
1 cup milk, boiled and cooled

In a heavy skillet over medium heat, roast the farina in two tablespoons of ghee until it turns light pink in color. Remove it from the stove, and let it cool. In a small skillet, toast the cashew pieces in a tablespoon of ghee to a light brown color, add the raisins, and let them plump up. Remove it from the stove. In a heavy skillet, combine the sugar with one and one-quarter cups of water and the food coloring, and cook over medium heat to a one-string consistency syrup (215°F to 220° F on a candy thermometer). The liquid sugar may be pulled into brittle threads. To test, take a small amount of the syrup in a spoon, and drop it from about two inches above the pot. If it spins a long thread as it drips, it is done.

Add the farina, cardamom, cashews and raisins, and the remaining ghee to the syrup, and stir continuously as it cooks. Remove it from the stove when it thickens and starts leaving the sides of the skillet as you stir. After it has cooled down, wet your palm with milk, and shape the mixture into small balls. Let them cool, and store them in an airtight container.

Makes 18 to 20.

Rava Kesari: Semolina Pudding

Here is an unbelievably easy dessert that can be prepared in less than twenty minutes. It's made with farina or cream of wheat, which is readily available in every U.S. supermarket. A few drops of food coloring give it a festive look.

½ cup ghee
10 cashew nuts, coarsely chopped
20 raisins
2½ cups milk
A few drops orange food coloring (optional)
1 cup farina or cream of wheat
2 cups sugar
1 teaspoon powdered cardamom

Heat two tablespoons of the ghee in a skillet, and fry the cashews until they are golden brown. Add the raisins, and let them plump up. Remove it from the stove, and set it aside. Add food coloring to the milk, and stir well. In a large, heavy skillet, toast the farina in two teaspoons of ghee until it turns pink. Add the milk, and cook over medium heat, stirring continuously, for five to seven minutes. When farina starts to thicken, stir in the sugar and the remaining ghee, and reduce the heat to medium-low. Stir continually to prevent lumps from forming. When it is dry, in about six to eight minutes, sprinkle it with cardamom, and add the cashew nut and raisin mixture. Stir well to combine.

Scoops of warm *rava kesari* may be served in small bowls. Or spread it on a greased plate; after it has cooled down, cut it into squares or other desired shapes.

Makes 20 to 25 pieces.

Semiya Kesari: Kesari may also be prepared with broken pieces of very thin Indian vermicelli, called *semiya*. Proceed with the recipe as described above.

Jilebis: Urad *Dal Pretzels in Rose-Flavored Sugar Syrup*

In sweet shops all over India, small piles of bright-orange *jilebis* are always at the front of the glass display cabinets. While the slightly sour and sweet version is popular in the north, the purely sweet *jilebi* (some call it *jangiri*), flavored with the essence of fragrant pink roses, is the favored version in the south. What is amazing about this sweet is the fact that its basic ingredient is *urad* dal, the same old small, grayish-white beans that make salty *idlis* and crispy *dosas* and add a nutty crunch to dishes when toasted in oil and added as a garnish.

2 cups *urad* dal
¼ cup long-grain rice
2½ cups sugar
A few drops orange food coloring **or** saffron
A few drops rose essence
4 cups ghee **or** oil

Soak the dal and the rice for an hour, rinse them in several changes of water until the water runs clear, and drain. Using a food processor grind them into a very fine, thick batter. In a heavy skillet, combine the sugar with one cup of water and the food coloring, and cook over medium heat to a one-string consistency syrup (215°F to 220°F on a candy thermometer). The liquid sugar may be pulled into brittle threads. To test, take a small amount of the syrup in a spoon, and drop it from about two inches above the pot. If it spins a long thread as it drips, it is done.

Add the rose essence, reduce the heat to very low, and keep the syrup warm. In another heavy skillet, heat the ghee or oil to 325°F over medium heat. Fill a large squeeze bottle (or a pastry bag fitted with a three-sixteenths inch diameter plain tube) with the batter. When the ghee is hot, slowly squeeze the batter into small, two-layer rounds. Each *jilebi* should be about two to two and a half inches wide. With a slotted spoon, turn them, and cook on both sides. Fry them until they are golden and crispy, then remove them from the ghee, and put them directly into the syrup. Turn the *jilebi* with a tong to coat them evenly with the syrup. Remove them from the syrup after two or three minutes, and place them on a platter. Repeat with the remaining batter. Always put hot *jilebi* in warm syrup for good absorption.

Makes 20 to 25.

Neyyil Varattiya Pazzam: Caramelized Plantains

When there were plenty of ripe plantains, my mother always made this simple and sinfully delicious dessert.

2 ripe plantains
¾ cup sugar
⅓ cup ghee

Peel the plantains, and slit each one vertically into two long pieces. Cut each piece into half-inch slices. In a skillet, combine the sugar and plantain pieces, and cook over medium heat, stirring gently so that the pieces are not mashed. When the sugar melts, the plantains will start caramelizing to become a golden-brown color. Add ghee, two tablespoons at a time, and keep stirring gently for six to eight minutes. Remove them from the stove, and let them cool. They taste great warm or cold.

Serving suggestion: To add an exotic touch to this dish, flame them at this point, if you like. Heat a ladle by holding it over a gas flame or by resting it on the edge of a hotplate. Then, away from the heat, pour a little liqueur or brandy into it, return it to the heat to warm the spirit, move away from the stove, and then set fire to it. Carry the flaming ladle to the table over the pan, and pour the flames over the caramelized plantains. After the flames have subsided, serve with a scoop or two of French vanilla or caramel ice cream. Naturally, this serving suggestion is not traditional.

Makes 4 servings.

Porikadala Laddu: *Laddu* with Puffed *Chana* Dal Flour

Here is a simpler version of *laddu,* made with powdered puffed *chana* dal. Your guests will never believe that it takes less than twenty minutes to prepare this delicious dessert.

1½ cups ghee
1 tablespoon slivered almonds
1 tablespoon cashew nut pieces
2 cups puffed *chana* dal, finely powdered
2 cups sugar, powdered in a blender
1 teaspoon cardamom powder

Heat a tablespoon of ghee in a skillet over medium heat, and fry the nuts until they are golden brown. Remove them from the stove, and set aside. Reserve another tablespoon of ghee to grease your palm when shaping the *laddus.* In a heavy skillet, heat the remaining ghee over medium-low heat. While the ghee is heating, combine the puffed *chana* dal powder, sugar, and cardamom, and mix well. Processing the dry ingredients together in a food processor will blend them perfectly; or use a handheld sifter to do this job. In a slow stream, add the powdered mix to the hot ghee, and keep stirring. Remove the pan from the stove, stir in the toasted nuts, and mix well. Smear the palm of your hand with ghee, and shape the mixture into small balls. For a festive look, place the balls in small, colorful paper muffin cups.

Makes 12 to 16.

Chapter Twelve
Glittering Festivals and Revered Offerings

Pageantry and grandeur reach their greatest heights during Kerala's temple festivals and celebrations. Our religious calendar is crowded with innumerable festivals, both big and small, throughout the year. Several special dishes are prepared as offerings at temple festivals. In addition, every major family celebration, whether it is the birth of a baby, a marriage, or an anniversary, is also an occasion for serving or making a gift of food. This chapter is devoted to traditional festival fare and foods that are prepared only on special occasions. Although description of every single festival and celebration is beyond the scope of this book, I have included certain special recipes that are prepared for religious, seasonal, and family festivals. Several of these recipes are prepared only once a year, or for a particular festival or celebration.

Temple Festival Recipes

Temple festivals are times for prayer, for pageantry, and for grand processions. For the inhabitants of the fertile valleys, plains, and rolling hills of southern India, almost every river, forest, and hill has its own spiritual presence that is intertwined with our religious beliefs. In Hindu beliefs, God came to Earth in various incarnations, endowed with human vices as well as virtues. We worship the many such aspects of God through prayers, sacrifices, and offerings.

During festivals, Kerala temples are decorated with fresh flower garlands, and as the sun goes down, rows and rows of tiny oil lamps positioned throughout the outer walls are lit. During festivals, the deities are bedecked with gold ornaments, and when the inner shrine opens for prayers at dusk, the antique crowns and age-old jewelry sparkle in the ineffable glow of bronze oil lamps and burning camphor cubes. Evening prayers are accompanied by the performance of several drummers and pipers.

Throughout the day, both classical and folk music are played, and dancers perform at the temple. The classical dance drama *Kathakali* continues until dawn. Some festivals include grand fireworks that light up the night sky in a rainbow of colors. Others boast processions of large floats as high as fifty feet, accompanied by several bands. At the grandest festivals, there are several elephants, sometimes more than thirty, elaborately decorated with gold-plated headdresses and colorful parasols. The elephant in the middle carries a decorated idol under a golden parasol, and they all sway to the rhythm of the band and lead the procession.

The forests of the Western Ghats mountain range are home to these elephants. They are captured and trained for several months before they are brought to the temple festivals. They are well trained, and they obey the commands of their caretakers. Even small children approach to feed them bunches of bananas and chunks of jaggery (Indian brown sugar).

The processions stops at designated points, and the drummers and pipers render a loud serenade as the festivities come to a climax. At this point, the riders on top of the elephants stand up and slowly wave their peacock feather fans and mohair whisks. At some festivals, just in front of the decorated elephants are several rows of *thalapoli*—young girls in colorful dresses, holding oil lamps and metal platters of flowers. The processional route is always crowded with spectators, and outside the temple walls, vendors sell various goods—toys for the children, glass bangles and flower garlands for the women, and several different snacks for everyone. The sharing of food, particularly the food offered to the deities, is a part of all temple festivals.

The offerings at temples are always the most excellent food. The fragrant aromas emanating from *thidappilli* (temple kitchen) and the excitement of waiting to receive a small serving from the priest are some of the fondest food memories of my childhood. It is hard to concentrate on one's prayers as the priest walks past with a bell-metal *uruli* full of *nivedyam* (food offering). The subtle fragrance of *neypaayasam* (rice pudding sweetened with raw sugar, enriched with ghee, and flavored with toasted coconut flakes) or the enticing aroma of *neyyappams* (panfried sweet rice cakes) would test one's concentration at prayer.

Interestingly enough, the offering of *nivedyam* is always hidden from the eyes of the devotees. As the priest enters the *sreekovil* (sanctum sanctorum) with the *nivedyam*, he closes the thick wooden door behind him. For the next several minutes, all one can hear is soft chanting in Sanskrit as he makes the ceremonial offering of food. Then he pulls open the wooden door, and the many small bells attached to the door chime together, producing a pleasant sound. And as the *mesanthi* (head priest) conclude the rituals with oil lamps, fragrant flowers, and the burning of camphor cubes, his assistant walk past the devotees with an *uruli* full of *nivedyam* with a few leaves of holy basil on top—proof of divine blessings. During festival days, both the quantity and the quality of *nivedyam* improve, and they are prepared with the best ingredients available.

Many Hindu temples are famous for their special *nivedyam*. Following are six recipes for these temple delicacies. The *paayasam* recipes are included in the chapter on puddings.

Neyyappam: Rice and Brown-Sugar Griddle Cakes

This rice-flour griddle cake sweetened with brown sugar is an important offering at many Kerala temples. My sister Rathi often made a meal out of these delicious *appam*. Traditionally, *neyyappam* is made in an *appakkara*, a bronze pan, about eight inches in diameter, with three or five large cavities. The pan is heated, and a spoonful of ghee is poured into each cavity. The batter is poured on top of hot ghee and cooked over medium heat. When the bottom is cooked, the *appam* is turned over, and the other side is cooked.

Alternatives for the pan are the Swedish *aebleskiver* pan or the Scandinavian blini pan. In the absence of these special skillets, *neyyappams* may be cooked on a griddle or a small skillet.

1 cup long-grain rice
1 medium-sized ripe banana, peeled and sliced
1 cup jaggery **or** brown sugar
1 teaspoon cardamom powder
1 tablespoon thinly sliced coconut pieces (optional)
1 cup ghee
(Temple recipe does not include ripe bananas.)

Soak the rice in water for a couple of hours, then rinse it in several changes of water until the water runs clear, and drain. In a blender, combine the rice, banana, and jaggery (or brown sugar) with just enough water to grind it into a fine, smooth, thick batter. Stir in the cardamom powder and coconut slices. This batter should have the consistency of a thick pancake batter.

Heat a heavy griddle, preferably cast iron, over medium heat. Smear the surface with a little ghee, and pour in a quarter-cup of batter. As the batter is thick, it will not spread into a large circle; it will be like a small pancake. Pour a half-teaspoon of ghee on top of each *neyyappam*. When the bottom is cooked (in a minute or so), turn it over, and cook the other side. When done, *neyyappams* are golden brown in color. Remove them from the griddle, and drain.

Makes 12 to 15.

Serving Suggestion: *Appams* may be served either warm or at room temperature. If you are serving them as a dessert, stack three small pancakes on a dessert plate, and top them with a scoop of vanilla or praline ice cream. Sprinkle with powdered sugar.

Thirattipaal or *Naalikera Poornam:* Dark Coconut Fudge

Thirattipaal is another traditional temple offering during the Navarathri festival. This buttery, flaky sweet literally melts in your mouth.

2½ cups freshly grated coconut
⅛ cup heavy cream **or** whole milk
1 cup jaggery brown sugar
1 teaspoon crushed cardamom
⅛ cup ghee

In a food processor, grind the grated coconut and cream (or milk) together to make a thick, coarse puree. Fresh coconut is very moist and does not require a lot of liquid to puree. In a large, heavy skillet, melt the jaggery (or brown sugar) along with one tablespoon of water. When the syrup starts bubbling, stir in the coconut puree, and keep stirring. Sprinkle it with cardamom, and pour in ghee, a couple of teaspoons at a time. Cook over low heat, stirring continuously. When the ghee is absorbed, add more ghee, and continue until all of it is used up. Cook for twelve to fifteen minutes, until the mixture thickens and starts leaving the sides of the pan as you stir. Remove it from the stove, and transfer it to a serving bowl. When it has cooled down to room temperature, take two tablespoons of *thirattipaal,* and shape it into a small ball. Then slightly flatten the ball, and place it in a storage container. Repeat with the remaining *thirattipaal.*

Makes 20 to 22.

Serving suggestion: A golden scoop of *thirattipaal* tastes great by itself. To make it look a bit more attractive, place each serving in a small paper baking cup. It may also be served warm with two scoops of vanilla or praline ice cream for dessert.

Kadala: Spicy Brown Chickpeas

This simple bean dish is a traditional offering at temples during the nine-day Navarathri festival. It is a healthy snack, and it also makes a good side dish for a brunch. Whole garbanzo beans may be substituted for brown Indian chickpeas.

2 cup Indian chickpeas **or** garbanzo beans
½ teaspoon turmeric powder
Salt to taste
1 tablespoon vegetable oil
1 teaspoon mustard seeds
2 dried red cayenne, serrano, or Thai chilies, halved, **or** ½ teaspoon crushed red pepper
¼ teaspoon asafetida powder (optional)
12 to 15 fresh curry leaves
2 fresh green chilies (serrano or Thai), thinly chopped (less for a milder taste)

Wash the chickpeas, and soak them overnight. Rinse them in several changes of water until the water runs clear. Place them in a saucepan, and add water to cover. Sprinkle them with turmeric, and cook over medium heat until they are very soft (or cook in a pressure cooker for six minutes or so, following the manufacturer's directions). Drain well, sprinkle with salt, and set aside. Heat the oil in a large skillet, and add the mustard seeds. When the mustard seeds start sputtering, add the halved red peppers, asafetida powder, curry leaves, and green chilies, and panfry. Add the drained chickpeas to the pan, and mix well. Panfry while stirring continuously for a minute or two. Remove them from the stove. Serve warm or cold.

Makes 6 to 8 servings.

Variations

This dish may be prepared with canned garbanzo beans. Wash the beans under running water, and drain well. Sprinkle them with salt and turmeric, and proceed with the recipe above.

Coconut-Mango *Sundal*: Another variation is to add grated coconut and raw mango slices to the beans. To prepare this recipe, fry the spices, and add two teaspoons of fresh lemon juice along with the drained chickpeas. Panfry for a minute or two while stirring continuously. Remove from them the stove. Add one medium-sized raw green mango (cut into small cubes) and half a cup of freshly grated coconut, and stir gently to mix. Garnish with chopped cilantro leaves. Serve warm or cold.

Modakam (Madhura Kozhukkatta): Steamed Sweet Coconut Balls

Steamed rice balls stuffed with a sweet coconut filling are believed to be a favorite of Lord Ganapathi, the destroyer of all obstacles. There is a myth about this sweet in my hometown—when someone has a splitting migraine headache, he or she prays and offers a large *modakam* (almost the size of a large grapefruit) at the Ganapathi temple. The belief is that the headache will be cured in no time.

1 cup jaggery or brown sugar
2 cups freshly grated coconut
3 tablespoons ghee plus 1 tablespoon for greasing your hand
¼ cup vegetable oil
2 cups rice flour

Melt the jaggery or brown sugar along with a tablespoon of water in a heavy skillet over medium heat. When the syrup starts bubbling, stir in the grated coconut and the ghee. Cook over medium heat, stirring continuously. It will thicken and start leaving the sides of the pan as you stir. Remove it from the stove, and let it cool.

Heat two cups of water in a small saucepan. When it starts bubbling, add the oil and the rice flour in a slow stream, stirring continuously. This will prevent lumps from forming. When all of the water has evaporated and the dough has thickened, remove it from the stove, and let it cool. Place the cool dough in a food processor, and knead it well.

Grease the palm of your hand with a touch of ghee. Put a tablespoon of dough in your palm, and flatten it into a three-inch disk. Place a large tablespoon of the coconut filling in the middle of the disk, and form the *modakam* into a smooth, round ball with the filling inside. Repeat with the remaining dough and filling.

Heat four cups of water in a steamer over medium heat. The water level should be below the insert and should not touch it. Place the *modakams* in a single layer on the insert, cover, and steam for twenty-five to thirty minutes. Serve warm.

Makes 20 to 25.

Paanakam: Sweet and Spicy Drink

Paanakam is believed to be the favorite drink of Lord Subrahmanya, and it is prepared as a food offering at festivals dedicated to him. Although considered a celestial favorite, it is also a refreshing, cool drink on a hot summer day anywhere in the world. The traditional recipe includes flavorings such as sandalwood and a fragrant root called *raamacham*. It tastes quite delicious even when these ingredients are substituted with crushed cardamom.

1 cup jaggery **or** brown sugar
1 pitcher cold water
½ teaspoon ground cardamom seeds
½ teaspoon ginger powder

Stir the jaggery (or brown sugar) into a pitcher of water until it has completely dissolved. Sprinkle with cardamom powder and ginger powder, and stir well. Serve over ice cubes for a cool, refreshing drink on hot summer afternoons.

Makes one pitcher.

Vellapayaru: Red Beans Sweetened With Brown Sugar

Here is a typical temple sweet that is very easy to prepare. It is a traditional *nivedyam* during the Navarathri festival—a distant cousin to baked beans with molasses!

2 cups small red beans
1 cup jaggery **or** brown sugar
4 tablespoons ghee

Soak the red beans in water for eight hours (or overnight). Rinse them in several changes of water until the water runs clear, and drain. Transfer them to a saucepan, add four cups of water, and bring it to a boil. Reduce the heat to medium, and cook until the beans are very soft to the touch and can be easily mashed between two fingers (about forty to fifty minutes). If necessary, add more water, and cook until the beans are soft. If any water is remaining after the beans are well cooked, drain it. (Alternatively, the beans may be cooked in a pressure cooker, following the manufacturer's directions. They will cook in about six to eight minutes.)

In a heavy skillet, melt the jaggery (or brown sugar) along with a couple of teaspoons of water. When the sugar melts and the liquid starts bubbling, stir in the drained beans and the ghee. Cook over low heat, stirring occasionally, until the beans have absorbed the syrup and are completely dry. Remove it form the stove, and let it rest a few minutes before serving.

Makes 2½ cups.

Paripputenga: Sweetened *Chana* Dal

This simple sweet is a must during the Navarathri festival in my hometown. The main ingredient is puffed *chana* dal, called *porikadala* or *pottukadala*, which is available in Indian grocery stores. This sweet is also a must at weddings in Tamil Nadu. Being on the border of Kerala and Tamil Nadu, the food of my hometown shows the influences of both.

¾ cup jaggery **or** brown sugar
2 cups puffed *chana* dal *(porikadala)*
2 tablespoons fresh coconut pieces, thinly sliced
1½ tablespoons ghee

Melt the jaggery or brown sugar along with two tablespoons of water in a heavy skillet over medium heat. Cook until the thick syrup reaches approximately 245°F to 250°F degrees on a candy thermometer. To test the syrup, drop half a spoonful of syrup into a cup of cold water. The syrup forms a firm ball when dropped into chilled water. It will not flatten when removed from water, but it remains malleable and will flatten when squeezed. Remove it from the stove, and stir in the *porikadala*, the coconut pieces, and the ghee. Wet your hands with cold water, pick up a handful of the mixture, and roll into a small ball. Repeat with the remaining mixture. These balls will harden as they cool. Store them in airtight containers.

Makes 20 to 22.

Seasonal Festival Recipes

Every season ushers in a new festival filled with fun and excitement, each a true celebration of the bounties of nature. The gods of the seasons—wind, rain, and sunshine—are still the main providers in India, where agriculture remains the foundation of the nation's economy. Those who sow seeds on the cold earth are making an act of faith, without the certainty of success. The need to persuade nature to be favorable became a matter of life or death. For the propitiation of the powerful elements of nature, we developed a pantheon of deities endowed with formidable capabilities. We appeal to the forces of nature in the form of offerings, prayers, and festivals.

Harvests mark the safe gathering of the food that would carry a sedentary household safely through the monsoon months. The sacred nature of the harvest is unspoken; favorable harvests are always considered to have a spiritual connection, and they are believed to be the result of divine intervention. At harvest festivals, the fruits of the harvest itself take pride of place at the feast. These festivals follow a traditional pattern, although details vary from region to region and household to household. New clothes, dance, music, and ritual all contribute to their joyful rhythm.

Seasonal festivals have a different beat, with most festivities taking place around the house. Each of the seasonal festivals has its very own special dishes. Thiruvonam, celebrated in late August or early September (depending on the lunar calendar), is the most important seasonal festival. Food offerings are presented to God before the family partakes of festive meals. At Thiruvonam, the special offering is a simple steamed rice cake filled with sweetened coconut flakes. Puthiri, the harvest festival, celebrates the cooking and eating of the newly harvested rice.

As we celebrate the bounty of tropical summer with a sumptuous feast, we also prepare a special rice soup: Vishu *kanji*. At both Thiruvonam and Vishu, feasts are prepared with mostly seasonal ingredients. Recipes for these are included in previous chapters. During the Thiruvathira festival we prepare some special dishes with arrowroot flour and root vegetables. At the height of monsoon season, there are more rituals and special dishes; medicinal porridges and healthy dishes prepared with leaf vegetables and bran are the specialties of this season.

Puthiri Avil: Pounded Rice with Milk, Sugar, Ghee, and Raisins

This dish captures the exuberance of Kerala's countryside at harvest time. During years past, rich, sweet *puthiri* was prepared only once a year, to celebrate the spring harvest. Fresh kernels of flattened rice moistened with warm milk and golden ghee, sweetened with sugar and honey and garnished with crushed cardamom and raisins, was a delicious treat, and it still is.

In our home, the ritual of Puthiri always started with a prayer. My mother lighted incense sticks and placed a platter of new *avil* (pounded rice), bananas, and flowers in front of a bronze oil lamp. Then she lighted some camphor cubes and made a ceremonial offering. After that, she prepared *puthiri* in a large silver bowl. She poured the warm milk into the bowl and stirred in sugar and honey. Then she combined the pounded rice and milk. Raisins and crushed cardamom went in next. Then, for a final touch, she drizzled a tablespoon of golden ghee (clarified butter) on top. *Puthiri avil* is very tasty dish that makes a good breakfast—or try it as a sweet snack.

2 cups *avil* (pounded rice) (available at Indian groceries)
2½ cups whole milk
¾ cup sugar
½ cup honey
1 teaspoon crushed cardamom
1 tablespoon raisins
2 tablespoons ghee

Wash and rinse the pounded rice, and spread it on paper towels to dry. Bring the milk to a rolling boil in a saucepan over medium heat. Remove it from the heat, and keep it covered. In a large bowl, combine the warm milk and sugar, and stir until all of the sugar is dissolved. Pour honey into the milk. Add the pounded rice, and mix well. Sprinkle in the cardamom and raisins, and stir gently. Drizzle ghee on top. Serve warm.

Makes 4 to 4½ cups.

Ela Ada: Rice Flour and Coconut Cakes Steamed in Plantain Leaves

During the festival of Thiruvonam, children dressed in festive clothes would collect flowers to decorate the courtyard with a *pookkalam*—a large flower design. In the middle of the flower design, we would place pyramidal images of Onathappan and decorate them with fresh flowers. Mothers offer ripe plantains and steamed flat cakes made with sweet coconut and rice to the lord. Sweetened coconut flakes are encased in a layer of rice batter spread on toasted banana leaves and then steam-cooked to make these delicate flat cakes. As it cooks, *ela ada* absorbs the aroma of the toasted banana leaves.

1 cup long-grain rice
1 cup jaggery **or** brown sugar
2½ cups freshly grated coconut
2 tablespoons ghee
10 to 15 banana leaf pieces cut into 6- to 7-inch squares

Soak the rice for two to three hours, then rinse it in several changes of water until the water runs clear. Grind the rice in a blender with just enough water to make a thick batter (of pancake-batter consistency). In a heavy, large skillet, melt the jaggery (or brown sugar) along with a tablespoon of water. Stir in the grated coconut, and cook for ten to fifteen minutes over medium heat, stirring constantly. When the mixture begins to thicken, add the ghee, and stir well. Remove it from the stove, and let it cool to room temperature.

With a pair of tongs, pick up one piece of banana leaf at a time, and toast it over a medium flame, holding it high, for ten seconds. The leaf will turn dark and become more pliable. Spread a small ladleful of rice batter evenly on the toasted leaf. Place a tablespoon of sweetened coconut over this, and spread evenly. Fold the banana leaf in the middle, and press in the sides to close it well. Repeat this process with the remaining leaves and filling.

Bring water to boil in a steamer pot. Line the steamer insert with banana leaves, and place the stuffed banana leaves flat inside. Reduce the heat to medium, and steam-cook for fifteen to twenty minutes. Remove them from the steamer, peel off the banana leaf wrappers, and serve.

Makes 12 to 15 pieces.

Thiruvathira Koottu: Mixed Root Vegetables and Plantain with Fresh Coconut

This simple mixed vegetable dish is prepared especially for the Thiruvathira celebration. The traditional recipe requires certain root vegetables called *koorka, cherukizangu,* and *kaachil* (different varieties of tropical yams). Vegetables typically used for this dish are not generally available in colder climates. Since I believe that the authenticity and quality of the recipe would have to be sacrificed with changes, I have left this recipe in its original form. Potatoes, yam, taro, and cassava may be used as substitutes. Other vegetables used are ash gourd and green plantain.

1 cup each of cubed *koorka, cherukizangu,* and *kaachil*
1 medium-sized plantain, peeled and cut into cubes
A small piece of ash gourd, cut into cubes
Salt to taste
½ teaspoon turmeric powder
½ teaspoon dried red cayenne, serrano, or Thai chili powder
1½ cups freshly grated coconut
2 tablespoons coconut oil
12 to 15 fresh curry leaves

Combine all cut vegetables in a saucepan, and add enough water to cover. Add salt, turmeric, and red pepper powder, and cook over medium heat until the vegetables become soft to the touch. Sprinkle grated coconut over the cooked vegetables, and stir gently. Garnish with coconut oil and fresh curry leaves.

Makes 6 to 8 servings.

Thiruvathira Puzukku: Mixed Vegetables with Red Beans and Coconut

This warm salad is prepared with various root vegetables and red beans at the Thiruvathira festival. It is garnished with coconut oil and curry leaves.

1 cup each cubed root vegetables such as potatoes, yam, taro, and cassava
   (*koorka, kaachil,* and telinga potatoes are used in the traditional dish)
1 medium-sized green plantain, peeled and cut into cubes
Salt to taste
¼ teaspoon turmeric powder
¼ teaspoon dried red cayenne, serrano, or Thai chili powder
½ cup red beans
1½ cups freshly grated coconut
¼ teaspoon cumin seeds
3 fresh green chilies (serrano or Thai) (less for a milder taste)
2 tablespoons coconut oil
12 to 15 fresh curry leaves

In a saucepan, bring four cups of water to a boil. Transfer the cut vegetables to the saucepan, add salt, turmeric, and red chili powder, and cook over medium heat until the vegetables are fork tender.

Soak the red beans in water for six to eight hours. Rinse them in several changes of water until the water runs clear, and drain. Transfer them to a saucepan, add two cups of water, and bring to a boil. Reduce the heat to medium, and cook until the beans are very soft to the touch and can be easily mashed between two fingers (about forty to fifty minutes). If necessary, add more water, and cook until the beans are soft. (Alternatively, the beans may be cooked in a pressure cooker, following the manufacturer's directions. They will take about six to eight minutes to cook). Season with salt and add the cooked red beans to the vegetables.

In a blender, grind the coconut, cumin, and green chilies into a coarse, thick puree. Combine the puree with the vegetables, and stir gently. Bring to a boil, reduce the heat, and simmer for five minutes over medium-low heat. Remove from the stove, add the coconut oil and curry leaves, and stir gently.

This dish is traditionally served with cooked cracked wheat or *nivara* rice or other cooked grains such as *chama* (Indian wild rice).

Makes 6 to 8 servings.

Madhura Koova Varattiyathu: Arrowroot Pudding with Milk, Sugar, and Cardamom

Arrowroot flour is pure starch, and when boiled in water or milk, it yields a transparent and pleasant-tasting jelly. Three different dishes are prepared with this flour during the Thiruvathira festival.

1 cup arrowroot powder
3 cups whole milk
½ cup sugar
1 teaspoon crushed cardamom seeds

Mix the arrowroot powder and one cup of milk in a heavy saucepan, and stir. Add the remaining milk and sugar, and stir well. Cook this liquid over medium heat, stirring continually. Sprinkle on the cardamom powder, and keep stirring. It will thicken and start leaving the sides of the pot as it is stirred. When it has thickened, remove it from the stove, and spread it evenly in a well-greased pan. Let it cool down to room temperature. Cut it into one-inch squares, and serve.

Makes 20 to 22 pieces.

Variations

The same flour that yields this mildly sweet gelatin-like dessert, when combined with buttermilk and spices, evolves into a salty, spicy dish.

1 cup arrowroot powder
3 cups buttermilk
Salt to taste
1 tablespoon vegetable oil
1 teaspoon mustard seeds
1 tablespoon *urad* dal
½ tablespoon *chana* dal
1 dried red cayenne, serrano, or Thai chili, halved
12 to 15 fresh curry leaves
1 teaspoon grated fresh ginger

Mix the arrowroot flour and one cup of buttermilk in a heavy saucepan. Add the remaining buttermilk and salt, and stir well.
    Heat the oil in a skillet, and add the mustard seeds. When the mustard seeds start sputtering, add the dal and the halved chili pepper. A minute later, add the curry leaves, and ginger, and panfry for a minute, Remove it from the stove. Pour it over the buttermilk mixture, and cook over medium heat, stirring continually. It will thicken and start leaving the sides of the pot as you stir. Remove it from the stove, and spread it evenly in a well-greased pan. Let it cool, cut it into one-inch squares, and serve.

Makes 20 to 22 pieces.

Koova Paayasam: The same flour is cooked here as a pudding. *Koova paayasam* is a must for Thiruvathira at the home of the royal family.

1 cup jaggery **or** brown sugar
1 cup arrowroot powder
2 tablespoons ghee
4 cups fresh coconut milk
1 teaspoon crushed cardamom

In a heavy saucepan, combine the jaggery (or brown sugar) with just enough water to cover. Cook over medium-low heat. Combine the arrowroot flour with just enough water to make a thick batter. When the jaggery melts and start bubbling, stir the arrowroot liquid into the syrup, and keep stirring. Stir in the ghee. Cook for about eight to ten minutes, stirring continuously. When the sweetened arrowroot starts leaving the sides of the skillet as you stir, pour in the coconut milk, and stir well. Reduce the heat to low, and cook until the liquid starts simmering. Simmer for five minutes. Remove it from the stove, and sprinkle it with cardamom powder. The paayasam will have a porridge-like consistency.

Makes 6 to 8 servings.

Ettangadi: Roasted Vegetables and Red Beans with Coconut, Sesame, and Brown Sugar

Ettangadi is a root vegetable and bean dish that is traditionally served at the Thiruvathira festival. It is prepared only once a year, just for this festival. It uses five kinds of tropical yams, red beans, and plantains. Vegetables typically used for this dish are not generally available in colder climates. Since I believe that the authenticity and quality of the recipe would have to be sacrificed with changes, I have left the recipe in its original form. Potatoes, yams, taro, and cassava may be used as substitutes.

1 cup *koorka*
1 small *cherukizangu*
1 sweet potato
3 or 4 taro roots
1 small *kaachil*
1 medium-sized green plantain
1 cup red beans
½ cup fresh grated coconut
4 tablespoons dry-roasted sesame seeds
1 ripe plantain
3 cups brown sugar

Roast all of the root vegetables and the green plantain in an oven. Traditionally, they are roasted over fire. When they have cooled, peel off the skin, and cut them into cubes. Combine the cubed vegetables and plantains in a saucepan.

Wash the red beans in several changes of water until the water runs clear, and drain. Dry roast the red beans in a heavy skillet. Bring three cups of water to a boil in a saucepan, and stir in the dry-roasted beans. Reduce the heat to medium, and cook until the beans are very soft to the touch and can be easily mashed between two fingers. (Alternatively, the beans may be cooked in a pressure cooker, following the manufacturer's directions. They will take about six to eight minutes to cook.) Add the cooked red beans, grated coconut, 8 tablespoons of water, and toasted sesame seeds to the vegetables, and cook over medium heat for another five minutes. Cut the ripe plantain into thin slices, add them to the pan, and set it aside. In a heavy, large skillet, heat the brown sugar with a few spoons of water, and make a thick syrup. Combine the cooked vegetable and fruit mixture with the syrup.

Makes 6 to 8 servings.

Vishu *Kanji:* Rice Soup with Coconut Milk

A special rice soup made with a combination of both parboiled and long-grain rice in coconut milk is prepared and served only once a year, during the summer festival of Vishu. The addition of *puliavarakka,* a legume similar to lima beans, adds a bite to this soup.

½ cup parboiled rice
½ cup long-grain rice
1 cup *puliavarakka** or fresh or frozen lima beans
3 cups coconut milk
Salt to taste

Separately wash both types of rice in several changes of water until the water runs clear. Since parboiled rice takes longer to cook, it is preferable to cook the two varieties in separate pans and then combine them. In two separate saucepans, bring three cups water to a boil, and add the cleaned rice. Lower the heat to medium, and cook until the rice is very soft. After both varieties of rice have cooked, combine them in one pot, and set it aside. In a saucepan, cook the toasted *puliavarakka* with coconut milk. When it is cooked, transfer it to the rice pot, add salt, and stir well. Just before serving, stir the *kanji* gently. If it is too thick for your taste, add a little boiling water, and stir. Serve hot with *pappadam* and *chakka puzukku.*

Makes 6 to 8 servings.

*Puliavarakka is a flat bean, slightly smaller than a lima bean. These beans have a slightly tart taste. Substitute with lima beans.

Thalu Kootan: Taro Stems with Fresh Coconut in Spicy Sauce

This simple curry of taro stems in a coconut and tamarind sauce is a once-a-year dish that is prepared on the first Tuesday and Friday of the month during the monsoon season.

2 cups taro plant stems, peeled and cubed
Salt to taste
½ teaspoon turmeric powder
1 tablespoon tamarind concentrate
2 tablespoons jaggery or brown sugar
1 cup freshly grated coconut
4 fresh green serrano or Thai chilies (less for a milder taste)
2 tablespoons coconut oil
1 teaspoon mustard seeds
1 teaspoon *urad* dal
12 to 15 fresh curry leaves
2 *pappadams,* cut into thin strips

In a saucepan, bring four cups of water to a boil, and add the taro stem along with salt and turmeric. Cook over medium heat until it is fork tender. Add the tamarind concentrate and jaggery (brown sugar), and simmer for five minutes.

In a blender, grind the fresh coconut and green chilies into a fine puree. Stir this puree into the taro mixture, and simmer until it bubbles and rises to the top. Remove it from the stove.

Heat the oil in a skillet, and add the mustard seeds. When the mustard seeds start sputtering, add the *urad* dal, curry leaves, and *pappadam* pieces to it. The *pappadam* pieces will puff up. Remove the spice mixture from the stove, and use it to garnish the curry.

Makes 6 to 8 servings.

Chuttathu: Bran Cakes with Coconut and Brown Sugar

These bran-flour cakes are cooked in folded banana leaves over a hot griddle. This once-a-year dish is prepared on the first Tuesday and Friday of the month during the monsoon season.

2 cups rice bran*
1 cup freshly grated coconut
¼ teaspoon salt
1 cup jaggery or brown sugar
Banana leaves, cut into large squares
⅓ cup vegetable oil

Combine the bran, coconut, salt, and jaggery (or brown sugar), and mix well. Smear a piece of banana leaf with oil, and place two tablespoons of the mixture in the middle. Spread it with your fingers into a thin layer, and fold the banana leaf in the middle. Repeat the process until all of the dough is used.

Heat a griddle, and spread on it half a tablespoon of oil. Place the folded banana leaf pieces on the griddle, and cook on both sides. The leaves will change color as they cook. Remove them after about five minutes, and let them cool. Peel off the banana leaves, and serve hot.

Makes 20 griddle cakes.

*If bran is not available, substitute with either wheat flour or rice flour.

Celebrations of Life Recipes

The richness of cultural histories and symbolic rituals is threaded through our celebrations of life, whether it is the birth of a baby, a marriage, or the observance of an anniversary. As both the royalty and the Nayars followed the matrilineal system, the very close bond between sister and brother—or, for that matter, between an uncle and his nieces and nephews—is often reaffirmed in some ancient ceremonies.

Celebrations of life also have their own special dishes. Sumptuous vegetarian feasts are a must at all celebrations. In addition to these feasts, we prepare sweet *kozhukkatta* (steamed sweet rice balls) to celebrate the crawling baby; *paal kanji* (sweet rice gruel cooked in milk) and *thirattipittu* (steamed sweet rice) to celebrate the coming of age of young girls; and *ingithayir* (a simple chutney of ginger, green chilies, and yogurt), *chatha pulisseri* (simple squash curry in buttermilk sauce), and *ellunda* (a sesame seed and brown-sugar sweet) as we honor the ancestors on their death anniversaries.

Ammini Kozhukkatta: Steamed Sweet Rice Balls

It is not just the major events in one's life that get celebrated; we celebrate even the small events. In my extended family, we celebrate when a baby starts crawling on its knees! Most of our old homes have huge teak doors to all rooms. The bottom part of the entry to each room is covered with a smooth and slightly elevated wooden piece called an *ummarappadi*. When a baby starts crawling and climbs over this wooden piece to enter the next room, it is an occasion for celebration! We celebrate this event by showering the baby with tiny, sweet rice dumplings. As the poor, confused child starts crying, the adults laugh and pick the child up from the floor, all the while enjoying the little dumplings.

1 cup long-grain rice
½ cup jaggery **or** brown sugar
2 tablespoons thinly sliced fresh coconut
⅓ cup ghee
1 teaspoon crushed cardamom

Soak the rice for two to three hours. Wash it in several changes of water until water runs clear, and drain. In a blender, grind the rice along with the jaggery (or brown sugar) and just enough water to form a batter of pancake-batter consistency. Toast the coconut in a teaspoon of the ghee, and set it aside.

Combine the rice batter and the remaining ghee in a saucepan, and cook the mixture over medium heat, stirring constantly. As the batter begins to thicken (in about six to eight minutes), sprinkle it with crushed cardamom and toasted coconut, and keep stirring. When the batter has cooked down to a dough-like consistency (in about four to five minutes), remove it from the stove, and set it aside to cool for a few minutes.

Shape the cooled dough into large marble-sized balls. Heat water in a heavy pot fitted with a steamer insert. Line the steamer insert with fresh banana leaves or a piece of cheesecloth, and spread the dough balls in a single layer. Cover tightly, and steam for twenty to thirty minutes over medium heat.

Makes 20 to 25 pieces.

Thirandu Kalyaanam: Coming-of-Age Ceremony

As girls attain puberty around the age of twelve or thirteen, they are given a coming-of-age ceremony called *Thirandu Kalyaanam*. The festivities lasted for four days. In ancient times, it was a form of ceremonial announcement to the society that one of the young girls of the family had reached marriageable age. Guests were invited to the house for feasts every day. Having personally gone through this ceremony, I can assure you that it was indeed an embarrassing ordeal for a teenager. Little did I know then that the passage into womanhood was also celebrated in other societies, thousands of miles away.

Getting my first period itself was confusing, and when my family wanted to celebrate it, I was mortified. But my mother wanted a big celebration for her firstborn. No one bothered to pay any attention to my tears and silent protests. Naturally, I succumbed to their wishes—who was I to question or disrespect the decisions of my elders?

The house was filled with relatives, and the head cook of our *tharavad* (matrilineal joint family) was called in to pour a few spoons of oil on my head. It was one of those unwritten rules of matrilineal traditions; he had the right to pour oil on my head and receive a present of money from my maternal uncle. One obsession of our community is bathing. We bathe in the morning and again in the evening, and several times during any and all ceremonies. Needless to say, I had to go for a dip in the pond around nine at night, and I was given a *vaalkannadi* (bronze mirror, considered an auspicious symbol) that I was to hold in my hands for the entire four days.

A room in the western wing of our home was cleaned, and the floor was decorated with rice-flour designs. A thick woolen blanket was spread inside the design and covered with a fine cotton *mundu* (two-piece Kerala sari). This was to be my seat—and my bed as well—for the next three days.

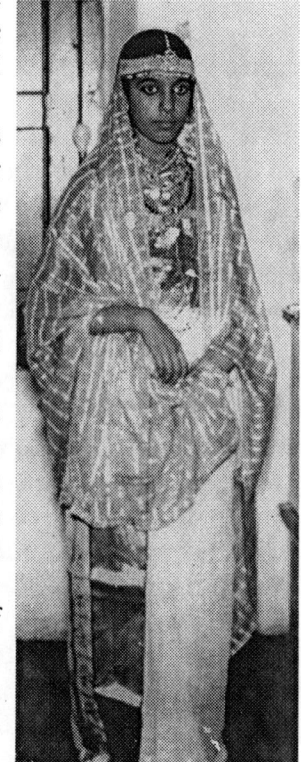

The big events were on the third and fourth days. The whole extended-family clan was invited. The menu for the feast on the third day was unique; it is served only at this celebration. Guests sat down in front of boat-shaped bowls *(thadas)* made with layers of plantain stems held together with the stems of coconut palm leaves. Next to each bowl was placed a small piece of banana leaf and a jackfruit-leaf spoon: a folded single jackfruit leaf pinned with the stems of coconut palm leaves. We had disposable bowls, spoons, and plates—all made from nature's bounty. A few fresh coconut slices, pieces of jaggery (Indian brown sugar), and a couple of crispy fried *pappadams* were served on the banana leaves. The bowls were filled with piping-hot *paalkanji*—rice cooked in milk and sweetened with sugar.

The ceremonies did not end with this unusual lunch. In the afternoon, women and girls gathered in our living room for another celebration. I sat on a mat spread on the floor. There was a large bronze lamp at the center of the room, and a banana leaf was spread in front. My *ammayi* (maternal uncle's wife) made a ceremonial presentation of *thirattipittu*, a simple steamed rice-flour dish sweetened with brown sugar. This is another dish, just like *paalkanji*, that is prepared only on the third day of this celebration. Platters of other sweets were placed around it. Girls and women formed a large circle around it and performed the traditional hand-clapping folk dance *kaikottikali*. Afterward, everyone enjoyed the sweets.

The fourth day was celebrated almost like a wedding, except there was no groom. I was dressed—after another early-morning bath, of course—in traditional attire: off-white, hand-woven cotton fabric, with a touch of color added as a wide golden border, draped around the waist, and a bright, colorful top. And this is the only occasion when girls in our community cover part of their hair with a piece of colorful fabric. But it was altogether a different story when it came to jewelry; any color lacking in my clothing was more than compensated with ornaments.

My aunt brought out the family jewels from my grandmother's iron safe. Family jewels are treasured possessions, often handed down from generation to generation. They are part of every celebration; they have their own cherished place in every auspicious event. She first took out grandmother's *kantasaram* (a choker made with gold crescent moon-shaped units set with red rubies and strung on either side of a beautiful ruby pendant) and placed it around my neck. That was just the beginning. Below that came an assortment of fine jewelry: *poothaali, mullamottu mala, Kuziminni, nagapadathali,* (the quintessential Kerala jewel), *and maangamala.* Last, she took out the two elaborate multi-strand necklaces worn only on this occasion in our family: *vattu mala,* a multi-strand garland of rounds, and *avilu mala,* several strands shaped like flattened rice, both hanging from ornate clasps. My ears, forehead, hands, and ankles were also adorned with more finery, and I felt like a walking display of jewelry.

I was taken to the temple, accompanied by sisters and cousins. My cousin held a pretty, colorful umbrella above my head. A Nagaswaram band (drums and wind instruments) and two young boys holding *valum parichayum* (swords and shields) walked in front of us—probably a symbolic representation of our hereditary warrior lineage. When we got back, I sat down, and guests brought me presents of money and jewelry. A lavish vegetarian feast was served around noon. I couldn't wait any longer for the guests to leave; I was anxious to take off the jewelry.

Today, this ceremony has lost its old social significance. However, in the remote villages of Kerala, it is still celebrated as a significant event in the life of a girl with special feasts and traditional gifts.

Paal Kanji: Rice Soup with Milk and Sugar

During the third day of the *Thirandu Kalyaanam* (coming of age) celebration of young girls, guests are served *paal kanji* along with coconut slices, jaggery chunks, and deep-fried *pappadams.* The soup is served in a *thada*—a bowl made of plantain stems held together with the stems of coconut palm leaves. The soup spoons are made of folded jackfruit leaves pinned with stems of coconut palm leaves.

3 cups whole milk
1 cup parboiled rice
3 cups water
½ cup sugar

In a heavy saucepan, bring the milk to a rolling boil. Reduce the heat, and simmer for ten minutes, stirring occasionally. Remove the pot from the stove, and keep it covered. Wash the rice in several changes of water until the water runs clear. In a saucepan, bring three cups of water to a boil, and add the cleaned rice. Lower the heat to medium, and cook, stirring frequently, for about forty minutes. Add more water as necessary, if it is absorbed too quickly. After forty minutes, pour in the boiled milk, and stir well. Continue to cook over medium heat for another ten to fifteen minutes, until the rice is fully cooked. Stir in the sugar, and keep it covered until it is time to serve. Just before serving, stir the *kanji* gently. Serve it with fresh coconut slices, jaggery chunks, and deep-fried *pappadams.*

Makes 6 to 8 servings.

Thirattipittu: Steamed Rice Flour Sweetened With Brown Sugar

Thirattipittu is a simple steamed rice-flour sweet that is prepared only on this occasion. Later, it is served to the guests.

2 cups rice flour
1 cup jaggery or brown sugar
2 teaspoons crushed cardamom
4 teaspoons ghee

In a heavy skillet, dry roast the rice flour over low to medium heat, stirring continuously, until it turns pink (about five to six minutes). Remove the pan from the stove, and let the flour cool to room temperature. When it is cool, sprinkle about half a cup of water over the flour, a few tablespoons at a time, and mix thoroughly. It is ideal to use clean hands to mix the flour and water. It should be wet but not lumpy. Add a few more drops of water if necessary.

Bring water to a boil in a heavy saucepan or a steamer. Spread cheesecloth over the steamer insert, and spread the rice flour over the cheesecloth. Cover and steam for fifteen to twenty minutes. Remove it from the stove, and spread it on a tray or platter to cool.

In a heavy skillet, mix the jaggery (or brown sugar) with a couple of tablespoons of water, and cook over medium heat to make a thick syrup of firm-ball consistency (approximately 245°F to 250°F on a candy thermometer). Remove the skillet from the stove, add the steamed rice flour, and mix thoroughly. Sprinkle it with crushed cardamom, pour on the ghee, and stir it well. Serve warm or at room temperature.

Makes 3 to 3½ cups.

Celebrating Ancestors: Food Traditions of the Days of the Dead

The somber event of death is observed with a fifteen-day mourning period. In times past, until the ritual cremation of the dead body, no one in the family ate or drank anything. During the following days, only very simple food was served, and fried foods, considered festive, were forbidden. At the close of the mourning period, the life of the demised was celebrated in a ceremony called *Adiyanthiram*. It was a way of expressing appreciation for the help and support of neighbors and friends. Feeding poor people on this day is another custom that is still observed. Annual death anniversaries are observed with religious rituals and gifts of food.

When I was growing up, my maternal grandmother's *sradham* (death anniversary) was a major event at our home. My grandmother passed away before I was born, but her *sradham* still brings back many fond memories of joint-family life, and of celebrations on a grand scale.

Every year, my mother and her siblings gathered at our ancestral home for their mother's death anniversary. All five of them performed the religious rites before dawn, making offerings to the gods for the peace of Grandmother's soul. At the crack of dawn, we children leaned against the iron railings of large windows and watched them feed cooked rice sprinkled with black sesame seeds to crows. Crows are considered messengers of the dead; the more crows that came to eat the rice, the happier were the departed souls.

Offering gifts to Brahmans is a big part of most Hindu ceremonies. My grandmother was a generous lady, and in her honor, plenty of uncooked food was offered to six Brahmans. The food was always uncooked, as Brahmans are considered a higher caste than the Nayars and were not allowed to eat food prepared by us. While Mother and her siblings performed religious rites, others in the family spread six long banana leaves, about five feet long, on the floor. They filled the leaves with rice, vegetables, and various dals. Milk, yogurt, and ghee were served in *donnas,* small pails made with fresh banana leaves. Gathered were essentially all of the necessary ingredients for cooking an elaborate vegetarian meal. The Brahmans sat on leaf-shaped wooden planks in front of the banana leaves, and my mother, aunt, and uncles offered them these gifts in Grandmother's name. Then all of us walked around them and bowed down our heads to receive their blessing.

The feast at noon included several vegetarian dishes and desserts. The *sradham sadya* always included some special dishes: *ingithayir,* a simple chutney made with ginger, green chilies, and yogurt; *pulisseri,* a simple squash curry in sour buttermilk sauce; and *ellunda,* a sesame seed and brown-sugar sweet.

Ingithayir: Ginger and Green Chilies in Yogurt

This ginger and yogurt chutney is a must at the annual death anniversary observances of departed family members. Traditionally, it is served in very small servings.

½ cup freshly grated ginger
4 fresh green serrano or Thai chilies (less for a milder taste)
Salt to taste
1 cup plain yogurt
1 tablespoon coconut oil
½ teaspoon mustard seeds
1 dried red cayenne, serrano, or Thai chili, halved
10 to 12 fresh curry leaves

Grind the ginger, green chilies, salt, and a couple of tablespoons of water together in a blender to make a smooth, thick puree. Combine the puree with the yogurt, and stir well.

Heat the oil in a skillet, and add the mustard seeds. When they start sputtering, add the red pepper and curry leaves, and remove it from the stove. Pour over the chutney, and stir well.

Makes one and a half cups.

Chatha Pulisseri: Ash Gourd in Buttermilk Sauce

This simple squash curry in a buttermilk sauce is another a must at death-anniversary observances. It is a watery curry, and it is usually served over rice. *Pulisseri* may also be prepared with ripe mangoes or telinga potatoes.

2 cups ash gourd pieces, cubed
Salt to taste
½ teaspoon turmeric powder
1 cup finely grated coconut
4 fresh green serrano or Thai chilies (less for a milder taste)
1½ cups buttermilk
¼ cup sour cream
1 tablespoons coconut oil
½ teaspoon mustard seeds
1 dried red cayenne, serrano, or Thai chili, halved
10 to 12 fresh curry leaves

Place the vegetable cubes in a heavy saucepan, and pour in one cup of water. Add salt and turmeric, and cook over medium heat until the vegetables are fork tender. Meanwhile, in a blender, grind the coconut, green chilies, and buttermilk together to form a smooth puree. Add this to the cooking vegetables, and simmer for five minutes. Beat the sour cream together with a couple of tablespoons of water, and pour it into the simmering curry. When the liquid in the pot starts bubbling, remove it from the stove. Heat the oil in a skillet, and add the mustard seeds. When they start sputtering, add the red pepper and curry leaves, and remove it from the stove. Pour it over the curry, and stir well. Cover and set aside. Serve hot with plain rice.

Sour cream is not used in the traditional recipe. As the buttermilk available at supermarkets is not as sour as homemade buttermilk, addition of sour cream is called for in this recipe.

Makes 6 to 8 servings.

Ellunda: Sesame Seed and Brown-Sugar Candy

Ellunda is another must at death anniversary observances. It is traditionally made with black sesame seeds and jaggery. It is preferable to use either black or brown sesame seeds to prepare this sweet.

2 cups sesame seeds
¾ cup jaggery or brown sugar
¼ cup ghee

In a heavy skillet, dry roast the sesame seeds over medium heat. As they become toasted, the seeds will start popping. Stir continuously, and roast for five to six minutes until you smell the toasted fragrance. Do not allow them to burn; if over-roasted, sesame seeds will taste bitter. Remove them from the stove, and spread them on a large plate. In a heavy skillet, mix the jaggery (or brown sugar) with a couple of tablespoons of water, and cook over medium heat to make a thick syrup (approximately 235°F to 240°F on a candy thermometer.) To test the syrup, drop half a spoonful of the syrup into a cup of cold water. It will form a soft ball, but it will flatten like a pancake after a few moments in your hand. Add the toasted sesame seeds to the syrup, and stir well. Let it cool down a little. Smear a little ghee on the palm of your hand, pick up a handful of the mixture, and roll it into a ball one to one and a half inch in diameter. Repeat with the remaining mixture. Store the *ellunda* in airtight containers.

Makes 30 to 32 pieces.

Appendix I: Recipe Index

Sacred Food: Rice and Rituals	80
Choru: Plain Boiled Rice	90
Kanji: Rice Soup	91
Thayir Choru: Yogurt Rice	93
Thenga Choru: Coconut Rice	94
Naraanga Choru: Lemon Rice	95
Pothichoru: Spiced Rice in Banana-Leaf Packets	96
The World of Curries	98
Popular Curries	100
Neyyum Parippum: Mashed Mung Dal with Ghee	103
Erisseri: Butternut Squash and Mung Dal in Coconut Cumin Sauce	103
Varutha Erisseri: Green Plantains in Toasted Coconut and Cumin Sauce	105
Kaalan: Ripe Plantains with Coconut, Green Chilies, and Yogurt	106
Oolan: Vegetables in Coconut-Milk Sauce	107
Aviyal: Mixed Vegetable Medley in Coconut Cumin Sauce	108
Sambar: Vegetables and *Tuvar* Dal in a Spicy Tamarind Sauce	109
Varutharacha Sambar: Vegetables and Tuvar Dal in a Toasted-Coconut and Tamarind Sauce	112
Thakkali Rasam: Tomato and *Tuvar* Dal Soup	113
Tomato *Pachadi:* Tomatoes in a Fresh Coconut and Yogurt Sauce	115
Okra *Kichadi:* Fried Okra in a Coconut and Mustard Sauce	116

Seasonal Curries — 118
Moloshyam: Vegetables in Coconut and Cumin Sauce — 119
Pulinkari: Vegetables with Spicy Tuvar Dal — 121
Vazuthaninga Varutharacha Kootan: Eggplant in Spicy Toasted-Coconut Sauce — 122
Paavakka Varutharacha Kootan: Bitter Gourd in Spicy Toasted-Coconut Sauce — 124
Koottu Curry: Butternut Squash and *Chana* Dal in Coconut-Cumin Sauce — 125
Cheera Udachathu: Spicy Mashed Spinach — 126
Maampaza Pachadi: Ripe Mangoes in a Coconut and Mustard Sauce — 127
Kadachakka Masalakkari: Breadfruit in Spicy Coconut Sauce — 128
Vellarikka Tharichathu: Cucumbers in a Mustard and Coconut Sauce — 129
Urulakkizangu Stew: Potato Stew — 132
Brown Stew: Potatoes in Spicy Coconut Milk — 133
Kadalakari: Spicy Chickpea Curry — 135
Kurumulaku Rasam: Black Pepper Soup — 136
Mulaku Varutha Puli: Onions and Green Chilies in Spicy Tamarind Sauce — 137
Uppuparippu: Mung Dal with Fresh Green Chilies and Curry Leaves — 138
Mathan Puzukku: Pumpkin and Red Beans with Coconut and Curry Leaves — 139

Curries from the Madapilli (Royal Kitchen) — 142
Ellukari: Vegetables in Spicy Coconut and Sesame Sauce — 144
Pacha Sambar: Sambar with Fresh Green Spices — 146
Varuthupperi Kootaan: Fried Plantains in Coconut Yogurt Sauce — 147
Chakka Madhura Curry: Sweet Jackfruit Curry — 148
Pappadavalli: Fried Pappadams in Spicy Sauce — 149
Varikkasseri: Green Bananas and Taro Root in Coconut Buttermilk Sauce — 150
Karutha Moloshyam: Telinga Potatoes *(Suran)* in Black Pepper and Coconut Sauce — 150
Kaattu Kootan: Green Bananas, Cucumber, and Yam in a Sweet and Sour Sauce — 151
Maampaza Kaalan: Ripe Mangoes in Coconut Yogurt Sauce — 152

Kurukku Kaalan: Vegetables in Slow-Cooked Sour Buttermilk Sauce	153

Hot off the Skillet: *Mezukkupurattis* and *Thorans* — 155

Kaya Mezukkupuratti: Panfried Green Plantains with Curry Leaves	155
Kaya and *Achinga Mezukkupuratti:* Panfried Green Plantains and Fresh Black-Eyed Peas with Mustard Seeds and Curry Leaves	156
Chena Mezukkupuratti: Telinga Potatoes Panfried with Mustard Seeds and Curry Leaves	157
Vellapayaru Mezukkupuratti: Red Beans Panfried with Curry Leaves and Mustard	158
Vellapayaru and *Kaya Tholi Mezukkupuratti:* Panfried Red Beans and Plantain Skins	159
Muthira Upperi: Horse Gram Beans Panfried with Mustard and Curry Leaves	160
Paavakka Mezukkupuratti: Bitter Gourd Panfried with Spices	161
Masala Niracha Paavakka: Bitter Gourd Stuffed with Spicy Onion	162
Kadachakka Mezukkupuratti: Breadfruit Panfried with Curry Leaves	163
Beans *Thoran:* Panfried Green Beans with Fresh Coconut and Mustard Seeds	163
Mottakoozu Thoran: Cabbage Panfried with Green Chilies and Coconut	164
Urulakizzangu Thoran: Potatoes Panfried with Green Chilies and Coconut	165
Idichakka Thoran: Tender Jackfruit Seasoned with Green Chilies, Mustard Seeds, and Coconut	166

Chutneys and Pickles — 168

Naalikera Chutney: Coconut Chutney	168
Ulli Chammanthi: Shallot Chutney	170
Manga Chammanthi: Fresh Mango Chutney	171
Adamaanga Chutney: Mango Chutney with Dried Spiced Mangoes	171
Thakkali Chutney: Fresh Tomato Chutney	172
Puliingi: Ginger and Green Chilies in a Tamarind Sauce	173

Mulagu Pachadi: Green Chiles in Spicy Tamarind
and Brown Sugar Sauce   174
Kothamallipodi: Spicy Fresh Coriander Chutney Powder   175
Chammanthipodi: Spicy Coconut Chutney Powder   176
Podi: Spice Powder Served With Dosa and Idli   177
Veppilakatti: Spicy Lemon Leaf Chutney Powder   177
Naranga Curry: Lemon Pickle   179
Vadugappuli Naranga Curry: Bitter Lemon Pickle   180
Nellikkakari: Gooseberry Pickle   181
Vedinellikka: Dry Gooseberry Pickle   181
Chethumaangakari: Green Mango Pickle   183
Uluva Maanga Curry: Mango Pickle
with Fenugreek and Cayenne Pepper   184
Ennamaanga: Deep-fried Mangoes with Spices in Sesame Oil   185
Uppumaanga: Mangoes in Brine   186
Kadumaanga: Tender Mango Pickle   187
Adamaanga: Dried, Spiced Mango Pieces   187

Accompaniments and Sun-Dried Preserves   190

Varuthupperi: Green Plantain Chips   191
Sarkara Upperi: Sweet Plantain Chips   192
Chena Varuthathu: Telinga Potato Chips   193
Pappadams: Fried *Urad* Dal Wafers   194
Chakka Varuthathu: -Jackfruit Chips   194
Kadachakka Varuthathu: Breadfruit Chips   195
Pazzam Nurukku: Steamed Ripe Plantains   196
Neyyu: Ghee or Clarified Butter   196
Thayir, Mooru, and *Sambharam:* Yogurt, Buttermilk,
and Spicy Yogurt Drink   197
Decoction Coffee: South Indian Coffee   198
Arikondattam: Spicy Rice Crisps   199
Ari Pappadams: Rice Wafers   200
Vendakka Kondattam: Okra Crisps   201
Paavakka Kondattam: Spicy Bitter-Gourd Crisps   202
Mulagu Kondattam: Green Chili Crisps   203
Maangaathera: Dried Ripe Mango Preserve   204
Chakka Pappadams: Jackfruit Wafers   204

Paayasams (Puddings) — 206

    Paal Paayasam: Rice Pudding — 207
    Neypaayasam: Rice Pudding with Brown Sugar and Ghee — 208
    Idichu Pizinja Paayasam: Rice and Mung Dal Pudding
    with Coconut Milk — 209
    Paal Ada Pradhaman: Rice Pudding
    with Steamed Rice Flakes — 210
    Avil Paayasam: Pounded Rice Pudding — 211
    Gothambu Pradhaman: Wheat Pudding — 212
    Semiya Paayasam: Vermicelli Pudding — 213
    Kadala Pradhaman: Chana Dal Pudding
    with Brown Sugar and Coconut Milk — 214
    Pazza Pradhaman: Ripe Plantain Pudding — 216
    Chakka Pradhaman: Jackfruit Pudding — 218

Breakfasts and Brunches — 221

    Puttu: Steamed Rice Flour and Fresh Coconut Logs — 221
    Noolpittu (Idiappam): Fresh Rice Noodles
    with Coconut Filling — 222
    Vellayappam: Rice and Coconut Milk Pancakes — 223
    Naalikera Dosa: Rice and Coconut Pancakes — 225
    Dosa: Rice and *Urad* Dal Pancakes — 226
    Masala Dosa: Rice and *Urad* Dal Pancakes Stuffed
    with Spicy Potatoes and Onions — 229
    Idli: Steamed Rice and *Urad* Dal Cakes — 230
    Idli Uppuma: Idli Panfried with Green Chilies,
    Curry Leaves, and Mustard Seeds — 232
    Oothappam: Spicy Pancakes — 232
    Ada: Thick Pancakes with Rice and a Mix of Dal — 233
    Uzunnu Vada: Deep-Fried *Urad* Dal Fritters — 234
    Tayir Vada: Vada in Spicy Yogurt Sauce — 235
    Uppuma: Farina Spiced with Green Chilies, Ginger,
    and Curry Leaves — 236
    Mixed Vegetable *Uppuma:* Spicy Farina
    with Mixed Vegetables — 237
    Kozhukkatta: Steamed Rice and Fresh Coconut Balls — 238

Savory Snacks 241

    Murukku: Rice and *Urad* Dal Pretzel 241
    Cheeda: Fried Spicy Rice and *Urad* Dal Balls 243
    Omappodi: Deep-Fried *Besan* Strings 244
    Kara Mixture: Spicy, Crunchy Mix 245
    Pappadavada (Thatta): Deep-Fried Spicy Rice
    and *Urad* Dal Disks 247
    Thengavada: Deep-Fried Spicy Rice and Coconut Disks 248
    Ribbon *Pokavada:* Spicy Rice and *Besan* Ribbons 248
    Urulakkizangu Bondas: Spicy Potato Fritters 249
    Bajji or *Pokavadas:* Vegetable Fritters 251
    Parippu Vadas: Deep-Fried Spicy *Tuvar* Dal Fritters 252
    Sevaka: Panfried Spicy Rice Noodles 253
    Puli Avil: Pounded Rice Spiced with Tamarind
    and Mustard Seeds 255
    Kannanaadan: Semi-Ripe Plantains Panfried
    with Mustard Seeds and Curry Leaves 255

Desserts: Sweet Treats 257

    Manoharam: Fried Rice and *Urad* Dal Strings Sweetened
    with Brown Sugar 261
    Vellacheeda: Rice, Dal, and Brown Sugar Balls
    with Cardamom and Sesame Seeds 262
    Cheruparippu Poornam: Mung Dal Fudge 263
    Ubbidu: Sweet Wheat-Flour Flat Bread 264
    Avil Nanachathu: Pounded Rice Sweetened
    with Brown Sugar and Fresh Coconut 265
    Pazza Palahaaram: Banana Pancakes 266
    Oralappam: Rice, Coconut, and Mung Dal Balls 266
    Poruvalanga: Rice and Mung Dal Balls 268
    Kumbilappam: Jackfruit Jam in Rice Cones Steamed
    in Banana Leaves 269
    Sugiyan: Deep-Fried Sweet Mung Dal Balls 270
    Mysorepak: Besan Fudge 271
    Laddu: Sweetened *Besan* Bead Balls with Cashews and Raisins 272
    Gothambu Halvah: Wheat-Flour Fudge with Cashews
    and Cardamom 274
    Badusha: Cream and Flour Disks in Sugar Syrup 275

Naalikera Burfi: Fresh Coconut Fudge	276
Paalgova: Milk Fudge	276
Rava Laddu: Sweet Semolina Balls with Cardamom and Raisins	277
Rava Kesari: Semolina Pudding	278
Jilebis: Urad Dal Pretzels in Rose-Flavored Sugar Syrup	279
Neyyil Varattiya Pazzam: Caramelized Plantains	280
Porikadala Laddu: Laddu with Puffed *Chana* Dal Flour	281

Glittering Festivals and Revered Offerings — 282

Neyyappam: Rice and Brown-Sugar Griddle Cakes	284
Thirattipaal or *Naalikera Poornam:* Dark Coconut Fudge	285
Kadala: Spicy Brown Chickpeas	286
Modakam (Madhura Kozhukkatta): Steamed Sweet Coconut Balls	287
Paanakam: Sweet and Spicy Drink	288
Vellapayaru: Red Beans Sweetened With Brown Sugar	288
Paripputenga: Sweetened Puffed *Chana* Dal	289
Puthiri Avil: Pounded Rice with Milk, Sugar, Ghee, and Raisins	290
Ela Ada: Rice Flour and Coconut Cakes Steamed in Plantain Leaves	291
Thiruvathira Koottu: Mixed Root Vegetables and Plantain with Fresh Coconut	292
Thiruvathira Puzukku: Mixed Vegetables with Red Beans and Coconut	293
Madhura Koova Varattiyathu: Arrowroot Pudding with Milk, Sugar, and Cardamom	294
Ettangadi: Roasted Vegetables and Red Beans with Coconut, Sesame, and Brown Sugar	296
Vishu Kanji: Rice Soup with Coconut Milk	297
Thalu Kootan: Taro Stems with Fresh Coconut in Spicy Sauce	298
Chuttathu: Bran Cakes with Coconut and Brown Sugar	298
Ammini Kozhukkatta: Steamed Sweet Rice Balls	300
Paal Kanji: Rice Soup with Milk and Sugar	303
Thirattipittu: Steamed Rice Flour Sweetened With Brown Sugar	303
Ingithayir: Ginger and Green Chilies in Yogurt	305
Chatha Pulisseri: Ash Gourd in Buttermilk Sauce	306
Ellunda: Sesame Seed and Brown-Sugar Candy	307

Appendix II:
Menu Suggestions

Those who are new to the vegetarian cuisine of southwest India may find it somewhat daunting to start preparing a complete meal. But you don't have to cook an entire traditional meal to enjoy this cuisine. Rather, you might try one of the chutneys as a party dip, or maybe an appetizer or two as part of a buffet. Use one of the breakfast dishes at your next brunch, or serve a *thoran* instead of plain green beans at dinner.

My goal in compiling these recipes is to retain authentic tastes and traditions while making the flavors and festivals of my region more approachable to all. In order to make it easy and accessible, I offer traditional menus along with suggestions for ways to incorporate side dishes into an otherwise Western meal.

Having lived for fourteen years in Texas, both my husband and I are huge fans of anything Texan. When we lived in New York, every year during the summer, we loved to throw a Texas dinner party with a South Indian accent. Our menus were often a combination of truly Texan fare along with a few South Indian dishes. These are two totally different cooking styles that, for all of their differences, are both earthy, vibrant cuisines that share the heartiness of spices, the interplay of sweet and acidic, and the use hot chili peppers.

We served authentic Texas beer and freshly made margaritas for drinks. Spread among the platters of tortilla chips, fresh salsa, homemade guacamole, and refried beans, there were plantain banana chips and *bondas* made with potatoes, cilantro, and corn served with tomato chutney and *mulagu pachadi*. Texas chili, barbecued briskets, and sausages naturally got the top billing in the dinner menu. But if I was serving rice, it was either Spanish rice or South Indian lemon rice. Instead of potato salad, often I made a bowl of potato *thoran*, or a platter of cabbage *thoran* in the place of coleslaw. And after a spicy meal, guests had a choice of Mexican chocolate cake with a hint of cinnamon or a bowl of pecan praline ice cream served with warm, caramelized ripe plantains.

I offer you a few suggested menus. To the beginner, the number of dishes may seem overwhelming at first, but most of them can be prepared ahead of time and warmed up just before serving. This is because no one dish dominates as the main course.

Sample Menus

Mix-and-Match Cocktail Party

It's easy to incorporate some Indian snacks and sweets into a cocktail party menu, particularly since many can be prepared a day or two in advance. Here are some suggestions for snacks, chutneys, and sweets you can incorporate into your cocktail party menu. Try one or two from each group, and you can add more as you get more comfortable with this cuisine.

Snacks:
Green Plantain Chips *(Varuthupperi)*
Spicy Rice and *Besan* Flour Ribbons (Ribbon *Pokavada)*
Rice and *Urad* Dal Pretzels *(Murukku)*
Spicy-Crunchy Mix *(Kara* Mixture)
Deep-Fried Spicy Potato Fritters with Tomato Chutney and Green Chilies in a Spicy Tamarind and Brown Sugar Sauce *(Bonda* with Tomato Chutney and *Mulagu Pachadi)*
Vegetable Fritters with Coconut and Fresh Cilantro Chutney (Vegetable *Pokavada* with *Naalikera* Chutney with Fresh Cilantro Leaves)
Deep-Fried *Urad* Dal Fritters with Coconut Chutney *(Uzunnu Vada* with *Naalikera* Chutney)

Sweets:
Caramelized Ripe Plantains *(Neyyil Varattiya Pazzam)*
Semolina Pudding *(Rava Kesari)*
Fresh Coconut Fudge *(Naalikera Burfi)*
Besan Fudge *(Mysorepak)*

Brunch

Skipping breakfast, and serving brunch instead, is unheard of in Kerala. This is because lunch is our main meal. However, several breakfast dishes in combination with lunch dishes make great brunch spreads.

Brunch Menu 1:
Coconut Rice *(Thenga Choru)*
Panfried Green Beans with Fresh Coconut and Mustard Seeds (Beans *Thoran*)
Spicy *Tuvar* Dal Fritters in Tomato and *Tuvar* Dal Soup *(Parippu Vada* with *Rasam)*
Green Plantain Chips *(Varuthupperi)*
Deep-Fried Sweet Mung Dal Balls *(Sugiyan)*
Rice Pudding *(Paal Paayasam)*

Brunch Menu 2:
Rice and *Urad* Dal Pancakes Stuffed with Spicy Potatoes and Onions *(Masala Dosa)*
Deep-Fried *Urad* Dal Fritters *(Uzunnu Vada)*
Vegetables and *Tuvar* Dal in a Spicy Tamarind Sauce *(Sambar)*
Coconut Chutney *(Naalikera* Chutney)
Semolina Pudding *(Rava Kesari)*

Brunch Menu 3:
Vegetable Fritters *(Pokavada)*
Lemon Rice *(Naranga Choru)*
Potatoes Panfried with Green Chilies and Coconut *(Urulakizzangu Thoran)*
Spicy Mashed Spinach *(Cheera Udachathu)*
Fried *Urad* Dal Wafers *(Pappadams)*

Festive Brunch Menu:
Rice and *Urad* Dal Pretzels *(Murukku)*
Deep-Fried Spicy Potato Balls with Tomato Chutney *(Bonda* with *Thakkali* Chutney)
Spicy Farina with Mixed Vegetables (Mixed Vegetable *Uppuma*)
Deep-Fried Spicy *Tuvar* Dal Fritters in Tomato and *Tuvar* Dal Soup *(Parippu Vada* in *Rasam)*
Yogurt Rice *(Thayir Choru)*
Cabbage Panfried with Green Chilies and Coconut *(Mottakoozu Thoran)*
Green Chilies in a Spicy Tamarind and Brown Sugar Sauce *(Mulagu Pachadi)*
Lemon Pickle *(Naranga* Curry)
Sweet Wheat-Flour Flatbread *(Ubbidu)*
Besan Fudge *(Mysorepak)*
Vermicelli Pudding *(Semiya Paayasam)*

Sadya: A Traditional Feast

I have always felt that somehow, time stands still in Kerala, especially when it comes to food. No matter what, the same dishes continue to be prepared and served in the same old combination. No one ever gets tired of them. And when it comes to religious or family celebrations, they continue to be celebrated in the same way by every generation in a family, and the same festive dishes are prepared year after year—traditions and recipes are passed on from one generation to the other. The following is a traditional feast menu.

Plain Rice *(Choru)*
Mashed Mung Dal with Ghee *(Neyyum Parippum)*
Butternut Squash and Mung Dal in Coconut Cumin Sauce *(Erisseri)*
Ripe Plantains with Coconut, Green Chilies, and Yogurt *(Kaalan)*
Vegetables in Coconut Milk Sauce *(Oolan)*
Mixed Vegetable Medley in Coconut Cumin Sauce *(Aviyal)*
Vegetables and Tuvar Dal in Spicy Tamarind Sauce *(Sambar)*
Tomato and Tuvar Dal Soup *(Rasam)*
Tomatoes in Fresh Coconut and Yogurt Sauce *(Pachadi)*
Fried Okra in Coconut-Mustard Sauce *(Kichadi)*
Panfried Green Plantains and Fresh Black-Eyed Peas with Mustard Seeds and Curry Leaves *(Kaya* and *Achinga Mezukkupuratti)*
Panfried Green Beans with Fresh Coconut and Mustard Seeds (Beans *Thoran)*
Ginger and Green Chilies in a Tamarind Sauce *(Puliingi)*
Lemon Pickle *(Naranga* Curry*)*
Green Plantain Chips *(Varuthupperi)*
Sweet Banana Chips *(Sarkara Upperi)*
Telinga Potato Chips *(Chena Varuthathu)*
Steamed Ripe Plantains *(Pazzam Nurukku)*
Fried *Urad* Dal Wafers *(Pappadams)*
Ripe Plantain Pudding *(Pazza Pradhaman)*
Chana Dal Pudding with Brown Sugar and Coconut Milk *(Kadala Pradhaman)*

Appendix III:
Cooking Measurements and Syrup Consistencies

Cooking Measurement Conversion Chart

Dry Measures

3 teaspoons	1 tablespoon	½ ounce	14.3 grams
2 tablespoons	⅛ cup	1 fluid ounce	28.35 grams
4 tablespoons	¼ cup	2 fluid ounces	56.7 grams
5⅓ tablespoons	⅓ cup	2.6 fluid ounces	75.6 grams
8 tablespoons	½ cup	4 ounces	113.4 grams
12 tablespoons	¾ cup	6 ounces	.375 pound
32 tablespoons	2 cups	16 ounces	1 pound
64 tablespoons	4 cups	32 ounces	2 pounds

Liquid Measures

1 cup	8 fluid ounces	½ pint	237 ml
2 cups	16 fluid ounces	1 pint	473 ml
4 cups	32 fluid ounces	1 quart	946 ml
2 pints	32 fluid ounces	1 quart	0.946 liters
4 quarts	128 fluid ounces	1 gallon	3.785 liters
1 tablespoon	½ fluid ounce	15 grams	15 ml
2 tablespoons	1 fluid ounce	30 grams	29.6 ml
8 tablespoons	4 fluid ounces	¼ pint	118.5 ml

Sugar Syrup Consistencies

Thread Stage: 215°F–220°F
At this relatively low temperature, there is still a lot of water left in the syrup. The liquid sugar may be pulled into brittle threads between the fingers. Or take a small amount of the syrup in a spoon, and drop it from about two inches above the pot. Let it drip into the pan. If it spins a long thread, like a spider web, it's done.

Soft-Ball Stage: 235°F–240°F
A small amount of syrup dropped into chilled water forms a soft, flexible ball, but flattens like a pancake after a few moments in your hand.

Firm-Ball Stage: 245°F–250°F
The syrup forms a firm ball when dropped into chilled water. It will not flatten when removed from water, but remains malleable and will flatten when squeezed.

Hard-Ball Stage: 250°F–265°F
At this stage, the syrup will form thick, ropy threads as it drips from the spoon. The sugar concentration is rather high now, which means there's less and less moisture in the sugar syrup. Syrup dropped into ice water may be formed into a hard ball which holds its shape on removal. The ball will be hard, but you can still change its shape by squashing it.

Appendix IV:
Resources and Ordering Information

The best way to find an Indian grocery store in your neighborhood is to visit the following Web sites, which list addresses, phone numbers, and directions to several stores in the United States.

http://www.thokalath.com/grocery/index.php
http://www.cuisinecuisine.com/IndianGroceryStoresinUS.htm
http://www.searchindia.com/search/groc.html

Many Indian stores in the United States also have their own Web sites and mail-order services. Some major mail-order sources for Indian ingredients and appliances are:

http://www.hosindia.com/
http://www.patelbrothersusa.com/index_main.asp
http://www.sisshopping.com/ (specializes in South Indian products)
http://www.innoconcepts.com/ (Specializes in appliances)
http://www.adrianascaravan.com/
http://www.namaste.com/

A Selective Bibliography

Books in English

Achaya, K. T. *Indian Food: A Historical Companion*. Oxford University Press, 1994.

Achaya, K. T. *A Historical Dictionary of Indian Food*. Oxford India Paperbacks, 1998.

Achaya, K. T. *The Story of Our Food*. Sangam Books Ltd, 2001

Adigal, Prince Ilango. *Silappathikaram,* translated by Alain Danielou. New Directions Books, 1965.

Aiyangar, S. Krishnaswami. *South India and Her Muhammadan Invaders.* Asian Education Services (reprint), 1991.

Alexander, William A. *Gender-Efficient Kerala*, a paper presented at the Sixth Symposium on Gender Research, University of Kiel, Germany, 2002.

Bahauddin, K.M. *Kerala Muslims*. Kottyam, Kerala: Sahithya Pravarthaka Cooperative Society, 1992.

Begley, Vimala and Richard Daniel De Puma (ed.). *Rome and India: The Ancient Sea Trade.* University of Wisconsin Press, 1991.

Bristow, Sir Robert. *The Cochin Saga*. London: Cassell & Company, 1959.

Buruiere, Andre, Christiane Kalpisch-Zuber, Martine Segalen, and Francoise Zonabend (ed.). *A History of the Family,* Volumes I and II. Harvard University Press, 1996.

Buchanan, Francis. *A Journey from Madras through the Countries of Mysore, Canara, and Malabar*. New Delhi and Madras: Asia Educational Services, New Delhi & Madras 1999 (first published in London in 1807).

Capatti, Alberto and Massimo Montanari. *Italian Cuisine: A Cultural History.* Columbia University Press, 2003.

Casson, Lionel. *The Periplus Maris Erythrei.* Princeton University Press, 1989.

Casson, Lionel. *The Ancient Mariners.* Princeton University Press, 1991.

Chellaiah, J. V. *Pattuppattu: Ten Tamil Idylls, Translated into English Verse.* Colombo General Publishers, 1947.

Corn, Charles. *The Scents of Eden: A History of the Spice Trade.* Kodansha International, 1998.

Chaudhuri, K. N. *Trade and Civilization in the Indian Ocean.* Cambridge University Press, 1985.

Dalby, Andrew. *Dangerous Tastes: The Story of Spices.* University of California Press, 2000.

Davidson, Alan. *The Oxford Companion to Food.* Oxford University Press, 1999.

Day, Francis. *The Land of the Perumals; or Cochin: Its Past and Its Present.* New Delhi and Madras: Asia Educational Services, 1990 (first published in 1863).

Dikshitar, V. R. Ramachandra. *Pre-historic South India.* New Delhi: Cosmo Publications, 1981 (first published in 1951).

Disney, A. R. *Twilight of the Pepper Empire: Portuguese Trade in Southwest India in the Early Seventeenth Century.* Harvard University Press, 1978.

Dos Passos, John. *The Portugal Story: Three Centuries of Exploration and Discovery.* Doubleday, 1969.

Fawcett, F. *Nayars of Malabar.* New Delhi and Madras: Asia Educational Services, 1990 (reprinted from 1901 edition).

Goitein, S. D. *Letters of Medieval Jewish Traders,* Princeton University Press, 1973.

Green, Aliza. *The Bean Bible.* Running Press, 2000.

Hart, George L. and Hank Heifetz (trans. and ed.). *The Purananuru: The Four Hundred Songs of War and Wisdom: An Anthology of Poems from Classical Tamil.* Columbia University Press, 1999.

Hutchinson, Sir Joseph (ed.). *Evolutionary Studies in World Crops: Diversity and Change in the Indian Subcontinent.* Cambridge University Press, 1974.

Iyengar, T. R. Shesa. *Dravidian India.* New Delhi: Asian Educational Services, 1982.

Iyer, L. K. Anantha Krishna. *The Cochin Tribes and Castes, Volume I and II*. London: Higginbotham & Co., 1912.

De Langhe, Edmond and Pierre De Maret. "Tracking the Banana: Its Significance in Early Agriculture," in Chris Gosden and Jon Hather (ed.), *The Prehistory of Food: Appetites for Change*. Routledge, 1999.

Levathes, Louise. *When China Ruled the Seas: The Treasure Fleet of the Dragon Throne*. Oxford University Press, 1994.

Lombard, Denys and Jean Aubin (ed.). *Asian Merchants and Businessmen in the Indian Ocean and the Chinese Sea*. Oxford University Press, 2000.

Luard, Elisabeth. *Sacred Food: Cooking for Spiritual Nourishment*. Chicago Review Press, 2001.

Malekandathil, Pius. *Portuguese Cochin and the Maritime Trade of India 1500–1663*. Delhi: Manohar Publishers, 2001.

Mathews, Johnsy. *Economy and Society in Medieval Malabar AD 1500–1600*. Kerala: St. Mary's Press and Book Depot.

Menon, C. Achyuta. *The Cochin State Manual*.

Menon, K. P. Padmanabha, *History of Kerala, Volumes 1, 2, and 3 Cochin Government Press*, 1924.

Miller, Roland E. *Mappila Muslims of Kerala*. London: Sangam Books Limited, 1992.

Mills, J. V. G. (tr.). *Ying-Yai Sheng-Lan: The Overall Survey of the Ocean Shores*, by Ma Huan. Hakluyt Society (Cambridge University Press), 1970.

Mote, Frederick W. and Dennis Twitchett (eds.). *The Cambridge History of China, Volumes 7 and 8: The Ming Dynasty 1368–1644*. Cambridge University Press, 1988.

Owen, Sri. *The Rice Book*. St. Martin Griffin, 1996.

Pillai, K. N. Sivaraja. *The Chronology of the Early Tamils*. New Delhi: Asian Educational Services, 1984.

Playne, Somerset and J. W. Bond (comp.) and Arnold Wright (ed.). *Southern India: Its History, People, and Industrial Resources*. New Delhi and Chennai: Asia Educational Services, 2004 (first published by Foreign and Colonial Compiling and Publishing Co., London, 1914–1915).

Prakash, Om. *Food and Drinks in Ancient India*. Delhi: Munshi Ram Manohar Lal, 1961.

Ramachandran, Rathi, Narayanan, Girija and Ramachandran, Ammini (ed.). *History of Medieval Kerala*. New Delhi: Pragati Publications, 2005.

Robinson, Francis (ed.). *The Cambridge Illustrated History of the Islamic World*. Cambridge University Press, 1996.

Rubies, Joan-Pau *Travel and Ethnology in the Renaissance: South India through European Eyes, 1250–1625*. Cambridge University Press, 2000.

Sastri, K. A. Nilakanta. *A History of South India*. Oxford India Paperbacks, 1975.

Schoff, Wilfred H. (trans. and ann.). *The Periplus of the Erythraean Sea*. Munshiram Manoharlal Publishers Pvt. Ltd., 2001.

Segal, J. B. *A History of the Jews of Cochin*. Vallentine Mitchell, 1993.

Merchant-Prince Shattan. *Manimekalai,* trans. by Alain Danielou. New Directions Books, 1989.

Merchant-Prince Shattan. *Manimekalai,* trans. by Sridharan K. Guruswamy and S. Srinivasan. Madras: Dr. U. V. Swaminatha Aiyar Library, 1964.

Swahn, J. O. *The Lore of Spices*. Crescent Books, 1991.

Tannahill, Reay. *Food in History*. Three Rivers Press, 1988.

Tate, Desmond. *Tropical Fruit*. Archipelago Press, 1999.

Toussaint-Samat, Maguelonne. *History of Food,* trans. by Anthea Bell. Blackwell Publishers, Inc., 1992.

Turner, Jack. *Spice: The History of a Temptation*. Alfred A. Knopf, 2004.

Two Mohammedan Travelers. *Ancient Accounts of India and China*, trans. by Esuebius Renaudot. New Delhi: Asian Educational Services, 1995 (first published in 1733).

Vaughn, J. G. and C. A. Geissler. *The New Oxford Book of Food Plants*. Oxford University Press, 1997.

Villiers, Alan. *Monsoon Seas: The Story of the Indian Ocean*. McGraw-Hill, 1952.

Books in Malayalam

Andronov, M. S. *Draavida Bhaashakal (Dravidian Languages)*, translated into English from Russian by D. M. Segal and further translated into Malayalam by Dr. V. R. Prabodhachandran and P. E. Daamodaran Namboothiri. Kerala: Kerala Bhaasha Institute, 1990.

Balakrishnan, P. K. *Jaathivyavasthithiyum Kerala Charithravum (Class System and Kerala History)*. Kerala: Sahithya Pravarthaka Sahakarana Sangham, 1983.

Joseph, M. P. *Malayaalathile Parakeeya Padangal (Foreign Words and Terms in Malayalam)*. Kerala: Kerala Bhasha Institute, 1984.

Kumaran, K. *Kerala Charithram (Kerala History)*. Mangalore, India: United Publishers, 1999.

Menon, K. P. Padmanabha. *Kochi Rajya Charithram (History of the Kingdom of Kochi)*. Kerala: Mathrubhumi Press, 1914.

Menon, Puthezathu Rama. *Sakthan Thampuran*. Sulabha Books, 2003 (first published in 1942).

Panikkasseri, Velaayudhan. *Sancharikalum Charithrakaaranmarum (Travelers and Historians)*, Volume I. Kerala: National Book Stall, 1971.

Panikkasseri, Velaayudhan. *Sancharikalum Charithrakaaranmarum (Travelers and Historians)*, Volume II. Kerala: National Book Stall, 1977.

Raghunathan, R. *Malayaala Bhashoolpathi Vivaranaathmaka Soochika (Origin of Malayalam Language: A Descriptive Bibliography)*. Kerala: Kerala Bhaasha Institute, 1989.

Thampuran, Rama Varma (Appan). *Sanghakkali*.

Varier, Raghava and Rajan Gurukkal. *Keralacharithram (Kerala History)*. Vallathol Vidayppedham, 1991.

About the Author

Born in Kerala, India, Ammini Ramachandran moved to the United States in the early 1970s. She was born into a Nayar joint family, and both her grandfather and her father-in-law were members of the royal family of Kochi. Because of this heritage, she has personal access to the authentic vegetarian recipes of both the royalty and the Nayars of central Kerala. During her many visits home over the years, she has studied this traditional cuisine from native cooks who have lived and cooked in this region for their entire lives.

Having lived in the United States for over three decades, she is also familiar with western cooking methods and is therefore uniquely able to adapt these traditional recipes to western styles of cooking and eating. In addition, she knows how to integrate these recipes into a western-style menu and is able to suggest ways for American home cooks to expand their repertoire without having to cook an entire menu of dishes from this book at any given meal.

A financial analyst turned freelance food writer, Ammini has devoted her time over the past seven years to researching and writing about the ancient spice trade and its influences on Kerala's cuisine and culture. She is a member of International Association of Culinary Professionals (IACP), Association for the Study of Food and Society and Culinary Historians of New York. She has contributed to the *Food History Primer* published by IACP. She writes a column on spices for www.sallys-place.com, the premier Web site for food, beverages, and travel. Her recipes and articles have appeared in *The Providence Journal*, *Flavor & Fortune*, *Sacred Waters*, www.leitesculinaria.com, www.thingsasian.com, and www.chintha.com. Her Web site, www.peppertrail.com, provides a virtual tour of Kerala's history, cuisine, and culture.

She holds a diploma in article writing from the School of Careers, Berkshire, UK; a BSc in chemistry and physics from Kerala University; and an MBA from Southern Methodist University in Dallas, Texas. She lives in Plano, Texas.

Index

Accompaniments
    breadfruit chips, 194–195
    buttermilk, 197
    decoction coffee, 198–199
    fried *urad* dal wafers, 194
    ghee, 196–197
    green plantain chips, 191–192
    jackfruit chips, 194–195
    spicy yogurt drink, 197–198
    steamed ripe plantains, 196
    sweet plantain chips, 192–193
    telinga potato chips, 193
    yogurt, 197
Adamaanga chutney, mango chutney with dried spiced mangoes, 171–172
Adamaanga, dried, spiced mango pieces, 187–189
Adas, thick pancakes with rice and a mix of dal, 78, 233–234
Ajowan (*omam* or *ayamodakam*), 56
Almond, chutney, 170
Ancient trade with the east
    Chinese trade, 30–31
    Southeast Asia trade, 30
Appakkara, appams, 78
Arab trade, 21
Arikondattam, spicy rice crisps, 199–200
Arrowroot
    flour (*koova podi*), 51–52
    pudding with milk, sugar, and cardamom, 294–296
Asafetida (*kaayam*), 56–58
Ash gourd (*elevan* or *kumbalanga*), 68
    in buttermilk sauce, 306–307

Avil nanachathu, pounded rice sweetened with brown sugar and fresh coconut, 265
Avil paayasam, pounded rice pudding, 211
Aviyal, mixed vegetable medley in coconut cumin sauce, 108–109

Badusha, cream and flour disks in sugar syrup, 275–276
Banana pancakes, 266
Bajji (pokavadas), vegetable fritters, 251–252
Beans *thoran,* panfried green beans with fresh coconut and mustard seeds, 163–164
Besan, 51, 257
    bead balls with cashews and raisins, 272–274
    deep fried strings, 244–245
    fudge, 271–272
    spicy ribbons with rice, 248–249
Betel leaves, 102–103
Bitter gourd or bitter melon (*paavakka* or *kaippaka*), 68–69
    panfried with spices, 161–162
    spicy crisps, 202
    in spicy toasted coconut sauce, 124–125
    stuffed with spicy onion, 162–163
Black-eyed peas
    crisps, 203
    with panfried plantains, mustard seeds, and curry leaves, 156–157
    with plantains and telinga potatoes, 140

Black pepper (*kurumulaku*), 58
  soup, 136–137
Breadfruit (*kadachakka*), 67
  chips, 195–196
  panfried with curry leaves, 163
  in spicy coconut sauce, 128–129
Breakfast
  fresh rice noodles with coconut filling, 222–223
  godambu pancakes, 228
  rava pancakes, 227–228
  rice and coconut milk pancakes, 223–225
  rice and coconut pancakes, 225–226
  rice and *urad* dal pancakes, 226–227, 229
  spicy pancakes, 232–233
  steamed rice and *urad* dal cakes, 230–231
  steamed rice flour and fresh coconut logs, 221–222
  thick pancakes with rice and a mix of dal, 233–234
Brunch
  cracked-wheat *uppuma*, 237
  deep-fried *urad* dal fritters, 234–235
  farina spiced with green chilies, ginger, and curry leaves, 236–237
  semiya uppumma, 237
  spicy farina with mixed vegetables, 237–238
  steamed rice and fresh coconut balls, 238–240
  vada in spicy yogurt sauce, 235
Buttermilk (*mooru*), 54, 197
  sauce, 153–154, 306–307
Butternut squash
  with *chana* dal in a coconut cumin sauce, 125–126
  and mung dal in a coconut cumin sauce, 103–104

Cabbage, panfried with green chilies and coconut, 164–165
Candy, sesame seed and brown sugar, 307
Cardamom seeds (*elakkaya*), 58–59
  balls with rice, dal, brown sugar, and sesame seeds, 262–263
  sweet and spicy drink, 288
Cayenne pepper, with mango pickle and fenugreek, 184–185
Celebration of a life cycle, 13–16
  celebration of ancestors. *See* Celebration of ancestors recipes
  coming of age ceremony, 300–303
  recipes. *See* Celebration of life recipes
  rice soup with milk and sugar, 303
  steamed rice flour sweetened with brown sugar, 303–304
Celebration of life recipes, 299
  steamed sweet rice balls, 300
Celebration of ancestors recipes, 303–305
  ash gourd in buttermilk sauce, 306–307
  ginger and green chilies in yogurt, 305–306
  sesame seed and brown sugar candy, 307
Chakka madhura curry, sweet jackfruit curry, 148–149
Chakka pappadams, jackfruit wafers, 204–205
Chakka pradhaman, jackfruit pudding, 218–219
Chakka varuthathu, jackfruit chips, 194–195
Chakka varattiyathu, jackfruit jam, 219–220
Chammanthipodi, spicy coconut chutney powder, 176
Chana dal, 49
  with butternut squash in a coconut cumin sauce, 125–126

pudding with brown sugar and coconut milk, 214
puffed, 49, 289
Chana flour (*kadalamavu*). *See* Besan
Chatha pulisseri, ash gourd in buttermilk sauce, 306–307
Cheeda, fried spicy rice and *urad* dal balls, 243–244
Cheera udachathu, spicy mashed spinach, 126–127
Chena mezukkupuratti, telinga potatoes panfried with mustard seeds and curry leaves, 157–158
   with bananas, 158
   with jackfruit seeds, 158
Chena varuthathu, telinga potato chips, 193
Cheruparippu murukku, rice and mung dal pretzels, 243
Cheruparippu poornam, mung dal fudge, 263–264
Chethumaangakari, green mango pickle, 183–184
Chili, 39
Chili pepper (*kappal mulagu*), 60
Choru, plain boiled rice, 90–91
Christian settlements, 28
Chutney
   almond, 170
   coconut, 168–170
   fresh tomato, 172–173
   ginger and green chilies in a tamarind sauce, 173–174
   ginger and yogurt, 305–306
   green chilies in spicy tamarind and brown sugar sauce, 174–175
   powder. *See* Chutney powders
   shallot, 170–171
   varieties of, 168
Chutney powders
   coconut, 176
   coriander, 175
   lemon leaf, 177–178

Chuttathu, bran cakes with coconut and brown sugar, 298–299
Coconut (*nalikeram*), 4, 45
   with balls of rice and mung dal, 266–267
   with balls of steamed rice, 239–240
   with bran cakes and brown sugar, 298–299
   breaking a, 46
   cakes with rice flour steamed in plantain leaves, 291–292
   chutney, 168–170
   chutney powder, 176
   extracting milk from, 46–47
   fried disks with rice, 248
   fudge, 276, 285
   with jackfruit, green chilies, and mustard seeds, 166–167
   and mango *sundal*, 286–287
   oil (*velichenna*), 52
   pancakes, 225–226
   with panfried cabbage and green chilies, 164–165
   with panfried green beans and mustard seeds, 163–164
   with panfried potatoes and green chilies, 165–166
   with pumpkin, red beans, and curry leaves, 139
   rice, 94–95
   in steamed rice flour logs, 221–222
   steamed sweet balls, 287
   with taro stems in spicy sauce, 298
   with vegetables and red beans, 293–294
   with vegetables, red beans, sesame, and brown sugar, 296–297
Coffee, 198–199
Cooking and dining traditions, 7–9
Cooking bananas (*kaya*), 67
Cooking methods
   boiling, 76
   deep-frying, 76–77

dry roasting, 76
panfrying at low heat, 76
salting while deep-frying, 77
seasoning or tempering (*kaduku varakkal*), 76
simmering, 76
steaming, 75
Coriander leaves or cilantro (*pachakothamalli*), 68
   chutney powder, 175
Coriander seeds (*kothamalli*), 60–61
Cowpeas or small red beans (*vellapayaru*), 51
Cucumbers, 68
   with green plantains and yam in a sweet and sour sauce, 151–152
   in mustard and coconut sauce, 129–130
Cumin seeds (*jeerakam*), 61–62
Curries
   from the *madapilli*, 99. *See also* Curries from the *madapilli*
   popular, 99. *See also* Popular curries
   seasonal, 99. *See also* Seasonal curries
   serving suggestions, 99
   types of, 99
Curries from the *madapilli*, 99, 142–144
   fried *pappadams* in spicy sauce, 149
   fried plantains in coconut yogurt sauce, 147–148
   green bananas and taro root in coconut buttermilk sauce, 150
   green plantains, cucumber, and yam in a sweet and sour sauce, 151–152
   ripe mangoes in coconut yogurt sauce, 152–153
   sambar with fresh green spices, 146–147
   sweet jackfruit curry, 148–149
   telinga potatoes in black pepper and coconut sauce, 150–151
   vegetables in slow-cooked sour buttermilk sauce, 153–154
   vegetables in spicy coconut and sesame sauce, 144–145
Curry leaves (*kariveppila*), 68
   with mung dal and green chilies, 138
   with panfried breadfruit, 163
   with panfried horse gram beans and mustard seeds, 160–161
   with panfried *idli*, 232
   with panfried *koorka* and mustard seeds, 158
   with panfried plantains, 155–156
   with panfried plantains and mustard seeds, 255–256
   with panfried plantains, black-eyed peas, and mustard seeds, 156–157
   with panfried red beans and mustard seeds, 158–159
   with panfried telinga potatoes and mustard seeds, 157–158
   with pumpkin, red beans, and coconut, 139

Deepavali festival, 261
Desserts
   banana pancakes, 266
   besan fudge, 271–272
   caramelized plantains, 280
   cream and flour disks in sugar syrup, 275–276
   deep-fried sweet mung dal balls, 270–271
   fresh coconut fudge, 276
   fried rice and *urad* dal strings sweetened with brown sugar, 261–262
   jackfruit jam in rice cones steamed in banana leaves, 269–270
   laddu with puffed *chana* dal flour, 281
   milk fudge, 276–277
   mung dal fudge, 263–264
   rice and mung dal balls, 268

rice, coconut, and mung dal balls, 266–267
rice, dal, and brown sugar balls with cardamom and sesame seeds, 262–263
semolina pudding, 278–279
sweetened *besan* bead balls with cashews and raisins, 272–274
sweet semolina balls with cardamom and raisins, 277–278
sweet wheat flour flatbread, 264–265
urad dal pretzels in rose-flavored sugar syrup, 279–280
wheat flour fudge with cashews and cardamom, 274–275

Dosa kallu
   adas, 78
   dosas, 78

Dosas, rice and *urad* dal pancakes, 78, 177, 226–227
   godambu, 228
   masala, 229
   onion, 227
   rava, 227–228

Drumstick or moringa (*muringakka*), 70
Dutch Protestants, 38

Eggplant, in spicy toasted coconut sauce, 122–123
Ela ada, rice flour and coconut cakes steamed in plantain leaves, 291–292
Elephant's foot yam or telinga potato (*chena*), 70
Ellukari, vegetables in spicy coconut and sesame sauce, 144–145
Ellunda, sesame seed and brown sugar candy, 307
Ennamaanga, deep fried mangoes with spices in sesame oil, 185
Erisseri, butternut squash and mung dal in coconut cumin sauce, 103–104

Ettangadi, roasted vegetables and red beans with coconut, sesame, and brown sugar, 296–297

Farina. *See also* Semolina (*rava*)
   spiced with green chilies, ginger, and curry leaves, 236
   spicy with mixed vegetables, 237–238

Fenugreek (*ulava*), 62–63
   with mango pickle and cayenne pepper, 184–185

Flaked or pounded rice (*avil*), 45, 84
   with milk, sugar, ghee, and raisins, 290–291
   pudding, 211
   spiced with tamarind and mustard seeds, 255
   sweetened with brown sugar and fresh coconut, 265

Flavored rice dishes
   coconut rice, 94–95
   lemon rice, 95
   spiced rice in banana-leaf packets, 96–97
   yogurt rice, 93–94

Flours
   arrowroot (*koova podi*), 51–52
   chana or *besan* (*kadalamavu*), 51
   rice (*arippodi*), 51. *See also* Rice flour
   urad (*uzunnu podi*), 51
   wheat (*gothambu mavu*), 51

Fruits
   breadfruit (*kadachakka*), 67
   cooking bananas (*kaya*), 67
   gooseberry (*nellikka*), 71–72
   jackfruit (*chakka*), 72–73
   lemons (*cherunaranga*), 73
   mango (*maanga*), 73
   plantains (*nenthra kaya*), 73–74
   tamarind (*puli*), 74

Ghee (*neyyu*), 54, 196–197
    mashed mung dal with, 103
    with rice pudding and brown sugar, 208
Ginger (*inji*), 70–71
    with green chilies in a tamarind sauce, 173–174
    with green chilies in yogurt, 305–306
Gooseberry (*nellikka*), 71–72
    pickle, 181–182
Gothambu halvah, wheat flour fudge with cashews and cardamom, 274–275
Gothambu pradhaman, wheat pudding, 212
Gourds, 68
Gram and dal (beans, peas, and lentils)
    chana dal, 49
    cooking, 48–49
    cowpeas or small red beans (*vellapayaru*), 51
    horse gram (*muthira* or *kollu*), 50
    Indian chickpeas, 49. *See also* Indian chickpeas
    major branches of legumes, 48
    mung and mung dal (*cherupayaru* and *cheruparippu*), 50
    puffed *chana* dal (*porikadala*), 49
    tuvar or *toor* dal (*tuvara parippu*), 50
    urad dal (*uzunnu parippu*), 50
Green beans, panfried with fresh coconut and mustard seeds, 163–164
Green chilies (*pacha mulagu*), 72
    crisps, 203–204
    with ginger in a tamarind sauce, 173–174
    with ginger in yogurt, 305–306
    with jackfruit, mustard seeds, and coconut, 166–167
    and onions in spicy tamarind sauce, 137–138
    with panfried cabbage and coconut, 164–165
    with panfried *idli*, 232
    with panfried potatoes and coconut, 165–166
    with plantains, coconut, and yogurt, 106–107
    in spicy tamarind and brown sugar sauce, 174–175
Herbs
    coriander leaves or cilantro (*pachakothamalli*), 68
    curry leaves (*kariveppila*), 68
Horse gram (*muthira* or *kollu*), 50

Idichu pizinja paayasam, rice and mung dal pudding with coconut milk, 209
Idli pathram, idlis, 78–79
Idlis, 78–79, 177, 230
    panfried with green chilies, curry leaves and mustard seeds, 232
    Raamasseri idli, 231
    spicy pancakes, 232–233
Indian chickpeas, 49
    spicy brown, 286
    spicy curry, 135–136
Indian cuisine, regional differences, 3
Indian grocery stores, 42–43
Influence of foreign trade, on agriculture and cuisine, 39–41
Ingithayir, ginger and green chilies in yogurt, 305–306

Jackfruit (*chakka*), 72–73
    curry, 148–149
    jam, 219–220
    pudding, 218
    puzukku, 141
    seasoned with green chilies, mustard seeds, and coconut, 166–167
    wafers, 204
Jaggery (*sarkara*), 47
    sweets with, 261–270
Jams
    ripe mango, 218

ripe plantain, 216–217
Jelebis, urad dal pretzels in rose-flavored sugar syrup, 279–280
Jewish settlements, 27–28
Jews, 35–36

Kaalan, ripe plantains with coconut, green chilies, and yogurt, 106–107
Kaatu Kootan, green plantains, cucumber, and yam in a sweet and sour sauce, 151–152
Kadachakka masalakkari, breadfruit in spicy coconut sauce, 128–129
Kadachakka mezukkupuratti, breadfruit panfried with curry leaves, 163
Kadachakka varuthathu, breadfruit chips, 195–196
Kadalakari, spicy chickpea curry, 135–136
Kadala pradhaman, chana dal pudding with brown sugar and coconut milk, 214
Kadala, spicy brown chickpeas, 286
Kalavara (pantry) staples
  coconut (*nalikeram*), 45
  flaked or pounded rice (*avil*), 45
  jaggery (*sarkara*), 47
  popped rice (*malar*), 45
  rice (*ari*), 43–44
  salt (*uppu*), 47–48
Kanji, rice soup, 91–92, 160
  and coconut chutney, 169
  with coconut milk, 297
  with milk and sugar, 303
Kannanaadan, panfried plantains with mustard seeds and curry leaves, 255–256
Karutha moloshyam, telinga potatoes in black pepper and coconut sauce, 150–151
Kathir festival, 87
Kara mixture, 245–246
Kaya and *achinga mezukkupuratti,* panfried plantains with black-eyed peas,

mustard seeds, and curry leaves, 155–156
Kaya mezukkupuratti, panfried plantains with curry leaves, 155–156
Kerala
  ancient trade with the east, 30–31
  ancient trade with the west, 20
  Arab trade, 21
  Christian settlements, 28
  Jewish settlements, 27–28
  and King Solomon, 20
  Kochi. *See* Kochi
  maritime trade route, 21–22
  matrilineal system, 10–13
  Muslim settlements, 27
  port of Muziris, 19, 20
  Roman trade, 22–25, 28–29
  spice trade, 19
  trade during the colonial era, 31–33
  unification of, 34–35
Kichadi, fried okra in a coconut and mustard sauce, 116–117
Kitchens, traditional, 4–6
Kochi
  under British rule, 34
  curries from the royal kitchen of, 142–154
  and Dutch Protestants, 38
  Dutch trade, 33
  and Jews, 35–36
  and Portuguese Catholics, 36–37
  Portuguese trade, 32
  and Muslims, 38
  royalty of, 34
  and Syrian Christians, 36
Koorka mezukkupuratti, koorka panfried with mustard seeds and curry leaves, 158
Kootu curry, butternut squash and *chana* dal in a coconut-cumin sauce, 125–126
Kothamalipodi, spicy fresh coriander chutney powder, 175

Kozhukkatta, steamed rice and fresh coconut balls, 238–240
Kudumaanga, tender mango pickle, 187
Kumbilappam, jackfruit jam in rice cones steamed in banana leaves, 269–270
Kurukku kaalan, vegetables in slow-cooked sour buttermilk sauce, 153–154
Kurumulaku rasam, black pepper soup, 136–137

Laddu, sweetened *besan* bead balls with cashews and raisins, 272–274
Lemon leaves (*narakathinte ela*), 73
   chutney powder, 177–178
Lemon rice, 95
Lemons (*cherunaranga*), 73
   pickle, 179–180, 181
Lotus stem crisps, 202–203

Maampaza kaalan, ripe mangoes in coconut yogurt sauce, 152–153
Maampaza pachadi, mangoes in coconut and mustard sauce, 127–128
Maampaza pradhaman, ripe mango pudding, 217–218
Maanga chammanthi, fresh mango chutney, 171
Maangathera, dried ripe mango preserve, 204
Maanga varattiyathu, ripe mango jam, 218
Mango (*maanga*), 73
   chutney, 171–172
   in coconut and mustard sauce, 127–128
   and coconut *sundal*, 286–287
   in coconut yogurt sauce, 152–153
   jam, 218
   pickles, 182–189
   pudding, 217–218
Manoharam, fried rice and *urad* dal strings sweetened with brown sugar, 261–262

Maritime trade route, discovery of, 21–22
Masala, 98
Masala niracha paavakka, bitter gourd stuffed with spicy onion, 162–163
Matrilineal system, 10–13
Melons, 68
Mezukkupurattis. See also Thorans
   bitter gourd stuffed with spicy onion, 162–163
   horse gram beans panfried with mustard seeds and curry leaves, 160–161
   panfried bitter gourd with spices, 161–162
   panfried breadfruit with curry leaves, 163
   panfried *koorka* with mustard seeds and curry leaves, 158
   panfried plantains with black-eyed peas, mustard seeds, and curry leaves, 156–157
   panfried plantains with curry leaves, 155–156
   panfried red beans and plantain skins, 159–160
   panfried red beans with curry leaves and mustard seeds, 158–159
   panfried telinga potatoes with mustard seeds and curry leaves, 157–158
Milk and milk products, 53
   buttermilk (*mooru*), 54
   fudge, 276–277
   ghee (*neyyu*), 54
   yogurt or curd (*thayir*), 54
Modakam (*madhura kozhukkatta*), steamed sweet coconut balls, 287
Moloshyam, vegetables in coconut and cumin sauce, 119–120
Monsoon treats, 130–132
   black pepper soup, 136–137
   brown stew, 133–134

mung dal with green chilies and curry leaves, 138
onions and green chilies in spicy tamarind sauce, 137–138
potato stew, 132–133
pumpkin and red beans with coconut and curry leaves, 139
puzukku with jackfruit, 141
puzzuku with plantains, telinga potatoes, and black-eyed peas, 140
spicy chickpea curry, 135–136
Mottokoozu thoran, cabbage panfried with green chilies and coconut, 164–165
Mudhura koova varattiyathu, arrowroot pudding with milk, sugar, and cardamom, 294–295
Mulagu kondattam, green chili crisps, 203–204
Mulagu pachadi, green chilies in spicy tamarind and brown sugar sauce, 174–175
Mulaku varutha puli, onions and green chilies in spicy tamarind sauce, 137–138
Mung (*cherupayaru*), 50
Mung dal (*cheruparippu*), 50
  balls with rice, 268
  balls with rice and coconut, 266–267
  and butternut squash in coconut cumin sauce, 103–104
  deep-fried sweet balls, 270–271
  fudge, 263–264
  with green chilies and curry leaves, 138
  mashed with ghee, 103
  pudding with brown sugar and coconut milk, 215
  and rice pudding with coconut milk, 209
Murukku naazi or snack press, 79
Murukku, rice and *urad* dal pretzels, 241–243
Muslims, 38

Muslim settlements, 27
Mustard, and coconut sauce, 127–128
Mustard seeds (*kaduku*), 63–65
  with jackfruit, green chilies, and coconut, 166–167
  with panfried green beans and fresh coconut, 163–164
  with panfried horse gram beans and curry leaves, 160–161
  with panfried *idli,* 232
  with panfried *koorka* and curry leaves, 158
  with panfried plantains and curry leaves, 255–256
  with panfried plantains, black-eyed peas, and curry leaves, 156–157
  with panfried red beans and curry leaves, 158–159
  with panfried telinga potatoes and curry leaves, 157–158
  with pounded rice and tamarind, 255
Muthira upperi, horse gram beans panfried with mustard seeds and curry leaves, 160–161
Mysorepak, besan fudge, 271–272

Naalikera burfi, fresh coconut fudge, 276
Naalikera chutney, coconut chutney, 168–170
Naalikera dosa, rice and coconut pancakes, 225–226
Naranga curry, lemon pickle, 179–180
Navarathri festival, 258–260, 272, 285
Nellikkakari, gooseberry pickle, 181
Neypaayasaam, rice pudding with brown sugar and ghee, 208
Neyyappam, rice and brown sugar griddle cakes, 283, 284–285
Neyyil varattiya pazzam, caramelized plantains, 280
Neyyum parippum, mashed mung dal with ghee, 103

Nira Festival, 82–83
Noolpittu (idiapam), fresh rice noodles with coconut filling, 222–223

Okra
  crisps, 201–202
  fried in coconut and mustard sauce, 116–117
Oils
  coconut (*velichenna*), 52
  sesame (*nallenna*), 52–53
Omappodi, deep-fried *besan* strings, 244–245
Onam festival, 83, 179, 196, 290
  during early centuries, 85–87
  and the Hindu mythology, 85
  kaalan, 106–107
  sadya, 84–85
Onions
  bitter gourd stuffed with, 162–163
  and green chilies in spicy tamarind sauce, 137–138
  pancakes, 227
Oolan, vegetables in coconut milk sauce, 107–108
Oothappam, spicy pancakes, 232–233
Oralappam, rice, coconut, and mung dal balls, 266–277

Paal ada pradhaman, rice pudding with steamed rice flakes, 210–211
Paalgova, milk fudge, 276–277
Paal kanji, rice soup with milk and sugar, 303
Paal paayasam, rice pudding, 207–208
Paanakam, sweet and spicy drink, 288
Paavakka kondattam, spicy bitter gourd crisps, 202
Paavakka mezukkupuratti, panfried bitter gourd with spices, 161–162
Paavakka varutharacha kootan, bitter gourd in spicy toasted coconut sauce, 124–125

Pacha sambar, sambar with fresh green spices, 146–147
Pancakes
  banana, 266
  godambu, 228
  rava, 227–228
  rice and coconut, 225–226
  rice and coconut milk, 223–225
  rice and *urad* dal, 226–227
  rice and *urad* dal stuffed with spicy potatoes and onions, 226–227
  onion, 227
  spicy, 232–233
Pantry, traditional, 6–7
Pappadams, 194
  fried in spicy sauce, 149
Pappadavada (thatta), deep-fried spicy rice and *urad* dal disks, 247
Pappadavalli, fried *pappadams* in spicy sauce, 149
Paradesi Synagogue, 35
Parippu pradhaman, mung dal pudding with brown sugar and coconut milk, 215
Paripputenga, sweetened puffed *chana* dal, 289
Payaru kondattam, black-eyed pea crisps, 203
Pazzam nurukku, steamed ripe plantains, 196
Pazzam varattiyathu, ripe plantain jam, 216–217
Pazza palahaaram, banana pancakes, 266
Pazza pradhaman, ripe plantain pudding, 216
Pickles, 178
  apple, 184
  deep fried mangoes with spices in sesame oil, 185
  dried, spiced mango pieces, 187–189
  gooseberry, 181
  green mango, 183–184
  lemon, 179–180, 181

mangoes in brine, 186
mango with fenugreek and cayenne pepper, 184–185
tender mango, 187
Plantains (*nenthra kaya*), 73–74
    caramelized, 280
    chips, 191–193
    with coconut, green chilies, and yogurt, 106–107
    with cucumber and yam in a sweet and sour sauce, 151–152
    fried in coconut yogurt sauce, 147–148
    jam, 216–217
    panfried with black-eyed peas, mustard seeds, and curry leaves, 155–156
    panfried with curry leaves, 155–156
    panfried with mustard seeds and curry leaves, 255–256
    pudding, 216
    and red beans and coconut, 293–294
    in spicy coconut and sesame sauce, 144–145
    steamed, 196
    and taro root in coconut buttermilk sauce, 150
    with telinga potatoes and black-eyed peas, 140
    in toasted coconut and cumin sauce, 105
    with vegetables and fresh coconut, 292–293
    with vegetables in slow-cooked sour buttermilk sauce, 153–154
Plantain skins, with panfried red beans, 159–160
Podi, spice powder with *dosa* and *idli*, 177
Pokavadas, vegetable fritters, 251–252
Popped rice (*malar*), 45
Popular curries, 99, 100–101
    butternut squash and mung dal in coconut cumin sauce, 103–104
    green plantains in toasted coconut and cumin sauce, 105
    mashed mung dal with ghee, 103
    mixed vegetable medley in coconut cumin sauce, 108–109
    ripe plantains with coconut, green chilies, and yogurt, 106–107
    tomato and *tuvar* dal soup, 113–115
    vegetables and *tuvar* dal in a spicy tamarind sauce, 109–111
    vegetables and *tuvar* dal in a toasted coconut and tamarind sauce, 112–113
    vegetables in coconut milk sauce, 107–108
Porikadala laddu, *laddu* with puffed *chana* dal flour, 281
Port of Muziris, 20
    location of, 26
Portuguese Catholics, 36–37
Poruvalanga, rice and mung dal balls, 268
Potatoes
    panfried with green chilies and coconut, 165–166
    in spicy coconut milk, 133–134
    spicy fritters, 249–250
    stew, 132–133
    telinga. *See* Telinga potatoes
Pothichoru, spiced rice in banana-leaf packets, 96–97
Preserves
    black-eyed peas, 203
    dried ripe mango, 204
    green chili crisps, 203–204
    jackfruit wafers, 204–205
    lotus stem crisps, 202–203
    okra crisps, 201–202
    rice wafers, 200–201
    spicy bitter gourd crisps, 202
    spicy rice crisps, 199–200
Pretzels
    rice and mung dal, 243
    rice and *urad* dal, 241–243

urad dal, 279–280
Puddings
   chana dal with brown sugar and coconut milk, 214
   jackfruit, 218–219
   mango, 217
   mung dal with brown sugar and coconut milk, 215
   plantain, 216
   pounded rice, 211
   rice, 207–206
   rice and mung dal with coconut milk, 209
   rice with brown sugar and ghee, 208
   rice with steamed rice flakes, 210–211
   semolina, 278–279
   vermicelli, 213
   wheat, 212
Puffed *chana* dal (*porikadala*), 49
   sweetened, 289
Puli avil, pounded rice spiced with tamarind and mustard seeds, 255
Pulinkari, vegetables with spicy *tuvar* dal, 121–122
Puli sevaka, *sevaka* with tamarind concentrate, 254
Pullingi, ginger and green chilies in a tamarind sauce, 173–174
Pumpkins, 68, 69
   and red beans with coconut and curry leaves, 139–141
Puthiri avil, pounded rice with milk, sugar, ghee, and raisins, 290–291
Puthiri festival, 82–83, 84, 209, 290
Puttu kudam, puttu, 79
Puzukku
   with jackfruit, 141
   with plantains, telinga potatoes, and black-eyed peas, 140
   pumpkin and red beans with coconut and curry leaves, 139

Rasam powder, 115
Rava kesari, semolina pudding, 278–279
Rava laddu, sweet semolina balls with cardamom and raisins, 277–278
Red beans
   and pumpkin with coconut and curry leaves, 139
   panfried with curry leaves and mustard seeds, 158–159
   panfried with plantain skins, 159–160
   sweetened with brown sugar, 288–289
   with vegetables and coconut, 293–294
   with vegetables, coconut, sesame, and brown sugar, 296–297
Ribbon *pokkavada*, spicy rice and *besan* ribbons, 248–249
Rice (*ari*), 4
   balls with coconut and mung dal, 266–267
   balls with dal, brown sugar, cardamom, and sesame seeds, 262–263
   balls with fresh coconut, 238–240
   balls with mung dal, 268
   breakfast cakes (*idli*), 230–231
   brief history of, 44–45
   coconut, 94–95
   cultivation of, 80–81
   festivals. *See* Rice festivals
   flaked or pounded (*avil*), 45, 84
   flour. *See* Rice flour (*arippodi*)
   fragrant (*jeeraka chamban*), 43
   fried balls with *urad* dal, 243–244
   fried disks with *urad* dal, 247
   fried strings with *urad* dal sweetened with brown sugar, 261–262
   griddle cakes with brown sugar, 284–285
   hand-pounded and parboiled (*kaikuthari*), 44
   lemon, 95
   medium-to long-grain (*unakkalari*), 43, 44, 88

and monsoon season, 131
and mung dal pudding with coconut milk, 208
names for, 89
noodles with coconut filling, 222–223
ordinary parboiled (*puzukkalari*), 43
other uses of, 81–82
pancakes, 223–227, 229, 233–234
panfried noodles, 253–254
plain boiled, 90–91
popped (*malar*), 45
pretzels, 241–243
pudding, 207–208, 209, 210–211
in social rituals, 88–89
soup, 91–92, 160, 197, 297, 303
spiced in banana-leaf packets, 96–97
spicy crisps, 199–200
steamed sweet balls, 300
in temple rituals, 87–88
wafers, 200–201
yogurt, 93–94

Rice festivals
Kathir, 87
Nira, 82–83
Onam, 83, 84
Puthiri, 82–83, 84
Vishu, 82

Rice flour (*arippodi*), 51
cakes with coconut steamed in plantain leaves, 291–292
steamed and sweetened with brown sugar, 303–304
steamed with fresh coconut, 221–222

Roman trade, 22–23
archeological evidence of, 26–27
literary evidence of, 23–25
revival of, 28–29

Sadya, 84–85, 100, 119, 193
serving a, 101–103
Salt (*uppu*), 47–48
Sambar powder, 111

Sambar, vegetables and *tuvar* dal in tamarind sauce, 109–111
with fresh green spices, 146–147
Sambharam, spicy yogurt drink, 197–198
Sarkara upperi, sweet plantain chips, 192–193
Sauces
black pepper and coconut, 150–151
buttermilk, 306–307
coconut and cumin, 103–104, 105, 108–109, 119–120, 125–126
coconut and mustard, 127–128, 129–130
coconut and sesame, 144–145
coconut and yogurt, 115–116, 147–148, 152–153
coconut buttermilk, 150
coconut milk, 107–108, 133–134
sour buttermilk, 153–154
spicy, 149, 298
spicy tamarind, 109–111, 112–113, 137–138, 174–175
spicy toasted coconut, 122–123, 124–125, 128–129
spicy yogurt, 235
sweet and sour, 151–152
tamarind, 109–111, 173–174
Seasonal curries, 99
bitter gourd in spicy toasted coconut sauce, 124–125
breadfruit in spicy coconut sauce, 128–129
butternut squash and *chana* dal in a coconut-cumin sauce, 125–126
cucumbers in mustard and coconut sauce, 129–130
eggplant in spicy toasted coconut sauce, 122–123
mangoes in coconut and mustard sauce, 127–128
spicy mashed spinach, 126–127
vegetables in coconut and cumin sauce, 119–120

vegetables with spicy *tuvar* dal, 121–122
and Vishu festival, 118–119
Seasonal festivals, 10
Seasonal festivals recipes, 289–290
   arrowroot pudding with milk, sugar, and cardamom, 294–295
   bran cakes with coconut and brown sugar, 298–299
   mixed root vegetables and plantain with fresh coconut, 292–293
   mixed vegetables with red beans and coconut, 293–294
   pounded rice with milk, sugar, ghee, and raisins, 290–291
   rice flour and coconut cakes steamed in plantain leaves, 291–292
   rice soup with coconut milk, 297
   roasted vegetables and red beans with coconut, sesame, and brown sugar, 296–297
   taro stems with fresh coconut in spicy sauce, 298
Semiya
   noodles, 52
   pudding, 213
   uppuma, 237
Semiya paayasam, vermicelli pudding, 213
Semolina (*rava*), 52. *See also* Farina
   pudding, 278–279
   sweet balls with cardamom and raisins, 277–278
Sesame oil (*nallenna*), 52–53
Sesame seeds (*ellu*), 65
   balls with rice, dal, brown sugar, and cardamom, 262–263
   and brown sugar candy, 307
   with vegetables, red beans, coconut, and brown sugar, 296–297
Sevaka, panfried spicy rice noodles, 253–254
Shallot chutney, 170–171

Snacks
   deep-fried *besan* strings, 244–245
   deep-fried spicy rice and coconut disks, 248
   deep-fried spicy rice and *urad* dal disks, 247
   deep-fried spicy *tuvar* dal fritters, 252–253
   fried spicy rice and *urad* dal balls, 243–244
   panfried spicy rice noodles, 253–254
   plantains panfried with mustard seeds and curry leaves, 255–256
   pounded rice spiced with tamarind and mustard seeds, 255
   rice and mung dal pretzels, 243
   rice and *urad* dal pretzels, 241–243
   spicy, crunchy mix, 245–246
   spicy potato fritters, 249–250
   vegetable fritters, 251–252
Snake gourd (*padavalanga*), 69–70
Soups
   black pepper, 136–137
   rice, 91–92, 297, 303
   tomato and *tuvar* dal soup, 113–115
Spices, 54–56
   ajowan (*omam* or *ayamodakam*), 56
   asafetida (*kaayam*), 56–58
   black pepper (*kurumulaku*), 58
   cardamom seeds (*elakkaya*), 58–59
   chili pepper (*kappal mulagu*), 60
   coriander seeds (*kothamalli*), 60–61
   cumin seeds (*jeerakam*), 61–62
   fenugreek (*ulava*), 62–63
   ginger (*inji*), 70–71
   mustard seeds (*kaduku*), 63–65
   sesame seeds (*ellu*), 65
   turmeric powder (*manja podi*), 65–67
Spice trade
   Marco Polo, 29
   and the Portuguese, 29
   and the Venetians, 29

Spinach, spicy mashed, 126–127
Squash, 68
Stews
    brown, 133–134
    potato, 132–133
Sugiyan, deep-fried sweet mung dal balls, 270–271
Suran. *See* Telinga potatoes
Sweet treats. *See* Desserts
Syrian Christians, 36

Tamarind (*puli*), 74
    with pounded rice and mustard seeds, 255
    sauce, 109–111, 112–113, 137–138, 173–174, 174–175
Taro root (*chembu*), 74
    with green bananas in coconut buttermilk sauce, 150
Taro stems, with fresh coconut in spicy sauce, 298
Tayir vada, *vada* in spicy yogurt sauce, 235
Telinga potatoes
    in black pepper and coconut sauce, 150–151
    chips, 193
    panfried with mustard seeds and curry leaves, 157–158
    with plantains and black-eyed peas, 140
    in spicy coconut and sesame sauce, 144–145
    with vegetables in slow-cooked sour buttermilk sauce, 153–154
Temple festivals, and festive fare, 9
Temple festivals recipes, 282–284
    coconut-mango *sundal*, 286–287
    dark coconut fudge, 285
    red beans sweetened with brown sugar, 288–289
    rice and brown sugar griddle cakes, 283, 284–285
    spicy brown chickpeas, 286
    steamed sweet coconut balls, 287
    sweet and spicy drink, 288
    sweetened puffed *chana* dal, 289
Thakkali chutney, fresh tomato chutney, 172–173
Thakkali rasam, tomato and *tuvar* dal soup, 113–115
Thalu kootan, taro stems with fresh coconut in spicy sauce, 298
Thamaravalayam kondattam, lotus stem crisps, 202–203
Thayir choru, yogurt rice, 93–94
Thayir sevaka, *sevaka* with yogurt, 254
Thenga choru, coconut rice, 94–95
Thengavada, deep-fried spicy rice and coconut disks, 248
Thirandu Kalyaanam, coming of age ceremony, 300–303
Thirattipaal, dark coconut fudge, 285
Thirattipittu, steamed rice flour sweetened with brown sugar, 303–304
Thiruvathira koottu, mixed root vegetables and plantain with fresh coconut, 292–293
Thiruvathira puzukku, mixed vegetables with red beans and coconut, 293–294
Thiruvathira festival, 290
Thiruvonam festival. *See* Onam festival
Thorans, 155. *See also* Mezukkupuratti
    cabbage panfried with green chilies and coconut, 164–165
    jackfruit seasoned with green chilies, mustard seeds, and coconut, 166–167
    panfried green beans with fresh coconut and mustard seeds, 163–164
    potatoes panfried with green chilies and coconut, 165–166
Tomatoes
    chutney, 172–173
    in a fresh coconut and yogurt sauce, 115–116

and *tuvar* dal soup, 113
Tomato *pachadi,* tomatoes in a fresh coconut and yogurt sauce, 115–116
Trade during the colonial era
    British colonization of India, 33
    Dutch trade, 33
    Portuguese trade, 31–32
Turmeric powder (*manja podi*), 65–67
Tuvar or *toor* dal (*tuvara parippu*), 50
    fritters, 252–253
    and tomato soup, 113–115
    vegetables with, 121–122
    with vegetables in tamarind sauce, 109–111
    with vegetables in coconut and tamarind sauce, 112–113

Ubbidu, sweet wheat flour flatbread, 264–265
Uli chammanthi, shallot chutney, 170–171
Uluva maanga curry, mango pickle with fenugreek and cayenne pepper, 184–185
Uppuma khozukkata, khozukkata with *tuvar* dal, 239–240
Uppumaanga, mangoes in brine, 186
Uppuparippu, mung dal with green chilies and curry leaves, 138
Urad dal (*uzunnu parippu*), 50
    breakfast cakes (*idli*), 230–231
    fried balls with rice, 234–244
    fried disks with rice, 247
    fried strings with rice and sweetened with brown sugar, 261–262
    fried wafers, 194
    fritters, 234–235
    pancakes, 226–227, 229
    pretzels, 241–243, 279–280
    spice powder, 177
Urad flour (*uzunnu podi*), 51
Urulakkizangu stew, potato stew, 132–133

Urulakizzangu bondas, spicy potato fritters, 249–250
Urulakizzangu thoran, potatoes panfried with green chilies and coconut, 165–166
Utensils
    appakkara, 78, 284
    appliances, 77
    dosa kallu, 78
    idli pathram, 78
    murukku naazi or snack press, 79
    puttu kudam, 79
    vellayappam chatti, 79
Uzunnu vada, deep-fried *urad* dal fritters, 234–235

Vadugappuli naranga curry, bitter lemon pickle, 180
Varikasseri, green bananas and taro root in coconut buttermilk sauce, 150
Varutha erisseri, green plantains in toasted coconut and cumin sauce, 105
Varutharacha sambar, vegetables and *tuvar* dal in coconut and tamarind sauce, 112–113
Varuthupperi, green plantain chips, 191–192
Varuthupperi kootan, fried plantains in coconut yogurt sauce, 147–148
Vazuthaninga varutharacha kootan, eggplant in spicy toasted coconut sauce, 122–123
Vedinellikka, dry gooseberry pickle, 181–182
Vellapayaru, red beans sweetened with brown sugar, 288–289
Vendakka kondattam, okra crisps, 201–202
Veppilakatti, spice lemon leaf chutney powder, 177–178
Vegetables
    ash gourd (*elevan* or *kumbalanga*), 68
    bitter gourd or bitter melon (*paavakka* or *kaippaka*), 68–69

bondas, 250–251
   in coconut cumin sauce, 108–109, 119–120
   in coconut milk, 107–108
cucumbers, 68
drumstick or moringa (*muringakka*), 70
elephant's foot yam or telinga potato (*chena*), 70
fritters, 251–252
gourds, 68
green chilies (*pacha mulagu*), 72
melons, 68
   with plantain and fresh coconut, 292–293
pumpkin (*mathanga*), 68, 69
   with red beans, coconut, sesame, and brown sugar, 296–297
   in slow-cooked sour buttermilk sauce, 153–154
snake gourd (*padavalanga*), 69–70
   in spicy coconut and sesame sauce, 144–145
spicy farina with, 237–238
with spicy *tuvar* dal, 121–122
squash, 68
taro root (*chembu*), 74
   and *tuvar* dal in coconut and tamarind sauce, 112–113
   and *tuvar* dal in spicy tamarind sauce, 109–111
yams (*cherukizangu, kaachil,* and *koorka*), 75
yellow cucumber (*vellarikka*), 69
Vegetarianism, 53
Vellacheeda, rice, dal, and brown sugar balls with cardamom and sesame seeds, 262–263

Vellapayaru mezukkupuratti, panfried red beans with curry leaves and mustard seeds, 158–159
Vellapayaru and *kaya tholi mezukkupuratti,* panfried red beans and plantain skins, 159–160
Vellarikka tharichathu, cucumbers in mustard and coconut sauce, 129–130
Vellayappam, rice and coconut milk pancakes, 223–225
Vellayappam chatti (*vellayappam* pan), 79
Vishu festival, 82, 118–119, 290
   sadya, 119
Vishu *kanji,* rice soup with coconut milk, 297
Venetian spice monopoly, 29
Vermicelli. *See Semiya*

Wheat pudding, 212
Wheat flour (*gothambu mavu*), 51
   fudge, 274–275

Yams (*cherukizangu, kaachil,* and *koorka*), 75
   with green plantains and cucumber in a sweet and sour sauce, 151–152
Yellow cucumber (*vellarikka*), 69
Yogurt or curd (*thayir*), 54, 197
   drink, 197–198
   with ginger and green chilies, 305–306
   with *sevaka,* 254
   with plantains, coconut, and green chilies, 106–107
   rice, 93–94
   sauce, 115–116, 147–148, 152–153, 235

978-0-595-40976-1
0-595-40976-8

Made in the USA
Coppell, TX
22 November 2024